Essays from
Contemporary Culture

Essays from Contemporary Culture

Fifth Edition

Katherine Anne Ackley
Professor Emerita
University of Wisconsin
at Stevens Point

THOMSON
HEINLE

Australia   Canada   Mexico   Singapore   Spain   United Kingdom   United States

THOMSON

HEINLE

Essays from Contemporary Culture, Fifth Edition
Katherine Anne Ackley

Publisher: *Michael Rosenberg*
Acquisitions Editor: *Dickson Musslewhite*
Developmental Editor: *Cathy Richard Dodson*
Production Editor: *Eunice Yeates-Fogle*
Marketing Manager: *Katrina Byrd*
Executive Marketing Manager: *Carrie Brandon*
Director of Marketing: *Lisa Kimball*
Manufacturing Manager: *Marcia Locke*
Cover Design: *Brian Salisbury*
Composition: *ATLIS Graphics & Design*
Project Management: *Hearthside Publishing Services*
Printer: *Transcontinental Printing*

Printed in Canada.
1   2   3   4   5   6   06   05   04   03

For more information, contact Heinle, 25 Thomson Place, Boston, MA 02210 USA,
or you can visit our Internet site at http://www.heinle.com

ISBN: 0-8384-0677-7

Library of Congress Catalog Card Number: 2003105931

Cover Art, "Meander," 23″ × 36″, © 2002 by Lucy Turner.
Used with permission of the artist.

Credits begin on page 403, which constitutes a continuation of the copyright page.

For my grandchildren
Elizabeth Anne Schilling
Lucas Konrad Schilling
Che Aaron James White
Zackary Idir Yahi
Celia Fatima Yahi

CONTENTS

Chapter 8   POPULAR CULTURE   267

Chapter 9   PREJUDICE AND DISCRIMINATION   329

Chapter 10   TERRORISM, WAR, AND VIOLENCE   369

Rhetorical Table of Contents

Note: Some essays appear in more than one category.

ARGUMENT/PERSUASION

CAUSE/EFFECT ANALYSIS

PREFACE

Essays from Contemporary Culture, Fifth Edition, is a collection of writings on topics that range from the highly personal to the culturally and socially significant. The underlying assumption of the book is that what students read, think, and write about is inextricably linked with who they are and how they behave as responsible human beings in relation to their classmates, their families, and/or the communities in which they live and work. The textbook is designed to engage student interest and encourage their responses to the writers' treatment of their subjects. The reader response questions, questions for discussion, and writing topics ask students to comment on or give informed opinions about topics that matter to them in a variety of forums, such as expressive writing, classroom discussion and formal essays.

The selections in this textbook by and large represent contemporary responses to not only enduring social issues and the varieties of human experience but also to more recent phenomena such as the 9/11/01 terrorist attacks against the United States and physician-assisted suicide. Such social issues as euthanasia, media violence, and what constitutes moral or ethical behavior have gained prominence in the public forum, while prejudice, discrimination, and violence continue to be pressing social problems. The contemporaneity of the readings in this book, which address issues that students may have to face themselves, speaks to the relevance of this textbook to students' lives beyond the classroom. While many of the readings are written, appropriately, in a serious manner, many of them explore matters of interest and importance with humor and lightheartedness. A balance of gravity with levity helps keep these issues in their proper perspective.

All of the works are written from the particular viewpoint of their writers, of course, and many are meant to be controversial. Controversy is useful because it requires that students question what they read, learn to challenge writers whose opinions they disagree with, explore their own thoughts and develop their own positions on important issues. The readings come from a variety of sources including newspapers, magazines, books, and the Internet; and though they vary in style, tone, and purpose, all in one way or another respond to particular issues of importance in contemporary culture. The readings also represent a broad range of rhetorical modes, including reflective, personal writing as well as argument, analysis, and opinion.

In response to suggestions from instructors who used and reviewed the fourth edition of *Essays from Contemporary Culture,* several changes have been made in this edition. Two new features to the book are a chapter on reading and writing critically and graphic images in each of the other nine chapters. Chapter 1 provides both guidelines for reading thoroughly and thoughtfully and directions for organizing and developing an essay, including an annotated student essay. Chapter 1 also includes a group of readings focused on the appropriateness of Abraham Lincoln's "Gettysburg Address" to the first anniversary of the 9/11/01 terrorist attacks. As for the graphic images, each chapter begins with two images related to the theme of the chapter, followed by questions for discussion or writing. Further, questions for discussion in the readings retained from the fourth edition have been revised to call for higher order responses rather than simple recall, and the same principle governs discussion questions for the new readings and stories. Most of the discussion questions can also serve as writing prompts, for either in-class writing or out-of-class assignments.

In addition to retaining works in the fourth edition by such highly respected writers as Bruce Catton, Kate Chopin, Annie Dillard, Ellen Goodman, William Raspberry, Roger Rosenblatt, and E. B. White, the fifth edition includes eighteen new essays and four new short stories. Writers of the new pieces include William Safire, Patricia J. Williams, Garry Wills, and Howard Zinn; short story authors who have been added are Toni Cade Bambara, Sandra Cisneros, Susan Glaspell, and Charles Johnson. Also, several academic essays have been included by writers David Arnold, Dorothy E. Denning, and Lorri Nandrea.

The seventy-five selections in this edition of *Essays from Contemporary Culture* are arranged in ten chapters that move thematically from generally personal issues to matters of significance to society at large, though all have appeals on both levels. The chapters "Transitions," "Insights," "Self-perception," "Role Models and Heroes," and "Gendered Relationships" contain selections that cover a wide range of topics that appeal to students' own personal experiences or concerns. "Ethics, Morals, and Values," "Popular Culture," "Prejudice and Discrimination," and "Terrorism, War, and Violence" also contain readings that are likely to touch students' own lives, but the selections address topics that have larger social implications. Indeed, a number of essays express opposing viewpoints on controversial topics. For instance, "Popular Culture" contains pieces by writers who hold differing opinions on the subject of how graphic content in movies and music affect behavior, while clustered readings on euthanasia represent different approaches to this highly charged issue. Finally, the textbook includes seven short stories by frequently anthologized creative writers. These stories explore in fiction the same topics that other writers explore by arguing, explaining, defining, analyzing, or commenting on. They provide an additional insight or perspective that is often profound and highly moving.

Students are invited to read these essays, commentaries, and stories, to think about them, and to respond to them. To assist in those purposes, questions about their personal reactions to the piece and questions for class discussion follow each selection. Students are asked for their personal reaction to the article first because subjective responses usually come before objective analyses of readings. Students would benefit by recording these personal responses in a journal or notebook, whether or not instructors ask students to share them in classroom discussion. After responding on a subjective level, students are asked to look back through the essay and answer questions about the author's purpose and meaning and the ways in which those are achieved. At the end of each chapter are writing suggestions that ask students to respond to individual writers, make connections between and among them, or write on some other topic related to the theme of the chapter.

The instructor's manual that accompanies this textbook begins with a general discussion of how to use the book, including ways to encourage students to participate in class and small-group discussions. The manual also provides answers, where appropriate, to the questions for discussion that follow each reading. Finally, for those instructors wishing to work on vocabulary, the instructor's manual includes a list of suggested vocabulary words for each of the readings.

I am grateful to the following reviewers for their input on the fifth edition of this book:

Marcia L. Laskey, *Cardinal Stritch University*
Matthew Novack, *California Polytechnic State University*

Katherine Anne Ackley
Professor Emerita
University of Wisconsin-Stevens Point

Essays from
Contemporary Culture

READING AND WRITING CRITICALLY

READING CRITICALLY

Learning to be a critical reader is an excellent step in the process of learning to write well. As a critical reader, your goals are, first, to understand what you are reading and, second, to assess or evaluate it. That is, you must clearly understand what you have read before you can examine it. Then you have a solid basis for moving beyond comprehension to evaluation. To reach the point where you are comfortable expressing your own views on an issue or topic, you must read with a critical eye what others have written on the same subject. As a critical reader, you must assess the evidence, details, or arguments the author has supplied to support or illustrate those ideas. Reading critically requires that you distinguish between fact and opinion, and it also requires that you sort out the evidence an author uses and evaluate that evidence in terms of its relevance, accuracy, and importance. Thus, reading critically means active engagement in what you read.

The following guidelines suggest ways to get the most from your reading. If you read the assigned selections carefully and critically, you will be prepared to express your own views, in your own voice, on the suggestions for discussion and writing that accompany the reading selections.

Title

The title usually suggests the subject of the piece, but it can also tell you something about how the subject will be treated. It may reflect the author's tone, or it may indicate the position the author has taken on the subject. For instance, several of the titles in Chapter 6, on role models and heroes, give clear indications of what you can expect to read in the essays. You expect to read about one particular teacher who had an effect on Nicholas Gage in his essay "The Teacher Who Changed My Life," while Bruce Catton's "Grant and Lee: A Study in Contrasts" is obviously a comparison/contrast essay on two people named Grant and Lee. If you are familiar with those two leaders of opposing sides in the American Civil War, then you have an even greater sense of what to expect in Catton's essay. If nothing else, the title should pique curiosity or attract attention. The titles of Roger Wilkins's "I Became Her Target" and Scott M. Fisher's "Lessons from Two Ghosts" are both intriguing enough to engage interest in reading the essays if only to find out what the titles mean.

Author

Next, learn something about the author. If information about the author is provided, read it. Knowing who the author is, the author's other publications, and the author's profession, for example, gives you an idea of the authority from which he or she writes. Often in magazines, journals, and collections of essays, such as those you will use in many of your college courses, the headnote tells you about the author. The headnote is that information located between the title and the beginning of the essay and is usually highlighted or set off from the body of the essay itself.

Purpose

As early into the essay as possible, determine the purpose. Good writers have a clear purpose in mind as they plan and draft their writing. Most nonfiction writing falls into the categories of persuasive, expository, and expressive writing. These forms are used to achieve different goals, and they involve different strategies for achieving those goals. In persuasive writing, the emphasis is on the reader: The writer's purpose is to convince the reader of the validity of his or her position on an issue and sometimes even move the reader to action. In expository writing, the goal is to inform or explain objectively; the emphasis is on ideas, events, or objects themselves, not on how the writer feels about them. Much of the writing in college textbooks is expository, as are newspaper and magazine articles, professional journal articles, and nonfiction books. Expository writing can take many forms, including cause/effect analysis, comparison/contrast, definition, and classification. In expressive writing, the emphasis is on the writer's feelings and subjective view of the world. The writer's focus is on personal feelings about or attitude toward his or her subject. The kind of writing you do in a journal or diary is expressive. Persuasive, expository, and expressive writing often overlap, but usually a writer has one main purpose. From the opening paragraphs of a written work, you should be able to determine its general purpose or aim. A clearly implied or stated purpose helps the writer to shape the writing, and it helps the reader to understand and evaluate the work.

Audience

Try to determine the original audience for the essay. Writers make assumptions about the people they are writing for, and these assumptions influence the tone they use, the evidence they select, and how they organize and develop their writing. These assumptions even influence their sentence structure, word choice and diction level. Knowing whom the writer is addressing helps you to understand the writer's point of view and explains the choices the writer has made. In writing for college courses, students usually assume a general audience of people like themselves who are reasonably intelligent and interested in what they have to say. Professional writers or scholars, however, often write for specific audiences, depending on the nature of the publication in which their writing appears. Writers want to know if their audience will be sympathetic or opposed to their position. Knowing the likely position of their readers helps writers make decisions about what tone to use and what details to include. Knowing whether their audience is familiar with what they are writing about—whether the audience is specialized or general—also governs what kind and how much evidence to use.

Thesis

As you begin reading, look for the thesis, which states the main idea or point of the entire essay. Sometimes it is in the form of a single sentence, the thesis statement, and sometimes it is stated in several sentences. If the main idea is not explicitly stated, then it should be clearly implied. Whether the thesis is explicit or implicit, it is a necessary component of a clearly written work. A thesis helps the writer to focus the writing and guides the organization and development of key ideas. It also helps provide direction to the reader and assists in the reader's understanding of the piece.

Key Ideas

As you read, locate key ideas and supporting evidence or details. For this step in your critical reading, underline or highlight the major points of the essay. One important tool for an active, critical reader is a pen or pencil so that you can underline, star, or in some way highlight major points of development. Look for topic sentences of paragraphs. Just as the thesis statement answers the question "What is this essay about?" so the topic sentence answers the question "What is this paragraph about?" If a topic sentence is not clearly stated, it should be clearly implied.

Marginal Notes

An excellent aid to reading critically is to write in the margins your comments, responses, or thoughts as you read. Note the words, phrases, or entire passages that you believe are important. Make notes about the evidence or details that support major points. If you have a question about something, mark it for later consideration. If you are not sure of the meaning of the word, circle it and look it up in a dictionary after you have finished reading. Finally, highlight any passages that you find particularly well written, thought provoking, or otherwise striking.

Summary

When you have finished reading, briefly summarize what you have read. This is the point at which you test your understanding of the material. Look at your notations, and try to put in your own words what the writing is about and the main points the writer made. If you can accurately summarize a piece of writing, then you probably have a good idea of its meaning. Summarizing also helps you to recall the piece later, perhaps in class or in small group discussions.

Evaluation

Another big step in critical reading is to evaluate what you have read. When you are sure that you understand and can summarize the reading objectively, you are ready to respond to it. There are a number of ways to evaluate something, depending on its purpose. Among the questions you can ask in assessing how well an essay is written are the following:

- Does the introduction give you enough information to get you easily into the essay?
- Does the author achieve the stated or implied purpose?
- Is the essay organized?
- Is the thesis or main idea thoroughly explained, developed, or argued?
- Has the writer supplied enough details, examples, or other evidence to fully support or illustrate the thesis?
- If it is an argument or persuasion essay, is the evidence convincing? Is the argument logical and reasonable? Are you persuaded to the writer's position?
- If it is a descriptive essay, has the writer conveyed the essence of the thing to you with appropriately vivid words?
- For any piece of writing, what questions do you have about any of the writer's assertions? Do you wish to challenge the writer on any points?
- Does the conclusion leave you satisfied that the writer has accomplished the purpose for the essay?
- Is the writing clear?
- Is the language colorful, engaging, and lively?

WRITING CRITICALLY

Learning to be a critical reader also helps you become a better writer. If you pay attention to the ways in which professional writers and scholars use language, structure their essays, and develop their ideas, you will learn some valuable lessons for your own writing. The process of writing encompasses several stages and a number of considerations. The content of your essay, how well you organize and develop it, your awareness of audience and style, and how well you construct sentences and paragraphs all go into producing a piece of writing that you can be proud of.

Familiarity with Subject

One of your goals in any writing assignment is to demonstrate your knowledge or understanding of your subject. If you have a choice of subject matter, select a topic that interests you and that you have some familiarity with. If your subject is assigned to you, take the time to understand it thoroughly. If you are not knowledgeable about your subject, it will show through in your writing and weaken your effectiveness.

Applying the Standards for Critical Reading

In your own writing, you will do well to pay attention to all the components that go into reading critically.

Title

Your title should reflect what the essay is about, but try to make it catchy, clever, or colorful. Your title is the first thing that your audience will read, so you want it to engage their interest.

Audience

Have a clear audience in mind. If your instructor lets you choose your own audience, select one that would find your paper intriguing. For instance, you might imagine an audience opposed to your point of view in an argumentative paper or an audience unfamiliar with your topic in an expository essay. Often your peers are your audience. In all cases, however, use language that is appropriate for that audience, and write in a style that is engaging and convincing. Use a vocabulary that is colorful, intelligent, and imaginative but not overwrought or stifled.

Thesis

Whenever possible, state your thesis clearly and early in your paper so that your readers know your central purpose. Remember that your thesis indicates the central idea of your paper, suggests the direction that your argument will go, states your position on the topic, or asks a question that you will answer in the course of your paper.

Organization

In addition to a thesis, your paper will have a number of paragraphs in the body that illustrate, develop, or explain the thesis. Ensure that each paragraph in the body of the paper has a topic sentence, focuses on a single idea, and provides details to illustrate, amplify, or comment on that idea. Make sure that you use transitional devices to move from point to point and from paragraph to paragraph so that readers can easily follow the development of your essay.

Purpose and Rhetorical Strategy

Writers use many different strategies for organizing and developing their ideas, depending on their purpose. Whether their purpose is persuasive, expository, or expressive, writers must be focused and clear if they want to engage their readers. They can achieve clarity or coherence with good organization and logical development of ideas. Writers seldom use any one method—or even consciously think about the particular pattern or mode of development they are using. Instead, they first decide what their purpose for writing is, and then they use whatever patterns best achieve that purpose. Whatever your purpose, however, there are some fairly standard ways of organizing your writing.

Argument/Persuasion

Argument is a mode of persuasion in which the goal is to convince readers of the validity of the writer's position (argument) or move readers to accept the author's view and even act on it (persuasion). In argument, writers set forth an assertion (often called a proposition) and then offer proof to convince readers that the assertion is valid or true. In persuasion, writers go a step further and offer a course of action, with the ultimate goal of making the readers take action. The supporting evidence or proof must be so convincing that readers cannot help but agree that the author's position is valid. The reasoning process must be so logical that readers inevitably draw the same conclusions that the author does from the evidence.

A writer's primary concern in the argument mode is to maintain an assertion he or she believes in strongly. This position or assertion should be stated clearly at the beginning of the essay. It is also helpful to have an explanation of why the writer believes this—for example, that the position is worth upholding or endorsing because it has some bearing on the lives of readers or the general common good of a community or a society. The argument will be more effective if it is organized with the least convincing or least important point first and then builds to its strongest point. This pattern lends

emphasis to the most important points, and it engages readers in the unfold-
ing process of the argument as the writer move through increasingly more
compelling proofs.

A successful argument also gives evidence of some sort, such as statistics, observations or testimony of experts, personal narratives, or other supporting proof, for every important point. Writers need to convince readers by
taking them from where they are on an issue to where the writers want the
readers to be. The only way to do this is to provide evidence that convinces
readers that the position is right or true. For examples of arguments by writers with opposing views on an issue, see "The Quality of Mercy Killing" by
Roger Rosenblatt, " First and Last, Do No Harm" by Charles Krauthammer, and
"Living Is the Mystery" by M. Scott Peck, all in Chapter 2. Some other essays
that use argument/persuasion are David A. Kaplan's "Infamy and Immortality,"
Tricia Rose's "Rap Music and the Demonization of Young Black Males," and
Stephen Steinberg's, "The Affirmative Action Debate."

Cause/Effect Analysis

A writer who wants to explain why something happened or show what happened as a result of something—or perhaps both—is doing cause/effect analysis. This kind of analysis is used frequently in news broadcasts and in
magazine and newspaper articles to explain things, such as the chain of events
that led to a particular action, the effects of a particular event or crisis, or both
causes and effects of a specific situation. Cause/effect analysis is also used frequently to argue. A writer who argues, for example, that offering sex education in schools or making contraceptives readily available to high school
students would be more effective in reducing the number of teenage pregnancies than a policy against showing explicit sex scenes on prime-time television is using the strategy of causal analysis. This writer would have to sort
out possible causes to explain the high rate of teenage pregnancies, to determine which are likely the most responsible and which are contributing factors, and then to conjecture the likely results if the recommendation were
followed. Wendell Berry's "Men and Women in Search of Common Ground,"
John Davidson's "Menace to Society," Alan Thein Durning's "Can't Live Without It," and Brent Staples's "Just Walk on By: A Black Man Ponders His Power
to Alter Public Space" are just some of the essays in this textbook that illustrate cause/effect analysis.

Comparison/Contrast

Another strategy for developing ideas is to show similarities and differences
between two things. Comparison/contrast can be useful in an argument when
the writer supports one of two possible choices and needs to explain the reasons for that choice. In an expository essay—that is, one in which the purpose is to explain something—comparison/contrast can be useful to
demonstrate a thorough understanding of the subject. When comparing or

contrasting, the purpose will usually be one of two things: to show each of two subjects distinctly by considering both side by side, or to evaluate or judge two things. An analogy is a useful kind of comparison when seeking to explain something complicated or unfamiliar by showing its similarities to something less complicated or more familiar. Among the essays in this book using the strategy of comparison/contrast are Bruce Catton's "Grant and Lee: A Study in Contrasts," Annie Dillard's "Living Like Weasels," Deborah Tannen's "Sex, Lies, and Conversation," and E. B. White's "Once More to the Lake."

Classification/Division

Classification is the sorting of information and ideas into categories or groups; division is the breaking of information, ideas, or concepts into parts to better understand them. A writer may use classification to explain how a particular class of people, things, or ideas can be separated into groups and labeled according to what those groups have in common that distinguishes them from other groups in their class. A writer may use division to make a large, complex subject easier to understand by dividing it into smaller, more manageable parts. The following essays employ classification, division, or both as an organizing pattern: Frank Conroy's "Think About It: Ways We Know, and Don't," Martin Luther King, Jr.'s "Pilgrimage to Nonviolence," Gerald F. Kreyche's "Have We Lost Our Sense of Humor?" and Noel Perrin's "The Androgynous Male."

Definition

Writers often need to define as they inform or argue. Definition is the process of making clear the precise meaning or significance of a thing. In definition, a writer conveys the essential characteristics of something by distinguishing it from all other things in its class. You are familiar with dictionary definitions of words. Writers employ a similar technique to clarify or explain, but usually with more detail than dictionaries give. In addition to providing brief definitions of terms, writers may provide extended definitions—that is, take the meaning of a word beyond its dictionary definition or beyond the limits of a simple definition. An extended definition may go for a paragraph or two or even the length of an entire essay. A writer using abstract terms or concepts unfamiliar to an audience will find the extended definition to be a useful tool. Frank Conroy's "Think About It: Ways We Know, and Don't," Scott Fisher's "Lessons from Two Ghosts," Ellen Goodman's "It's Failure, Not Success," Martin Luther King, Jr.'s "Pilgrimage to Nonviolence," and Noel Perrin's "The Androgynous Male" are among the essays illustrating how writers use definition as part of their rhetorical strategy.

Exemplification

Examples and illustrations are crucial to writing, no matter what the primary purpose. Without examples, writing will stay at the general or abstract level and leave readers only vaguely understanding what the writer means. Examples make the writer's meaning clear and help to make writing more interesting, livelier, and engaging than an essay without details. Examples may be brief and numerous or extended and limited in number, and they even may take the form of a narrative. Much of Lini S. Kadaba's "What's in a Name?" consists of examples that illustrate her thesis. So do Gerald F. Kreyche's "Have We Lost Our Sense of Humor?" Nancy Mairs's "On Being a Cripple," Mary Crow Dog's "A Woman from He-Dog," and Deborah Tannen's "Sex, Lies, and Conversation." It would be difficult to find an effective piece of writing that does not use examples of some sort.

Narration

Narration is the recreation of an experience for a specific purpose. It may be a brief anecdote, a story, or a case history. Writers use narration for a variety of purposes: to explain something, to illustrate a particular point, to report information, to entertain, or to persuade. Often a narrative is only one part of a written work, but occasionally it may be the entire means of development. When they write their stories, journalists are accustomed to asking a series of questions that help make a narrative complete: What happened? Who did it happen to? When did it happen? Where did it happen? Why did it happen? How did it happen—that is, under what circumstances or in what way did it happen? George Orwell's "Shooting an Elephant," Lynn Randall's "Grandma's Story," and Roger Wilkins's "I Became Her Target" are readings in this book that rely in large part on narration. Narration is often combined with description.

Description

Description is depicting in words a person, place, or thing by appealing to the senses—that is, by evoking through words certain sights, smells, sounds, or tactile sensations. Description is an almost indispensable part of our writing, and it certainly is inextricably linked with narration. As with narration and all other kinds of writing, description has a purpose. Description may be objective, to convey information without bias; or it may be subjective, to express feelings, impressions, or attitudes about a person, place, or thing. For good descriptive passages, see Annie Dillard's "Living Like Weasels," Nicholas Gage's "The Teacher Who Changed My Life," and E. B. White's "Once More to the Lake."

Sentence-Level Skills

Finally, pay attention to sentence-level skill. A good writer demonstrates the ability to construct effective sentences that are varied in structure and length. Make sure that words are spelled correctly and that sentences are punctuated according to standard conventions. Leave time to proofread and edit your paper before handing it in.

Self-Evaluation

Apply the questions that appear in the discussion of evaluation in the *Reading Critically* section presented earlier. Ask yourself if you have a clearly stated central idea, if your paragraphs are fully developed with specific and detailed statements, if your overall organizing pattern is clear, if your writing is understandable and intelligent, and if the language used is appropriate and idiomatic. Here is the list again, modified to suit an evaluation of your own work:

- Does your introduction give enough information to get your readers easily into the essay?
- Do you achieve your stated or implied purpose?
- Is your essay organized?
- Is your thesis or main idea thoroughly explained, developed, or argued?
- Have you supplied enough details, examples, or other evidence to fully support or illustrate the thesis?
- If it is an argument or persuasion essay, is the evidence convincing? Is the argument logical and reasonable?
- If it is a descriptive essay, have you conveyed the essence of the thing with appropriately vivid words?
- Can you anticipate questions that your readers might have about or challenges they might make to any of your assertions? If so, can you revise your paper to address those potential questions or challenges?
- Does your conclusion bring your paper to a satisfactory closure?
- Is your writing clear?
- Have you used colorful, engaging, and lively language?

ILLUSTRATION: READING CRITICALLY AND WRITING WELL

For examples of how both student and professional writers can read the same work and then write their own critical perspectives on it, read the following group of essays. First, read Abraham Lincoln's "The Gettysburg Address." Next, read the student essay for one perspective on the applicability of Lincoln's Civil War words to the United States in 2002. Then, applying the guidelines for reading critically that have been outlined here, read Garry Wills's "How to Speak to a Nation's Suffering" and William Safire's "A Spirit Reborn" for critical responses to "The Gettysburg Address" by two well-known professional writers. Notice how a piece of writing more than 140 years old has relevance to today's world and remains as fresh and timely in its own way today as it did when it was first written.

The Gettysburg Address
Abraham Lincoln

Fourscore and seven years ago our fathers brought forth on this continent a new nation, conceived in liberty and dedicated to the proposition that all men are created equal.

Now we are engaged in a great civil war, testing whether that nation or any nation so conceived and so dedicated can long endure. We are met on a great battlefield of that war. We have come to dedicate a portion of that field as a final resting-place for those who here gave their lives that that nation might live. It is altogether fitting and proper that we should do this.

But in a larger sense, we cannot dedicate, we cannot consecrate, we cannot hallow this ground. The brave men, living and dead who struggled here have consecrated it far above our poor power to add or detract. The world will little note nor long remember what we say here, but it can never forget what they did here. It is for us the living, rather, to be dedicated here to the unfinished work which they who fought here have thus far so nobly advanced. It is rather for us to be here dedicated to the great task remaining before us—that from these honored dead we take increased devotion to that cause for which they gave the last full measure of devotion—that we here highly resolve that these dead shall not have died in vain, that this nation under God shall have a new birth of freedom, and that government of the people, by the people, for the people shall not perish from the earth.

Josanne's introduction begins with a general statement and becomes more specific as she moves toward her thesis. Josanne frames her thesis in the form of a question.

The Gettysburg Address and the War

Against Terrorism

Josanne Begley

Time changes everything. As each second passes, a change occurs somewhere: a baby is born, a discovery is made, a tragic event occurs—it only takes a moment. But does it follow that, because the physical world changes with time, therefore the ideas of great thinkers and leaders of the past are no longer relevant? Can the words of a speech that is over 140 years old have any significance to today's world? What can "The Gettysburg Address" possibly say to a nation at war with terrorism?

The paragraph focuses on trials that America has survived, connecting the Civil War with the war on terrorism.

Ever since the American founders established a nation based on the principle that all men and women are created equal and are entitled to be free, its enemies have tried its ability to survive. At war internally, the United States even put itself to the test during the Civil War over the issue of slavery. Many people gave their lives in that long fight to preserve the freedom for all people that is a hallmark of this country. More recently, terrorists put America to the test when they used its own airplanes as flying bombs and crashed three of them into the World Trade Center and the Pentagon, along with another one that was diverted into a field in Pennsylvania. That trial, too, was not without sacrifices.

Josanne discusses the Gettysburg Address and quotes a passage whose words she will refer to later.

After a bloody battle at Gettysburg during the Civil War, President Abraham Lincoln delivered his famous address to dedicate a cemetery at the site of the battle. The Confederacy was fighting for the right to own and use slaves, but President Lincoln knew that slavery went against the principles of freedom and equality that the nation was built upon. In his speech, Lincoln charged the people of the Union to carry on the fight for which so many lives had already been given:

> The world will little note nor long remember what we say here, but it can

never forget what they did here. It
is for us the living, rather, to be
dedicated here to the unfinished work
which they who fought here have thus
far so nobly advanced. It is rather
for us to be here dedicated to the
great task remaining before us—that
from these honored dead we take
increased devotion to that cause for
which they gave the last full measure
of devotion—that we here highly
resolve that these dead shall not
have died in vain.

Lincoln realized that those who gave their
lives at the battle of Gettysburg died for a
cause they believed in, and his speech to
those assembled for the dedication of the
cemetery reiterated the need for the living
to carry on the battle with renewed and even
stronger commitment.

After the terrorist attacks on September
11, 2001, America is once again fighting for
freedom, this time not only for the right of
each human being to live his or her life as
he or she sees fit but also to live that
life without the constant fear of a
terrorist attack. Obviously the war against
terrorism is different from the Civil War.
This war has a nebulous and widespread
enemy; there is no one specific country to
target but rather specific persons and their
followers whose goal it is to destroy the
United States. The war on terrorism is
likely to be protracted far beyond the

Note how the first sentence makes the transition into the new paragraph and shifts the focus to the war on terrorism. Josanne contrasts the Civil War with the war on terrorism but then highlights the relevance of Lincoln's words at Gettysburg to the events of September 11, 2001.

number of years it took to fight the Civil War. The goal of this war—eradicating terrorism—is not easy to achieve, but that does not mean that the country will not fight for it. We must not and will not let the thousands of people who lost their lives on that eleventh day of September to "have died in vain." As buildings were burning and crumbling into rubble, brave police officers and courageous firemen "gave the last full measure of devotion" as they tried to save the lives of innocent people trapped in those buildings. Hearing the horrendous news about the attacks on New York and the Pentagon, people on another hijacked plane rallied together and saved untold numbers of lives by giving up their own. Like the dead at Gettysburg, these people in New York, Washington, D.C., and Pennsylvania died heroic deaths.

Josanne's conclusion answers the question posed in her thesis and continues to emphasize the relevance of Lincoln's words to today's battle.

Lincoln's words at Gettysburg do indeed have strong relevance for us today. As a nation, we "can never forget" what those who died on September 11, 2001, did. We must commit ourselves "to the task remaining before us." We must complete "the unfinished work" that was begun that day of fighting to preserve our basic liberties and to eliminate terrorism. We must resolve, as Lincoln put it to his audience over 140 years ago, "that this nation under God shall have a new birth of freedom, and that government of the people, by the people, for the people shall not perish from the earth."

How to Speak to a Nation's Suffering
Garry Wills

*Garry Wills, a professor of history at Northwestern University, is
the author of* Lincoln at Gettysburg:The Words that Remade America, *(1992) for which he won the Pulitzer Prize, and, most recently,* Why I Am a Catholic *(2002)."How to Speak to a Nation's
Suffering" appeared in the August 18, 2002, issue of* The New
York Times.

It is said that the greatest works of art achieve universality through a paradoxical specificity—that Hamlet becomes more Everyman the more he is made
the Prince of Denmark. However that applies to other works of art, it is certainly true of one masterpiece, the Gettysburg Address, which will be read
aloud twice, by politicians of both parties, on the anniversary of the attack on
the World Trade Center and the Pentagon.

Although the Gettysburg Address was criticized early on for dealing in
"glittering generalities," it was what would be called today a site-specific artifact. "We are met on a great battlefield . . . to dedicate a portion of that field
. . . as a final resting-place for those who here gave their lives . . . who struggled here   The world will little note nor long remember what we say here
but it can never forget what they did here. . . . It is for us, the living, rather, to
be dedicated here to the unfinished work."

It is also time-specific: Not only are we met "here," but the day is accurately placed in the flow of time that matters to the polity, coming as it does
87 years after the signing of the Declaration of Independence.

4   Though Lincoln referred reverentially to the Declaration of Independence, he did not think it adequate simply to read the document over the
dead bodies at Gettysburg. He had to think its meaning into the new situation.
He wanted to know everything he could about that new situation—to know
ahead of time, for instance, what "that field" would look like when he got
there. So he called to the White House the landscape architect—another great
artist, William Saunders—who had laid out the burial ground where Lincoln
would be speaking. Lincoln learned at this conference that Saunders had
adapted the semicircular rows of identical graves to the curve of the land,
making sure that no one state or regiment or officer was favored over any others. Literally "embodied" in the very earth that these men had made sacred
was the truth that "all men are created equal."The pattern of these graves was
not completed when Lincoln rose to speak above it, but he knew what Saunders's vision for the cemetery was, and he gave it even more precise focus
and explication.

Those rows on rows of dead offered a potential indictment of the living.
Why had they been sacrificed in such numbers? About 6,000 were left dead at
battle's end, with many more to die very soon of wounds contracted there.

The loss of men to both armies—killed, wounded, captured or missing—ran to 50,000, taking out of action a quarter of the Northern forces engaged there and a third of the Southern.

How was Lincoln to find meaning in such a cruel tally? He actually used the scale of payment in dead bodies to boost the value of the thing being purchased. His argument was that the Union would not be worth preserving at that price unless the battle vindicated the entire principle of self-rule ("that the government of the people, by the people, for the people shall not perish from the earth"). And self-rule was not worth this terrible expenditure unless it, in turn, was based on "the proposition that all men are created equal."

By linking the deaths with the Declaration, issued 87 years earlier, Lincoln engaged in a kind of beneficent opportunism. He was redefining the nature of the Union in terms not used in the Constitution. He smuggled into that founding document the language of Jefferson, that "all men are created equal." Only if this truth were at stake could meaning be commensurate with the toll of deaths at Gettysburg. And later generations would have to honor this meaning if they were to keep faith with the dead, with "those who here gave their lives that that nation might live." The dead had set a task for the living—that we "take increased devotion to that cause for which they gave the last full measure of devotion." Lincoln was creatively upping the ante of the whole American project. Dr. Martin Luther King, Jr., understood the nature of the commitment Lincoln made for "that nation." He would say that the 1963 march on Washington came to cash the check issued by the Declaration (which was reissued when Lincoln repeated Jefferson's words). And just as Lincoln did not merely read the Declaration of Independence over the dead, Dr. King did not just read the Gettysburg Address in the shadow of the Lincoln Memorial. He, too, thought the old document into his immediate situation. As Lincoln had begun "Fourscore and seven years ago," Dr. King began "Five score years ago," adding links to the chain of meanings wrought from national suffering and trial. In this way does creativity give birth to further creativity, Jefferson's to Lincoln's, Lincoln's to King's.

PERSONAL RESPONSE

In what ways, if any, do you find Lincoln's "The Gettysburg Address" comforting as you recall the events of September 11, 2001?

QUESTIONS FOR DISCUSSION

1. What do you understand Wills to mean by "paradoxical specificity" (paragraph 1). How does he use the "The Gettysburg Address" to illustrate his point?

2. What do you think Wills means when he says that Lincoln "had to think its [Declaration of Independence] meaning into the new situation" (paragraph 4)? Why do you think he brings in the reference to Dr. Martin Luther King, Jr., in his closing paragraph?

3. In what way did "[t]hose rows on rows of dead [offer] a potential indictment of the living" (paragraph 5)? How is that point relevant to the events of September 11, 2001?

4. To what extent do you agree with Wills when he says that "Lincoln engaged in a kind of beneficent opportunism" (paragraph 7)?

A Spirit Reborn
William Safire

William Safire has been a writer for The New York Times *since 1963. Winner of the 1978 Pulitzer Prize for distinguished commentary, he also writes a Sunday column, "On Language," that has appeared in* The New York Times Magazine *since 1979. Among the many books he has published are* Freedom *(1987),* Lend Me Your Ears *(1992),* The First Dissident *(1992),* Sleeper Spy *(1995), and* Scandalmonger *(2000). This opinion piece appeared in* The New York Times Online *on September 9, 2002.*

Abraham Lincoln's words at the dedication of the Gettysburg cemetery will be the speech repeated at the commemoration of Sept. 11 by the governor of New York and by countless other speakers across the nation.

The lips of many listeners will silently form many of the famous phrases. "Fourscore and seven years ago"—a sonorous way of recalling the founding of the nation 87 years before he spoke—is a phrase many now recite by rote, as is "the last full measure of devotion."

But the selection of this poetic political sermon as the oratorical centerpiece of our observance need not be only an exercise in historical evocation, nonpolitical correctness and patriotic solemnity. What makes this particular speech so relevant for repetition on this first anniversary of the worst bloodbath on our territory since Antietam Creek's waters ran red is this: Now, as then, a national spirit rose from the ashes of destruction.

4   Here is how to listen to Lincoln's all-too-familiar speech with new ears.

In those 266 words, you will hear the word dedicate five times. The first two times refer to the nation's dedication to two ideals mentioned in the Declaration of Independence, the original ideal of "liberty" and the ideal that became central to the Civil War: "that all men are created equal."

The third, or middle, dedication is directed to the specific consecration of the site of the battle of Gettysburg: "to dedicate a portion of that field as a final resting-place." The fourth and fifth times Lincoln repeated dedicate reaffirmed those dual ideals for which the dead being honored fought: "to the unfinished work" and then "to the great tasks remaining before us" of securing freedom and equality.

Those five pillars of dedication rested on a fundament of religious metaphor. From a president not known for his piety—indeed, often criticized for his supposed lack of faith—came a speech rooted in the theme of national resurrection. The speech is grounded in conception, birth, death and rebirth.

8   Consider the barrage of images of birth in the opening sentence. The nation was "conceived in liberty," and "brought forth"—that is, delivered into life—by "our fathers" with all "created" equal. (In the 19th century, both "men" and "fathers" were taken to embrace women and mothers.) The nation was born.

Then, in the middle dedication to those who sacrificed themselves, come images of death: "final resting place" and "brave men, living and dead."

Finally, the nation's spirit rises from this scene of death: "that this nation under God shall have a new birth of freedom." Conception, birth, death, rebirth. The nation, purified in this fiery trial of war, is resurrected. Through the sacrifice of its sons, the sundered nation would be reborn as one.

An irreverent aside: All speechwriters stand on the shoulders of orators past. Lincoln's memorable conclusion was taken from a fine oration by the Rev. Theodore Parker at an 1850 Boston antislavery convention. That social reformer defined the transcendental "idea of freedom" to be "a government of all the people, by all the people, for all the people."

12   Lincoln, 13 years later, dropped the "alls" and made the phrase his own. (A little judicious borrowing by presidents from previous orators shall not perish from the earth.) In delivering that final note, the Union's defender is said to have thrice stressed the noun "people" rather than the prepositions "of," "by" and "for." What is to be emphasized is not rhetorical rhythm but the reminder that our government's legitimacy springs from America's citizens; the people, not the rulers, are sovereign. Not all nations have yet grasped that.

Do not listen on Sept. 11 only to Lincoln's famous words and comforting cadences. Think about how Lincoln's message encompasses but goes beyond paying "fitting and proper" respect to the dead and the bereaved. His sermon at Gettysburg reminds "us the living" of our "unfinished work" and "the great task remaining before us"—to resolve that this generation's response to the deaths of thousands of our people leads to "a new birth of freedom."

PERSONAL RESPONSE

Have you had a renewed sense of nationalism or patriotism since September 11, 2001?

QUESTIONS FOR DISCUSSION

1. Explore the implications of the statement that "a national spirit rose from the ashes of destruction" (paragraph 3).
2. Discuss the difference it makes if Lincoln stressed the word *people* instead of the prepositions *of, by,* and *for* in his conclusion to "The Gettysburg Address" (paragraph 12).
3. How effective do you find Safire's directions on "how to listen to Lincoln's all-too-familiar speech with new ears" (paragraph 4). Do you now have a different understanding of or way of thinking about the speech?

2

ETHICS, MORALS, AND VALUES

Ethics, morals, and values, though different in their dictionary definitions, are closely related in meaning and are often used interchangeably. According to the *American Heritage Dictionary, ethics* are the rules or standards governing the conduct of a person or members of a profession, as in *medical* or *legal ethics. Morals* are also related to rules of conduct, but in a broader sense than ethics. Morals have to do with habits of conduct regarding standards of right and wrong, as in *a person of loose morals* or *a decline in public morals.* Finally, *values,* in the context of ethics and morals, have to do with principles, standards, or qualities that are considered to be worthwhile or desirable, as in *family values.* The authors represented in this chapter explore guidelines for ethical and moral behavior. Their essays focus on subjects that involve standards of conduct, standards of right and wrong, or standards of worthwhile behavior.

The chapter begins with Lorri G. Nandrea's "Having No Hand in the Matter," which explores the way the hand has functioned as a signifier of individual responsibility (or guilt). She considers such matters as agency, ethics, and responsibility in the case of crimes that take place because of negligence, distancing, or a failure to prevent something that will not be directly attributable to anybody. Nandrea concludes that the large, impersonal networks in which we are now involved make it necessary to think about ethics in a way that does not depend on individuality or personal contact (the "hand" model).

Ellen Goodman's "It's Failure, Not Success" takes exception to a definition of success advanced in a popular self-help book of the late 1980s. Such books are still being published, which makes her observations relevant today. Maintaining that it is not all right to be greedy or dishonest, even if one becomes rich as a result, Goodman explains where she draws the line between what is moral and what is immoral. Next, Christina Hoff Sommers, in "Are We Living in a Moral Stone Age?" laments what she sees as a lack of moral standards in young people today. Her remarks are sure to draw strong responses from readers. Kurt Wiesenfeld, a physics professor at Georgia Tech, echoes Sommers's complaint as he discusses the behavior of students who disregard the connection between grades and performance by asking for a higher grade than the one they deserve at the end of the semester. In "Making the Grade," he explains the connection he sees among such student behavior, the superficial values of American society, an erosion in academic standards, and the potentially fatal effects of these things.

Commenting on individual responsibility to the larger community, David A. Kaplan, in "Infamy and Immortality," raises an interesting question about how long a man who behaved unethically must be punished for his actions. Discussing the case of "Shoeless Joe" Jackson, Kaplan argues that this legendary baseball player deserves, finally, to be admitted to the Baseball Hall of Fame. Jackson may have let down a nation of baseball fans, but enough time has passed, Kaplan believes, to honor the man for his achievements.

Three selections in this chapter provide differing viewpoints on the controversial matter of euthanasia, an act that many believe has serious ethical and moral implications. Roger Rosenblatt, in "The Quality of Mercy Killing," discusses the controversial case of Roswell Gilbert's mercy killing of his wife, which received widespread news coverage and provoked heated public debate. Rosenblatt calls for passion and understanding in such tragic cases while acknowledging the wrenching moral dilemmas they pose. Next, Charles Krauthammer, in "First and Last, Do No Harm," takes the position that allowing doctors to aid people in committing suicide is unconscionable. Finally, M. Scott Peck, in "Living Is the Mystery," argues that the issue is far too complicated to be easily resolved.

The chapter ends with a short story by Susan Glaspell that focuses on an ethical dilemma involving murder. Two women, left alone in the kitchen of another woman suspected of having murdered her husband, piece together a likely scenario of the woman's life and what must have precipitated the murder. "A Jury of Her Peers" is likely to promote lively discussion about situational ethics and the differences between men's and women's view of justice.

1. Where do you think children learn to cheat?
2. Under what circumstances, if any, do you think cheating is justified?
3. In your experience as a student, have you witnessed cheating? What do you think motivates students to cheat?

DISCUSSION QUESTIONS/WRITING TOPICS

1. In what ways do hands reveal emotion? How do gestures indicate guilt, shame, humility, rage, or despair?
2. Create a scenario for which the image in this photograph could serve as an illustration.

Having No Hand in the Matter

Lorri G. Nandrea

Lorri Nandrea, an Assistant Professor of English at the University of Wisconsin—Stevens Point, grew up in Colorado and lived in various parts of California before earning her Ph.D. at Northwestern University in 1999. She presented an earlier version of this paper at a graduate student conference, "Anonymity," held at Harvard University in March, 1997. The paper was originally inspired by a seminar, "Is it a Tragedy?" given at Northwestern University in 1996 by the French dramatist and feminist theorist Hélène Cixous. Nandrea reports that her ideas for the essay were influenced by the astute comments and questions of the undergraduates in her discussion sections as well as by Professor Cixous's riveting lectures.

Picture, if you will, a theater; setting: the scene of the crime. Six acts, with several hundreds of years in between. Thus, we will require a number of stage hands. But in fact it is the hands I want to stage: five acts are five fingers, counting down to the sixth, the zero hour, the last minute of our time. The first fingers trace the shifting alliances between the hand, the name, and the concept of agency;[1] the last point to the way new forms of anonymous agency erase the role of the hand, defeat our current models of justice, and require us to reinvent the world—quickly, before it is too late. As all the ghosts who cross our stage remind us, "there is really such a thing as *too late*" (Cixous, "Is It a Tragedy?").

ACT I: AESCHYLUS

ORESTES: Bear me witness—show me the way, Apollo!
Did I strike her down with justice?
Strike I did, I don't deny it, no.
But how does our bloody work impress you now?—
Just or not? Decide.

APOLLO: Just,
I say to you and your high court, Athena . . .
This is [Zeus's] justice—omnipotent, I warn you.

---

[1] The *Oxford English Dictionary* defines "agent" as "one who (or that which) acts or exerts power"; "agency" is "the faculty of an agent or of acting; active working or operation," but can also mean "action or instrumentality embodied or personified as concrete existence." In other words, the word can refer to an individual's power of acting (individual agency), or more generally to "that which acts."

> . . . no oath can match
> the power of the father.

(Aeschylus 258-59)

In 458 B.C., the Greek dramatist Aeschylus wrote a trilogy of plays which stage a transition from archaic models of justice to a court system in which we can recognize our own. Specifically, the plays imagine the movement from the principles of *Dikê* (might makes right: Zeus's justice, the law of the father) and vengeance (the moral imperative to redeem a crime by another crime; to exchange violence for violence and life for life) to a system based on law, rhetoric, and consensus: reason and persuasion take the place of pain and passion. In the first play, Queen Clytaemnestra kills her husband, King Agamemnon, who sacrificed their daughter, Iphigeneia. In the second play, her son, Orestes, obeying the injunctions of a vengeful god, murders his mother to revenge the death of his father. In the third play, this tragic hero is hounded by the Furies, three ancient, magical, mythical women who arise wailing and shrieking to hunt down and torture those who have committed blood crimes, in particular, crimes against the mother. On the brink of madness, Orestes is rescued by Apollo, who appeals to Athena, goddess of reason, to end the cycle of violence. Athena founds a civilized court to replace the barbarism of individual revenge: "I will appoint the judges of manslaughter,/swear them in, and found a tribunal here/for all time to come," she declares, and indeed, we recognize the elements of her system: "My contestants,/summon your trusted witnesses and proofs,/your defenders under oath to help your cause./And I will pick the finest men of Athens,/return and decide the issue fairly, truly—/bound to our oaths, our spirits bent on justice" (253). But the Furies are infuriated, and to keep them from destroying her new system and enlist their tremendous power to support it, Athena must find some way to appease the Furies. To do so, she consigns them to the underground: "By all my rights I promise you your seat/in the depths of earth, yours by all rights—/stationed at hearths equipped with glistening thrones" (267). She promises the Furies that they will be forever remembered and revered, "covered with praise," and hence re-names them; no longer the Furies, they will now be called Eumenides, the kindly ones. Finally, after much persuasion, the Furies relent. The Furies betray us, and then we betray them.

FURIES: Zeus, you say . . .
            charged Orestes here to avenge his father's death
            and spurn his mother's rights?
APOLLO: —Not the same
            for a noble man to die, covered with praise,
            his sceptre the gift of god—murdered, at that,
            by a woman's hand, no arrows whipping in
            from a distance as an Amazon would fight.

(Aeschylus 632-635)

Agamemnon was killed by a *woman's* hand, I thought at first, this is the disgrace; but no: killed by a woman's *hand,* no arrows whipping in from a distance. At issue is the fact of contact—the crime of contact—the *hand* that tears open, breaks through the sacred frontier of the other's body, spilling the blood that, the Furies wail, "wets the ground, and you can never bring it back, dear god, the Earth drinks, and the running life is gone" (243). Crimes committed from a respectful distance, Apollo insinuates, are another matter altogether. An Other than matter, perhaps; distance appears to purify crime, eliminating the mutual contamination of the victim by the touch of the criminal and the criminal by the blood of the victim. Likewise, Athena attempts to purify justice of its tainted association with the intimate, material violence of the Furies by founding her court on the lofty "Crag of Ares, where the Amazons/pitched their tents . . ." (262), the Amazons who shoot from a distance. Like Apollo, the court repudiates contact, repressing the Furies and the abject, maternal power they represent: these repulsive old women are "driven under the earth, condemned, like so much filth" (268). The Law erects itself upon the buried bodies of these murdered mothers, who are made to comply in their own burial through Athena's arts of persuasion and the magic of re-naming. The furious kindly ones go underground and we leave them there, we forget them, but they remember; at home in our unconscious, they resurrect themselves, returning as the anonymous dark mothers that haunt us in bad dreams.

4   Athena's court, to which we are heirs, repudiates the unending cycle of vengeance, and the messy bodies of victim and criminal; instead it relies on words which function to assign the crime, to distribute guilt and innocence among individuals who can be named murderers or victims, then to determine reasonable retribution and restitution. Yet if the court disembodies justice, it affirms the embodiment of crime; it locates guilt at the point of contact, linking the name to the crime through the hand: as Orestes states, "The law condemns the man of the violent hand" (461). Moreover, its arbitrations rely in many ways on conscience; that is, on an archaic fear of the Furies who have only gone inside: "Hold out your hands, if they are clean/no fury of ours will stalk you, you will go through life unscathed. But show us the guilty—one like this/who hides his reeking hands,/and up from the outraged dead we rise. . . ." (312–17).

ACT II: MACBETH

LADY M.:   . . . Go get some water
              And wash this filthy witness from your hand.

              . . .

MACBETH: Will all great Neptune's ocean wash this blood
              Clean from my hand? No; this hand will rather
              The multitudinous seas incarnadine,
              Making the green one red.

(Shakespeare, Macbeth *II. ii. 43–60)*

LADY M.:   Here's the smell of blood still. All the perfumes of Arabia will not
sweeten this little hand.

(V. i. 50–51)

Bloody hands mark the murderer: the victim's blood, a "filthy witness,"
leaves little room for doubt. A material signifier preserved and revived by the
Furies, it is not a mark that is easily erased. If, like O. J. Simpson, you are not
caught red handed, perhaps a pair of gloves gives you away; or fingerprints
that testify to the former presence of this one here or that one there, allowing
the law to point to say, You had a hand in this matter. For literature, the law,
the Western cultural imaginary, the hand functions as symbol and signifier of
individual agency understood within the paradigm of contact, a paradigm coordinated by the "complicated and ambiguous act of touching" (Cixous, "Is it a
Tragedy?"). The work of hands—a theft, a murder, a painting—retains their
traces; conversely, hands image the connection between persons and their
acts or products, between the world and the individual will. In fact it is the
combination of hand and name that produces the signature, which binds the
individual to his or her legal identity. The trace of the hand thus forestalls
anonymity; it is an intimate and individual remainder which in a certain sense
guarantees the name, guarantees that even if a name is not known, it exists or
existed, it is possible. This is the promise the court makes to the victim: Apart
from false and sometimes horrifying equivalencies calculated by the law
($20,000 for your child's life), the semblance of justice offered to victims in
our time is recognition, acknowledgement, naming. Verso: this model of justice
does not permit us to call a crime a crime if it has no signatory, if the criminal's name is not just unknown but nonexistent; if it has been committed
anonymously in the most radical sense, by no one's hand.

ACT III: DOSTOYEVSKY

In Fyodor Dostoyevsky's 1871 novel *The Devils, or, The Possessed,* Stavrogin
returns to the house in which he has raped the landlady's young daughter,
Matryosha, who, not understanding what has happened and having no name
for this crime has accused herself of "killing God."

*There was no one there except Matryosha. . . . I saw her looking out. But I pretended
not to have noticed . . . It positively gave me pleasure not to talk to Matryosha
but to keep her in suspense. . . . I waited for a whole hour. . . . She stood and
gazed [at me] in silence. . . . Then suddenly she raised her tiny fist and began
shaking it at me. . . . Her face was full of such despair which was quite
unbearable to see on the face of a child. . . . I left her, went back to my room, . . .
[and] remained as though waiting for something. . . . She went out through the
door onto the wooden landing . . . I ran up to my door at once, opened it a
little and was just in time to see Matryosha go into the tiny box-room, which
was like a hen-coop. . . . A very curious thought flashed through my mind. . . . I*

moved my chair quietly away from the window....I picked up a book, but put
it down again and began looking at a tiny red spider on the leaf of a
geranium and lost count of the time. I remember everything to the very last
moment....

Twenty minutes had passed since she went out of the room. My guess was assuming
the aspect of reality. But I decided to wait for exactly another quarter of an hour.
...Then I got up, put on my hat, buttoned my overcoat and looked round the
room to make sure that I had left no trace of my presence there....[I] went up to
the little box-room. It was closed....I knew that it was never bolted, but I did not
want to open it. I stood on tiptoe and began looking through the chink....I
looked through the chink a long time, for it was very dark there, but not so dark
as to prevent me...from seeing what I wanted...At last I decided to leave.

(689–92)

Matryosha, of course, has killed herself. When he writes this confession, Stavrogin realizes, due to the relentless prosecution of internal Furies, that he has committed an unforgivable crime, the murder of a child. He stresses "to what an extent I was quite clearly in the full possession of my mental faculties and how much I am responsible for everything" (692). Still, no court could define his series of non-actions as a murder, for it was a crime of no contact; yet neither was it simply a sin of omission. Matryosha was intentionally murdered through distances, silences, and waiting; through no actions; through a kind of negative contact. Stavrogin tries to publish his confession, encouraging authorities to prosecute him, but realizes in despair that "legally [he has] nothing to fear, [at least] not to any considerable extent" (697). Still he tries, through naming himself a criminal and Matryosha a victim, to achieve a kind of justice: at least there will "remain those who will know everything and they will look at me and I at them" (697). Ironically, the confession was suppressed by the editors when the novel was first published, and from later editions by Dostoyevsky himself. Nonetheless, even in versions of the novel where readers do not quite understand why, the Furies finally catch up with Stavrogin and he hangs himself.

8   In this act, we witness the disappearance of the hand from the scene of the crime. Yet the Furies are still there below the stage, and through their agency something vaguely resembling justice is achieved; moreover the series of murderous non-actions has an individual author who can name himself— who can recognize himself as such. But not for long.

ACT IV: ANONYMOUS

Blood, and gold. One, as it circulates, traces the history of the circulation of the other. Astonishingly, blood, unlike hands, can be exchanged. Thus, hemophiliacs can live; due to advances in medical technology, they can even build up their coagulant capacities in a prophylactic fashion by using specially manufactured plasma concentrates. These concentrates are manufactured from

enormous stocks of donated blood: four to five thousand donors are required
to produce one industrial lot. Thus, these products carry extremely high risks
for viral contamination: "When one of the five thousand donors contributing
to an industrial lot . . . is seropositive for AIDS, the entire lot [will be] contaminated" unless the lot has been subjected to heat treatments that destroy the
virus (Kramer 83). By the mid-eighties, most of the doctors treating hemophiliacs knew this. By the late eighties many of these doctors knew, and all could
have known, that AIDS is a fatal disease transmissible by transfusions. Some of
the doctors and pharmaceutical companies involved in manufacturing and dis-
tributing plasma products also knew that their stocks were in fact contaminated, and that contamination could be reversed through investing in heat
treatments. But for complicated reasons that boil down to the love of gold,
they sold the deadly products to the hemophiliacs anyway. In France, thirteen
hundred hemophiliacs, most of them children, were infected with AIDS; approximately half have died. In the U.S., approximately eight thousand hemophiliacs have died or are dying from AIDS. Similar crises have erupted in Japan
and Canada.

   Gold and blood. The hemophiliac's lives were too expensive; they have
been "assassinated, discarded for money; they have been sacrificed" to the
profit motive, and those who might have saved them refuse responsibility for
their deaths (Cixous, "Is It a Tragedy?"). We were in doubt, they say; then, when
it becomes clear that there was really no room for doubt, someone else is at
fault, everyone is at fault, no one is at fault. In France, the director of the National Center for Blood Transfusion claimed that "although it was statistically
shown that all the Center's lots were contaminated, it was up to the 'supervisory authorities'—and not to him, to take the responsibility and ban them.
[These authorities] claimed that they hadn't banned them because it was up
to the Health Secretary. The Health Secretary said that it was up to the Minister for Social Affairs. The Minister for Social Affairs claimed that medicine was
'not my specialty.' The Prime Minister said that he didn't know" (Kramer 83).
As in the recent Enron scandals, it was difficult to know where in the chain of
authority the charges would start or stop; moreover, it was difficult for victims
or their families to prosecute anyone, since an appropriate charge could not
be found. The crime could not be identified, because it did not fit into existing
legal definitions: it was, in fact, "a deed without a name" (Shakespeare, *Macbeth* IV. i. 49). In 1989, the government of France offered victims $20,000 in
compensation if they agreed not to file complaints. In 1996, American pharmaceutical companies offered $100,000 under similar conditions. In France, trials
were at last held on charges of merchandising fraud; two doctors served light
prison sentences and are now once again working in prestigious medical positions. Just or not? Decide.

   As in Dostoyevsky, these crimes were committed by distances: by positively not speaking, not seeing, not acting, not touching. The effacement of the
hand corresponds to the erasure of the name, creating and complicating various dimensions of anonymity: the potentially benevolent anonymity of the
blood donors, the potentially protective anonymity of the too many people

involved in the large capitalist and socialist systems that produce and distribute blood products—an anonymity which made it possible to point vaguely in another direction when one asks who is to blame—and the tragic anonymity of the victims, who were not treated as precious living particularities but as a nameless, faceless set of statistics and dollar signs; as red ink rather than red blood. Sadly, too, this is a crime which should be seen not as an isolated incident but as a symptom; the symptom of a new ethical disease and the sign of a terrifying collapse of conscience. No one wanted to kill the children, but they could be murdered anyway; due to the uniquely postmodern distances between deciders, decisions, and their material effects, no one had to put a hand in the matter. And no one did: the Furies, it seems, have been conquered by market values. There is no tragic hero, here, no guilty one to recognize his flaws; only systems which act anonymously, thousands of faceless victims and a generalized tragic condition in which the language of guilt and responsibility must be transformed.

ACT V: "THE WORLD HAS BECOME A CLENCHED FIST"
OR
HÉLÈNE CIXOUS AWAKENS THE FURIES

FURIES: So, you have killed,
            Even if you did not want to kill.
            And what the killing consisted in, I'll tell you:
            You did nothing to prevent [their] death
            . . . and not to kill is not not to kill,
            To not kill is to do everything possible not to kill.
            Did you do everything possible not to kill?
            No. Did you want—not to *kill?*
            . . .

FURIES: Listen to this question.
            All of our children were deprived of their bloom.
            Though your hands are covered with blood
            You say you didn't kill.
            Whose fault is it, then?
            Who will answer that one?

X2:   There is no blood on our hands . . .
            Did I ever touch so much as a hair on anybody's head?
            I never administered cure or poison to anyone . . .
            the fault is not ours. Moreover, its no one's, there was no fault. There was
                only natural homicide. Without any will behind it. That's life. That's
                science.
            That's the job. That's the accident.

FURIES: Back in our days, everything was simple.
            The guilty were guilty.
            . . . Conscience! Conscience, do you remember?
            In the past, oftentimes, people

Talking in their sleep, or in a delirium, let's say,
Would accuse themselves, and, wandering through the night,
Scrubbing their stained hands,
Would thus reveal their hidden crimes . . .
What has changed in the universe
Is the structure of the human soul.

(Cixous, The Perjured City *69-73)*

12   In her recent play *The Perjured City (La ville parjure),* based on the events I have related, Hélène Cixous chooses to call the two criminal doctors "X1" and "X2," partly to avoid prosecution for libel. Yet these non-names imply a continuing series of culpability—X3 is me, X4 is you—and also refuse to distinguish the criminals. These are the ones history should forget, she implies: it is the victims whose names should be remembered, and it is the mother of two dead hemophiliac boys who becomes the heroine of the tragedy. What does the mother want? Justice. But what form can justice take? To have the children back is impossible: as Aeschylus's chorus wails, "a man's life-blood/is dark and mortal./Once it wets the earth/what song can sing it back?" (Aeschylus 142). With these lines, the chorus captures the paradox at the heart of the concept of justice. To "justify" the margins—to square things off, or set things straight, or balance things out in an even manner—may be possible in space, but will always be impossible in time, because time moves only forward; what is done cannot be undone. Hence history has ragged margins: the present is always out of joint with the past; the two cannot be brought into line. Justice always comes after; it tries too late, and if it is inevitably belated, how can it ever be achieved?

CHORUS: With a coffin on each side
She wants something,
Something that doesn't exist.
Something to counter despair.
She wants the wondrous thing,
The star hidden behind the stars.
Will her day ever dawn?
No human person has ever seen it,
And yet her pseudonym is engraved
In the memory of all hearts.
We all sigh: "Justice, O beloved,"
Dear and radiant image,
O Divine Non-Entity, . . .
It is you she wants, O Justice,
She wants Justice to love her.

(Cixous, The Perjured City *20)*

And yet we in the present feel that the past has a claim on us, that it is part of our ethical responsibility to try to right the wrongs of the past. So we try somehow to compensate. We may make monuments or write a book; we may try somehow to pay, and indeed in *The Perjured City* Aeschylus appears to ask the Mother if she would accept a sum of money in recompense for the loss of her child. She refuses: no amount of money could possibly equal an individual life; the very idea violates our sense of human value.

When the principles of "civilized" justice fail her, the Mother decides she wants revenge; Aeschylus (a character in Cixous's play) awakens the Furies and bring them up to the surface of our world. The Furies hunt down and torture the doctors, but when they appear before her, bloody and wounded, the Mother stops the Furies. What she wants is not death for death or pain for pain. The men are not *evil*, after all; they are unethical, cowardly, dishonest, irresponsible and thoughtless, but in all these things they are quite ordinary, not at all out of the common; they are products of a system they failed to resist.

In place of revenge, the Mother decides that the greatest service to the victims (the children and herself) would be recognition, acknowledgement, and remembrance. If she cannot achieve justice, the Mother at least wants truth, or really honesty: not the truth of fact, but the truth of understanding, the truth that transpires between people, not as answer, but as question, or honest plea: forgive me. Above all, the Mother wants to be able to forgive. In the endeavor to bring forth truth, the play stages a tribunal that resembles the recent Truth Courts in South Africa, courts that radically re-define the goals of justice as truth, recognition, and reconciliation rather than accusation, prosecution, and punishment. In this respect, the act of witnessing—to bear witness, to record and preserve the truth—becomes the primary activity of justice. Indeed, it is this process of ratification that is often the most deeply desired outcome for the victims of large-scale, systemic historical tragedies. When one watches documentary films of the Nazi War Crimes Trials, it is clear that the Holocaust survivors await just this, with enormous hope and expectation; they are seeking not revenge, but validation of the truth of their experience—and this is exactly what does not happen. The criminals steadfastly refuse to admit that they did what they did or that what they did was wrong, and the enormous disappointment of the victims is palpable in their faces, often concealed behind disbelieving, despairing hands; they weep whether or not the criminal is condemned; this is not cathartic; this is not what they wanted. Truth remains unachieved; the murderers will not admit that a crime has been committed; they cannot ask forgiveness; they cannot acknowledge their own guilt. This inability is in part psychological, but is also encouraged by the workings of the law: it is in the criminals' interest not to admit guilt; not to tell the truth. Thus within Athena's court of law, truth is often paralyzed: working to assemble an objective narrative of facts and evidence which may be affirmed or denied by reason, courts often forestall the emergence of a meaningful subjective truth, and hence obliterate the possibility of forgiveness.

X1:   ...Where is the man who can say: Out of compulsion for profit, I caused
thirteen hundred children to die, or, I did not cause them not to die. Besides,
   it's
not really thirteen hundred, its only two hundred ninety who are dead at the
moment. Besides, when misfortune stepped in insidiously, science was telling
   us
that only one tenth of those affected might succumb, that's to say, therefore,
   one
hundred and thirty. But Madame, if I had done that, I would deserve death.
That's why nothing in the world can ever make me confess. I'm not ashamed
   to
say that I have money in my blood, but not in my head. For me to kill, the
   word
money and its ardent syllables would have had to cause convulsions in my
   brain.
But I have a cool head. Look at my hand, I have white, straight fingers.
If I had done that, do you believe that it wouldn't show?

(Cixous, The Perjured City *105)*

16   In the end, this crime can neither be named and remembered nor for-
given and forgotten; there is no redemption, no resolution, only a theater and
a terrifying sense that we, like Aeschylus, are bearing witness to the complete
and sudden replacement of one ethical world by another—or perhaps we are
watching an old and defunct ethical world implode, leaving our vulnerable
bodies flailing in an ethical void, a black hole swiftly swallowing things that
matter.

VI. LOOK, NO HANDS
OR
WRITING INTO THE VOID

CHORUS: And I say: unjust Justice is not an inevitable fate.
      And it is not true that everything was settled a long time ago,
      For ever and ever.

(Cixous, The Perjured City *24)*

      A nostalgia for the handmade, associated with the accelerated disappear-
ance of the hand from all production processes, certainly results from the encroaching anonymity of objects, machine-made things which carry little
evidence of their humanity. On the other side, we find the failure of the world
to register our fingers, our having been there; graffiti and vandalism can be
seen as spectacular acts of protest against a world that seems inflexibly pre-
fabricated. I do not want to advocate nostalgia for the hand—voice—name

model of individual agency, which has clearly been rendered unworkable in this our world. And yet at the moment we are confronted with a volatile situation in which widespread cynicism about this model has outraced the responsiveness of systems founded upon it. We mistake O. J. Simpson for a model of criminal guilt, whose hands do or do not fit these gloves. Meanwhile, behind our back, as we name individual criminals who appear to have killed for a reason, or for no reason, true enormities are not committed, not crimes but criminal failures in which thousands of people die because the place of the Furies has been infected by the profit motive.

In our time, it seems essential that the redistribution of individual agency among systems which act anonymously does not become a cynical ruse for the absence of individual care. The very distances that immaterialize our relations in late capitalist societies also exponentially multiply the ways in which we affect one another, catching us altogether in a great volatile worldwide web. How can we, as collections of anonymous particles that compose together such large and powerful anonymous agencies, cultivate a sense of responsibility for the unknowable masses who may be affected by our actions and our failures? As the eighteenth-century philosopher David Hume argued, it is not really individuality that threatens the fabric of society but partiality, the cultivation of specific sympathies for those with whom I am in contact, those who are not anonymous for me. This ethos is inadequate to our time. How can one learn to care namelessly for the nameless others, even for those who are dead or not yet born; how can the forms of anonymous agency produced by our capitalist systems be suffused with a fundamental respect for life that cannot be overridden by financial considerations? We need new ethics, new concepts of justice that help us think not just contact but distance and absences; that foster fidelity to the absent one, to those we will never see and never know. This fidelity cannot take the form of an indiscriminate general love for everything, which is equivalent to having no love at all. Instead, it must be based on a sense of the incomparable value of the particular: a particular love for each fragile, mortal, irreplaceable particular, no matter who, or where, or what it may be.

In addition to extending our sympathy to encompass the stranger, this new ethics must involve an understanding of justice as a perpetually unfinished transaction between the past, the present, and the future; an ongoing tension that can never be completely resolved. Martin Luther King's *Letter from Birmingham Jail* was a letter addressed directly to a group of his contemporaries, it is true; but it is a double letter that is always also addressed to a future that will never finally arrive. "One day the South will recognize its real heroes," King writes (721), and we who read the letter today recognize that line makes a demand upon us: King's "one day" is our day, now. King asks us, the future, to promise that this recognition, a form of justice *will have been* achieved. Underneath this demand one hears the bittersweet echo of an urgent human question, "Will this have been worthwhile?" King's enormous faith in the future, his ability to value the nameless ones, led him to sacrifice his present on our behalf; to work toward a justice that could not be guaranteed, a better world that he himself would never see or know. It is temporarily up to us to make his sacrifice have been worthwhile. It is up to us, the future readers, to recognize, to answer, to act, and then to pass the letter on to a future remains before us; to make it possible for that future to receive and reply.

20   The philosopher Jacques Derrida has argued that all just decisions will be based on a sense of ethical responsibility to those who "remain before" us: both those who are dead, and those who are not yet born; all those outside of the living present. In order to achieve such a position, we must work against a growing tendency to see the present as outside of history, or to see history as a series of unconnected presents—especially when these tendencies function to distance us from some of the atrocities of the recent past (because we didn't have a hand in them, we don't want to see ourselves as responsible for them in any way). We must also work against the tendency to doubt the existence of the future, or to disclaim the power our actions exert upon the future. Indeed, the present exerts shaping force on both past and present: the present determines what will be possible or not be possible in the future; in the past, what will or will not have been worthwhile.

In place of an ethics based on contact—on the hand, perhaps we need an ethics based on writing—on the letter: a mode of connection that, unlike the hand, can take place across distances and absences and hence compete with the networks of gold. Writing travels from past to present to future; it can function to link moments in time, to create virtual relations between a past and a present and a series of future readers. Like our capitalist systems, writing can be impersonal; one often writes blindly, for readers who are likely to remain nameless, invisible, unknown. But unlike the overly efficient systems of capitalist reproduction, writing allows time for care; writing encourages one to imagine the act of addressing anonymous others as dear. An ethics of writing would require care, and a sense of responsibility—for both our acts of authorship and our failures to protest, even when our words no longer bear the trace of a single hand.

WORKS CITED

Aeschylus. *The Oresteia*. Trans. Robert Fagles. New York: Penguin, 1979.

Cixous, Hélène. "Is It a Tragedy?" Seminar (CLS D-90). Northwestern University, Evanston, IL, Fall 1996.

—. *The Perjured City, or, The Awakening of the Furies*. Trans. Bernadette Fort. Unpublished manuscript, 1994. In *The Plays of Hélène Cixous*. New York: Routledge, 2003.

Derrida, Jacques. *Specters of Marx*. Trans. Peggy Kamuf. New York: Routledge, 1994.

Dostoyevsky, Fyodor. *The Devils, or, The Possessed*. Trans. David Magarshack. New York: Penguin, 1971.

King, Martin Luther, Jr. "Letter from Birmingham Jail." *The Dolphin Reader.*
    Ed. Douglas Hunt. Boston: Houghton Mifflin, 1986. 707–22.

Kramer, Jane. "Bad Blood." *New Yorker* 11 Oct. 1993:74–95.

Shakespeare, William. *Macbeth. The Riverside Shakespeare.* Ed.
    G. Blakemore Evans. Boston: Houghton Mifflin, 1974. 1312–42.

READER RESPONSE

Imagine that you have just been the victim of a crime. In the wake of this
crime, what would you want? If you have, in fact, been a victim, think back
to how you felt at that time: What did you want? Did you get what you
wanted? If so, how? If not, why not?

QUESTIONS FOR DISCUSSION

1. Why does this article refer so often to the theater—both in the literary
   texts it discusses and in its own style and structure? Do you see special
   connections between the theater and the concept of agency, or the question of justice?
2. What do you think is Nandrea's purpose in this article? Do you think her
   style facilitates her purpose? Does the style effectively target you as an audience? Choose lines or passages to illustrate your responses.
3. Nandrea discusses the "affair of the contaminated blood," and she mentions the Enron scandal and the O. J. Simpson trial. Can you think of other
   current events that illustrate the connection between the hand and criminal agency and/or show that this model is inadequate in our time?
4. Consider Nandrea's statement about truth in the court system: "Thus
   within Athena's court of law, truth is often paralyzed: working to assemble an objective narrative of facts and evidence which may be affirmed or
   denied by reason, courts often forestall the emergence of a meaningful
   subjective truth, and hence obliterate the possibility of forgiveness." Do
   you agree that the court system can function to impede honesty and
   hence "obliterate the possibility of forgiveness"? How or why? Is this an
   important failure?
5. What are the pros and cons of basing your ethics on concern for "anonymous" others (those you do not know personally, those who are not part
   of your present)? What kinds of thinking, or what kinds of actions, might
   help us to feel such a concern? Do you agree that *writing* could act out
   this ethics? If not, why not? If so, how?
6. Choose one of the literary works that Nandrea mentions (Aeschylus's *The
   Oresteia,* Shakespeare's *Macbeth,* Dostoyevsky's *The Possessed,* or the
   plays of Hélène Cixous), and find out more about this work and author
   through Internet or library research. Write up your findings to present to

the other students in your class to help them better understand (or, perhaps, critique) the interpretations offered in this essay.

It's Failure, Not Success
Ellen Goodman

Ellen Goodman began her career as a reporter for Newsweek
and worked for the Detroit Free Press *before becoming a columnist for the* Boston Globe *in 1967. Her column, "At Large," has
been syndicated by the Washington Post Writers Group since
1976. In 1980 she won a Pulitzer Prize for distinguished commentary. Her books include a study of human change,* Turning
Points *(1979), and, with co-author Patricia O'Brien,* I Know Just
What You Mean: The Power of Friendship in Women's Lives *(2000).
Many of her columns have been collected in* Close to Home
(1979), At Large *(1981),* Keeping in Touch *(1985),* Making Sense
(1989), and Value Judgments *(1993). "It's Failure, Not Success"
was published in the* Boston Globe *in 1987.*

I knew a man who went into therapy about three years ago because, as he
put it, he couldn't live with himself any longer. I didn't blame him. The guy
was a bigot, a tyrant and a creep.

In any case, I ran into him again after he'd finished therapy. He was still a
bigot, a tyrant and a creep, but . . . he had learned to live with himself.

Now, I suppose this was an accomplishment of sorts. I mean, nobody
else could live with him. But it seems to me that there are an awful lot of people running around and writing around these days encouraging us to feel
good about what we should feel terrible about, and to accept in ourselves
what we should change.

4   The only thing they seem to disapprove of is disapproval. The only judgment they make is against being judgmental, and they assure us that we have
nothing to feel guilty about except guilt itself. It seems to me that they are all
intent on proving that I'm OK and You're OK, when in fact, I may be perfectly
dreadful and you may be unforgivably dreary, and it may be—gasp!—*wrong*.

What brings on my sudden attack of judgmentitis is success, or rather,
Success!—the latest in a series of exclamation-point books all concerned with
How to Make It.

In this one, Michael Korda is writing a recipe book for success. Like the
other authors, he leapfrogs right over the "Shoulds" and into the "Hows." He

eliminates value judgments and edits out moral questions as if he were Fanny Farmer and the subject was the making of a blueberry pie.

It's not that I have any reason to doubt Mr. Korda's advice on the way to achieve success. It may very well be that successful men wear handkerchiefs stuffed neatly in their breast pockets, and that successful single women should carry suitcases to the office on Fridays whether or not they are going away for the weekend.

8   He may be realistic when he says that "successful people generally have very low expectations of others." And he may be only slightly cynical when he writes: "One of the best ways to ensure success is to develop expensive tastes or marry someone who has them."

And he may be helpful with his handy hints on how to sit next to someone you are about to overpower.

But he simply finesses the issues of right and wrong—silly words, embarrassing words that have been excised like warts from the shiny surface of the new how-to books. To Korda, guilt is not a prod, but an enemy that he slays on page four. Right off the bat, he tells the would-be successful reader that:

- It's OK to be greedy.
- It's OK to look out for Number One.
- It's OK to be Machiavellian (if you can get away with it).
- It's OK to recognize that honesty is not always the best policy (provided you don't go around saying so.)
- And it's always OK to be rich.

Well, in fact, it's not OK. It's not OK to be greedy, Machiavellian, dishonest. It's not always OK to be rich. There is a qualitative difference between succeeding by making napalm or by making penicillin. There is a difference between climbing the ladder of success, and macheteing a path to the top.

12   Only someone with the moral perspective of a mushroom could assure us that this was all OK. It seems to me that most Americans harbor ambivalence toward success, not for neurotic reasons, but out of a realistic perception of what it demands.

Success is expensive in terms of time and energy and altered behavior— the sort of behavior he describes in the grossest of terms: "If you can undermine your boss and replace him, fine, do so, but never express anything but respect and loyalty for him while you're doing it."

This author—whose *Power!* topped the best-seller list last year—is intent on helping rid us of that ambivalence which is a signal from our conscience. He is like the other "Win!" "Me First!" writers, who try to make us comfortable when we should be uncomfortable.

They are all Doctor Feelgoods, offering us placebo prescriptions instead of strong medicine. They give us a way to live with ourselves, perhaps, but not a way to live with each other. They teach us a whole lot more about "Failure!" than about success.

READER RESPONSE

Explain your own position on Goodman's statement in paragraph 11 that "[i]t's not always OK to be rich."

QUESTIONS FOR DISCUSSION

1. To what extent do you agree with Goodman's opinion of Michael Korda's definition of success? To what extent do you agree with Korda's definition?
2. To what extent do you agree with Goodman's definition of success?
3. Summarize the complaints Goodman has about how-to-make-it books and the "Me First!" attitude they promote. What do you think she means in paragraph 15 when she writes, "They are all Doctor Feelgoods, offering us placebo prescriptions instead of strong medicine"?
4. Describe the tone of this piece. For example, what effect do you think Goodman wants to achieve when she uses figurative language such as "excised like warts" (paragraph 10) and "someone with the moral perspective of a mushroom" (paragraph 12)? What level of diction are words like "creep" (paragraph 1) and "gasp!" (paragraph 4)?

Are We Living in a Moral Stone Age?
Christina Hoff Sommers

Christina Hoff Sommers is a professor of philosophy at Clark University. Her books include Vice and Virtue in Everyday Life: Introductory Readings in Ethics *(1987),* Who Stole Feminism?: How Women Have Betrayed Women *(1994), and* The War Against Boys *(2000). Sommers delivered "Are We Living in a Moral Stone Age?" at a national leadership institute sponsored by Hillsdale College, which later published it in the March 1998 edition of* Imprimis.

We hear a lot today about how Johnny can't read, how he can't write, and the trouble he is having finding France on a map. It is also true that Johnny is having difficulty distinguishing right from wrong. Along with illiteracy and innumeracy, we must add deep moral confusion to the list of educational problems. Increasingly, today's young people know little or nothing about the Western moral tradition.

This was recently demonstrated by *Tonight Show* host Jay Leno. Leno frequently does "man-on-the-street" interviews, and one night he collared some young people to ask them questions about the Bible. "Can you name one of the Ten Commandments?" he asked two college-age women. One replied, "Freedom of speech?" Mr. Leno said to the other, "Complete this sentence: Let he who is without sin. . . ." Her response was, "have a good time?" Mr. Leno then turned to a young man and asked, "Who, according to the Bible, was eaten by a whale?" The confident answer was, "Pinocchio."

As with many humorous anecdotes, the underlying reality is not funny at all. These young people are morally confused. They are the students I and other teachers of ethics see every day. Like most professors, I am acutely aware of the "hole in the moral ozone." One of the best things our schools can do for America is to set about repairing it—by confronting the moral nihilism that is now the norm for so many students.

4   I believe that schools at all levels can do a lot to improve the moral climate of our society. They can help restore civility and community if they commit themselves and if they have the courage to act.

CONCEPTUAL MORAL CHAOS

When you have as many conversations with young people as I do, you come away both exhilarated and depressed. Still, there is a great deal of simple good-heartedness, instinctive fair-mindedness, and spontaneous generosity of spirit in them. Most of the students I meet are basically decent individuals. They form wonderful friendships and seem to be considerate of and grateful to their parents—more so than the baby boomers were.

In many ways they are more likable than the baby boomers—they are less fascinated with themselves and more able to laugh at their faults. An astonishing number are doing volunteer work (70 percent of college students, according to one annual survey of freshmen). They donate blood to the Red Cross in record numbers and deliver food to housebound elderly people. They spend summer vacations working with deaf children or doing volunteer work in Mexico. This is a generation of kids that, despite relatively little moral guidance or religious training, is putting compassion into practice.

Conceptually and culturally, however, today's young people live in a moral haze. Ask one of them if there are such things as "right" and "wrong," and suddenly you are confronted with a confused, tongue-tied, nervous, and insecure individual. The same person who works weekends for Meals on Wheels, who volunteers for a suicide prevention hotline or a domestic violence shelter might tell you, "Well, there really is no such thing as right or wrong. It's kind of like whatever works best for the individual. Each person has to work it out for himself. "The trouble is that this kind of answer, which is so common as to be typical, is no better than the moral philosophy of a sociopath.

8   I often meet students incapable of making even one single confident moral judgment. And it's getting worse. The things students now say are more and more unhinged. Recently, several of my students objected to philosopher

Immanuel Kant's "principle of humanity"—the doctrine that asserts the unique dignity and worth of every human life. They told me that if they were faced with the choice between saving their pet or a human being, they would choose the former.

We have been thrown back into a moral Stone Age; many young people are totally unaffected by thousands of years of moral experience and moral progress. The notion of objective moral truths is in disrepute. And this mistrust of objectivity has begun to spill over into other areas of knowledge. Today, the concept of objective truth in science and history is also being impugned. An undergraduate at Williams College recently reported that her classmates, who had been taught that "all knowledge is a social construct," were doubtful that the Holocaust ever occurred. One of her classmates said, "Although the Holocaust may not have happened, it's a perfectly reasonable conceptual hallucination."

A creative writing teacher at Pasadena City College wrote an article in the *Chronicle of Higher Education* about what it is like to teach Shirley Jackson's celebrated short story "The Lottery" to today's college students. It is a tale of a small farming community that seems normal in every way; its people are hardworking and friendly. As the plot progresses, however, the reader learns this village carries out an annual lottery in which the loser is stoned to death.

It is a shocking lesson about primitive rituals in a modern American setting. In the past, the students had always understood "The Lottery" as a warning about the dangers of mindless conformity, but now they merely think that it is "Neat!" or "Cool!" Today, not one of the teacher's current students will go out on a limb and take a stand against human sacrifice.

THE LOSS OF TRUTH

12 It was not always thus. When Thomas Jefferson wrote that all men have the right to "life, liberty, and the pursuit of happiness," he did not say, "At least that is my opinion." He declared it as an objective truth. When Elizabeth Cady Stanton amended the Declaration of Independence by changing the phrase "all men" to "all men and women," she was not merely giving an opinion; she was insisting that females are endowed with the same rights and entitlements as males.

The assertions of both Jefferson and Stanton were made in the same spirit—as self-evident truths and not as personal judgments. Today's young people enjoy the fruits of the battles fought by these leaders, but they themselves are not being given the intellectual and moral training to argue for and to justify truth. In fact, the kind of education they are getting is systematically undermining their common sense about what is true and right.

Let me be concrete and specific: Men and women died courageously fighting the Nazis. They included American soldiers, Allied soldiers, and resistance fighters. Because brave people took risks to do what was right and necessary, Hitler was eventually defeated. Today, with the assault on objective truth, many college students find themselves unable to say *why* the United States was on the right side in that war. Some even doubt that America *was* in the right. To add insult to injury, they are not even sure that the salient events of the Second World War ever took place. They simply lack confidence in the objectivity of history.

Too many young people are morally confused, ill-informed, and adrift. This confusion gets worse rather than better once they go to college. If they are attending an elite school, they can actually lose their common sense and become clever and adroit intellectuals in the worst sense. George Orwell reputedly said, "Some ideas are so absurd that only an intellectual could believe them." Well, the students of such intellectuals are in the same boat. Orwell did not know about the tenured radicals of the 1990s, but he was presciently aware that they were on the way.

THE GREAT RELEARNING

16   The problem is not that young people are ignorant, distrustful, cruel, or treacherous. And it is not that they are moral skeptics. They just talk that way. To put it bluntly, they are conceptually clueless. The problem I am speaking about is *cognitive*. Our students are suffering from "cognitive moral confusion."

What is to be done? How can we improve their knowledge and understanding of moral history? How can we restore their confidence in the great moral ideals? How can we help them become morally articulate, morally literate, and morally self-confident?

In the late 1960s, a group of hippies living in the Haight-Ashbury District of San Francisco decided that hygiene was a middle class hang-up that they could best do without. So, they decided to live without it. For example, baths and showers, while not actually banned, were frowned upon. The essayist and novelist Tom Wolfe was intrigued by these hippies who, he said, "sought nothing less than to sweep aside all codes and restraints of the past and start out from zero."

Before long, the hippies' aversion to modern hygiene had consequences that were as unpleasant as they were unforeseen. Wolfe describes them: "At the Haight-Ashbury Free Clinic there were doctors who were treating disease no living doctor had ever encountered before, diseases that had disappeared so long ago they had never even picked up Latin names, such as the mange, the grunge, the itch, the twitch, the thrush, the scroff, the rot." The itching and the manginess eventually began to vex the hippies, leading them to seek help from the local free clinics. Step by step, they had to rediscover for themselves the rudiments of modern hygiene. Wolfe refers to this as the "Great Relearning."

20   The Great Relearning is what has to happen whenever earnest reformers extirpate too much. When, "starting from zero," they jettison basic social practices and institutions, abandon common routines, defy common sense, reason, conventional wisdom—and, sometimes, sanity itself.

We saw this with the most politically extreme experiments of our century: Marxism, Maoism, and fascism. Each movement had its share of zealots and social engineers who believed in "starting from zero." They had faith in a new order and ruthlessly cast aside traditional arrangements. Among the unforeseen consequences were mass suffering and genocide. Russians and Eastern Europeans are just beginning their own "Great Relearning." They now realize, to their dismay, that starting from zero is a calamity and that the structural damage wrought by the political zealots has handicapped their societies for decades to come. They are also learning that it is far easier to tear apart a social fabric than it is to piece it together again.

America, too, has had its share of revolutionary developments—not so much political as moral. We are living through a great experiment in "moral deregulation," an experiment whose first principle seems to be: "Conventional morality is oppressive." What is right is what works for us. We question everything. We casually, even gleefully, throw out old-fashioned customs and practices. Oscar Wilde once said, "I can resist everything except temptation." Many in the Sixties generation made succumbing to temptation and license their philosophy of life.

We now jokingly call looters "non-traditional shoppers." Killers are described as "morally challenged"—again jokingly, but the truth behind the jokes is that moral deregulation is the order of the day. We poke fun at our own society for its lack of moral clarity. In our own way, we are as down and out as those poor hippies knocking at the door of the free clinic.

24   We need our own Great Relearning. Here, I am going to propose a few ideas on how we might carry out this relearning. I am going to propose something that could be called "moral conservationism." It is based on this premise: We are born into a moral environment just as we are born into a natural environment. Just as there are basic environmental necessities, like clean air, safe food, fresh water, there are basic moral necessities. What is a society without civility, honesty, consideration, self-discipline? Without a population educated to be civil, considerate, and respectful of one another, what will we end up with? Not much. For as long as philosophers and theologians have written about ethics, they have stressed the moral basics. We live in a moral environment. We must respect and protect it. We must acquaint our children with it. We must make them aware it is precious and fragile.

I have suggestions for specific reforms. They are far from revolutionary, and indeed some are pretty obvious. They are "common sense," but unfortunately, we live in an age when common sense is becoming increasingly hard to come by.

We must encourage and honor institutions like Hillsdale College, St. Johns College, and Providence College, to name a few, that accept the responsibility of providing a classical moral education for their students. The last few decades of the twentieth century have seen a steady erosion of knowledge and a steady increase in moral relativism. This is partly due to the diffidence of many teachers who are confused by all the talk about pluralism. Such teachers actually believe that it is wrong to "indoctrinate" our children in our own culture and moral tradition.

Of course, there are pressing moral issues around which there is no consensus; as a modern pluralistic society we are arguing about all sorts of things. This is understandable. Moral dilemmas arise in every generation. But, long ago, we achieved consensus on many basic moral questions. Cheating, cowardice, and cruelty are wrong. As one pundit put it, "The Ten Commandments are not the Ten Highly Tentative Suggestions."

28   While it is true that we must debate controversial issues, we must not forget there exists a core of noncontroversial ethical issues that were settled a long time ago. We must make students aware that there is a standard of ethical ideals that all civilizations worthy of the name have discovered. We must encourage them to read the Bible, Aristotle's *Ethics,* Shakespeare's *King Lear,* the Koran, and the *Analects* of Confucius. When they read almost any great work, they will encounter these basic moral values: integrity, respect for human life, self control, honesty, courage, and self-sacrifice. All the world's major religions proffer some version of the Golden Rule, if only in its negative form: Do not do unto others as you would not have them do unto you.

We must teach the literary classics. We must bring the great books and the great ideas back into the core of the curriculum. We must transmit the best of our political and cultural heritage. Franz Kafka once said that a great work of literature melts the "frozen sea within us." There are also any number of works of art and works of philosophy that have the same effect.

American children have a right to their moral heritage. They should know the Bible. They should be familiar with the moral truths in the tragedies of Shakespeare, in the political ideas of Jefferson, Madison, and Lincoln. They should be exposed to the exquisite moral sensibility in the novels of Jane Austen, George Eliot, and Mark Twain, to mention some of my favorites. These great works are their birthright.

This is not to say that a good literary, artistic, and philosophical education suffices to create ethical human beings; nor is it to suggest that teaching the classics is all we need to do to repair the moral ozone. What we know is that we cannot, in good conscience, allow our children to remain morally illiterate. All healthy societies pass along their moral and cultural traditions to their children.

32   And so I come to another basic reform: Teachers, professors, and other social critics should be encouraged to moderate their attacks on our culture and its institutions. They should be encouraged to treat great literary works as literature and not as reactionary political tracts. In many classrooms today, students only learn to "uncover" the allegedly racist, sexist, and elitist elements in the great books.

Meanwhile, pundits, social critics, radical feminists, and other intellectuals on the cultural left never seem to tire of running down our society and its institutions and traditions. We are a society overrun by determined advocacy groups that overstate the weaknesses of our society and show very little appreciation for its merits and strengths. I would urge those professors and teachers who use their classrooms to disparage America to consider the possibility that they are doing more harm than good. Their goal may be to create sensitive, critical citizens, but what they are actually doing is producing confusion and cynicism. Their goal may be to improve students' awareness of the plight of exploited peoples, but what they are actually doing is producing kids who are capable of doubting that the Holocaust took place and kids who are incapable of articulating moral objections to human sacrifice.

In my opinion, we are today not unlike those confused, scrofulous hippies of the late 1960s who finally showed up at the doors of the free clinics in Haight-Ashbury to get their dose of traditional medicine. I hope we have the good sense to follow their example. We need to take an active stand against the divisive unlearning that is corrupting the integrity of our society.

William Butler Yeats talked of the "center" and warned us that it is not holding. Others talk of the threats to our social fabric and tradition. But we are still a sound society; in more than one sense, we have inherited a very healthy constitution from our founding fathers. We know how to dispel the moral confusion and get back our bearings and our confidence. We have traditions and institutions of proven strength and efficacy, and we are still strong.

36   We need to bring back the great books and the great ideas. We need to transmit the best of our political and cultural heritage. We need to refrain from cynical attacks against our traditions and institutions. We need to expose the folly of all the schemes for starting from zero. We need to teach our young people to understand, respect, and protect the institutions that protect us and preserve our kindly, free, and democratic society.

This we can do. And when we engage in the Great Relearning that is so badly needed today, we will find that the lives of our morally enlightened children will be saner, safer, more dignified, and more humane.

READER RESPONSE

Freewrite for a few minutes in response to Sommers's essay. In the context of what she has to say here, where would you position yourself morally? Do you consider yourself an ethical person? Explain your answer.

QUESTIONS FOR DISCUSSION

1. How does Sommers define "moral Stone Age" (paragraph 9)? What do you understand her to mean by "moral nihilism" (paragraph 3)?

2. Answer the question Sommers raises in paragraph 7: Are there such things as "right" and "wrong"? Do you agree with Sommers that "the notion of objective moral truths is in disrepute" (paragraph 9)?

3. Discuss your response to Sommers's assertion in paragraph 15 that "[t]oo many young people are morally confused, ill-informed, and adrift. This confusion gets worse rather than better once they go to college."

4. State in your own words what you understand Sommers to mean by "Great Relearning," and then locate her suggestions for "how we might carry out this relearning" (paragraph 24). Discuss your response to her suggestions.

Making the Grade

Kurt Wiesenfeld

Kurt Wiesenfeld is a physicist who teaches at Georgia Tech in Atlanta. He wrote this essay for the "My Turn" column of the June 17, 1996, issue of Newsweek.

It was a rookie error. After 10 years I should have known better, but I went to my office the day after final grades were posted. There was a tentative knock on the door. "Professor Wiesenfeld? I took your Physics 2121 class? I flunked it? I wonder if there's anything I can do to improve my grade?" I thought: "Why are you asking me? Isn't it too late to worry about it? Do you dislike making declarative statements?"

After the student gave his tale of woe and left, the phone rang. "I got a D in your class. Is there any way you can change it to 'Incomplete'?" Then the e-mail assault began. "I'm shy about coming in to talk to you, but I'm not shy about asking for a better grade. Anyway, it's worth a try." The next day I had three phone messages from students asking *me* to call *them*. I didn't.

Time was, when you received a grade, that was it. You might groan and moan, but you accepted it as the outcome of your efforts or lack thereof (and, yes, sometimes a tough grader). In the last few years, however, some students have developed a disgruntled-consumer approach. If they don't like their grade, they go to the "return" counter to trade it in for something better.

4   What alarms me is their indifference toward grades as an indication of personal effort and performance. Many, when pressed about why they think they deserve a better grade, admit they don't deserve one but would like one anyway. Having been raised on gold stars for effort and smiley faces for self-esteem, they've learned that they can get by without hard work and real talent if they can talk the professor into giving them a break. This attitude is beyond

cynicism. There's a weird innocence to the assumption that one expects (even deserves) a better grade simply by begging for it. With that outlook, I guess I shouldn't be as flabbergasted as I was that 12 students asked me to change their grades *after* final grades were posted.

That's 10 percent of my class who let three months of midterms, quizzes and lab reports slide until long past remedy. My graduate student calls it hyperrational thinking: if effort and intelligence don't matter, why should deadlines? What matters is getting a better grade through an unearned bonus, the academic equivalent of a freebie T-shirt or toaster giveaway. Rewards are disconnected from the quality of one's work. An act and its consequences are unrelated, random events.

Their arguments for wheedling better grades often ignore academic performance. Perhaps they feel it's not relevant. "If my grade isn't raised to a D I'll lose my scholarship." "If you don't give me a C, I'll flunk out." One sincerely overwrought student pleaded, "If I don't pass, my life is over." This is tough stuff to deal with. Apparently, I'm responsible for someone's losing a scholarship, flunking out or deciding whether life has meaning. Perhaps these students see me as a commodities broker with something they want—a grade. Though intrinsically worthless, grades, if properly manipulated, can be traded for what has value: a degree, which means a job, which means money. The one thing college actually offers—a chance to learn—is considered irrelevant, even less than worthless, because of the long hours and hard work required.

In a society saturated with surface values, love of knowledge for its own sake does sound eccentric. The benefits of fame and wealth are more obvious. So is it right to blame students for reflecting the superficial values saturating our society?

8   Yes, of course it's right. These guys had better take themselves seriously now, because our country will be forced to take them seriously later, when the stakes are much higher. They must recognize that their attitude is not only self-destructive, but socially destructive. The erosion of quality control—giving appropriate grades for actual accomplishments—is a major concern in my department. One colleague noted that a physics major could obtain a degree without ever answering a written exam question completely. How? By pulling in enough partial credit and extra credit. And by getting breaks on grades.

But what happens once she or he graduates and gets a job? That's when the misfortunes of eroding academic standards multiply. We lament that schoolchildren get "kicked upstairs" until they graduate from high school despite being illiterate and mathematically inept, but we seem unconcerned with college graduates whose less blatant deficiencies are far more harmful if their accreditation exceeds their qualifications.

Most of my students are science and engineering majors. If they're good at getting partial credit but not at getting the answer right, then the new bridge breaks or the new drug doesn't work. One finds examples here in Atlanta. Last year a light tower in the Olympic Stadium collapsed, killing a worker. It collapsed because an engineer miscalculated how much weight it could hold. A new 12-story dormitory could develop dangerous cracks due to a foundation that's uneven by more than six inches. The error resulted from incorrect data being fed into a computer. I drive past that dorm daily on my way to work, wondering if a foundation crushed under kilotons of weight is repairable or if this structure will have to be demolished. Two 10,000-pound steel beams at the new natatorium collapsed in March, crashing into the student athletic complex. (Should we give partial credit since no one was hurt?) Those are real-world consequences of errors and lack of expertise.

But the lesson is lost on the grade-grousing 10 percent. Say that you won't (not can't, but won't) change the grade they deserve to what they want, and they're frequently bewildered or angry. They don't think it's fair that they're judged according to their performance, not their desires or "potential." They don't think it's fair that they should jeopardize their scholarships or be in danger of flunking out simply because they could not or did not do their work. But it's more than fair; it's necessary to help preserve a minimum standard of quality that our society needs to maintain safety and integrity. I don't know if the 13th-hour students will learn that lesson, but I've learned mine. From now on, after final grades are posted, I'll lie low until the next quarter starts.

READER RESPONSE

Have you ever asked a teacher for a higher grade or received a grade you felt you did not deserve? If not, do you know of anyone who has? Explain the circumstances.

QUESTIONS FOR DISCUSSION

1. To what extent do you think that Wiesenfeld has a legitimate complaint about students asking for a better grade?
2. To what extent do you agree with this statement: "The one thing college actually offers—a chance to learn—is considered irrelevant, even less than worthless, because of the long hours and hard work required" (paragraph 6)?
3. Wiesenfeld asks, "So is it right to blame students for reflecting the superficial values saturating our society?" (paragraph 7) and then answers, "Yes, of course it's right" (paragraph 8). To what extent do you agree with him?
4. Wiesenfeld seems to suggest that "gold stars for effort and smiley faces for self-esteem" are not worthwhile incentives or rewards for students (paragraph 4). What does he see as the effect of such rewards? Do you agree with him?

Infamy and Immortality

David A. Kaplan

David A. Kaplan received his law degree from New York University Law School in 1981 and practiced law for several years before becoming a freelance writer. In addition to the law, he has written extensively on a variety of subjects, including baseball, ethics, film, politics, and television. His work has appeared in the Washington Post, The New York Times, New York Newsday, *and* The Nation. *Kaplan joined* Newsweek *magazine as legal affairs editor in 1989 and has been a senior editor since 1992. "Infamy and Immortality" appeared in the August 2, 1999, issue of* Newsweek.

It is, and always will be, simply, The Fix. And "Shoeless Joe" will forever be the name associated with it. In the autumn of 1919, in a nation just over the Great War, the Cincinnati Reds and Chicago White Sox assembled for the World Series. The Sox were the big draw, the greatest baseball team theretofore assembled—including "Shoeless" Joe Jackson in left. The owner was Charles Comiskey, a tightwad so cheap that he wouldn't pay for his team's uniforms to be cleaned—thus leading the players to call themselves the Black Sox. All of this alone made for a momentous time. But there was a final, tragic ingredient to the games about to begin. Eight members of the Black Sox had agreed to throw the World Series.

And so they did. After the scheme was revealed, Jackson and seven other Sox players were banished for life by baseball's first commissioner, the iron-fisted Kenesaw Mountain Landis. Yet because Jackson is one of the best ever to play, many fans have long argued he still deserves a place in the Hall of Fame. That debate resonated this past Sunday, when the seven newest members were inducted in Cooperstown, N.Y.

Now there is a chance that Joseph Jefferson Jackson—dead since 1951—may get to the promised land. Spurred by the pleas of a pair of 80-year-old Hall of Famers, Ted Williams and Bob Feller, baseball commissioner Bud Selig is reviewing the Black Sox case and will decide by the end of the season whether to remove Jackson from the sport's "ineligible list." Selig, a baseball-history buff, says he's "long been interested in the case." He has "a gut sense" of what to do, he told *Newsweek*—but won't offer any hints. "I'm trying to have as open a mind as possible."

4   Selig's ruling would only be half the ballgame, for it still would be up to the Hall to consider Jackson for induction. But the commissioner's choice is still profound: can a sin be so old that we may ultimately pardon it, or does the gravity of the offense require that the punishment be everlasting? Selig also faces a political problem. If he decides to reinstate Jackson, he will

inevitably have to revisit the question of Pete Rose's eligibility. Rose, the all-time leader in hits, was banned for life in 1989 by Commissioner Bart Giamatti for betting on baseball.

The Fix has fascinated authors, filmmakers and ethicists for 80 years. In 1988 John Sayles made a whole movie about the Sox calling it "Eight Men Out." F. Scott Fitzgerald invoked Arnold Rothstein, the mobster who bankrolled the bribes, in "The Great Gatsby." "It never occurred to me," he wrote, "that one man could play with the faith of 50 million people." But it is not Rothstein's name that's synonymous with the worst scandal to sully American sports. That ignominy belongs to Shoeless Joe.

Taught how to hit by a Confederate war veteran, armed with his special 48-ounce bat, "Black Betsy"—made from a hickory tree and darkened with to-bacco juice—Jackson is the man Babe Ruth called the "greatest hitter" he ever saw. (Jackson earned his nickname playing in stocking feet in the minors.) He's the player who first visits Kevin Costner's cornfield in "Field of Dreams," when a voice commands, "If you build it, he will come." And then there's the most memorable line uttered about The Fix. As Jackson left a courtroom after testifying, the story goes, a boy clutched at his sleeve and pleaded: "Say it ain't so, Joe. Say it ain't so."

But it was. Chicago first baseman Chick Gandil hatched the idea to dump the 1919 Series for $100,000. Among his co-conspirators was Jackson, who took $5,000 and complained when he didn't get the other $15,000 he'd been promised. After the White Sox lost—missing plays, throwing fat pitches—there was speculation about a fix. But it wasn't till a year later that Jackson, and others, confessed. Though a jury acquitted them of any crime, Landis expelled them from baseball anyway.

8   Jackson came to embody the public's mixed emotions about the scandal's resolution. Yes, he took the cash, but he tried to give it back soon after. He went on to have a stupendous World Series, hitting .375 to lead all players. This suggested he had little role in throwing the games. Moreover, Jackson's lifetime batting average (.356) is the third-best ever, and his fielding was so good his glove was called "the place triples go to die." He surely deserved to be punished, but, Williams asks, has he not served out his "sentence"? Williams believes Jackson took the money, but that he was "taken advantage of" by the gamblers. As to Shoeless Joe's qualifications, "I believe I know a little about hit-ting," the last man to hit .400 wrote to Selig. Feller told *Newsweek* that "if *any-one* doesn't belong in the Hall, it's Comiskey. He refused to pay the players the bonuses they were entitled to."

The case comes down to instinct. Giamatti avoided the controversy alto-gether, remarking he wouldn't "play God with history." Selig seems bolder. In a country that gives second chances to countless miscreants—Richard Nixon, Marv Albert, Latrell Sprewell—why not a salute to Shoeless Joe? His part in The Fix will always be remembered. It must be. But should not this baseball immortal at long last be celebrated?

READER RESPONSE

Do you think "Shoeless Joe" Jackson should be inducted into the Baseball Hall of Fame? Explain your answer.

QUESTIONS FOR DISCUSSION

1. Summarize in your own words the effects of the 1919 Black Sox scandal. What are the implications of the boy's plea, "Say it ain't so, Joe" (paragraph 6)? How did Jackson "embody the public's mixed emotions about the scandal's resolution" (paragraph 8)?
2. Explain the ethical dilemma of the "Shoeless Joe" Jackson controversy. In what way is Pete Rose's situation related to Jackson's (paragraph 4)?
3. Respond to this question: "[C]an a sin be so old that we may ultimately pardon it, or does the gravity of the offense require that the punishment be everlasting?" (paragraph 4). What sins, in your opinion, are unpardonable no matter how much time passes? What sins do you think might be pardoned after a suitable period of time?
4. How persuaded are you by Kaplan's argument? How do you answer his final question, "But should not this baseball immortal at long last be celebrated?" (paragraph 9).

The Quality of Mercy Killing
Roger Rosenblatt

Roger Rosenblatt has been a contributing editor for Time, Life, Family Circle, The New Republic, Vanity Fair, *and* Men's Journal. *He has written and performed two one-man off-Broadway shows and has won Peabody and Emmy awards for his essays on PBS's* The News Hour with Jim Lehrer. *His books include* The Man in the Water: Essays and Stories *(1994),* Coming Apart; A Memoir of the Harvard Wars of 1969 *(1997),* Rules for Aging *(2000), and* Where We Stand: 30 Reasons for Loving Our Country *(2002). "The Quality of Mercy Killing" was first published in the August 1985 issue of* Time.

If it were only a matter of law, the public would not feel stranded. He killed her, after all. Roswell Gilbert, a 76-year-old retired electronics engineer living in a seaside condominium in Fort Lauderdale, Fla., considered murdering his

wife Emily for at least a month before shooting her through the head with a
Luger as she sat on their couch. The Gilberts had been husband and wife for
51 years. They were married in 1934, the year after Calvin Coolidge died, the
year after Prohibition was lifted, the year that Hank Aaron was born. At 73,
Emily had Alzheimer's disease and osteoporosis; her spinal column was gradually collapsing. Roswell would not allow her to continue life as "a suffering animal," so he committed what is called a mercy killing. The jury saw only the
killing; they felt Gilbert had mercy on himself. He was sentenced to 25 years
with no chance of parole, which would make him 101 by the time he got out.
The Governor has been asked to grant clemency. Most Floridians polled hope
that Gilbert will go free.

Not that there ever was much of a legal or practical question involved.
Imagine the precedent set by freeing a killer simply because he killed for love.
Othello killed for love, though his passion was loaded with a different motive.
Does any feeling count, or is kindness alone an excuse for murder? Or age:
maybe someone has to be 76 and married 51 years to establish his sincerity.
There are an awful lot of old people and long marriages in Florida. A lot of
Alzheimer's disease and osteoporosis as well. Let Gilbert loose, the fear is, and
watch the run on Lugers.

Besides, the matter of mercy killing is getting rough and out of hand. Nobody seems to use poison anymore. In Fort Lauderdale two years ago, a 79-
year-old man shot his 62-year-old wife in the stairwell of a hospital; like Emily
Gilbert, she was suffering from Alzheimer's disease. In San Antonio four years
ago, a 69-year-old man shot his 72-year-old brother to death in a nursing
home. Last June a man in Miami put two bullets in the heart of his three-year-
old daughter who lay comatose after a freak accident. An organization that
studies mercy killings says that nine have occurred this year alone. You cannot
have a murder every time someone feels sorry for a loved one in pain. Any
fool knows that.

4   Yet you also feel foolish watching a case like Gilbert's (if any case can be
said to be like another) because, while both feet are planted firmly on the side
of the law and common sense, both are firmly planted on Gilbert's side as
well. The place the public really stands is nowhere: How can an act be equally
destructive of society and wholly human? The reason anyone would consider
going easy on Gilbert is that we can put ourselves in his shoes, can sit at his
wife's bedside day after day, watching the Florida sun gild the furniture and listening to the Atlantic lick the beach like a cat. Emily dozes. He looks at her in
a rare peaceful pose and is grateful for the quiet.

Or he dreams back to when such a scene would have been unimaginable: she, sharp as a tack, getting the better of him in an argument; he, strong
as a bull, showing off by swinging her into the air—on a beach, perhaps, like
the one in front of the condominium where old couples like themselves walk
in careful slow motion at the water's edge. Since the case became a cause,
photographs of the Gilberts have appeared on television, she in a formal
gown, he in tails; they, older, in a restaurant posing deadpan for a picture for

no reason, the way people do in restaurants. In a way the issue here *is* age: mind and body falling away like slabs of sand off a beach cliff. If biology declares war, have people no right to a pre-emptive strike? In the apartment he continues to stare at her who, from time to time, still believes they are traveling together in Spain.

Now he wonders about love. He loves his wife; he tells her so; he has told her so for 51 years. And he thinks of what he meant by that: her understanding of him, her understanding of others, her sense of fun. Illness has replaced those qualities in her with screams and a face of panic. Does he love her still? Of course, he says; he hates the disease, but he loves his wife. Or— and this seems hard—does he only love what he remembers of Emily? Is the frail doll in the bed an imposter? But no; this is Emily too, the same old Emily hidden somewhere under the decaying cells and in the folds of the painkillers. It is Emily and she is suffering and he swore he would always look after her.

He considers an irony: you always hurt the one you love. By what act or nonact would he be hurting his wife more? He remembers news stories he has read of distraught people in similar positions, pulling the plugs on sons and husbands or assisting in the suicides of desperate friends. He sympathizes, but with a purpose; he too is interested in precedents. Surely, he concludes, morality swings both ways here. What is moral for the group cannot always be moral for the individual, or there would be no individuality, no exceptions, even if the exceptions only prove the rule. Let the people have their rules. What harm would it do history to relieve Emily's pain? A little harm, perhaps, no more than that.

8   This is what we see in the Gilbert case, the fusion of our lives with theirs in one grand and pathetic cliché in which all lives look pretty much alike. We go round and round with Gilbert: Gilbert suddenly wondering if Emily might get better, if one of those white-coated geniuses will come up with a cure. Gilbert realizing that once Emily is gone, he will go too, since her way of life, however wretched, was their way of life. He is afraid for them both. In *The Merchant of Venice* Portia says that mercy is "twice blessed;/It blesses him that gives and him that takes." The murder committed, Gilbert does not feel blessed. At best, he feels he did right, which the outer world agrees with and denies.

Laws are unlikely to be changed by such cases: for every modification one can think of, there are too many loopholes and snares. What Gilbert did in fact erodes the whole basis of law, which is to keep people humane and civilized. Yet Gilbert was humane, civilized and wrong: a riddle. In the end we want the law intact and Gilbert free, so that society wins on both counts. What the case proves, however, is that society is helpless to do anything for Gilbert, for Emily or for itself. All we can do is recognize a real tragedy when we see one, and wonder, perhaps, if one bright morning in 1934 Gilbert read of a mercy killing in the papers, leaned earnestly across the breakfast table and told his new bride. "I couldn't do that. I could never do that."

READER RESPONSE

What is your reaction to the jury's finding Roswell Gilbert guilty of murder?

QUESTIONS FOR DISCUSSION

1. According to Rosenblatt, what is the dilemma posed by cases such as Gilbert's? What is the "riddle" mentioned in the last paragraph?
2. In paragraph 8, Rosenblatt quotes from the play alluded to in his title, Shakespeare's *The Merchant of Venice*. The lines immediately before those he quotes are: "The quality of mercy is not strained,/It droppeth as the gentle rain from heaven/Upon the place beneath." Explain the function of the allusion in the title and the lines Rosenblatt quotes in paragraph 8. What does the reference to Othello (paragraph 2) mean, and what purpose does it serve?
3. Do you think Rosenblatt's emotional appeal is too sentimental? Does the strong emotional appeal undercut his argument? What function do the closing sentences serve? Does Rosenblatt condone mercy killing? Does he imply that exceptions to the law should be made in some cases?
4. What is your position on the issue of mercy killing?
5. Rosenblatt writes in paragraph 5 that "[i]n a way the issue here *is* age." In what sense might age be the issue?

First and Last, Do No Harm
Charles Krauthammer

Charles Krauthammer has had a varied career as a political scientist, psychiatrist, journalist, speech writer, and television talk-show panelist. Since 1983, he has written essays for Time *magazine. He is also a contributing editor to* The New Republic, *and since 1985, he has contributed a weekly syndicated column to the* Washington Post. *In 1981, he won a Pulitzer Prize for commentary on politics and society. He has published one book,* Cutting Edges: Making Sense of the Eighties *(1985). This commentary appeared in the April 15, 1996, issue of* Time *after the Second Circuit Court of Appeals struck down a New York State law that prohibited physicians from helping their patients die. The Ninth Circuit Court in San Francisco made a similar ruling in the month before the New York ruling.*

"I will give no deadly medicine to anyone if asked."

The Hippocratic Oath

"**D**id you ask for your hemlock?" Thanks to appeals-court judges in New York and California, this question will now be in your future.

You will be old, infirm and, inevitably at some point, near death. You may or may not be in physical distress, but in an age of crushing health-care costs, you will be a burden to your loved ones, to say nothing of society. And thanks to courts that back in 1996 legalized doctor-assisted suicide for the first time in American history, all around you thousands of your aging contemporaries will be taking their life.

You may want to live those last few remaining weeks or months. You may have no intention of shortening your life. But now the question that before 1996 rarely arose—and when it did arise, only in the most hushed and guilty tones—will be raised routinely: Others are letting go; others are giving way; should not you too?

4   Of course, the judges who plumbed the depths of the Constitution to find the "right" to physician-assisted suicide—a right unfindable for 200 years—deny the possibility of such a nightmare scenario. Psychological pressure on the elderly and infirm to take drugs to hasten death? Why, "there should be none," breezily decrees the Second Circuit Court of Appeals.

King Canute had a better grip on reality. This nightmare scenario is not a hypothesis; it has been tested in Holland and proved a fact. Holland is the only jurisdiction in the Western world that heretofore permitted physician-assisted suicide. The practice is now widespread (perhaps 2,000 to 3,000 cases a year; the U.S. equivalent would be 40,000 to 60,000) and abused. Indeed, legalization has resulted in so much abuse—not just psychological pressure but a shocking number of cases of out-and-out *involuntary* euthanasia, inconvenient and defenseless patients simply put to death without their consent— that last year the Dutch government was forced to change its euthanasia laws.

Judge Roger Miner, writing for the Second Circuit, uncomprehendingly admits the reality of the nightmare: "It seems clear that some physicians [in the Netherlands] practice nonvoluntary euthanasia, although it is not legal to do so." Well, why would such things occur in the Netherlands? Are the people there morally inferior to Americans? Are the doctors somehow crueler and more uncaring?

Of course not. The obvious reason is that doctors there were relieved of the constraint of the law. The absolute ethical norm established since the time of Hippocrates—that doctors must not kill—was removed in the name of compassion, and the inevitable happened. Good, ordinary doctors, in their zeal to be ever more compassionate in terminating useless and suffering life, began killing people who did not even ask for it. Once given power heretofore reserved to God, some exceeded their narrow mandate and acted like God. Surprise.

8   In America the great moral barrier protecting us from such monstrous God-doctoring is the one separating passive from active euthanasia. Pulling the plug for the dying is permitted. Prescribing death-dealing drugs to those who are quite self-sustaining is not. It is this distinction that the judges are intent on destroying.

"Physicians do not fulfill the role of 'killer' by prescribing drugs to hasten death any more than they do by disconnecting life-support systems," writes Judge Miner. This is pernicious nonsense. There is a great difference between, say, not resuscitating a stopped heart—allowing nature to take its course—and actively killing someone. In the first case the person is dead. In the second he only wishes to be dead. And in the case of life sustained by artificial hydration or ventilation, pulling the plug simply prevents an artificial prolongation of the dying process. Prescribing hemlock initiates it.

The distinction is not just practical. It is also psychological. Killing is hard to do. The whole purpose of this case is to make it easier. How? By giving doctors who actively assist in suicide the blessing of the law and society.

After all, why did we need this ruling in the first place? In New York State, where this case was brought, not a single physician has been penalized for aiding a suicide since 1919. For 77 years, one can assume, some doctors have been quietly helping patients die. Why then the need for a legal ruling to make that official, a ruling that erases a fundamental ethical line and opens medical practice to unconscionable abuse?

12   The need comes from the modern craving for "authenticity." If you are going to do it, do it openly, proudly, unashamedly. But as a society, do we not want this most fearful act—killing—to be done fearfully? If it must be done at all—and in the most extreme and pitiable circumstances it will—let it be done with trembling, in shadow, in whispered acknowledgment that some fundamental norm is being violated, even if for the most compassionate ofreasons.

No more. These judges have now liberated us from the hypocrisy of the unenforced law. Damn them. Lack of enforcement is an expression of compassion, but the law is the last barrier to arrogance. And God knows that in this age of all-powerful medicine, arrogance is the greater danger. Every grandparent will soon know that too.

READER RESPONSE

Krauthammer asks, "[W]hy did we need this ruling in the first place?" (paragraph 11). Are you convinced that the Second Circuit ruling is necessary, or do you share Krauthammer's reservations?

QUESTIONS FOR DISCUSSION

1. In the matter of terminally ill patients, it was already legal for doctors to withhold or withdraw treatment at the patient's request, but the New York and California rulings allow a doctor to prescribe a lethal dose of medicine as long as the patient is in the final stages of a terminal disease, is mentally competent, and is able to take the medicine on his or her own. What dangers does Krauthammer see in the rulings? Do you believe his fears are reasonable?

2. What distinction does Krauthammer draw between what doctors were previously allowed to do under the law and what they are now legally free to do in New York and California?

3. Krauthammer calls the opinion of Judge Miner in the Second Circuit Court ruling "pernicious nonsense" (paragraph 9). What is your opinion of Judge Miner's statement? Do you agree with Krauthammer?

4. Discuss Krauthammer's comment that the ruling "erases a fundamental ethical line and opens medical practice to unconscionable abuse" (paragraph 11).

Living Is the Mystery

M. Scott Peck

M. Scott Peck is a physician and writer. His many books include The Road Less Traveled: A New Psychology of Love, Traditional Values, *and* Spiritual Growth *(1995),* People of the Lie: The Hope for Healing Human Evil *(1996),* The Road Less Traveled and Beyond: Spiritual Growth in an Age of Anxiety *(1997),* and Golf and the Spirit: Lessons for the Journey *(1999). This adaptation from his book* Denial of the Soul: Spiritual and Medical Perspectives on Euthanasia and Mortality *(1997) appeared in the "My Turn" column of the March 10, 1997, issue of* Newsweek *magazine.*

The current debate over euthanasia is often simplistic. The subject is complex. We don't even have a generally agreed-upon definition of the word. Is euthanasia solely an act committed by someone—a physician or family member—on someone else who is ill or dying? Or can the term also be used for someone who is ill or dying who kills himself without the assistance of another? Does euthanasia require the patient's consent? The family's consent? Is it separable from other forms of suicide or homicide? How does it differ from simply "pulling the plug"? If one type of euthanasia consists of refraining from the use of "heroic measures" to prolong life, how does one distinguish between those measures that are heroic and those that are standard treatment? What is the relationship between euthanasia and pain? Is there a distinction to be made between physical pain and emotional pain? How does one assess degrees of suffering? Above all, why are ethical issues involved, and what might they be?

I believe that all patients deserve fully adequate medical relief from physical pain. Emotional pain may be another matter. It is very difficult to say no to emotional demands of those suffering severe physical disease, but that doesn't mean it shouldn't be done. I have always resonated to two quotations: "Life is not a problem to be solved but a mystery to be lived" and "Life is what happens to us while we are making other plans." I find I need to remind myself of these quotations on a daily basis. Among other things, they point out to me that the loss of control, the irrationality, the mystery and the insecurity inherent in dying are also inherent to living. The emotional suffering involved in dealing with these realities strikes me as a very important segment of what I call existential suffering. It seems to me that "true euthanasia" patients suffer not so much from a problem of death as from a problem of life. I think they have a lot to learn from being assisted to face this problem rather than being assisted to kill themselves in order to avoid it.

More than anything else, our differing beliefs about the existence or nonexistence of the human soul make euthanasia a subject for passionate ethical and moral debate. I am of a position that dictates against a laissez-faire attitude toward euthanasia, or what could be termed "euthanasia on demand." While I am passionate about this position forged out of complexity, I am also profoundly aware that I do not know personally what it is like to be totally and permanently incapacitated or to live under a death sentence as a result of a very specific disease with a rapidly deteriorating course. In other words, I have not been there. All that I write here, therefore, should be taken with at least that much of a grain of salt.

4   If I were a jurist, my judgment would be to keep physician-assisted suicide illegal. This would be my decision for three reasons:

1) The other extreme—making assisted suicide so fully legal that it is considered a right—has, I believe, profound negative implications for society as a whole. My concern is not simply, as another author has put it, that "euthanasia breeds euthanasia" or that the floodgates would be opened. My primary concern is the message that would be given to society. It would be yet another secular message that we need not wrestle with God, another message denying the soul and telling us that this is solely our life to do with as we please. It would be a most discouraging message. It would not encourage us to face the natural existential suffering of life, to learn how to overcome it, to learn how to face emotional hardship—the kind of hardship that calls forth our courage. Instead, it would be a message that we are entitled to take the easy way out. It would be a message pushing our society further along the worst of the directions it has already been taking.

2) A decision for the middle ground legalizing assisted suicide under certain circumstances and not others would lead us into a legal quagmire. Despite their enormous expense and frustration, such quagmires might be all to the good if we were prepared to wallow in them. I do not believe that we are currently so prepared.

3) As a society, we are not yet ready to grapple with the euthanasia issue in a meaningful way. There are just too many even more important issues that need to be decided first: the right to physical pain relief, the right to hospice comfort care, the right to public education that is not wholly secular, the right to free discourse about the soul and human meaning, the right to education about the nature of existential suffering, the right to medical care in general, and the right to quasi-euthanasia for the chronically but not fatally ill. Only when we are clear about these matters, among others, will we be in a position to tackle the issue of legalizing physician-assisted suicide for the terminally ill.

8   I submit that the answer to the problem of assisted suicide lies not in more euthanasia but in more hospice care. The first order of business should be to establish that dying patients have a constitutional right to competent hospice care. Only *after* this right has been established does it make sense for the courts to turn their attention to the question of whether terminally ill patients should have an additional constitutional right to physician-assisted euthanasia.

I am not for rushing to resolve the euthanasia debate but for enlarging and heating it up. If we can do this, it is conceivable to me that historians of the future will mark the debate as a turning point in U.S. history, on a par with the Declaration of Independence. They will see it as a watershed time when a possibly moribund society almost magically became revitalized. It is both my experience and that of others that whenever we are willing to engage ourselves fully in the mystery of death, the experience is usually enlivening. I believe that the euthanasia debate, besides requiring that we confront certain societal problems, offers the greatest hope in forcing us to encounter our own souls—often for the first time.

READER RESPONSE

To what extent do you agree with Peck that physician-assisted suicide should remain illegal?

QUESTIONS FOR DISCUSSION

1. To what extent do you agree with Peck's reasons for why he believes physician-assisted suicide should remain illegal (paragraph 5–7)? How convincing do you find his reasoning?
2. What do you think of Peck's list of questions in his opening paragraph? Do his questions help to clarify the issue for you or make it more complicated? Select one or more of his points for class discussion, or pursue them in a writing assignment.
3. According to Peck, what role should hospices play in the lives of terminally ill patients? Do you agree with him?

A Jury of Her Peers
Susan Glaspell

Susan Glaspell (1876–1948) was a journalist before becoming a fiction writer and playwright. With her husband, George Cook, she founded the Provincetown Players in Cape Cod, Massachusetts. In 1931 she won the Pulitzer Prize for Alison's House, *a play based loosely on the life and family of Emily Dickinson. This story, based on her 1916 play* Trifles, *appeared in* The Best Short Stories of 1917 *and in 1999 was included in* The Best American Short Stories of the Century. *The play and the story were inspired by a murder that Glaspell covered while working as a reporter for the* Des Moines Daily News.

When Martha Hale opened the storm-door and got a cut of the north wind, she ran back for her big woolen scarf. As she hurriedly wound that round her head her eye made a scandalized sweep of her kitchen. It was no ordinary thing that called her away—it was probably further from ordinary than anything that had ever happened in Dickson County. But what her eye took in was that her kitchen was in no shape for leaving: her bread all ready for mixing, half the flour sifted and half unsifted.

She hated to see things half done; but she had been at that when the team from town stopped to get Mr. Hale, and then the sheriff came running in to say his wife wished Mrs. Hale would come too—adding, with a grin, that he guessed she was getting scary and wanted another woman along. So she had dropped everything right where it was.

"Martha!" now came her husband's impatient voice. "Don't keep folks waiting out here in the cold."

4   She again opened the storm-door, and this time joined the three men and the one woman waiting for her in the big two-seated buggy.

After she had the robes tucked around her she took another look at the woman who sat beside her on the back seat. She had met Mrs. Peters the year before at the county fair, and the thing she remembered about her was that she didn't seem like a sheriff's wife. She was small and thin and didn't have a strong voice. Mrs. Gorman, sheriff's wife before Gorman went out and Peters came in, had a voice that somehow seemed to be backing up the law with every word. But if Mrs. Peters didn't look like a sheriff's wife, Peters made it up in looking like a sheriff. He was to a dot the kind of man who could get himself elected sheriff—a heavy man with a big voice, who was particularly genial with the law-abiding, as if to make it plain that he knew the difference between criminals and non-criminals. And right there it came into Mrs. Hale's mind, with a stab, that this man who was so pleasant and lively with all of them was going to the Wrights' now as a sheriff.

"The country's not very pleasant this time of year," Mrs. Peters at last ventured, as if she felt they ought to be talking as well as the men.

Mrs. Hale scarcely finished her reply, for they had gone up a little hill and could see the Wright place now, and seeing it did not make her feel like talking. It looked very lonesome this cold March morning. It had always been a lonesome-looking place. It was down in a hollow, and the poplar trees around it were lonesome-looking trees. The men were looking at it and talking about what had happened. The county attorney was bending to one side of the buggy, and kept looking steadily at the place as they drew up to it.

8   "I'm glad you came with me," Mrs. Peters said nervously, as the two women were about to follow the men in through the kitchen door.

Even after she had her foot on the door-step, her hand on the knob, Martha Hale had a moment of feeling she could not cross that threshold. And the reason it seemed she couldn't cross it now was simply because she hadn't crossed it before. Time and time again it had been in her mind, "I ought to go over and see Minnie Foster"—she still thought of her as Minnie Foster, though for twenty years she had been Mrs. Wright. And then there was always something to do and Minnie Foster would go from her mind. But now she could come.

The men went over to the stove. The women stood close together by the door. Young Henderson, the county attorney, turned around and said, "Come up to the fire, ladies."

Mrs. Peters took a step forward, then stopped. "I'm not—cold," she said.

12   And so the two women stood by the door, at first not even so much as looking around the kitchen.

The men talked for a minute about what a good thing it was the sheriff had sent his deputy out that morning to make a fire for them, and then Sheriff Peters stepped back from the stove, unbuttoned his outer coat, and leaned his hands on the kitchen table in a way that seemed to mark the beginning of official business. "Now, Mr. Hale," he said in a sort of semi-official voice, "before we move things about, you tell Mr. Henderson just what it was you saw when you came here yesterday morning."

The county attorney was looking around the kitchen.

"By the way," he said, "has anything been moved?" He turned to the sheriff. "Are things just as you left them yesterday?"

16   Peters looked from cupboard to sink; from that to a small worn rocker a little to one side of the kitchen table.

"It's just the same."

"Somebody should have been left here yesterday," said the county attorney.

"Oh—yesterday," returned the sheriff, with a little gesture as of yesterday having been more than he could bear to think of. "When I had to send Frank to Morris Center for that man who went crazy—let me tell you. I had my hands full yesterday. I knew you could get back from Omaha by today, George, and as long as I went over everything here myself—"

20   "Well, Mr. Hale," said the county attorney, in a way of letting what was past and gone go, "tell just what happened when you came here yesterday morning."

Mrs. Hale, still leaning against the door, had that sinking feeling of the mother whose child is about to speak a piece. Lewis often wandered along and got things mixed up in a story. She hoped he would tell this straight and plain, and not say unnecessary things that would just make things harder for Minnie Foster. He didn't begin at once, and she noticed that he looked queer—as if standing in that kitchen and having to tell what he had seen there yesterday morning made him almost sick.

"Yes, Mr. Hale?" the county attorney reminded.

"Harry and I had started to town with a load of potatoes," Mrs. Hale's husband began.

24   Harry was Mrs. Hale's oldest boy. He wasn't with them now, for the very good reason that those potatoes never got to town yesterday and he was taking them this morning, so he hadn't been home when the sheriff stopped to say he wanted Mr. Hale to come over to the Wright place and tell the county attorney his story there, where he could point it all out. With all Mrs. Hale's other emotions came the fear now that maybe Harry wasn't dressed warm enough—they hadn't any of them realized how that north wind did bite.

"We come along this road," Hale was going on, with a motion of his hand to the road over which they had just come, "and as we got in sight of the house I says to Harry, 'I'm goin' to see if I can't get John Wright to take a telephone.' You see," he explained to Henderson, "unless I can get somebody to go in with me they won't come out this branch road except for a price I can't pay. I'd spoke to Wright about it once before; but he put me off, saying folks talked too much anyway, and all he asked was peace and quiet—guess you know about how much he talked himself. But I thought maybe if I went to the house and talked about it before his wife, and said all the women-folks liked the telephones, and that in this lonesome stretch of road it would be a good thing—well, I said to Harry that that was what I was going to say— though I said at the same time that I didn't know as what his wife wanted made much difference to John—"

Now there he was!—saying things he didn't need to say. Mrs. Hale tried to catch her husband's eye, but fortunately the county attorney interrupted with:

"Let's talk about that a little later, Mr. Hale. I do want to talk about that but, I'm anxious now to get along to just what happened when you got here."

28   When he began this time, it was very deliberately and carefully:

"I didn't see or hear anything. I knocked at the door. And still it was all quiet inside. I knew they must be up—it was past eight o'clock. So I knocked again, louder, and I thought I heard somebody say, 'Come in.' I wasn't sure— I'm not sure yet. But I opened the door—this door," jerking a hand toward the door by which the two women stood, "and there, in that rocker"—pointing to it—"sat Mrs. Wright."

Everyone in the kitchen looked at the rocker. It came into Mrs. Hale's mind that that rocker didn't look in the least like Minnie Foster—the Minnie Foster of twenty years before. It was a dingy red, with wooden rungs up the back, and the middle rung was gone, and the chair sagged to one side.

"How did she—look?" the county attorney was inquiring.

32   "Well," said Hale, "she looked—queer."

"How do you mean—queer?"

As he asked it he took out a note-book and pencil. Mrs. Hale did not like the sight of that pencil. She kept her eye fixed on her husband, as if to keep him from saying unnecessary things that would go into that note-book and make trouble.

Hale did speak guardedly, as if the pencil had affected him too.

36   "Well, as if she didn't know what she was going to do next. And kind of—done up."

"How did she seem to feel about your coming?"

"Why, I don't think she minded—one way or other. She didn't pay much attention. I said, 'Ho' do, Mrs. Wright? It's cold, ain't it?' And she said. 'Is it?'— and went on pleatin' at her apron.

"Well, I was surprised. She didn't ask me to come up to the stove, or to sit down, but just set there, not even lookin' at me. And so I said: 'I want to see John.'

40   "And then she—laughed. I guess you would call it a laugh.

"I thought of Harry and the team outside, so I said, a little sharp, 'Can I see John?' 'No,' says she—kind of dull like. 'Ain't he home?' says I. Then she looked at me. 'Yes,' says she, 'he's home.' 'Then why can't I see him?' I asked her, out of patience with her now. 'Cause he's dead' says she, just as quiet and dull—and fell to pleatin' her apron. 'Dead?' says, I, like you do when you can't take in what you've heard.

"She just nodded her head, not getting a bit excited, but rockin' back and forth.

"'Why—where is he?' says I, not knowing what to say.

44   "She just pointed upstairs—like this"—pointing to the room above.

"I got up, with the idea of going up there myself. By this time I—didn't know what to do. I walked from there to here; then I says: 'Why, what did he die of?'

"'He died of a rope around his neck,' says she; and just went on pleatin' at her apron."

Hale stopped speaking, and stood staring at the rocker, as if he were still seeing the woman who had sat there the morning before. Nobody spoke; it was as if every one were seeing the woman who had sat there the morning before.

48   "And what did you do then?" the county attorney at last broke the silence.

"I went out and called Harry. I thought I might—need help. I got Harry in, and we went upstairs." His voice fell almost to a whisper. "There he was— lying over the—"

"I think I'd rather have you go into that upstairs," the county attorney interrupted, "where you can point it all out. Just go on now with the rest of the story."

"Well, my first thought was to get that rope off. It looked—"

52   He stopped, his face twitching.

"But Harry, he went up to him, and he said. 'No, he's dead all right, and we'd better not touch anything.' So we went downstairs.

"She was still sitting that same way. 'Has anybody been notified?' I asked. 'No,' says she, unconcerned.

"'Who did this, Mrs. Wright?' said Harry. He said it businesslike, and she stopped pleatin' at her apron. 'I don't know,' she says. 'You don't know?' says Harry. 'Weren't you sleepin' in the bed with him?' 'Yes,' says she, 'but I was on the inside.' 'Somebody slipped a rope round his neck and strangled him, and you didn't wake up?' says Harry. 'I didn't wake up,' she said after him.

56   "We may have looked as if we didn't see how that could be, for after a minute she said, 'I sleep sound.'

"Harry was going to ask her more questions, but I said maybe that weren't our business; maybe we ought to let her tell her story first to the coroner or the sheriff. So Harry went fast as he could over to High Road—the Rivers' place, where there's a telephone."

"And what did she do when she knew you had gone for the coroner?" The attorney got his pencil in his hand all ready for writing.

"She moved from that chair to this one over here"—Hale pointed to a small chair in the corner—"and just sat there with her hands held together and lookin down. I got a feeling that I ought to make some conversation, so I said I had come in to see if John wanted to put in a telephone; and at that she started to laugh, and then she stopped and looked at me—scared."

60   At the sound of a moving pencil the man who was telling the story looked up.

"I dunno—maybe it wasn't scared," he hastened: "I wouldn't like to say it was. Soon Harry got back, and then Dr. Lloyd came, and you, Mr. Peters, and so I guess that's all I know that you don't."

He said that last with relief, and moved a little, as if relaxing. Everyone moved a little. The county attorney walked toward the stair door.

"I guess we'll go upstairs first—then out to the barn and around there."

64   He paused and looked around the kitchen.

"You're convinced there was nothing important here?" he asked the sheriff. "Nothing that would—point to any motive?"

The sheriff too looked all around, as if to re-convince himself.

"Nothing here but kitchen things," he said, with a little laugh for the insignificance of kitchen things.

68   The county attorney was looking at the cupboard—a peculiar, ungainly structure, half closet and half cupboard, the upper part of it being built in the wall, and the lower part just the old-fashioned kitchen cupboard. As if its queerness attracted him, he got a chair and opened the upper part and looked in. After a moment he drew his hand away sticky.

"Here's a nice mess," he said resentfully.

The two women had drawn nearer, and now the sheriff's wife spoke.

"Oh—her fruit," she said, looking to Mrs. Hale for sympathetic understanding.

72   She turned back to the county attorney and explained:"She worried about that when it turned so cold last night. She said the fire would go out and her jars might burst."

Mrs. Peters' husband broke into a laugh.

"Well, can you beat the women! Held for murder, and worrying about her preserves!"

The young attorney set his lips.

76   "I guess before we're through with her she may have something more serious than preserves to worry about."

"Oh, well," said Mrs. Hale's husband, with good-natured superiority, "women are used to worrying over trifles."

The two women moved a little closer together. Neither of them spoke. The county attorney seemed suddenly to remember his manners—and think of his future.

"And yet," said he, with the gallantry of a young politician,"for all their worries, what would we do without the ladies?"

80   The women did not speak, did not unbend. He went to the sink and began washing his hands. He turned to wipe them on the roller towel—whirled it for a cleaner place.

"Dirty towels! Not much of a housekeeper, would you say, ladies?"

He kicked his foot against some dirty pans under the sink.

"There's a great deal of work to be done on a farm," said Mrs. Hale stiffly.

84   "To be sure. And yet"—with a little bow to her—"I know there are some Dickson County farm-houses that do not have such roller towels." He gave it a pull to expose its full length again.

"Those towels get dirty awful quick. Men's hands aren't always as clean as they might be."

"Ah, loyal to your sex, I see," he laughed. He stopped and gave her a keen look,"But you and Mrs. Wright were neighbors. I suppose you were friends, too."

Martha Hale shook her head.

88   "I've seen little enough of her of late years. I've not been in this house— it's more than a year."

"And why was that? You didn't like her?"

"I liked her well enough," she replied with spirit."Farmers' wives have their hands full, Mr. Henderson. And then—" She looked around the kitchen.

"Yes?" he encouraged.

92   "It never seemed a very cheerful place," said she, more to herself than to him.

"No," he agreed;"I don't think anyone would call it cheerful. I shouldn't say she had the home-making instinct."

"Well, I don't know as Wright had, either," she muttered.

"You mean they didn't get on very well?" he was quick to ask.

96   "No; I don't mean anything," she answered, with decision. As she turned a little away from him, she added: "But I don't think a place would be any the cheerfuller for John Wright's bein' in it."

"I'd like to talk to you about that a little later, Mrs. Hale," he said. "I'm anxious to get the lay of things upstairs now."

He moved toward the stair door, followed by the two men.

"I suppose anything Mrs. Peters does'll be all right?" the sheriff inquired. "She was to take in some clothes for her, you know—and a few little things. We left in such a hurry yesterday."

100   The county attorney looked at the two women they were leaving alone there among the kitchen things.

"Yes—Mrs. Peters," he said, his glance resting on the woman who was not Mrs. Peters, the big farmer woman who stood behind the sheriff's wife. "Of course Mrs. Peters is one of us," he said, in a manner of entrusting responsibility. "And keep your eye out, Mrs. Peters, for anything that might be of use. No telling; you women might come upon a clue to the motive—and that's the thing we need."

Mr. Hale rubbed his face after the fashion of a showman getting ready for a pleasantry.

"But would the women know a clue if they did come upon it?" he said; and, having delivered himself of this, he followed the others through the stair door.

104   The women stood motionless and silent, listening to the footsteps, first upon the stairs, then in the room above them.

Then, as if releasing herself from something strange. Mrs. Hale began to arrange the dirty pans under the sink, which the county attorney's disdainful push of the foot had deranged.

"I'd hate to have men comin' into my kitchen," she said testily— "snoopin' round and criticizin'."

"Of course it's no more than their duty," said the sheriff's wife, in her manner of timid acquiescence.

108   "Duty's all right," replied Mrs. Hale bluffly; "but I guess that deputy sheriff that come out to make the fire might have got a little of this on." She gave the roller towel a pull. "Wish I'd thought of that sooner! Seems mean to talk about her for not having things slicked up, when she had to come away in such a hurry."

She looked around the kitchen. Certainly it was not "slicked up." Her eye was held by a bucket of sugar on a low shelf. The cover was off the wooden bucket, and beside it was a paper bag—half full.

Mrs. Hale moved toward it.

"She was putting this in there," she said to herself—slowly.

112   She thought of the flour in her kitchen at home—half sifted, half not sifted. She had been interrupted, and had left things half done. What had

interrupted Minnie Foster? Why had that work been left half done? She made a move as if to finish it,—unfinished things always bothered her,—and then she glanced around and saw that Mrs. Peters was watching her—and she didn't want Mrs. Peters to get that feeling she had got of work begun and then—for some reason—not finished.

"It's a shame about her fruit," she said, and walked toward the cupboard that the county attorney had opened, and got on the chair, murmuring: "I wonder if it's all gone."

It was a sorry enough looking sight, but "Here's one that's all right," she said at last. She held it toward the light. "This is cherries, too." She looked again. "I declare I believe that's the only one."

With a sigh, she got down from the chair, went to the sink, and wiped off the bottle.

116   "She'll feel awful bad, after all her hard work in the hot weather. I remember the afternoon I put up my cherries last summer."

She set the bottle on the table, and, with another sigh, started to sit down in the rocker. But she did not sit down. Something kept her from sitting down in that chair. She straightened—stepped back, and, half turned away, stood looking at it, seeing the woman who had sat there "pleatin' at her apron."

The thin voice of the sheriff's wife broke in upon her: "I must be getting those things from the front-room closet." She opened the door into the other room, started in, stepped back. "You coming with me, Mrs. Hale?" she asked nervously. "You—you could help me get them."

They were soon back—the stark coldness of that shut-up room was not a thing to linger in.

120   "My!" said Mrs. Peters, dropping the things on the table and hurrying to the stove.

Mrs. Hale stood examining the clothes the woman who was being detained in town had said she wanted.

"Wright was close!" she exclaimed, holding up a shabby black skirt that bore the marks of much making over. "I think maybe that's why she kept so much to herself. I s'pose she felt she couldn't do her part; and then, you don't enjoy things when you feel shabby. She used to wear pretty clothes and be lively—when she was Minnie Foster, one of the town girls, singing in the choir. But that—oh, that was twenty years ago."

With a carefulness in which there was something tender, she folded the shabby clothes and piled them at one corner of the table. She looked up at Mrs. Peters, and there was something in the other woman's look that irritated her.

124   "She don't care," she said to herself. "Much difference it makes to her whether Minnie Foster had pretty clothes when she was a girl."

Then she looked again, and she wasn't so sure; in fact, she hadn't at any time been perfectly sure about Mrs. Peters. She had that shrinking manner, and yet her eyes looked as if they could see a long way into things.

"This all you was to take in?" asked Mrs. Hale.

"No," said the sheriff's wife; "she said she wanted an apron. Funny thing to want," she ventured in her nervous little way, "for there's not much to get you dirty in jail, goodness knows. But I suppose just to make her feel more natural. If you're used to wearing an apron—. She said they were in the bottom drawer of this cupboard. Yes—here they are. And then her little shawl that always hung on the stair door."

128   She took the small gray shawl from behind the door leading upstairs, and stood a minute looking at it.

Suddenly Mrs. Hale took a quick step toward the other woman, "Mrs. Peters!"

"Yes, Mrs. Hale?"

"Do you think she—did it?"

132   A frightened look blurred the other thing in Mrs. Peters' eyes.

"Oh, I don't know," she said, in a voice that seemed to shrink away from the subject.

"Well, I don't think she did," affirmed Mrs. Hale stoutly. "Asking for an apron, and her little shawl. Worryin' about her fruit."

"Mr. Peters says—." Footsteps were heard in the room above; she stopped, looked up, then went on in a lowered voice: "Mr. Peters says—it looks bad for her. Mr. Henderson is awful sarcastic in a speech, and he's going to make fun of her saying she didn't—wake up."

136   For a moment Mrs. Hale had no answer. Then, "Well, I guess John Wright didn't wake up—when they was slippin' that rope under his neck," she muttered.

"No, it's strange," breathed Mrs. Peters. "They think it was such a—funny way to kill a man."

She began to laugh; at sound of the laugh, abruptly stopped.

"That's just what Mr. Hale said," said Mrs. Hale, in a resolutely natural voice. "There was a gun in the house. He says that's what he can't understand."

140   "Mr. Henderson said, coming out, that what was needed for the case was a motive. Something to show anger—or sudden feeling."

'Well, I don't see any signs of anger around here," said Mrs. Hale, "I don't—" She stopped. It was as if her mind tripped on something. Her eye was caught by a dish-towel in the middle of the kitchen table. Slowly she moved toward the table. One half of it was wiped clean, the other half messy. Her eyes made a slow, almost unwilling turn to the bucket of sugar and the half empty bag beside it. Things begun—and not finished.

After a moment she stepped back, and said, in that manner of releasing herself:

"Wonder how they're finding things upstairs? I hope she had it a little more red up up there. You know,"—she paused, and feeling gathered,—"it seems kind of sneaking: locking her up in town and coming out here to get her own house to turn against her!"

144   "But, Mrs. Hale," said the sheriff's wife, "the law is the law."

"I s'pose 'tis," answered Mrs. Hale shortly.

She turned to the stove, saying something about that fire not being much to brag of. She worked with it a minute, and when she straightened up she said aggressively:

"The law is the law—and a bad stove is a bad stove. How'd you like to cook on this?"—pointing with the poker to the broken lining. She opened the oven door and started to express her opinion of the oven; but she was swept into her own thoughts, thinking of what it would mean, year after year, to have that stove to wrestle with. The thought of Minnie Foster trying to bake in that oven—and the thought of her never going over to see Minnie Foster—.

148   She was startled by hearing Mrs. Peters say: "A person gets discouraged—and loses heart."

The sheriff's wife had looked from the stove to the sink—to the pail of water which had been carried in from outside. The two women stood there silent, above them the footsteps of the men who were looking for evidence against the woman who had worked in that kitchen. That look of seeing into things, of seeing through a thing to something else, was in the eyes of the sheriff's wife now. When Mrs. Hale next spoke to her, it was gently:

"Better loosen up your things, Mrs. Peters. We'll not feel them when we go out."

Mrs. Peters went to the back of the room to hang up the fur tippet she was wearing. A moment later she exclaimed, "Why, she was piecing a quilt," and held up a large sewing basket piled high with quilt pieces.

152   Mrs. Hale spread some of the blocks on the table.

"It's log-cabin pattern," she said, putting several of them together, "Pretty, isn't it?"

They were so engaged with the quilt that they did not hear the footsteps on the stairs. Just as the stair door opened Mrs. Hale was saying:

"Do you suppose she was going to quilt it or just knot it?"

156   The sheriff threw up his hands.

"They wonder whether she was going to quilt it or just knot it!"

There was a laugh for the ways of women, a warming of hands over the stove, and then the county attorney said briskly:

"Well, let's go right out to the barn and get that cleared up."

160   "I don't see as there's anything so strange," Mrs. Hale said resentfully, after the outside door had closed on the three men—"our taking up our time with little things while we're waiting for them to get the evidence. I don't see as it's anything to laugh about."

"Of course they've got awful important things on their minds," said the sheriff's wife apologetically.

They returned to an inspection of the block for the quilt. Mrs. Hale was looking at the fine, even sewing, and preoccupied with thoughts of the woman who had done that sewing, when she heard the sheriff's wife say, in a queer tone:

"Why, look at this one."

164   She turned to take the block held out to her.

"The sewing," said Mrs. Peters, in a troubled way, "All the rest of them have been so nice and even—but—this one. Why, it looks as if she didn't know what she was about!"

Their eyes met—something flashed to life, passed between them; then, as if with an effort, they seemed to pull away from each other. A moment Mrs. Hale sat there, her hands folded over that sewing which was so unlike all the rest of the sewing. Then she had pulled a knot and drawn the threads.

"Oh, what are you doing, Mrs. Hale?" asked the sheriff's wife, startled.

168   "Just pulling out a stitch or two that's not sewed very good," said Mrs. Hale mildly.

"I don't think we ought to touch things," Mrs. Peters said, a little helplessly.

"I'll just finish up this end," answered Mrs. Hale, still in that mild, matter-of-fact fashion.

She threaded a needle and started to replace bad sewing with good. For a little while she sewed in silence. Then, in that thin, timid voice, she heard:

172   "Mrs. Hale!"

"Yes, Mrs. Peters?"

'What do you suppose she was so—nervous about?"

"Oh, I don't know," said Mrs. Hale, as if dismissing a thing not important enough to spend much time on. "I don't know as she was—nervous. I sew awful queer sometimes when I'm just tired."

176   She cut a thread, and out of the corner of her eye looked up at Mrs. Peters. The small, lean face of the sheriff's wife seemed to have tightened up. Her eyes had that look of peering into something. But next moment she moved, and said in her thin, indecisive way:

"Well, I must get those clothes wrapped. They may be through sooner than we think. I wonder where I could find a piece of paper—and string."

"In that cupboard, maybe," suggested to Mrs. Hale, after a glance around.

One piece of the crazy sewing remained unripped. Mrs. Peter's back turned, Martha Hale now scrutinized that piece, compared it with the dainty, accurate sewing of the other blocks. The difference was startling. Holding this block made her feel queer, as if the distracted thoughts of the woman who had perhaps turned to it to try and quiet herself were communicating themselves to her.

180   Mrs. Peters' voice roused her.

"Here's a bird-cage," she said. "Did she have a bird, Mrs. Hale?"

"Why, I don't know whether she did or not." She turned to look at the cage Mrs. Peters was holding up. "I've not been here in so long." She sighed. "There was a man round last year selling canaries cheap—but I don't know as she took one. Maybe she did. She used to sing real pretty herself."

Mrs. Peters looked around the kitchen.

184   "Seems kind of funny to think of a bird here." She half laughed—an attempt to put up a barrier. "But she must have had one—or why would she have a cage? I wonder what happened to it."

"I suppose maybe the cat got it," suggested Mrs. Hale, resuming her sewing.

"No; she didn't have a cat. She's got that feeling some people have about cats—being afraid of them. When they brought her to our house yesterday, my cat got in the room, and she was real upset and asked me to take it out."

"My sister Bessie was like that," laughed Mrs. Hale.

188   The sheriff's wife did not reply. The silence made Mrs. Hale turn round. Mrs. Peters was examining the bird-cage.

"Look at this door," she said slowly. "It's broke. One hinge has been pulled apart."

Mrs. Hale came nearer.

"Looks as if someone must have been—rough with it."

192   Again their eyes met—startled, questioning, apprehensive. For a moment neither spoke nor stirred. Then Mrs. Hale, turning away, said brusquely:

"If they're going to find any evidence, I wish they'd be about it. I don't like this place."

"But I'm awful glad you came with me, Mrs. Hale." Mrs. Peters put the bird-cage on the table and sat down. "It would be lonesome for me—sitting here alone."

"Yes, it would, wouldn't it?" agreed Mrs. Hale, a certain determined naturalness in her voice. She had picked up the sewing, but now it dropped in her lap, and she murmured in a different voice: "But I tell you what I do wish, Mrs. Peters. I wish I had come over sometimes when she was here. I wish—I had."

196   "But of course you were awful busy, Mrs. Hale. Your house—and your children."

"I could've come," retorted Mrs. Hale shortly. "I stayed away because it weren't cheerful—and that's why I ought to have come. I"—she looked around—"I've never liked this place. Maybe because it's down in a hollow and you don't see the road. I don't know what it is, but it's a lonesome place, and always was. I wish I had come over to see Minnie Foster sometimes. I can see now—" She did not put it into words.

"Well, you mustn't reproach yourself," counseled Mrs. Peters. "Somehow, we just don't see how it is with other folks till—something comes up."

"Not having children makes less work," mused Mrs. Hale, after a silence, "but it makes a quiet house—and Wright out to work all day—and no company when he did come in. Did you know John Wright, Mrs. Peters?"

200   "Not to know him. I've seen him in town. They say he was a good man."

"Yes—good," conceded John Wright's neighbor grimly. "He didn't drink, and kept his word as well as most, I guess, and paid his debts. But he was a hard man, Mrs. Peters. Just to pass the time of day with him—." She stopped, shivered a little. "Like a raw wind that gets to the bone." Her eye fell upon the cage on the table before her, and she added, almost bitterly: "I should think she would've wanted a bird!"

Suddenly she leaned forward, looking intently at the cage. "But what do you s'pose went wrong with it?"

"I don't know," returned Mrs. Peters; "unless it got sick and died."

204   But after she said it she reached over and swung the broken door. Both women watched it as if somehow held by it.

"You didn't know—her?" Mrs. Hale asked, a gentler note in her voice.

"Not till they brought her yesterday," said the sheriff's wife.

"She—come to think of it, she was kind of like a bird herself. Real sweet and pretty, but kind of timid and—fluttery. How—she—did—change."

208   That held her for a long time. Finally, as if struck with a happy thought and relieved to get back to everyday things, she exclaimed:

"Tell you what, Mrs. Peters, why don't you take the quilt in with you? It might take up her mind."

"Why, I think that's a real nice idea, Mrs. Hale," agreed the sheriff's wife, as if she too were glad to come into the atmosphere of a simple kindness. "There couldn't possibly be any objection to that, could there? Now, just what will I take? I wonder if her patches are in here—and her things?"

They turned to the sewing basket.

212   "Here's some red," said Mrs. Hale, bringing out a roll of cloth. Underneath that was a box. "Here, maybe her scissors are in here—and her things." She held it up. "What a pretty box! I'll warrant that was something she had a long time ago—when she was a girl."

She held it in her hand a moment; then, with a little sigh, opened it.

Instantly her hand went to her nose.

"Why—!"

216   Mrs. Peters drew nearer—then turned away.

"There's something wrapped up in this piece of silk," faltered Mrs. Hale.

"This isn't her scissors," said Mrs. Peters, in a shrinking voice.

Her hand not steady, Mrs. Hale raised the piece of silk. "Oh, Mrs. Peters!" she cried. "It's—"

220   Mrs. Peters bent closer.

"It's the bird," she whispered.

"But, Mrs. Peters!" cried Mrs. Hale. "Look at it! Its neck—look at its neck! It's all—other side to."

She held the box away from her.

224   The sheriff's wife again bent closer.

"Somebody wrung its neck," said she, in a voice that was slow and deep.

And then again the eyes of the two women met—this time clung together in a look of dawning comprehension, of growing horror. Mrs. Peters looked from the dead bird to the broken door of the cage. Again their eyes met. And just then there was a sound at the outside door. Mrs. Hale slipped the box under the quilt pieces in the basket, and sank into the chair before it. Mrs. Peters stood holding to the table. The county attorney and the sheriff came in from outside.

"Well, ladies," said the county attorney, as one turning from serious things to little pleasantries, "have you decided whether she was going to quilt it or knot it?"

228   "We think," began the sheriff's wife in a flurried voice, "that she was going to—knot it."

He was too preoccupied to notice the change that came in her voice on that last.

"Well, that's very interesting, I'm sure," he said tolerantly. He caught sight of the bird-cage.

"Has the bird flown?"

232   "We think the cat got it," said Mrs. Hale in a voice curiously even.

He was walking up and down, as if thinking something out.

"Is there a cat?" he asked absently.

Mrs. Hale shot a look up at the sheriff's wife.

236   "Well, not now," said Mrs. Peters. "They're superstitious, you know; they leave."

She sank into her chair.

The county attorney did not heed her. "No sign at all of anyone having come in from the outside," he said to Peters, in the manner of continuing an interrupted conversation. "Their own rope. Now let's go upstairs again and go over it, piece by piece. It would have to have been someone who knew just the—"

The stair door closed behind them and their voices were lost.

240   The two women sat motionless, not looking at each other, but as if peering into something and at the same time holding back. When they spoke now it was as if they were afraid of what they were saying, but as if they could not help saying it.

"She liked the bird," said Martha Hale, low and slowly. "She was going to bury it in that pretty box."

"When I was a girl," said Mrs. Peters, under her breath, "my kitten—there was a boy took a hatchet, and before my eyes—before I could get there—" She covered her face an instant. "If they hadn't held me back I would have"— she caught herself, looked upstairs where footsteps were heard, and finished weakly—"hurt him."

Then they sat without speaking or moving.

244   "I wonder how it would seem," Mrs. Hale at last began, as if feeling her way over strange ground—"never to have had any children around?" Her eyes made a slow sweep of the kitchen, as if seeing what that kitchen had meant through all the years. "No, Wright wouldn't like the bird," she said after that— "a thing that sang. She used to sing. He killed that too." Her voice tightened.

Mrs. Peters moved uneasily.

"Of course we don't know who killed the bird."

"I knew John Wright," was Mrs. Hale's answer.

248   "It was an awful thing was done in this house that night, Mrs. Hale," said the sheriff's wife. "Killing a man while he slept—slipping a thing round his neck that choked the life out of him."

Mrs. Hale's hand went out to the bird cage.

"We don't know who killed him," whispered Mrs. Peters wildly. "We don't know."

Mrs. Hale had not moved. "If there had been years and years of—nothing, then a bird to sing to you, it would be awful—still—after the bird was still."

252   It was as if something within her not herself had spoken, and it found in Mrs. Peters something she did not know as herself.

"I know what stillness is," she said, in a queer, monotonous voice. "When we homesteaded in Dakota, and my first baby died—after he was two years old—and me with no other then—"

Mrs. Hale stirred.

"How soon do you suppose they'll be through looking for the evidence?"

256   "I know what stillness is," repeated Mrs. Peters, in just that same way. Then she too pulled back. "The law has got to punish crime, Mrs. Hale," she said in her tight little way.

"I wish you'd seen Minnie Foster," was the answer, "when she wore a white dress with blue ribbons, and stood up there in the choir and sang."

The picture of that girl, the fact that she had lived neighbor to that girl for twenty years, and had let her die for lack of life, was suddenly more than she could bear.

"Oh, I wish I'd come over here once in a while!" she cried. "That was a crime! Who's going to punish that?"

260   "We mustn't take on," said Mrs. Peters, with a frightened look toward the stairs.

"I might 'a' *known* she needed help! I tell you, it's queer, Mrs. Peters. We live close together, and we live far apart. We all go through the same things—it's all just a different kind of the same thing! If it weren't—why do you and I understand? Why do we know—what we know this minute?"

She dashed her hand across her eyes. Then, seeing the jar of fruit on the table she reached for it and choked out:

"If I was you I wouldn't tell her her fruit was gone! Tell her it ain't. Tell her it's all right—all of it. Here—take this in to prove it to her! She—she may never know whether it was broke or not."

264   She turned away.

Mrs. Peters reached out for the bottle of fruit as if she were glad to take it—as if touching a familiar thing, having something to do, could keep her from something else. She got up, looked about for something to wrap the fruit in, took a petticoat from the pile of clothes she had brought from the front room, and nervously started winding that round the bottle.

"My!" she began, in a high, false voice, "it's a good thing the men couldn't hear us! Getting all stirred up over a little thing like a—dead canary." She hurried over that. "As if that could have anything to do with—with—My, wouldn't they laugh?"

Footsteps were heard on the stairs.

268   "Maybe they would," muttered Mrs. Hale—"maybe they wouldn't."

"No, Peters," said the county attorney incisively; "it's all perfectly clear, except the reason for doing it. But you know juries when it comes to women. If there was some definite thing—something to show. Something to make a story about. A thing that would connect up with this clumsy way of doing it."

In a covert way Mrs. Hale looked at Mrs. Peters. Mrs. Peters was looking at her. Quickly they looked away from each other. The outer door opened and Mr. Hale came in.

"I've got the team round now," he said. "Pretty cold out there."

272   "I'm going to stay here awhile by myself," the county attorney suddenly announced. "You can send Frank out for me, can't you?" he asked the sheriff. "I want to go over everything. I'm not satisfied we can't do better."

Again, for one brief moment, the two women's eyes found one another. The sheriff came up to the table.

"Did you want to see what Mrs. Peters was going to take in?"

276   The county attorney picked up the apron. He laughed.

"Oh, I guess they're not very dangerous things the ladies have picked out."

Mrs. Hale's hand was on the sewing basket in which the box was concealed. She felt that she ought to take her hand off the basket. She did not seem able to. He picked up one of the quilt blocks which she had piled on to cover the box. Her eyes felt like fire. She had a feeling that if he took up the basket she would snatch it from him.

But he did not take it up. With another little laugh, he turned away, saying:

280   "No; Mrs. Peters doesn't need supervising. For that matter, a sheriff's wife is married to the law. Ever think of it that way, Mrs. Peters?"

Mrs. Peters was standing beside the table. Mrs. Hale shot a look up at her; but she could not see her face. Mrs. Peters had turned away. When she spoke, her voice was muffled.

"Not—just that way," she said.

"Married to the law!" chuckled Mrs. Peters' husband. He moved toward the door into the front room, and said to the county attorney:

284   "I just want you to come in here a minute, George. We ought to take a look at these windows."

"Oh—windows," said the county attorney scoffingly.

"We'll be right out, Mr. Hale," said the sheriff to the farmer, who was still waiting by the door.

Hale went to look after the horses. The sheriff followed the county attorney into the other room. Again—for one final moment—the two women were alone in that kitchen.

288   Martha Hale sprang up, her hands tight together, looking at that other woman, with whom it rested. At first she could not see her eyes, for the

sheriff's wife had not turned back since she turned away at that suggestion of being married to the law. But now Mrs. Hale made her turn back. Her eyes made her turn back. Slowly, unwillingly, Mrs. Peters turned her head until her eyes met the eyes of the other woman. There was a moment when they held each other in a steady, burning look in which there was no evasion or flinching. Then Martha Hale's eyes pointed the way to the basket in which was hidden the thing that would make certain the conviction of the other woman—that woman who was not there and yet who had been there with them all through that hour.

For a moment Mrs. Peters did not move. And then she did it. With a rush forward, she threw back the quilt pieces, got the box, tried to put it in her handbag. It was too big. Desperately she opened it, started to take the bird out. But there she broke—she could not touch the bird. She stood there help-less, foolish.

There was the sound of a knob turning in the inner door. Martha Hale snatched the box from the sheriff's wife, and got it in the pocket of her big coat just as the sheriff and the county attorney came back into the kitchen.

"Well, Henry," said the county attorney facetiously, "at least we found out that she was not going to quilt it. She was going to—what is it you call it, ladies?"

292   Mrs. Hale's hand was against the pocket of her coat.

"We call it—knot it, Mr. Henderson."

READER RESPONSE

The story seems to suggest that special circumstances to some extent justify or even condone extreme acts such as, in this case, murder. To what extent do you agree that violent responses, even murder, are understandable or jus-tifiable? Are there any conditions in which you might approve of such acts?

QUESTIONS FOR DISCUSSION

1. How are the men and women in this story characterized? How do the two women differ from one another? What do they have in common? How do they contrast with the men? What experiences do they have in common with Minnie Wright?
2. What do we learn of the two characters who never appear, the dead man John Wright and his wife Minnie Wright? How would you characterize their relationship based on what the other characters say about them?
3. How does the setting of the play help to develop the theme? Consider the weather, the time of year, the physical location of the Wright house, and the kitchen where Mrs. Hale and Mrs. Peters spend most of their time.

4. Discuss the implications of the following statement: "Oh, I wish I'd come over here once in a while!" she cried. "That was a crime! Who's going to punish that?" (paragraph 259).

5. Mr. Hale says at one point that "women are used to worrying over trifles." Yet it is "trifles" that lead the women to conclude that Mrs. Wright murdered her husband. What are these trifling things, and why do the women consider them to be important?

6. Discuss the extent to which you believe the women acted appropriately in carrying off evidence "that would make certain the conviction of the other woman." How does Mrs. Peters's being "married to the law" make her moral position especially problematic (paragraph 288)?

ADDITIONAL SUGGESTIONS FOR WRITING ABOUT ETHICS, MORALS, AND VALUES

1. Using Lorri G. Nandrea's "Having No Hand in the Matter" as a springboard for your own ideas, write a thoughtful, extended definition for the concept of justice. Use examples to illustrate and support your definition.

2. Write a reflection paper in response to the following assertion from Nandrea's "Having No Hand in the Matter": "We need new ethics, new concepts of justice that help us think not just contact but distance and absences; that foster fidelity to the absent one, to those we will never see and never know." You may want to explain why you do or do not agree with this assertion, what kinds of situations these new ethics should help us to address, or how we can be brought to feel responsible for the well-being of people we may never see and never know.

3. Working with a literary text that deals with a crime, analyze the "model of agency" that seems to determine the criminal's guilt (as explained in Lorri G. Nandrea's "Having No Hand in the Matter"). Does the crime fit the "hand" model? If so, how? If not, in what way is the criminal's guilt established? If the criminal gets away, is it because he or she "had no *hand* in the matter"? You also may want to analyze the manner in which the criminal is punished: Is he or she hounded by "internal furies," punished by revenge, or punished by a court that uses words, rhetoric, and a system of equivalences to assign the crime and compensate the victim?

4. In "Having No Hand in the Matter," Lorri G. Handrea discusses the "affair of the contaminated blood" *(affaire du sang contaminé)* without giving complete details. Beginning with the source that she cites, research these events further: What exactly happened, and why? What was the public's reaction to the scandal in France? In America? What were the political repercussions in each country, if any? How widely publicized was the scandal? Have any recent developments or further consequences occurred? Working with the sources you have found, write a research paper

in which you background the second half of this argument by giving your readers more information about the events on which it is based and offer your own thoughtful response to your findings.

5. Drawing on Ellen Goodman's "It's Failure, Not Success," explain your position concerning the Machiavellian philosophy that any means you have to use to get to the top are justifiable.

6. Define *success* or *failure* by using the example of a person (or people) you know personally or have read about. One person might illustrate how you define the term, or several people might represent different kinds of success. Is it possible for one person to be both a success and a failure?

7. With Ellen Goodman's "It's Failure, Not Success" in mind, explore the moral aspects of success by considering to what degree morality or ethics might be an issue in certain careers or professions.

8. Write a response to any of the charges against young people that Christina Hoff Sommers makes in "Are We Living in a Moral Stone Age?" To what extent do you agree with her?

9. Write to the editor of *Time* magazine in response to either Kurt Wiesenfeld's "Making the Grade" or Charles Krauthammer's "First and Last, Do No Harm."

10. Using Kurt Wiesenfeld's "Making the Grade" as a starting point for your thinking and discussion, write your own "My Turn" column on the subject of grades, teachers, and jobs. Consider whether you believe that grades and the job they lead to are more valuable or important than getting a good education. Consider, too, the matter of incentives such as the gold stars and smiley faces Wiesenfeld mentions. In what ways have teachers you have had rewarded you for effort, not results?

11. Drawing on Roger Rosenblatt's "The Quality of Mercy Killing," Charles Krauthammer's "First and Last, Do No Harm," and M. Scott Peck's "Living Is the Mystery," write an opinion paper on mercy killing. Include the example of the Gilbert or another mercy-killing case. Consider whether mercy killing is ever justified and, if so, under what circumstances it might be.

12. Taking into account what some of the writers in this chapter say about individual responsibility, moral or ethical choices, and positive values, write an essay about your personal definition of one of these abstract terms. Use examples to illustrate or make your definition concrete.

13. Choose a current event or life situation that seems to involve an injustice. You may want to look through a newspaper and find an article or two that you can use as sources in your paper (be sure to save the publication information, so you can cite them). Then write an argument in which you explain why this particular situation constitutes an injustice and how you think justice might best be achieved.

14. With Susan Glaspell's "A Jury of Her Peers" in mind, examine the issue of an individual's right to act according to conscience when that act would violate the law. Under what circumstances, aside from mercy killing,

might such a dilemma occur? When might the issue of individual freedom take precedence over the law, or should the law always be obeyed?

15. Explain how a specific person, institution, book, or course in school has had a strong effect on the formation of your own values.

16. Interview your parents (or other people who were young adults in a generation different from your own) about what they recall of their hopes, fears, formative values, and moral options. Then write an essay describing the results of your interviews and the conclusions you draw from them. Consider, for instance, how the experiences and beliefs of the people you interviewed are similar to and different from your own.

17. Define an abstract quality such as honor, duty, integrity, honesty, or moral responsibility by using specific examples to illustrate your general statements.

TRANSITIONS

Transition is a natural part of life, beginning with the most basic transition: birth. Our lives are characterized by change as we grow and develop from infancy to childhood, from childhood to adulthood, and from life to death. In each of these stages, we undergo change, make adjustments, and try to adapt. People make many other transitions as well, such as moving through levels of education, selecting or changing job or career paths, and making choices about whom to date, commit to, marry, or divorce. The physical movement from place to place is a common transition, from changing addresses within the same city to moving across the country or around the world.

Besides these obvious changes, emotional and psychological transitions occur as well. Such transitions may occur slowly, such as in the subtle, multi-faceted growth from innocence to maturity, or they may occur suddenly, such as when flashes of insight transform us from ignorance to knowledge. We make some of these transitions willingly; we find others difficult to make. But whether we welcome or resist transitions, they almost always affect us in significant ways.

While our personal transitions are of utmost importance to us, transitions that occur in our communities, our nation, and our world affect—and sometimes even determine—our personal transitions. For instance, entering a new millennium, a rare transition, was observed and celebrated by people around the world. What happens in other countries, such as war or political changes, can have a profound effect on our own country, while changes in political administrations at home, especially on the national level, also hold the possibility of tremendous change for the nation and for our own lives.

Inaugural addresses provide speakers and writers with an opportunity to comment on the important transitions they commemorate. This chapter opens with President John F. Kennedy's inaugural address, a speech that not only ushered in a new political climate but also inspired a generation of young people in significant ways. As you read his speech, consider how timely it remains today, more than forty years later. Several passages in the speech have become famous, such as that urging Americans to become active citizens and the unforgettable one beginning "Ask not what your country can do for you. . . ." Kennedy also urges the nations of the world to join together in the fight against the common enemies of tyranny, poverty, disease, and war.

Next, writing about a different kind of transition, Jennifer Crichton, in " 'Who Shall I Be?': The Allure of a Fresh Start," comments on the experience of students making the transition into college. Using both personal anecdotes and examples of people she knows, Crichton explains how going away to college offers an opportunity to create an entirely new identity. Although her essay focuses on the specific and personal transition she made, its general theme can be applied to any change in which people have an opportunity for a fresh start, such as moving from one neighborhood or city to another or going from being a student to starting a career. Richard Ford thinks that moving is not so bad. In "An Urge for Going," he maintains that moving makes him feel "safe and in possession of [him]self." In contrast, Lynn Randall, in "Grandma's Story," tells of an entirely different and involuntary move, the forced relocation of her grandparents and the bewilderment and insecurity that followed.

One very common transition that occurs with the passage of time is the loss of or change in a favorite retreat or particular place that is filled with warm memories and fond associations. E. B. White's classic essay "Once More to the Lake," written in August 1941 against a backdrop of war in Europe and domestic turmoil as the United States wrestled with whether to get involved, is a product of both memory and introspection. Returning with his son to the lake where his family vacationed annually when he was a boy, he looks for familiar sights and sounds, contemplates the changes wrought by the years that have passed, and considers their larger implications.

The last entry in this chapter is a short story written from the perspective of an adult looking back on childhood and the growth, both intellectual and emotional, that resulted from growing up. Larry Watson's short story "Silence" features an event that happened when the narrator was eight years old and suggests that the transition from childhood to adulthood may carry with it some unresolved issues. Looking back as an adult on that memorable day, the narrator makes a painful realization.

1. Comment on the significance of graduation day as a transitional marker.
2. Describe the feelings and thoughts you had about your past and your future when you graduated from high school.
3. Explain which graduation you think has more significance, high school or college, and why. Is one more important than another?

DISCUSSION QUESTIONS/WRITING SUGGESTIONS

1. How often have you moved? Are you looking forward to being settled in one place, or do you like the idea of moving from time to time?
2. How connected do you feel to your community or neighborhood? Do you plan to return to the town you grew up in when you are ready to start a career, or do you plan to go someplace completely different? Explain your answer.
3. How willing are you to relocate to anywhere a job will take you?
4. How prepared do you think you are for a sudden change in your life?

Inaugural Address
John F. Kennedy

John F. Kennedy (1917-1963) was an author, an officer in the U.S. Navy, a newspaper correspondent, a member of the U.S. House of Representatives, and a U.S. Senator before becoming the 35th president of the United States. His book Profiles in Courage *(1957), about Americans who had taken unpopular but moral stands, won the Pulitzer Prize for biography. President Kennedy was assassinated on November 23, 1963. This speech was delivered at his inauguration in Washington, D.C., on January 20, 1961.*

Vice President Johnson, Mr. Speaker, Mr. Chief Justice, President Eisenhower, Vice President Nixon, President Truman, reverend clergy, fellow citizens, we observe today not a victory of party, but a celebration of freedom—symbolizing an end, as well as a beginning—signifying renewal, as well as change. For I have sworn before you and Almighty God the same solemn oath our forebears prescribed nearly a century and three quarters ago.

The world is very different now. For man holds in his mortal hands the power to abolish all forms of human poverty and all forms of human life. And yet the same revolutionary beliefs for which our forebears fought are still at issue around the globe—the belief that the rights of man come not from the generosity of the state, but from the hand of God.

We dare not forget today that we are the heirs of that first revolution. Let the word go forth from this time and place, to friend and foe alike, that the torch has been passed to a new generation of Americans—born in this century, tempered by war, disciplined by a hard and bitter peace, proud of our ancient heritage—and unwilling to witness or permit the slow undoing of those human rights to which this Nation has always been committed, and to which we are committed today at home and around the world.

4 Let every nation know, whether it wishes us well or ill, that we shall pay any price, bear any burden, meet any hardship, support any friend, oppose any foe, in order to assure the survival and the success of liberty.

This much we pledge—and more.

To those old allies whose cultural and spiritual origins we share, we pledge the loyalty of faithful friends. United, there is little we cannot do in a host of cooperative ventures. Divided, there is little we can do—for we dare not meet a powerful challenge at odds and split asunder.

To those new states whom we welcome to the ranks of the free, we pledge our word that one form of colonial control shall not have passed away merely to be replaced by a far more iron tyranny. We shall not always expect to find them supporting our view. But we shall always hope to find them strongly supporting their own freedom—and to remember that, in the past, those who foolishly sought power by riding the back of the tiger ended up inside.

8   To those peoples in the huts and villages across the globe struggling to break the bonds of mass misery, we pledge our best efforts to help them help themselves, for whatever period is required—not because the Communists may be doing it, not because we seek their votes, but because it is right. If a free society cannot help the many who are poor, it cannot save the few who are rich.

To our sister republics south of our border, we offer a special pledge—to convert our good words into good deeds—in a new alliance for progress—to assist free men and free governments in casting off the chains of poverty. But this peaceful revolution of hope cannot become the prey of hostile powers. Let all our neighbors know that we shall join with them to oppose aggression or subversion anywhere in the Americas. And let every other power know that this hemisphere intends to remain the master of its own house.

To that world assembly of sovereign states, the United Nations, our last best hope in an age where the instruments of war have far outpaced the instruments of peace, we renew our pledge of support—to prevent it from becoming merely a forum for invective—to strengthen its shield of the new and the weak—and to enlarge the area in which its writ may run.

Finally, to those nations who would make themselves our adversary, we offer not a pledge but a request: that both sides begin anew the quest for peace, before the dark powers of destruction unleashed by science engulf all humanity in planned or accidental self-destruction.

12   We dare not tempt them with weakness. For only when our arms are sufficient beyond doubt can we be certain beyond doubt that they will never be employed.

But neither can two great and powerful groups of nations take comfort from our present course—both sides overburdened by the cost of modern weapons, both rightly alarmed by the steady spread of the deadly atom, yet both racing to alter that uncertain balance of terror that stays the hand of mankind's final war.

So let us begin anew—remembering on both sides that civility is not a sign of weakness, and sincerity is always subject to proof. Let us never negotiate out of fear. But let us never fear to negotiate.

Let both sides explore what problems unite us instead of belaboring those problems which divide us.

16   Let both sides, for the first time, formulate serious and precise proposals for the inspection and control of arms—and bring the absolute power to destroy other nations under the absolute control of all nations.

Let both sides seek to invoke the wonders of science instead of its terrors. Together let us explore the stars, conquer the deserts, eradicate disease, tap the ocean depths, and encourage the arts and commerce.

Let both sides unite to heed in all corners of the earth the command of Isaiah—to "undo the heavy burdens . . . and to let the oppressed go free."

And if a beachhead of cooperation may push back the jungle of suspicion, let both sides join in creating a new endeavor, not a new balance of power, but a new world of law, where the strong are just and the weak secure and the peace preserved.

20   All this will not be finished in the first 100 days. Nor will it be finished in the first 1,000 days, nor in the life of this administration, nor even perhaps in our lifetime on this planet. But let us begin.

In your hands, my fellow citizens, more than in mine, will rest the final success or failure of our course. Since this country was founded, each generation of Americans has been summoned to give testimony to its national loyalty. The graves of young Americans who answered the call to service surround the globe.

Now the trumpet summons us again—not as a call to bear arms, though arms we need; not as a call to battle, though embattled we are—but a call to bear the burden of a long twilight struggle, year in and year out, "rejoicing in hope, patient in tribulation"—a struggle against the common enemies of man: tyranny, poverty, disease, and war itself.

Can we forge against these enemies a grand and global alliance, North and South, East and West, that can assure a more fruitful life for all mankind? Will you join in that historic effort?

24   In the long history of the world, only a few generations have been granted the role of defending freedom in its hour of maximum danger. I do not shirk from this responsibility—I welcome it. I do not believe that any of us would exchange places with any other people or any other generation. The energy, the faith, the devotion which we bring to this endeavor will light our country and all who serve it—and the glow from that fire can truly light the world.

And so, my fellow Americans: ask not what your country can do for you—ask what you can do for your country.

My fellow citizens of the world: ask not what America will do for you, but what together we can do for the freedom of man.

Finally, whether you are citizens of America or citizens of the world, ask of us the same high standards of strength and sacrifice which we ask of you. With a good conscience our only sure reward, with history the final judge of our deeds, let us go forth to lead the land we love, asking His blessing and His help, but knowing that here on earth God's work must truly be our own.

READER RESPONSE

In paragraph 23, President Kennedy says, "I do not believe that any of us would exchange places with any other people or any other generation." Would you want to change places with any other people or live in another generation? Explain your answer.

QUESTIONS FOR DISCUSSION

1. To what degree is the United States still committed to the ideals that Kennedy mentions, such as "assur[ing] the survival and the success of liberty" (paragraph 4) and others throughout the speech?
2. President Kennedy mentions the arms race in several places. Is the arms race still an issue? What other national concerns does the president mention, and which are still national priorities?
3. Comment on the rhetorical strategies of the speech. How does President Kennedy engage his audience, convey his message, and ensure that his words will long be remembered?
4. In his opening paragraph, President Kennedy notes that his inauguration is "a celebration of freedom—symbolizing an end, as well as a beginning—signifying renewal, as well as change." In what ways is every presidential inauguration a new beginning and a symbol of both renewal and change?

"Who Shall I Be?": The Allure of a Fresh Start
Jennifer Crichton

Jennifer Crichton has published articles in a number of national magazines. Her book, Delivery: A Nurse-Midwife's Story *(1986), is a fictionalized account of life on the labor and delivery floor of a metropolitan hospital. She has also written* Family Reunion *(1997), a guide to planning and attending family reunions. In 2002, she completed her M.A. degree in English literature at Columbia University. This essay was published in* Ms. *magazine in 1984.*

The student is a soul in transit, coming from one place en route to someplace else. Moving is the American way, after all. Our guiding principle is the fresh start, our foundation the big move, and nothing seduces like the promise of a clean slate.

"Do you realize how many people saw me throw up at Bob Stonehill's party in tenth grade? A lot of people," says my friend Anne. "How many forgot about it? Maybe two or three. Do you know how much I wanted to go someplace where nobody knew I threw up all over Bob Stonehill's living room in tenth grade? Very much. This may not seem like much of a justification for going away to college, but it was for me." Going away to college gives us a chance to rinse off part of our past, to shake off our burdensome reputations.

We've already survived the crises of being known, allowing how American high schools are as notoriously well-organized as totalitarian regimes, complete with secret police, punishment without trial, and banishment. High school society loves a label, cruelly infatuated with pinning down every species of student. Hilary is a klutz, Julie is a slut, and Michele a gossiping bitch who eats like a pig.

4   No wonder so many of us can't wait to be free of our old identities and climb inside a new skin in college. Even flattering reputations can be as confining as a pair of too-tight shoes. But identity is tricky stuff, constructed with mirrors. How you see yourself is a composite reflection of how you appear to friends, family, and lovers. In college, the fact that familiar mirrors aren't throwing back a familiar picture is both liberating and disorienting (maybe that's why so many colleges have freshman "orientation week").   *Ha.*

"I guess you could call it an identity crisis," Andrea, a junior now, says of her freshman year. "It was the first time nobody knew who I was. I wasn't even anybody's daughter any more. I had always been the best and brightest—what was I going to do now, walk around the dorm with a sign around my neck saying 'Former High School Valedictorian'?"

For most of my college years, I was in hot pursuit of an identity crisis, especially after a Comparative Literature major informed me that the Chinese definition of "crisis" was "dangerous opportunity," with the emphasis on opportunity. On college applications, where there were blanks for your nickname, I carefully wrote "Rusty," although none of my friends (despite the fact that I have red hair) had ever, even for a whimsical moment, considered calling me that. I was the high-strung, sensitive, acne-blemished, antiauthoritarian, would-be writer. If I went through a day without some bizarre mood swing, people asked me what was wrong. I didn't even have the leeway to be the cheerful, smiling sort of girl I thought I might have it in me to be. My reputation seemed etched in stone, and I was pretty damn sick of it. As I pictured her, Rusty was the blithe spirit who would laugh everything off, shrug at perils as various as freshman mixers, bad grades, and cafeterias jammed with aloof strangers, and in general pass through a room with the vitality and appeal of a cool gust of wind.

what was your reputation in high school?

But when I arrived at college, Rusty had vaporized. She was simply not in the station wagon that drove me up to campus. Much of college had to do with filling in the blanks, but changing myself would not be so easy, so predictable, so cliché.

8   My parents, acting as anxious overseers on the hot, humid day I took my new self to college, seemed bound by a demonic ESP to sabotage my scarcely budding new identity. After a summer planning how I would metamorphose into the great American ideal, the normal teenage girl, I heard my mother tell my roommate, "I think you'll like Jenny—she's quite the oddball." Luckily, my roommate was saturated with all kinds of information the first day of college

had flung at her, and the last thing she was paying attention to were the off-the-cuff remarks this oddball's mother was making. My unmarked reputation kept its sheen as it waited for me to cautiously build it up according to plan. My parents left without any further blunders, except to brush my bangs from my eyes ("You'll get a headache, Sweetheart") and foist on what had been a blissfully bare dormitory room an excruciatingly ugly lamp from home. As soon as the station wagon became a distant mote of dust on the highway, I pulled my bangs back over my eyes in my New Wave fashion of choice, tossed the ugly lamp in the nearest trash can, and did what I came to college to do. Anonymous, alone, without even a name, I would start over and become the kind of person I was meant to be: like myself, but better, with all my failures, rejections, and sexual indiscretions relegated to a history I hoped none of my new acquaintances would ever hear of.

Why was it, I wondered, when *any* change seemed possible that year, had it been so impossible in high school? For one thing, people know us well enough to see when we're attempting a change, and change can look embarrassingly like a public admission of weakness. Our secret desires, and the fact that we're not entirely pleased with ourselves, are on display. To change in public under the scrutiny of the most hypercritical witnesses in the world—other high school students—is to risk failure ("Look how cool she's trying to be, the jerk!") or succeeding but betraying friends in the process ("I don't understand her any more," they say, hurt and angry) or feeling so much like a fraud that you're forced to back down. And while we live at home, parental expectations, from the lovingly hopeful to the intolerably ambitious, apply the pressure of an invisible but very effective mold.

Jacki dressed in nothing but baggy Levis and flannel shirts for what seemed to be the endless duration of high school, even though she came to a sort of truce with her developing woman's body in eleventh grade and wasn't averse any longer to looking pretty. Looking good in college was a fantasy she savored because in high school, "I didn't want to make the attempt in public and then fail," she explains now, looking pulled together and chic. "I thought everyone would think I was trying to look good but I only managed to look weird. And I didn't want a certain group of girls who were very image-conscious to think they'd won some kind of victory either, that I was changing to please them.

"So I waited for college, and wore nice, new clothes right off the bat so nobody would know me any other way. I had set my expectations too high, though—I sort of thought that I'd be transformed into a kind of femme fatale or something. When I wasn't measuring up to what I'd imagined, I almost ditched the whole thing until I realized that at least I wasn't sabotaging myself any more. When I ran into a friend from high school, even though I had gotten used to the nice way I looked, I was scared that she could see right through my disguise. That's how I felt for a long time: a slobby girl just pretending to be pulled together."

12   At first, any change can feel uncomfortably like a pretense, an affectation. Dana had been a punked-out druggy in high school, so worried about being considered a grind that she didn't use a fraction of her considerable vocabulary when she was around her anti-intellectual friends. She promised herself to get serious academically in college, but the first night she spent studying in the science library, she recalls, "I half-expected the other kids to look twice at me, as if my fish-out-of-water feeling was showing. Of course, it wasn't. But it was schizophrenic at first, as if I were an imposter only playing at being smart. But when you do something long enough that thing becomes *you*. It's not playing any more. It's what you are."

Wanting to change yourself finds its source in two wellsprings: self-hatred and self-affirmation. Self-affirmation takes what already exists in your personality (even if slightly stunted or twisted) and encourages its growth. Where self-affirmation is expansive, self-hatred is reductive, negating one's own personality while appropriating qualities external to it and applying them like thick pancake makeup.

Joan's thing was to hang out with rich kids with what can only be described as a vengeance. She dressed in Ralph Lauren, forayed to town for $75 haircuts, and complained about the tackiness of mutual friends. But after a late night of studying, Joan allowed her self-control to slip long enough to tell me of her upbringing. Her mother was a cocktail waitress and Joan had never even found out her father's name. She and her mother had trucked about from one Western trailer park to another, and Joan always went to school dogged by her wrong-side-of-the-tracks background. That Joan had come through her hardscrabble life with such strong intellectual achievement seemed a lot more creditable—not to mention interesting—than the effortless achievements of many of our more privileged classmates. Joan didn't think so, and, I suppose in fear I'd blow her cover (I never did), she cut me dead after her moment's indulgence in self-revelation. Joan was rootless and anxious, alienated not only from her background but, by extension, from herself, and paid a heavy psychic price. This wasn't change: this was lies. She scared me. But we learn a lot about friends from the kinds of masks they choose to wear.

After all, role-playing to some degree is the prerogative of youth. A woman of romance, rigorous academic, trendy New Waver, intense politico, unsentimental jock, by turn—we have the chance to experiment as we decide the kind of person we want to become. And a stereotypical role, adopted temporarily, can offer a refuge from the swirl of confusing choices available to us, by confining us to the limits of a type. Returning to my old self after playing a role, I find I'm slightly different, a little bit more than what I was. To contradict one's self is to transcend it.

16   As occasional fugitives from our families, we all sometimes do what Joan did. Sometimes you need a radical change in order to form an identity independent of your family, even if that change is a weird but transient reaction. My friend Lisa came from a family of feminists and academics. When she

returned home from school for Thanksgiving, dressed as a "ditsy dame" straight out of a beach-blanket-bingo movie, she asked me, "How do you think I look? I've been planning this since tenth grade. Isn't it great?" Well, er, yes, it was great—not because she looked like a Barbie doll incarnate but because nobody would ever automatically connect her life with that of her parents again.

Another friend, Dan, went from a Southern military academy to a Quaker college in the North to execute his scheme of becoming a serious intellectual. The transformation went awry after a few months, partly because his own self was too likably irrepressible. It wouldn't lie down and play dead. "I kept running into myself like a serpent chasing its tail," as he puts it. But his openness to change resulted in a peculiar amalgamation of cultures whose charm lies in his realizing that, while he's of his background, he's not identical to it. Most of our personalities and bodies are just as stubbornly averse to being extinguished, even if the fantasy of a symbolic suicide and a renaissance from the ashes takes its obsessive toll on our thoughts now and again. But a blank slate isn't the same as a blank self, and the point of the blank slate that college provides is not to erase the past, but to sketch out a new history with a revisionist's perspective and an optimist's acts.

And what of my changes? Well, when I was friendly and happy in college, nobody gaped as though I had sprouted a tail. I learned to laugh things off as Rusty might have done, and there was one particular counterman at the corner luncheonette who called me Red, which was the closest I came to being known as Rusty.

What became of Rusty? Senior year, I stared at an announcement stating the dates that banks would be recruiting on campus, and Rusty materialized for the first time since freshman year. Rusty was a Yuppie now, and I pictured her dressed in a navy-blue suit, looking uneasily like Mary Cunningham, setting her sights on Citibank. I was still the high-strung, oversensitive, would-be writer (I'm happy to report my skin did clear up), but a little better, who left the corporate world to Rusty. For myself, I have the slate of the rest of my life to write on.

READER RESPONSE

In what ways has college given you the opportunity for a fresh start? Have you made any changes in your behavior or appearance from when you were in high school? If so, explain what they are and why you have made them.

QUESTIONS FOR DISCUSSION

1. What do you think Crichton means by the statement "nothing seduces like the promise of a clean slate" (paragraph 1). In what sense can the fresh start of college be "both liberating and disorienting" (paragraph 4)? If you

have tried to start over—by going to college or by starting anew in some other way—explain what the experience meant to you. Was it liberating and/or disorienting?

2. Do you agree with Crichton that it is difficult to change in high school? Do you think it is more difficult to change in high school than during any other period of one's life? When else might it be difficult to change oneself?

3. Comment on Crichton's statement "we learn a lot about friends from the kinds of masks they choose to wear" (paragraph 14). In what ways do people "choose" to wear masks? Do your own friends wear masks? Do you?

4. Explain what you think Crichton means in paragraph 15 when she says, "To contradict one's self is to transcend it."

An Urge for Going
Richard Ford

Richard Ford is a writer on the move, as he explains in this essay, which was first published in the February 1992 issue of Harper's *magazine. He is a staff writer for* The New Yorker *and editor of* The Granta Book of the American Short Story. *His novel* Independence Day *won the 1995 Pulitzer Prize for fiction.*

I've read someplace that in our descending order of mighty and important human anxieties, Americans suffer the death of a spouse, the loss of a house by fire, and moving to be the worst three things that can happen to us.

So far, I've missed the worst of these—the first, unspeakable, and my house up in flames. Though, like most of us, I've contemplated burning my house *myself*—prior to the spring fix-up season or during those grinding "on-the-market" periods when prices sag and interest rates "skyrocket" and I brood over the sign on my lawn bitterly demanding "make offer."

But moving. Moving's another matter. Moving's not so bad. I've done it a lot.

4   Twenty times, probably, in twenty years (I'm sure I've forgotten a move or two). And always for excellent reasons. St. Louis to New York, New York to California, California to Chicago, Chicago to Michigan, Michigan to New Jersey, New Jersey to Vermont, Vermont to Montana, Montana to Mississippi, Mississippi to Montana, Montana to Montana to here—New Orleans, land of dreamy dreams, where I doubt I'll stay much longer.

To speed the getaways I've sacrificed valuable mortgage points, valuable rent deposits, valuable realtors' commissions, valuable capital gains write-offs. I've blown off exterminator contracts, forsaken new paint jobs, abandoned antique mirrors, oil paintings, ten-speeds, armoires, wedding presents, snow chains, and—unintentionally—my grandfather's gold-handled cane engraved with his name.

What are my excellent reasons? No different from the usual, I imagine. I've just put more of mine into motion. My wife got a better job, I got a better job, I needed to leave a bad job. I began to hate the suburbs and longed for the country, I began to hate New York and longed for the Berkshires, I got frightened of becoming a Californian and longed for the Middle West, I longed to live again in the place where I was born, then later I couldn't stand to live in the place where I was born. I missed the West. I missed the South. I missed the East Coast. I missed my pals. I got sick of their company.

Longing's at the heart of it, I guess. Longing that overtakes me like a fast car on the freeway and makes me willing to withstand a feeling of personal temporariness. Maybe, on a decidedly reduced scale, it's what a rock star feels, or a chewing-gum heiress, celebs who keep houses all over the globe, visit them often, but never fully live in any: a sense that life's short and profuse and mustn't be missed.

8   In the past, when people have asked me why I've moved so often, I've answered that if you were born in Mississippi you either believed you lived in the vivid center of a sunny universe, or you believed as I did that the world outside of there was the more magical, exotic place and *that's* what you needed to see. Or else I've said it was because my father was a traveling sales-man, and every Monday morning I would hear him whistling as he got ready to leave again: a happy weekend at home with his bag packed in the bed-room, then a happy workweek traveling, never seeming to suffer the wrench-pang of departure, never seeming to think life was disrupted or lonely.

I doubt now if either of those reasons is satisfactory. And, indeed, I'm suspicious of explanations that argue that any of us does anything because of a single reason, or two, or three.

Place, that old thorny-bush in our mind's backyard, is supposed to be im-portant to us Southerners. It's supposed to hold us. But where I grew up was a bland, unadhesive place—Jackson, Mississippi—a city in love with the subur-ban Zeitgeist, a city whose inert character I could never much get interested in. I just never seemed like enough of a native, and Jackson just never meant as much to me as it did to others. Other places just interested me more.

My most enduring memories of childhood are mental snapshots not of my hometown streets or its summery lawns but of roads leading out of town. Highway 51 to New Orleans. Highway 49 to the delta and the coast. Highway 80 to Vicksburg and darkest Alabama. These were my father's customary routes, along which I was often his invited company—I and my mother together.

12   Why these should be what I now recollect most vividly, instead of, say, an odor of verbena or watermelons in a tub on the Fourth of July, I don't know, other than to conjecture that we were on the move a lot, and that it mattered to me that my parents were my parents and that they loved me, more than *where* they loved me.

Home—real home—the important place that holds you, always meant that: affection, love.

Once my wife and I were stranded with car trouble in the town of Kearney, Nebraska, on a blurry, hot midsummer day late in the '70s. And when we'd eaten our dinner in a little, home-cook place at the edge of town not far from the interstate, we walked out into the breezy, warm air and stood and watched the sun go down beyond the ocean of cornfields and the shining Platte River. And as the shadows widened on, my wife said to me, drowsily, "I've just gotten so sleepy now. I've got to go home and go to sleep." "Home?" I said. "How far is that from here?" "Oh, you know," she said and shook her head and laughed at the absurdity of that idea. "Just back to the motel. Where else?"

Oh, I've stayed places, plenty of times. I've owned "homes," three or four, with likable landscapes, pleasant prospects, safe streets, folksy friends nearby. I've held down jobs, paid millages, served on juries, voted for mayors. As with all of us, some part of me is a stayer. *Transient* is a word of reproach; *impermanence* bears a taint, a suspicion that the gentleman in question isn't quite

well . . . solid, lacks a certain depth, can't be fully *known*, possibly has messy business left on the trail somewhere—another county, something hushed up.

16   Other people's permanences are certainly in our faces all the time; their lengthy lengths-of-stay at one address, their many-layered senses of place, their store of lorish, insider blab. Their commitment. Yet I don't for a minute concede their establishment to be any more established than mine, or their self-worth richer, or their savvy regarding risk management and reality any more meticulous. They don't know any more than I do. In fact, given where they've been and haven't been, they probably know less.

"But you," they might say, "you only get a superficial view of life living this way, skimming the top layer off things the way you do." And my answer is: Memory always needs replenishing, and anyway you misunderstand imagination and how it thrives in us by extending partial knowledge to complete any illusion of reality. "We live amid surfaces, and the true art of life is to skate well on them," Emerson wrote.

One never moves without an uneasiness that staying is the norm and that what you're after is something not just elusive but desperate, and that eventually you'll fail and have to stop. But those who'll tell you what you *have to do* say so only because that's what they've done and are glad about it—or worse, are not so glad. Finally, I'll be the judge. It'll be on my bill, not theirs.

On the first night I ever spent in the first house I ever owned, I said to my wife as we were going to sleep on a mattress on the bedroom floor amid boxes and paper and disheveled furniture, "Owning feels a lot like renting, doesn't it? You just can't leave when you want to." This was in New Jersey, 15 years ago—a nice, brown three-story stucco of a vaguely Flemish vernacular, on a prizable double lot on a prizable oak-lined street named for President Jefferson—a home that cost $117,500, and that now probably runs above a half million if you could buy it, which you can't. This was a house I eventually grew to feel so trapped in that one night I got stirringly drunk, roared downstairs with a can of white paint, and flung paint on everything—all over the living room, the rugs, the furniture, the walls, my wife, even all over our novelist friend who was visiting and who hasn't been back since. I wanted, I think, to desanctify "the home," get the *joujou* out of permanence. And, in fact, in two months' time we were gone from there, for good.

20   Today, when people ask me, people who banked their fires and their equity, "Don't you wish you'd hung onto that house on Jefferson? You'd have it half paid for now. You'd be rich!" my answer is, "Holy Jesus no! Don't you realize I'd have had to *live* in that house all this time? Life's too short." It's an odd thing to ask a man like me.

It may simply and finally be that the way most people feel when they're settled is the way I feel when I move: safe and in possession of myself. So much so that when I'm driving along some ribbony highway over a distant and heat-miraged American landscape, and happen to spy, far across the median strip, a U-Haul van humping its cargo toward some pay dirt far away, its beetle-browed driver alone in the buzzing capsule of his own fears and hopes and silent explanations of the future, who I think of is . . . me. He's me. And my heart goes out to him. It's never a wasted effort to realize that what we do is what anybody does, all of us clinging to our little singularities, making it in the slow lane toward someplace we badly need to go.

READER RESPONSE

Are your own sentiments about staying versus leaving closer to Ford's or to those who stay in one place permanently? Explain why you feel as you do.

QUESTIONS FOR DISCUSSION

1. To what extent do your own observations confirm the contrasts that Ford draws between people on the move and people who stay in one place?
2. Explain what you understand this quotation from Emerson to mean: " 'We live amid surfaces, and the true art of life is to skate well on them' " (paragraph 17).
3. How does Ford define *home?* How would you define it? Does home become more important at certain holidays or on special family occasions?

Grandma's Story

Lynn Randall

Lynn Randall is a Native American from the Oglala tribe who resides in Pine Ridge Village, South Dakota. The following narrative appeared in A Gathering of Spirits: A Collection by North American Indian Women *(1984). In it, Randall recounts a story she heard her grandmother tell many times.*

She never told me the year nor the season it happened. I don't even know what it's called in the history books, or if it's even in the history books. All I know is what she told me, and that Grandma called it "The Bombing Range Days."

She lay in bed that day, a little longer than usual. With nine kids underfoot and one on the way, the peace and quiet of early morning hours were a luxury she seldom enjoyed. She thought about all the chores that needed to be done that day and the chores that were left over from yesterday. Mentally, she made a list assigning each child to a job. Still there were chores left to do. Chores that would probably be left over for tomorrow. Inwardly she groaned, rolling over and smothering any sound escaping into her pillow. Sighing wearily she got up to make coffee. Stepping carefully over the bodies of her children sprawled all over the floor, she made her way into the kitchen. She put the last of the wood into the stove. As she poured the kerosene and lit the stove, she decided to let her husband sleep a while before asking him to fetch more wood for the afternoon meal. She put the coffee on the stove and started to mix the batter for pancakes.

The sun was barely warming the earth when the man came. Her husband had risen an hour ago and was out back chopping wood. The sound of the knocking frightened her; none of her friends or neighbors ever knocked. They always yelled by the gate, and she ran out to meet them. The knocking continued. Backing away from the door, she bumped against her eldest son. "Take it easy Mom, I'll get it," he assured her. The man at the door stood tall. He was dressed in a green hat. This was the dress of an Army man. She knew this and it frightened her more. "Where's your man?" he demanded of her. She could only nod towards the back. The man turned to leave and she followed. She listened in silent rage as the man told her husband they had until nightfall to get their belongings together and get out. "It isn't fair," she thought. "First they take all the good land away from us and put us here on this worthless tract of nothing-land; now they're taking that too." She listened on in newfound horror as the man explained what use the land would be to the Army. "New recruits need to be trained to fly and to know how to drop bombs. This worthless land will be perfect for this area of training. Tomorrow at eight o'clock, a squad of new recruits will be in for the first day of training." With that the man turned and left. She stared at her husband in shock and fear. Her husband's face reflected her own emotions. Together they quickly turned and ran toward the house, gathering objects as they ran.

4   Breathlessly she ran into the house shouting orders. Her oldest son, understanding immediately, ran out to help his father herd the cows together, heading them towards the boundary line. There wasn't much time and some would probably be lost or stolen before the day ended, but still they represented the food and money they would need later. The three oldest daughters started packing the household and personal items. The younger children were outside chasing and catching the hens and the old rooster, putting them in cardboard boxes, flour sacks, or whatever else would hold them. She ran out to hitch the team to the wagon. Almost immediately it began to fill. She started tearing apart the outhouse, throwing the planks down as she took them off. The wood was important, more useful than clothing, almost. Not paying attention to where she was walking, she stepped on a protruding nail. The nail was old and rusty. The pain was so great she found she couldn't stand on the foot for more than a few minutes. Sitting down, she cried in frustration, screaming at her children when they dared come close. Her husband, upon returning, found his wife sitting in the middle of a toilet, half-up half-down, crying her eyes out. He examined the wound, then bandaged it with an old sheet he found, soothing her as he worked. Lifting her gently, he put her in the already filled wagon.

Together they raced across the country to the boundary line. As they neared the line, she stared in shock at what she saw. Her friends and neighbors were all over, unloading their wagons in a pile next to the fence, then jumping back into their wagons and racing off for the next load. Unlike the friendly faces she was used to, their faces were grim and determined. Her husband finished unloading, then took her off the wagon, setting her down next to the load. He raced off in the direction of the house. She looked at the sun, it was sitting dangerously close to the west. She only hoped they had time to get everything of importance. Looking around she saw her neighbors' belongings all along the fence. The older women were clearing out spaces for the tents. Some of the children were gathering wood for the fires. Suddenly she realized her family hadn't eaten since last night and started searching through her stuff for pots and pans and food. Sending her young son off for some wood, she began preparing the evening meal.

It was well into the night when her husband returned with the last load. The coffee was hot, the soup long since done. She finished setting up the tent. Wearily she sat down, her leg throbbing in pain. Her swollen body ached with exhaustion. She watched as each of her children ate, then one by one crawled into the tent and to bed, till there was only herself and her husband. He hadn't said a word but only sat and stared into his coffee. Tears of frustration threatened her as she sat and looked at her husband. "What will happen now?" she asked. "Are we going to live on this hill, in this tent, the rest of our lives? Will we ever get to go back to our home?" He didn't answer her but only sat and stared into his cup. She looked at him for a while, then put her head down and cried.

For as long as I can remember I heard my grandma tell this story. Sometimes a friend would drop over and together they would tell tales of that day with horror or amusement, whatever mood they were in. I can never tell the story as she told it. Each time she told it, she would be able to raise some emotion in me. I would laugh with her or I would cry with her. She left us last summer.

READER RESPONSE

How do you think you would react in circumstances similar to those experienced by Randall's grandmother and her family?

QUESTIONS FOR DISCUSSION

1. How effectively does the opening paragraph introduce the narrative that follows? Did it spark your interest and make you want to keep reading?
2. Describe the living conditions of Grandma's family before and after the move. How did Grandma and her husband respond to the order to leave their home? What do you think were the answers to Grandma's questions to her husband in paragraph 6?
3. What does "Grandma's Story" reveal about oppression?
4. Although this is Grandma's story, it is told by someone who has heard it many times. What details help to characterize Grandma? How does Randall feel about her grandmother? How do you know?

Once More to the Lake
E. B. White

Elwyn Brooks White (1899–1985), a regular contributor to The New Yorker *and* Harper's *magazine, was one of the best-known essayists of the twentieth century. He is perhaps even better known for his children's books, including* Stuart Little *(1945),* Charlotte's Web *(1952), and* The Trumpet of the Swan *(1970). He was also responsible for revising* The Elements of Style *(1952), written by his former professor at Cornell University, William Strunk, Jr. Strunk and White's* The Elements of Style *is still widely consulted. In 1977, he published his collected essays, including "Once More to the Lake," which originally appeared in* One Man's Meat *(1941).*

One summer, along about 1904, my father rented a camp on a lake in Maine and took us all there for the month of August. We all got ringworm from some kittens and had to rub Pond's Extract on our arms and legs night and morning, and my father rolled over in a canoe with all his clothes on; but outside of that the vacation was a success and from then on none of us ever thought there was any place in the world like that lake in Maine. We returned summer after summer—always on August 1st for one month. I have since become a salt-water man, but sometimes in summer there are days when the restlessness of the tides and the fearful cold of the sea water and the incessant wind which blows across the afternoon and into the evening make me wish for the placidity of a lake in the woods. A few weeks ago this feeling got so strong I bought myself a couple of bass hooks and a spinner and returned to the lake where we used to go, for a week's fishing and to revisit old haunts.

I took along my son, who had never had any fresh water up his nose and who had seen lily pads only from train windows. On the journey over to the lake I began to wonder what it would be like. I wondered how time would have marred this unique, this holy spot—the coves and streams, the hills that the sun set behind, the camps and the paths behind the camps. I was sure that the tarred road would have found it out and I wondered in what other ways it would be desolated. It is strange how much you can remember about places like that once you allow your mind to return into the grooves which lead back. You remember one thing, and that suddenly reminds you of another thing. I guess I remembered clearest of all the early mornings, when the lake was cool and motionless, remembered how the bedroom smelled of the lumber it was made of and of the wet woods whose scent entered through the screen. The partitions in the camp were thin and did not extend clear to the top of the rooms, and as I was always the first up I would dress softly so as not to wake the others, and sneak out into the sweet outdoors and start out in the canoe, keeping close along the shore in the long shadows of the pines. I remembered being very careful never to rub my paddle against the gunwale for fear of disturbing the stillness of the cathedral.

The lake had never been what you would call a wild lake. There were cottages sprinkled around the shores, and it was in farming country although the shores of the lake were quite heavily wooded. Some of the cottages were owned by nearby farmers, and you would live at the shore and eat your meals at the farmhouse. That's what our family did. But although it wasn't wild, it was a fairly large and undisturbed lake and there were places in it which, to a child at least, seemed infinitely remote and primeval.

4   I was right about the tar: it led to within half a mile of the shore. But when I got back there, with my boy, and we settled into a camp near a farmhouse and into the kind of summertime I had known, I could tell that it was going to be pretty much the same as it had been before—I knew it, lying in bed the first morning, smelling the bedroom, and hearing the boy sneak quietly out and go off along the shore in a boat. I began to sustain the illusion that he was I, and therefore, by simple transposition, that I was my father. This

sensation persisted, kept cropping up all the time we were there. It was not an entirely new feeling, but in this setting it grew much stronger. I seemed to be living a dual existence. I would be in the middle of some simple act, I would be picking up a bait box or laying down a table fork, or I would be saying something, and suddenly it would be not I but my father who was saying the words or making the gesture. It gave me a creepy sensation.

We went fishing the first morning. I felt the same damp moss covering the worms in the bait can, and saw the dragonfly alight on the tip of my rod as it hovered a few inches from the surface of the water. It was the arrival of this fly that convinced me beyond any doubt that everything was as it always had been, that the years were a mirage and there had been no years. The small waves were the same, chucking the rowboat under the chin as we fished at anchor, and the boat was the same boat, the same color green and the ribs broken in the same places, and under the floorboards the same freshwater leavings and debris—the dead helgramite, the wisps of moss, the rusty discarded fishhook, the dried blood from yesterday's catch. We stared silently at the tips of our rods, at the dragonflies that came and went. I lowered the tip of mine into the water, tentatively, pensively dislodging the fly, which darted two feet away, poised, darted two feet back, and came to rest again a little farther up the rod. There had been no years between the ducking of this dragonfly and the other one—the one that was part of memory. I looked at the boy, who was silently watching his fly, and it was my hands that held his rod, my eyes watching. I felt dizzy and didn't know which rod I was at the end of.

We caught two bass, hauling them in briskly as though they were mackerel, pulling them over the side of the boat in a businesslike manner without any landing net, and stunning them with a blow on the back of the head. When we got back for a swim before lunch, the lake was exactly where we had left it, the same number of inches from the dock, and there was only the merest suggestion of a breeze. This seemed an utterly enchanted sea, this lake you could leave to its own devices for a few hours and come back to, and find that it had not stirred, this constant and trustworthy body of water. In the shallows, the dark, water-soaked sticks and twigs, smooth and old, were undulating in clusters on the bottom against the clean ribbed sand, and the track of the mussel was plain. A school of minnows swam by, each minnow with its small individual shadow, doubling the attendance, so clear and sharp in the sunlight. Some of the other campers were in swimming, along the shore, one of them with a cake of soap, and the water felt thin and clear and unsubstantial. Over the years there had been this person with the cake of soap, this cultist, and there he was. There had been no years.

Up to the farmhouse to dinner through the teeming, dusty field, the road under our sneakers was only a two-track road. The middle track was missing, the one with the marks of the hooves and the splotches of dried, flaky manure. There had always been three tracks to choose from in choosing which track to walk in; now the choice was narrowed down to two. For a moment I missed terribly the middle alternative. But the way led past the tennis court, and something about the way it lay there in the sun reassured me; the tape had loosened along the backline, the alleys were green with plantains and other weeds, and the net (installed in June and removed in September) sagged in the dry noon, and the whole place steamed with midday heat and hunger and emptiness. There was a choice of pie for dessert, and one was blueberry and one was apple, and the waitresses were the same country girls, there having been no passage of time, only the illusion of it as in a dropped curtain—the waitresses were still fifteen; their hair had been washed, that was the only difference—they had been to the movies and seen the pretty girls with the clean hair.

8   Summertime, oh summertime, pattern of life indelible, the fade-proof lake, the woods unshatterable, the pasture with the sweet-fern and the juniper forever and ever, summer without end; this was the background, and the life along the shore was the design, the cottages with their innocent and tranquil design, their tiny docks with the flagpole and the American flag floating against the white clouds in the blue sky, the little paths over the roots of the trees leading from camp to camp and the paths leading back to the outhouses and the can of lime for sprinkling, and at the souvenir counters at the store the miniature birch-bark canoes and the post cards that showed things looking a little better than they looked. This was the American family at play, escaping the city heat, wondering whether the newcomers in the camp at the head of the cover were "common" or "nice," wondering whether it was true that the people who drove up for Sunday dinner at the farmhouse were turned away because there wasn't enough chicken.

It seemed to me, as I kept remembering all this, that those times and those summers had been infinitely precious and worth saving. There had been jollity and peace and goodness. The arriving (at the beginning of August) had been so big a business in itself, at the railway station the farm wagon drawn up, the first smell of the pine-laden air, the first glimpse of the smiling farmer, and the great importance of the trunks and your father's enormous authority in such matters, and the feel of the wagon under you for the long ten-mile haul, and at the top of the last long hill catching the first view of the lake after eleven months of not seeing this cherished body of water. The shouts and cries of the other campers when they saw you, and the trunks to be unpacked, to give up their rich burden. (Arriving was less exciting nowadays, when you sneaked up in your car and parked it under a tree near the camp and took out the bags and in five minutes it was all over, no fuss, no loud wonderful fuss about trunks.)

Peace and goodness and jollity. The only thing that was wrong now, really, was the sound of the place, an unfamiliar nervous sound of the outboard motors. This was the note that jarred, the one thing that would sometimes break the illusion and set the years moving. In those other summertimes all motors were inboard; and when they were at a little distance, the noise they made was a sedative, an ingredient of summer sleep. They were one-cylinder and two-cylinder engines, and some were make-and-break and some were jump-spark, but they all made a sleepy sound across the lake. The one-lungers throbbed and fluttered, and the twin-cylinder ones purred and purred, and that was a quiet sound too. But now the campers all had outboards. In the daytime, in the hot mornings, these motors made a petulant, irritable sound; at night, in the still evening when the afterglow lit the water, they whined about one's ears like mosquitoes. My boy loved our rented outboard, and his great desire was to achieve singlehanded mastery over it, and authority, and he soon learned the trick of choking it a little (but not too much), and the adjustment of the needle valve. Watching him I would remember the things you could do with the old one-cylinder engine with the heavy flywheel, how you could have it eating out of your hand if you got really close to it spiritually. Motor boats in those days didn't have clutches, and you would make a landing by shutting off the motor at the proper time and coasting in with a dead rudder. But there was a way of reversing them, if you learned the trick, by cutting the switch and putting it on again exactly on the final dying revolution of the fly-wheel, so that it would kick back against compression and begin reversing. Approaching a dock in a strong following breeze, it was difficult to slow up sufficiently by the ordinary coasting method, and if a boy felt he had complete mastery over his motor, he was tempted to keep it running beyond its time and then reverse it a few feet from the dock. It took a cool nerve, because if you threw the switch a twentieth of a second too soon you could catch the flywheel when it still had speed enough to go up past center, and the boat would leap ahead, charging bull-fashion at the dock.

We had a good week at the camp. The bass were biting well and the sun shone endlessly, day after day. We would be tired at night and lie down in the accumulated heat of the little bedrooms after the long hot day and the breeze would stir almost imperceptibly outside and the smell of the swamp drift in through the rusty screens. Sleep would come easily and in the morning the red squirrel would be on the roof, tapping out his gay routine. I kept remembering everything, lying in bed in the mornings—the small steamboat that had a long rounded stern like the lip of a Ubangi, and how quietly she ran on the moonlight sails, when the older boys played their mandolins and the girls sang and we ate doughnuts dipped in sugar, and how sweet the music was on the water in the shining night, and what it had felt like to think about girls then. After breakfast we would go up to the store and the things were in the same place—the minnows in a bottle, the plugs and spinners disarranged and pawed over by the youngsters from the boys' camp, the Fig Newtons and the Beeman's gum. Outside, the road was tarred and cars stood in front of the store. Inside, all was just as it had always been, except there was more Coca-Cola and not so much Moxie and root beer and birch beer and sarsaparilla. We would walk out with a bottle of pop apiece and sometimes the pop would backfire up our noses and hurt. We explored the streams, quietly, where the turtles slid off the sunny logs and dug their way into the soft bottom; and we lay on the town wharf and fed worms to the tame bass. Everywhere we went I had trouble making out which was I, the one walking at my side, the one walking in my pants.

12   One afternoon while we were there at that lake a thunderstorm came up. It was like the revival of an old melodrama that I had seen long ago with childish awe. The second-act climax of the drama of the electrical disturbance over a lake in America had not changed in any important respect. This was the big scene, still the big scene. The whole thing was so familiar, the first feeling of oppression and heat and a general air around camp of not wanting to go very far away. In mid-afternoon (it was all the same) a curious darkening of the sky, and a lull in everything that had made life tick; and then the way the boats suddenly swung the other way at their moorings with the coming of a breeze out of the new quarter, and the premonitory rumble. Then the kettle drum, then the snare, then the bass drum and cymbals, then crackling light against the dark, and the gods grinning and licking their chops in the hills. Afterward the calm, the rain steadily rustling in the calm lake, the return of light and hope and spirits, and the campers running out in joy and relief to go swimming in the rain, their bright cries perpetuating the deathless joke about how they were getting simply drenched, and the children screaming with delight at the new sensation of bathing in the rain, and the joke about getting drenched linking the generations in a strong indestructible chain. And the comedian who waded in carrying an umbrella.

When the others went swimming my son said he was going in too. He pulled his dripping trunks from the line where they had hung all through the shower, and wrung them out. Languidly, and with no thought of going in, I watched him, his hard little body, skinny and bare, saw him wince slightly as he pulled up around his vitals the small, soggy, icy garment. As he buckled the swollen belt suddenly my groin felt the chill of death.

READER RESPONSE

In what ways do vacations function as transitions? What do you think is the purpose of a vacation?

QUESTIONS FOR DISCUSSION

1. White returns to the lake wondering how much of what he remembers from his youth is still the same. What things have not changed? What things have changed? What do the changes signify to White?
2. This essay is filled with descriptive passages of people, sights, and sounds. Locate passages that you consider to be particularly effective. For instance, how does White describe "the sound of the place" (paragraph 10)? How does that sound fit with his memories of the lake? Locate metaphors that White uses throughout the essay. How do they help to describe the lake and convey memories of his youth?

3. Why does White refer to his son as "the boy"? How does White's illusion that his son is he and he his father (paragraph 4) reinforce his strong nostalgia for this place he knew so well in his youth?
4. What do you think White was seeking when he returned to the lake? What do you think he found? How do you account for the final sentence? Explain how you arrived at your answers.

Silence

Larry Watson

Larry Watson teaches English at the University of Wisconsin at Stevens Point. His books include a chapbook of poetry, Leaving Dakota *(1984); two novels,* In a Dark Time *(1980) and* Montana 1948 *(1993), which won the Milkweed National Fiction Prize; and a collection of stories,* Justice *(1995). This short story appeared in* Cream City Review, *a publication of the University of Wisconsin at Milwaukee.*

I was eight years old when my father stole me, and on that day, I stopped speaking. I chose not to speak, yet once I made that decision, it gained its own power and was not easily unmade.

I remember still that sensation, of my tongue becoming a dry thickness in my mouth, of my throat dissolving into a tangle of slack muscles, and of silence itself, falling down from my brain like snow and smothering everything.

I was born in 1942, two years after my parents' marriage. At the time of my birth my father was in the Army and stationed in the Philippines, and my mother, to save on rent money, moved in with her father and mother. It was in my grandparents' house that I was born, in an upstairs bedroom of a white frame house in Pierce, a small town in western Wisconsin. That bedroom had been my mother's when she was a child, and she gave birth to me in her same, narrow childhood bed. The room still held some of the furniture, dolls, and toys of her girlhood, so into a child's world I was child born.

4   While my father was at war my mother stopped loving him. She did not fall in love with someone else, but in my father's absence she not only learned she could live without a husband—as she and so many women had to do—she went a step beyond and largely forgot about him altogether. Her task, at their initial separation, was to try to find some way not to think of her husband and the difficulty of their distance from each other, and at this she simply succeeded too well. Finally, when I was born I was not a reminder of her husband but another distraction, something else that kept her mind from him.

When my father came home in 1946, my mother had a new job (she was secretary and bookkeeper at a John Deere implement dealer), a new home (her old home actually), and son she had for four years raised without a father. At his return, my half-forgotten father, like a large hand trying to squeeze into a small glove, had to try to fit into her—*our*—life.

Before long the impossibility of resuming a relationship in which one partner no longer loves the other declared itself. Less than two years after he returned from the war, my father moved out. The fault, as my mother always admitted freely, was hers, but laying blame in broken marriages does nothing to restore them. I remember only this about my father's leaving: he moved out with the same green footlocker with which he moved in, and I felt a vague relief when he was gone, as though a stranger had once again resumed his proper distance.

If my father would have resented me that would have been understandable. I had, after all, assumed a place at his wife's side while he was away, and he saw me only once during my infancy. My grandfather had more to do with my learning-to-walk, learning-to-talk years than my father did. My father, however, was incapable of feeling any bitterness toward his own child, and he was determined, in spite of the divorce, to have a normal relationship with his son. And there was the problem. My mother naturally was given custody of me, and my father had me for only one day a week and that was always Saturday. He lived in Eau Claire, fifty miles from us, and he was a salesman of office supplies, on the road Monday through Friday. Sunday was set aside for Sunday School and services at Mt. Olivet Lutheran Church, and for dinners with my grandparents. Only Saturday was left. My father wanted me to spend more time with him, for us to do more than go to a matinee or the park, have an ice cream, and hurry back to my grandparents, and it was all right with my mother that we do more together, except for one matter. She would not allow my father to keep me overnight. I don't know why she made that resolution, but about it she was intransigent. And, naturally, denied that, it became exactly what my father wanted most. "For *God's sake,* Irene," he would say, his voice shifting, within one sentence, from an angry demand to a plea, "for God's sake, we're only talking about one night." She always said no.

8 So, because there was one point these reasonable people could not be reasonable about, on a sunny August morning (not a Saturday) in 1950, my father in his black Buick pulled up to the curb in front of my grandparents' house. My mother was at work, and I was playing in the trickle of water that ran through the gutter.

I was a solitary child and small for my age, no bigger than many six-year-olds. The first fact made it easy for my father to find me alone; the second made it easy for him to do what he did next. He got out of his car quickly, bent down, and without a word, picked me up. His hat fell off, and when he picked it up he did it hastily, carelessly, crushing and ruining the perfect crease of the crown, the precise roll of the brim. I knew, from the rough way he treated his hat as well as from the speed with which he picked me up and put me in his car, that something was wrong, and that this was not something arranged or approved in advance.

Through the car window I looked to the house, hoping to see my grandmother or grandfather come out, but no one came. The Buick's scratchy grey wool upholstery was warm and smelled of oily office machines and stale cigarette smoke.

"I've got some calls to make, Lewis," my father said as he drove speedily away. "How about you coming along to help me out?"

12   I said nothing. Without knowing I had made the decision, I had made my commitment to silence, and the apparatus for speech was already shut down.

My father, nervous and guilty, talked so much as we drove out of town that he did not notice that I wasn't talking. "I'll bet sales pick up with you along," he said. "I'll bet you bring me good luck." He continued to chatter on about his work, going through his list of calls and mentioning how I was going to charm a secretary or supervisor so she would triple her usual order. One secretary, Miss Zeller, my father said, would probably forget about business altogether and propose marriage to me. I could do worse than Miss Zeller, he said with a wink.

To say I was frightened through all this would not have been accurate. Although I knew my father had done something wrong, and although I did not know him well enough from our Saturday afternoons together to be completely comfortable in his presence, I was not afraid. Still, though my father plainly meant me no harm, I was uneasy. I had been taken forcefully from my home, and I did not belong in that black car, driving through that bright, dry, yellow landscape. I was surrounded by the unfamiliar sights of corn and wheat fields and the strange smells of road dust and barnyards and cut hay, and I had no idea of how I might put order back in my life. When we are eight years old we have so little power in the adult world. What can we do? We can refuse to eat, drink, or go to sleep. Or we can refuse to speak.

I don't remember the names of the towns along the Minnesota–Wisconsin border where we stopped that day, but I do remember, in bits and pieces, some of the offices we visited. We climbed stairs, a narrow flight of some rickety steps over a shoe store and a wide set of stone steps leading up to the heavy metal doors of a county court house. We opened doors, a succession of them with windows of opaque glass on which were printed in gilt letters the names of lawyers or accountants. From one second story window I leaned against a radiator and looked down at a small main street and tried to pick out my father's car from the row of diagonally-parked cars below. In another office a big white-haired woman with a long jaw and peculiar little rimless glasses cautioned my father to "keep the armies away from that boy." In a tiny, airless office that smelled of cigar smoke and whiskey from the bar below, my father put a roll of paper into an adding machine for an accountant who was nearly blind. All day long my father delivered tightly-wrapped reams of paper, boxes of envelopes, and stacks of long legal pads. He looked inside typewriters, dictaphones, and adding machines that weren't working, he gave away blue pencils with his company's name printed in silver letters, and he raised the height of an office chair for a short typist.

16   And I met Miss Zeller. She was young and pretty and she had wavy dark hair that fell to her shoulders so neatly it looked like a thick black cloth. She gave me a stick of Beeman's gum from her desk drawer, and she shook my hand and said, "Your dad is lucky to have such a big helper."

It was strange that she called "dad" the man I always referred to as "father."

"Are you helping him carry some of his heavy machines?" she teased.

I nodded and stared at the floor but said nothing.

20   My father made a joke that excused me. "Sure, he does all the lifting. He's the strong, silent type."

When we left Miss Zeller's office my father put his hand on my shoulder and asked heartily, "What do you think? Didn't I say she was something? Didn't I say you could do worse?"

I was becoming angry at my father's pretense, how he continued to make believe that I was with him because I wanted to be. Be quiet, I thought, just be quiet; if you think Miss Zeller is so wonderful why don't you marry her—marry her and leave me alone.

At some time during the day my father noticed I wasn't talking. Or perhaps he noticed all along and finally chose to acknowledge it. I know from my own experience as a parent that I am seldom ignorant of what goes on in the lives of my children; I only choose to remain quiet about what I know. And since my father knew that his act was the cause of my silence, he must have thought long and hard before bringing up the subject. "You know," he said, "if you ever want to be a salesman, one thing you got to have is the gift of gab. If you're inclined to let the cat have your tongue you're going to have trouble turning over those sales."

24   It was the wrong tactic. I resented hearing any advice on how to be a salesman, or any presumption that I might want to be one. At eight I didn't know what I wanted to be, but on that day I knew I did not want to be in any way like the man who stole children from in front of their own home.

Later, my father tried to approach my silence from another side. "What I can't figure out is how you turned into such a shy one," he said. "Now me, me you've never been able to shut up, not now and not when I was a boy. My dad used to say I liked to yak more than old Mrs. Monka." No matter how hard he tried to convince me otherwise, I kept telling myself that my silence was not the result of my nature but of his sin. Of course, when I was eight I had a much clearer sense of what was sin and what was not.

After all the calls had been made, we stopped for dinner at a small roadside cafe in Whitman, Wisconsin. Neither my mother nor my grandparents ever took me to a restaurant because they thought it was wasteful and indulgent to pay others to prepare food which you were perfectly capable of fixing for yourself. So, sitting in the booth by the window and looking over at the slices of pie and cake in the glass case was a special experience, even under those circumstances.

When the waitress asked for our order, my father, having by now caught on to the rules of the game, ordered for me. He told the waitress that I wanted a hot roast beef sandwich, peas, and a glass of milk. I did not; I wanted a fried ham sandwich and an orange soda.

28   As soon as the waitress left, my father leaned across the table and spoke sternly to me. "Look, Lewis, this is nonsense. All I want is for you and me to spend some time together. You're my son. Now, I'm going to take you back to your mother in a day or two. In the meantime, let's get along."

When my father got angry his face would flush and a vein that ran straight down his forehead stood out like a piece of string. His anger frightened me, and perhaps if he had asked me a question instead of making a statement I would have spoken at that moment. I don't know. I turned and looked out the window at the cars and trucks speeding by the Whitman Cafe.

Try not talking for a long time. Try to go an entire day without speaking. After a time speech recedes even from your thoughts; you no longer talk to yourself, and your thinking becomes airy and wordless. You begin to doubt whether the mechanism works any more. Imagine what it is like for an eight-year-old boy. My father went to the restroom, and I picked up the menu. On the cover were the words "The Whitman Cafe: The Best Food," and I tried, just to see if my voice still worked, to say those words out loud. First I moved my lips only, but then I whispered, very softly, "The Whitman Cafe: The Best Food," over and over. But see for yourself; whispering, so much like our regular exhalations of breath, is not at all the same as talking.

After dinner, my father leaned back in the booth, lit a cigarette (after first tapping it on the crystal of his watch, a gesture that always fascinated and baffled me) and, uncharacteristically, for my father did almost everything with enthusiasm, watched with detachment. For a long time, his silence matched mine until finally he spoke: "Do you want cake or pie? Just tell me what kind you want and you can have a piece. But you have to tell me. You have to say it out loud."

32   I left the Whitman Cafe without dessert.

My father lived in a hotel in Eau Claire called The Kingsbury. He moved in after he left my grandparents' house, and he never got around to moving out of the hotel. He became friends with the owner who gave him a special rate. The hotel was small and the rooms had the same kind of furniture you might find in someone's home. In my father's room were lace curtains that blew in and out the open window on the warm night I was there, a single bed with a white chenille bedspread, a bureau, a bedside table, a dark green overstuffed chair, a floor lamp, and, in one corner, a metal two-drawer filing cabinet and typing table that belonged to my father. Two typewriters were on the floor. A picture of me, taken at a studio when I was five, was on the bureau next to a carton of Chesterfields.

While we were alone in the room my father tried to explain why he had taken me away. I remember little of what he said, but it was a stammering, incoherent speech designed to appeal to powers of reason that I did not have and to a love that I did not feel. Those were discoveries I made while my father talked to me. He kept saying, "Do you understand? You do understand, don't you?" I kept shaking my head. As he spoke my father gripped my shoulders with hands that were always ink-stained from handling typewriter ribbons. I remember the pressure of his hands better than his words.

After the futile attempt to make clear his motives, my father gave up and told me it was time to get ready for bed. From a grocery bag he brought out a new pair of pajamas and a tooth brush he had bought for me. The pajamas were white, starchy cotton with blue piping and much too big for me, but I put them on. I sat on the edge of the bed, and then I was scared. I wondered if I *was* going to go home again. The prospect of sleeping in a strange bed in new pajamas made the idea of home recede, the way a train station seems to pull away from you as you stand outside on the platform of the train's last car.

36   At about 9:00 I was lying awake in bed, unable to sleep, and my father was sitting in the chair smoking when someone knocked on the door and called out, "Frank? It's Bob Wirth. Are you in there?"

When he heard the man's voice, my father's head slumped forward so suddenly it was as if the muscles in his neck had been cut. He looked up and his face had the ashen, worn look of a man who has not slept for days. My father walked slowly to the door, opened it, and stood aside. The man outside looked in the room for me, and when he saw me said, "The boy's mother wants him back, Frank."

My father took another step back and a short, lean man in a dark suit walked over to the bed and looked down at me. "Get up and get dressed," he said. "You're going back to your mama. We'll go call your grandpa and he'll come get you." The man standing over me was, he announced, the Eau Claire County sheriff.

I went into the bathroom to dress, and while I was in there, I heard the sheriff say to my father, "Jesus, Frank, this was stupid. This wasn't something to go and do."

40   Tiredly, my father said, "It's a long story, Bob. Someday I'll tell you about it."

That my father and the sheriff were friends pleased and relieved me.

After I dressed, the sheriff told me he'd take me down to the lobby to wait for my grandfather. My father, who was sitting on the portion of the unmade bed where I had been lying, waved at me as I was leaving and called out, "So long for now, Lewis."

In the small, unsteady elevator we rode down to the lobby. There, the sheriff deposited me in an old worn leather club chair. The back of the chair was against a pillar, and the front was in full view of the desk and the night clerk. "Now you sit right here," the sheriff told me. "I'm going to call your people, and then I'm going back upstairs to have a word with your papa."

44   In less than an hour my grandfather arrived, and when he saw me, he asked one question: "Are you all right?"

I nodded yes.

I fell asleep in the car on the way home, and when we got back to Pierce, my grandfather carried me into the house and to my bed, the second time that day I was lifted in the arms of an adult.

When I awoke the next morning my mother was sitting in a chair in my bedroom. I knew instantly she had been there all night, and now, back in my room, I was embarrassed by her presence.

48   Her first question was the same as my grandfather's. "Are you all right?"

"Yes," I said out loud.

I never saw my father again after that night. His rights of custody were revoked by a judge who believed that no one, not even a parent, has the right to steal someone away against his will. My father made no attempt to fight this ruling, and his acquiesence was the result, I believe, of my behavior toward him that day. I believe that with my silence I killed his love for me.

My father eventually remarried. He married a widow from Eau Claire who had two sons, and one of the sons was an All-State basketball player who won an athletic scholarship to the University of Minnesota where he went on to receive an All-American honorable mention. I remember feeling an odd pride that my father was this boy's stepfather, and I also felt that by following this boy's career I was somehow staying in touch with my father. My father died of a heart attack in 1974.

52   Now this is the strange part. All of us grieve, at some time in our lives, for our lost childhood, but in the sameness of all the days of the past only the unusual day, the day different from all the othr days, is likely to stand out in memory. And for me the day my father stole me is the day I remember best. As a result, when I wish I could be a boy again, I invariably, unwillingly, think of making business calls with my father. I miss those offices with their worn carpets and massive wooden desks. I miss the heavy black machines, the typewriters and dictaphones and adding machines. I miss the unsharpened pencils, the stacks of white paper, the smeary carbons and canary yellow legal pads, the embossed sheets of letter-head and the long envelopes. I miss my father.

READER RESPONSE

The narrator, Lewis, tells of one memorable day from his childhood that stands out precisely because it is different from all the other days. Is there one day in particular from your childhood that you recall? What makes that day stand out from all the rest?

QUESTIONS FOR DISCUSSION

1. Explain what, besides the boy's refusal to speak, the title "Silence" might refer to.
2. Although we cannot know for sure, because the story is told entirely from the son's point of view, how do you suppose the father sees his role as parent? How do you think he feels about his son? Is there any evidence in the text that suggests how the father feels?

3. What motivates the father to kidnap his son? Why does the son refuse to speak? Do you believe, as the eight-year-old Lewis did, that the boy's silence "killed his [father's] love" for his son (paragraph 50)? Are you sympathetic toward the father, the son, neither, or both? Explain your answer.
4. Explain in what ways the relationship of the father and son in this story is typical and in what ways it is not typical of father–son relationships in general.
5. Look closely at the concluding paragraph. Why does the narrator consider what he says there to be "the strange part"? Does it surprise you that he says he misses all of the places his father took him on that one day? Given the event he narrates and his feelings for his father when he was young, what do you make of his now saying, "I miss my father"? Explain your answer.

ADDITIONAL SUGGESTIONS FOR WRITING ABOUT TRANSITIONS

1. Explain what you think is your most important transition to date and why you think it is so significant. For instance, describe a memorable experience you have had as a new college student and how your life has changed as a result, or narrate the events surrounding a significant move you have made and the effects of that move on you.
2. Describe the image of yourself that you hope to have in college. Does it differ significantly from your old self, or is it the same? Have you undergone any changes at college in the way you act or your appearance? Why?
3. Go to a website that offers the complete texts of all the presidential inaugural addresses, and select one by a president who interests you. Read the address, and then provide a thoughtful analysis of its effectiveness, using your own criteria. Explain what your criteria are and how the speech measures up to them.
4. Compare the inaugural address of any other American president with that of John F. Kennedy, reprinted in this chapter. How are they similar? How do they differ?
5. If you have ever felt an urge to move somewhere and leave everything behind, explain why you would like to leave, what you would hope to find, and how you think your life would be different.
6. Explain how and why you chose the career goal you now have. If you have not yet selected a career goal, write an essay exploring possible career paths or explaining why you have not yet selected a goal.
7. Describe your favorite retreat or something you own that you would find unbearable to give up. Explain why it is important to you, and describe key memories associated with it.
8. Describe a memory from your childhood that a particular smell, taste, or other stimulus always triggers.

9. Narrate your experience of returning to a place from your childhood, such as a former home or an old play area. How did your memory of the place contrast with the way it looked when you revisited it?

10. Compare and contrast the treatment of the father–son relationship in E. B. White's "Once More to the Lake" and Larry Watson's "Silence."

11. The narrator in Larry Watson's "Silence" says, "All of us grieve . . . for our lost childhood, but . . . only the unusual day, the day different from all the other days, is likely to stand out in memory" (paragraph 52). Write an essay describing the one day in your childhood that stands out in your memory, and explain why it is significant.

12. Explain the circumstances that led to a moment of insight regarding your feelings for someone, perhaps a family member, an authority figure, or a friend.

13. Describe a ritual that you or your family perform at special times such as celebrations, illnesses, or family gatherings. If your family no longer performs a ritual it once did or has stopped observing a particular holiday or religious custom, explain the change, why you think it occurred, and how you feel about it.

14. Identify a major transition on a national or global scale, and analyze its impact on people. For instance, consider the viewpoints of people at the approach of the new millennium as the world moved from 1999 to 2000. What made that transition so strikingly different from the usual year-end activities? What fears, apprehensions, and/or hopes did people have as that significant event approached?

15. Analyze the terrorist attacks against New York and Washington on September 11, 2001, in terms of their serving as catalysts for change. Focus on a particular subject, such as personal change, a change in the community, a change in the nation, or a change on a global scale.

Chapter

4

INSIGHTS

While the nature of the insights varies, the selections in this chapter all fea
ture people who achieve a perception about something they had previously
not understood. It may be recognition of a lesson about themselves or someone else; some new awareness of an important, intangible aspect of their lives;
or a general philosophical understanding of the larger pattern of things.

In the first selection, Frank Conroy, drawing on personal experience,
shares his understanding of the ways in which insight happens. In "Think
About It: Ways We Know, and Don't," Conroy distinguishes between two ways
in which education occurs, and he concludes that "understanding does not always mean resolution." For some things, he writes, never being sure of the
answer Is "our special fate, our inexpressibly valuable condition," but for others, insight comes with "a kind of click, a resolving kind of click."

The other readings in this chapter illustrate how their writers (or, in the case of the short story, the central character) achieved an understanding and, possibly, a resolution, many of them with the kind of click Conroy describes. For instance, Annie Dillard, in "Living Like Weasels," describes her sudden encounter with a weasel. The experience is so stunning, her insight into the animal so startling, that she is led to reflect that she "could very calmly go wild." Next, Pat Mora's "To Gabriella, a Young Writer" is, in part, about what it means to be a Mexican American and what it means to be a woman, but more important, it is about what it means to be a writer. Addressing the thirteen-year-old daughter of a friend, Mora shares her insights into why she writes and how she goes about doing it well.

Roger Rosenblatt, in "The Silent Friendship of Men," reflects on the death of a friend and explains his insight into men's apparent uncommunicativeness. It is, he argues, an inherent part of their natures, and the important point about men's friendships is the fact of the friendships themselves. "The silence of men in general," he contends, "is over-talked about and overcriticized." Steven Doloff, in "Woodstock's Message Is Still True," illustrates yet another kind of insight as Doloff explains his belief that the 1969 Woodstock Music Festival embodied the American dream of spiritual community. His essay suggests that a reconsideration of that 1960s music festival might provide the younger generation of the 1990s a useful reminder of "the need to dream Walt Whitman's, the Rev. Dr. Martin Luther King's and Woodie Guthrie's optimistic American dreams and to find their own Woodstocks."

The next essay addresses the subject of alcohol abuse and its effect not only on one of its users but also on his victims. Michael Denne, writing from a jail cell, explores in "Learning the Hard Way" the responsibility he bears and the punishment he must take for driving while intoxicated.

The last two selections illustrate that insight into something else can also mean insight into oneself. In "Shooting an Elephant," George Orwell recounts an incident in Burma when, as a British policeman, he committed an act of unnecessary violence "solely to avoid looking a fool." Looking back on the incident, he realizes the experience gave him insight not only into the real nature of imperialism but also into his own character. Finally, in Kate Chopin's "The Story of an Hour," the central character achieves in one hour a momentous insight into her marriage, her relationship with her husband, and her potential to live life fully for her own self. The story's surprise ending adds a twist that readers are sure to find controversial.

1. Discuss the relationships among the abstract concepts "education," "knowledge," and "wisdom." How are they similar? How are they different? How are they closely connected?
2. How would you assess the quality of your education so far?
3. What do you feel most knowledgeable about?
4. Do you consider yourself to be wise?
5. Discuss the extent to which you believe people can be taught to think. Is thinking a learned skill, or is it something that comes naturally?

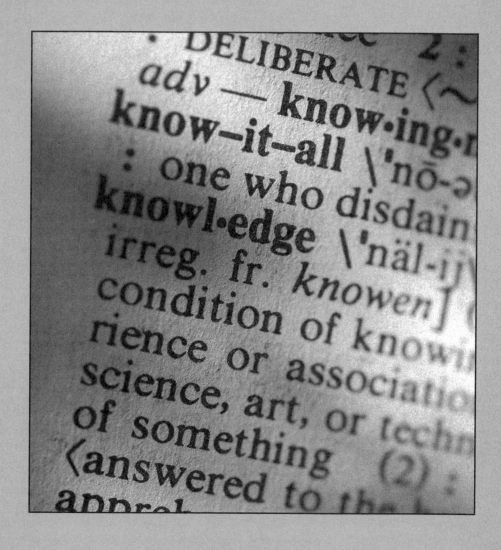

Think About It: Ways We Know, and Don't
Frank Conroy

*Frank Conroy has worked as a jazz pianist and often writes of
American music. His essays and stories have appeared in* The
New Yorker, Esquire, Harper's, *and* GQ. *His books include a novel-
istic autobiography,* Stop-time *(1967); a collection of short stories,* Midair *(1985); a novel,* Body and Soul *(1998); and* The
Eleventh Draft: Craft and the Writing Life from Iowa Writers' Workshop *(1999), a collection of 23 essays about writing from fiction
writers who at one time were Iowa Writers's Workshop students
or faculty members.* Dogs Bark, But the Caravan Rolls On: Observations Then and Now *(2002) is a collection of nonfiction essays.
This essay was first published in* Harper's *in 1988.*

When I was sixteen I worked selling hot dogs at a stand in the Fourteenth
Street subway station in New York City, one level above the trains and one below the street, where the crowds continually flowed back and forth. I worked
with three Puerto Rican men who could not speak English. I had no Spanish,
and although we understood each other well with regard to the tasks at hand,
sensing and adjusting to each other's body movements in the extremely confined space in which we operated, I felt isolated with no one to talk to. On my
break I came out from behind the counter and passed the time with two old
black men who ran a shoeshine stand in a dark corner of the corridor. It was a
poor location, half hidden by columns, and they didn't have much business. I
would sit with my back against the wall while they stood or moved around
their ancient elevated stand, talking to each other or to me, but always staring
into the distance as they did so.

As the weeks went by I realized that they never looked at anything in
their immediate vicinity—not at me or their stand or anybody who might
come within ten or fifteen feet. They did not look at approaching customers
once they were inside the perimeter. Save for the instant it took to discern the
color of the shoes, they did not even look at what they were doing while they
worked, but rubbed in polish, brushed, and buffed by feel while looking over
their shoulders, into the distance, as if awaiting the arrival of an important person. Of course there wasn't all that much distance in the underground station,
but their behavior was so focused and consistent they seemed somehow to
transcend the physical. A powerful mood was created, and I came almost to
believe that these men could see through walls, through girders, and around
corners to whatever hyperspace it was where whoever it was they were waiting and watching for would finally emerge. Their scattered talk was hip, ellipti-
cal, and hinted at mysteries beyond my white boy's ken, but it was the staring
off, the long, steady staring off, that had me hypnotized. I left for a better job,
with handshakes from both of them, without understanding what I had seen.

Perhaps ten years later, after playing jazz with black musicians in various Harlem clubs, hanging out uptown with a few young artists and intellectuals, I began to learn from them something of the extraordinarily varied and complex riffs and rituals embraced by different people to help themselves get through life in the ghetto. Fantasy of all kinds—from playful to dangerous—was in the very air of Harlem. It was the spice of uptown life.

4　　Only then did I understand the two shoeshine men. They were trapped in a demeaning situation in a dark corner in an underground corridor in a filthy subway system. Their continuous staring off was a kind of statement, a kind of dance. Our bodies are here, went the statement, but our souls are receiving nourishment from distant sources only we can see. They were powerful magic dancers, sorcerers almost, and thirty-five years later I can still feel the pressure of their spell.

The light bulb may appear over your head, is what I'm saying, but it may be a while before it actually goes on. Early in my attempts to learn jazz piano, I used to listen to recordings of a fine player named Red Garland, whose music I admired. I couldn't quite figure out what he was doing with his left hand, however; the chords eluded me. I went uptown to an obscure club where he was playing with his trio, caught him on his break, and simply asked him. "Sixths," he said cheerfully. And then he went away.

I didn't know what to make of it. The basic jazz chord is the seventh, which comes in various configurations, but it is what it is. I was a self-taught pianist, pretty shaky on theory and harmony, and when he said sixths I kept trying to fit the information into what I already knew, and it didn't fit. But it stuck in my mind—a tantalizing mystery.

A couple of years later, when I began playing with a bass player, I discovered more or less by accident that if the bass played the root and I played a sixth based on the fifth note of the scale, a very interesting chord involving both instruments emerged. Ordinarily, I suppose I would have skipped over the matter and not paid much attention, but I remembered Garland's remark and so I stopped and spent a week or two working out the voicings, and greatly strengthened my foundations as a player. I had remembered what I hadn't understood, you might say, until my life caught up with the information and the light bulb went on.

8　　I remember another, more complicated example from my sophomore year at a small liberal-arts college outside Philadelphia. I seemed never to be able to get up in time for breakfast in the dining hall. I would get coffee and a doughnut in the Coop instead—a basement area with about a dozen small tables where students could get something to eat at odd hours. Several mornings in a row I noticed a strange man sitting by himself with a cup of coffee. He was in his sixties, perhaps, and sat straight in his chair with very little extraneous movement. I guessed he was some sort of distinguished visitor to the college who had decided to put in some time at a student hangout. But no one ever sat with him. One morning I approached his table and asked if I could join him.

"Certainly," he said. "Please do." He had perhaps the clearest eyes I had ever seen, like blue ice, and to be held in their steady gaze was not, at first, an entirely comfortable experience. His eyes gave nothing away about himself while at the same time creating in me the eerie impression that he was looking directly into my soul. He asked a few quick questions, as if to put me at my ease, and we fell into conversation. He was William O. Douglas from the Supreme Court, and when he saw how startled I was he said, "Call me Bill. Now tell me what you're studying and why you get up so late in the morning." Thus began a series of talks that stretched over many weeks. The fact that I was an ignorant sophomore with literary pretensions who knew nothing about the law didn't seem to bother him. We talked about everything from Shakespeare to the possibility of life on other planets. One day I mentioned that I was going to have dinner with Judge Learned Hand. I explained that Hand was my girlfriend's grandfather. Douglas nodded, but I could tell he was surprised at the coincidence of my knowing the chief judge of the most important court in the country save the Supreme Court itself. After fifty years on the bench Judge Hand had become a famous man, both in and out of legal circles—a living legend, to his own dismay. "Tell him hello and give him my best regards," Douglas said.

Learned Hand, in his eighties, was a short, barrel-chested man with a large, square head, huge, thick, bristling eyebrows, and soft brown eyes. He radiated energy and would sometimes bark out remarks or questions in the living room as if he were in court. His humor was sharp, but often leavened with a touch of self-mockery. When something caught his funny bone he would burst out with explosive laughter—the laughter of a man who enjoyed laughing. He had a large repertoire of dramatic expressions involving the use of his eyebrows—very useful, he told me conspiratorially, when looking down on things from behind the bench. (The court stenographer could not record the movement of his eyebrows.) When I told him I'd been talking to William O. Douglas, they first shot up in exaggerated surprise, and then lowered and moved forward in a glower.

"*Justice* William O. Douglas, young man," he admonished. "Justice Douglas, if you please." About the Supreme Court in general, Hand insisted on a tone of profound respect. Little did I know that in private correspondence he had referred to the Court as "The Blessed Saints, Cherubim and Seraphim," "The Jolly Boys," "The Nine Tin Jesuses," "The Nine Blameless Ethiopians," and my particular favorite, "The Nine Blessed Chalices of the Sacred Effluvium."

12   Hand was badly stooped and had a lot of pain in his lower back. Martinis helped, but his strict Yankee wife approved of only one before dinner. It was my job to make the second and somehow slip it to him. If the pain was particularly acute he would get out of his chair and lie flat on the rug, still talking, and finish his point without missing a beat. He flattered me by asking for my impression of Justice Douglas, instructed me to convey his warmest regards, and then began talking about the Dennis case, which he described as a particularly tricky and difficult case involving the prosecution of eleven leaders of

the Communist party. He had just started in on the First Amendment and free speech when we were called into dinner.

William O. Douglas loved the outdoors with a passion, and we fell into the habit of having coffee in the Coop and then strolling under the trees down toward the duck pond. About the Dennis case, he said something to this effect: "Eleven Communists arrested by the government. Up to no good, said the government; dangerous people, violent overthrow, etc., First Amendment, said the defense, freedom of speech, etc." Douglas stopped walking. "Clear and present danger."

"What?" I asked. He often talked in a telegraphic manner, and one was expected to keep up with him. It was sometimes like listening to a man thinking out loud.

"Clear and present danger," he said. "That was the issue. Did they constitute a clear and present danger? I don't think so. I think everybody took the language pretty far in Dennis." He began walking, striding along quickly. Again, one was expected to keep up with him. "The F.B.I. was all over them. Phones tapped, constant surveillance. How could it be clear and present danger with the F.B.I. watching every move they made? That's a ginkgo," he said suddenly, pointing at a tree. "A beauty. You don't see those every day. Ask Hand about clear and present danger."

16   I was in fact reluctant to do so. Douglas's argument seemed to me to be crushing—the last word, really—and I didn't want to embarrass Judge Hand. But back in the living room, on the second martini, the old man asked about Douglas. I sort of scratched my nose and recapitulated the conversation by the ginkgo tree.

"What?" Hand shouted. "Speak up, sir, for heaven's sake."

"He said the F.B.I. was watching them all the time so there couldn't be a clear and present danger," I blurted out, blushing as I said it.

A terrible silence filled the room. Hand's eyebrows writhed on his face like two huge caterpillars. He leaned forward in the wing chair, his face settling, finally, into a grim expression. "I am astonished," he said softly, his eyes holding mine, "at Justice Douglas's newfound faith in the Federal Bureau of Investigation." His big, granite head moved even closer to mine, until I could smell the martini. "I had understood him to consider it a politically corrupt, incompetent organization, directed by a power-crazed lunatic." I realized I had been holding my breath throughout all of this, and as I relaxed, I saw the faintest trace of a smile cross Hand's face. Things are sometimes more complicated than they first appear, his smile seemed to say. The old man leaned back. "The proximity of the danger is something to think about. Ask him about that. See what he says."

20   I chewed the matter over as I returned to campus. Hand had pointed out some of Douglas's language about the F.B.I. from other sources that seemed to bear out his point. I thought about the words "clear and present danger," and the fact that if you looked at them closely they might not be as simple as they had first appeared. What degree of danger? Did the word "present" allude to

the proximity of the danger, or just the fact that the danger was there at all—that it wasn't an anticipated danger? Were there other hidden factors these great men were weighing of which I was unaware?

But Douglas was gone, back to Washington. (The writer in me is tempted to create a scene here—to invent one for dramatic purposes—but of course I can't do that.) My brief time as a messenger boy was over, and I felt a certain frustration, as if, with a few more exchanges, the matter of *Dennis* v. *United States* might have been resolved to my satisfaction. They'd left me high and dry. But, of course, it is precisely because the matter did not resolve that has caused me to think about it, off and on, all these years. "The Constitution," Hand used to say to me flatly, "is a piece of paper. The Bill of Rights is a piece of paper." It was many years before I understood what he meant. Documents alone do not keep democracy alive, nor maintain the state of law. There is no particular safety in them. Living men and women, generation after generation, must continually remake democracy and the law, and that involves an ongoing state of tension between the past and the present which will never completely resolve.

Education doesn't end until life ends, because you never know when you're going to understand something you hadn't understood before. For me, the magic dance of the shoeshine men was the kind of experience in which understanding came with a kind of click, a resolving kind of click. The same with the experience at the piano. What happened with Justice Douglas and Judge Hand was different, and makes the point that understanding does not always mean resolution. Indeed, in our intellectual lives, our creative lives, it is perhaps those problems that will never resolve that rightly claim the lion's share of our energies. The physical body exists in a constant state of tension as it maintains homeostasis, and so too does the active mind embrace the tension of never being certain, never being absolutely sure, never being done, as it engages the world. That is our special fate, our inexpressibly valuable condition.

READER RESPONSE

In your own words, explain what Conroy means by "a resolving kind of click" (paragraph 22). If you have ever experienced such a click, describe the circumstances.

QUESTIONS FOR DISCUSSION

1. What do you understand Conroy to mean by the "magic dance of the shoeshine men" (paragraph 22)? How did Red Garland's saying the word "sixths" to Conroy (paragraph 5) later strengthen Conroy's foundation on the piano?

2. Do Conroy's experiences with the shoeshine men and with what happened to him at the piano clearly illustrate one particular way of knowing?

3. Comment on Conroy's effectiveness in describing Justice Douglas and Judge Hand. Do you have clear images of both men? How do the viewpoints of Judge Hand and Justice Douglas differ on the Dennis case? What does Judge Hand mean when he says that the Constitution and the Bill of Rights are pieces of paper (paragraph 21)?

4. What lesson about education—about the ways of knowing—does Conroy learn from his experience with Justice Douglas and Judge Hand?

Living Like Weasels
Annie Dillard

Annie Dillard was a contributing editor for Harper's *from 1973 to 1981. In 1974 she published a book of poems,* Tickets for a Prayer Wheel, *and a volume of essays,* Pilgrim at Tinker Creek, *for which she won the Pulitzer Prize. Her other books include* Living with Fiction *(1982),* Encounters with Chinese Writers *(1984),* An American Childhood *(1987), and* For the Time Being *(1999). The selection that follows comes from* Teaching a Stone to Talk *(1982), a collection of her own narrative essays.*

A weasel is wild. Who knows what he thinks? He sleeps in his underground den, his tail draped over his nose. Sometimes he lives in his den for two days without leaving. Outside, he stalks rabbits, mice, muskrats, and birds, killing more bodies than he can eat warm, and often dragging the carcasses home. Obedient to instinct, he bites his prey at the neck, either splitting the jugular vein at the throat or crunching the brain at the base of the skull, and he does not let go. One naturalist refused to kill a weasel who was socketed into his hand deeply as a rattlesnake. The man could in no way pry the tiny weasel off, and he had to walk half a mile to water, the weasel dangling from his palm, and soak him off like a stubborn label.

And once, says Ernest Thompson Seton—once, a man shot an eagle out of the sky. He examined the eagle and found the dry skull of a weasel fixed by the jaws to his throat. The supposition is that the eagle had pounced on the weasel and the weasel swiveled and bit as instinct taught him, tooth to neck, and nearly won. I would like to have seen that eagle from the air a few weeks or months before he was shot: was the whole weasel still attached to his feathered throat, a fur pendant? Or did the eagle eat what he could reach, gutting the living weasel with his talons before his breast, bending his beak, cleaning the beautiful airborne bones?

I have been reading about weasels because I saw one last week. I startled a weasel who startled me, and we exchanged a long glance.

4   Twenty minutes from my house, through the woods by the quarry and across the highway, is Hollins Pond, a remarkable piece of shallowness, where I like to go at sunset and sit on a tree trunk. Hollins Pond is also called Murray's Pond; it covers two acres of bottomland near Tinker Creek with six inches of water and six thousand lily pads. In winter, brown-and-white steers stand in the middle of it, merely dampening their hooves; from the distant shore they look like miracle itself, complete with miracle's nonchalance. Now, in summer, the steers are gone. The water lilies have blossomed and spread to a green horizontal plane that is terra firma to plodding blackbirds, and tremulous ceiling to black leeches, crayfish, and carp.

This is, mind you, suburbia. It is a five-minute walk in three directions to rows of houses, though none is visible here. There's a 55 mph highway at one end of the pond, and a nesting pair of wood ducks at the other. Under every bush is a muskrat hole or a beer can. The far end is an alternating series of fields and woods, fields and woods, threaded everywhere with motorcycle tracks—in whose bare clay wild turtles lay eggs.

So. I had crossed the highway, stepped over two low barbed-wire fences, and traced the motorcycle path in all gratitude through the wild rose and poison ivy of the pond's shoreline up into high grassy fields. Then I cut down through the woods to the mossy fallen tree where I sit. This tree is excellent. It makes a dry, upholstered bench at the upper, marshy end of the pond, a plush jetty raised from the thorny shore between a shallow blue body of water and a deep blue body of sky.

The sun had just set. I was relaxed on the tree trunk, ensconced in the lap of lichen, watching the lily pads at my feet tremble and part dreamily over the thrusting path of a carp. A yellow bird appeared to my right and flew behind me. It caught my eye; I swiveled around—and the next instant, inexplicably, I was looking down at a weasel, who was looking up at me.

8   Weasel! I'd never seen one wild before. He was ten inches long, thin as a curve, a muscled ribbon, brown as fruitwood, soft-furred, alert. His face was fierce, small and pointed as a lizard's; he would have made a good arrowhead. There was just a dot of chin, maybe two brown hairs' worth, and then the pure white fur began that spread down his underside. He had two black eyes I didn't see, any more than you see a window.

The weasel was stunned into stillness as he was emerging from beneath an enormous shaggy wild rose bush four feet away. I was stunned into stillness twisted backward on the tree trunk. Our eyes locked, and someone threw away the key.

Our look was as if two lovers, or deadly enemies, met unexpectedly on an overgrown path when each had been thinking of something else: a clearing blow to the gut. It was also a bright blow to the brain, or a sudden beating of brains, with all the charge and intimate grate of rubbed balloons. It emptied our lungs. It felled the forest, moved the fields, and drained the pond; the world dismantled and tumbled into that black hole of eyes. If you and I looked at each other that way, our skills would split and drop to our shoulders. But we don't. We keep our skulls. So.

He disappeared. This was only last week, and already I don't remember what shattered the enchantment. I think I blinked, I think I retrieved my brain from the weasel's brain, and tried to memorize what I was seeing, and the weasel felt the yank of separation, the careening splashdown into real life and the urgent current of instinct. He vanished under the wild rose. I waited motionless, my mind suddenly full of data and my spirit with pleadings, but he didn't return.

12   Please do not tell me about "approach-avoidance conflicts." I tell you I've been in that weasel's brain for sixty seconds, and he was in mine. Brains are private places, muttering through unique and secret tapes—but the weasel and I both plugged into another tape simultaneously, for a sweet and shocking time. Can I help it if it was a blank?

What goes on in his brain the rest of the time? What does a weasel think about? He won't say. His journal is tracks in clay, a spray of feathers, mouse blood and bone: uncollected, unconnected, loose-leaf, and blown.

I would like to learn, or remember, how to live. I come to Hollins Pond not so much to learn how to live as, frankly, to forget about it. That is, I don't think I can learn from a wild animal how to live in particular—shall I suck warm blood, hold my tail high, walk with my footprints precisely over the prints of my hands?—but I might learn something of mindlessness, something of the purity without bias or motive. The weasel lives in necessity and we live in choice, hating necessity and dying at the last ignobly in its talons. I would like to live as I should, as the weasel lives as he should. And I suspect that for me the way is like the weasel's: open to time and death painlessly, noticing everything, remembering nothing, choosing the given with a fierce and pointed will.

I missed my chance. I should have gone for the throat. I should have lunged for that streak of white under the weasel's chin and held on, held on through mud and into the wild rose, held on for a dearer life. We could live under the wild rose wild as weasels, mute and uncomprehending. I could very calmly go wild. I could live two days in the den, curled, leaning on mouse fur, sniffing bird bones, blinking, licking, breathing musk, my hair tangled in the roots of grasses. Down is a good place to go, where the mind is single. Down is out, out of your ever-loving mind and back to your careless senses. I remember muteness as a prolonged and giddy fast, where every moment is a feast of utterance received. Time and events are merely poured, unremarked, and ingested directly, like blood pulsed into my gut through a jugular vein. Could two live that way? Could two live under the wild rose, and explore by the pond, so that the smooth mind of each is as everywhere present to the other, and as received and as unchallenged, as falling snow?

16   We could, you know. We can live any way we want. People take vows of poverty, chastity, and obedience—even of silence—by choice. The thing is to

stalk your calling in a certain skilled and supple way, to locate the most tender and live spot and plug into that pulse. This is yielding, not fighting. A weasel doesn't "attack" anything; a weasel lives as he's meant to, yielding at every moment to the perfect freedom of single necessity.

I think it would be well, and proper, and obedient, and pure, to grasp your one necessity and not let it go, to dangle from it limp wherever it takes you. Then even death, where you're going no matter how you live, cannot you part. Seize it and let it seize you up aloft even, till your eyes burn out and drop; let your musky flesh fall off in shreds, and let your very bones unhinge and scatter, loosened over fields, over fields and woods, lightly, thoughtless, from any height at all, from as high as eagles.

READER RESPONSE

Describe an experience you have had with something wild in its natural setting; if you have not had such an experience, reflect on an animal you have closely observed. What might you learn from that animal? From what other animal(s) besides weasels might humans learn something?

QUESTIONS FOR DISCUSSION

1. What do you understand Dillard's point to be in the anecdotes of the first two paragraphs about the nature of weasels.
2. Find passages that you believe are vividly descriptive, and explain what makes them effective. Where does Dillard use metaphor or other figurative language to create images or convey sensory experience?
3. Explain what you think Dillard means when she compares her meeting with the weasel to "two lovers, or deadly enemies" (paragraph 10) coming upon one another suddenly. In what way would the emotions generated by a sudden encounter between lovers and between enemies be the same? What do you think Dillard means by the last sentence of paragraph 8: "He had two black eyes I didn't see, any more than you see a window"?
4. Explain what Dillard finds attractive about the way weasels live. What does she think humans might learn from weasels? Do you agree with her?

To Gabriella, a Young Writer

Pat Mora

Pat Mora, who holds B.A. and M.A. degrees in English from the University of Texas at El Paso, is a prolific poet, children's

literature writer, and essayist. Her collections of poetry include
Chants *(1984),* Borders *(1986),* Communion *(1991),* Aunt Car-
men's Book of Practical Saints *(1997),* Confetti: Poems for Children
(1996), and This Big Sky *(1999). Among her many children's
books are* This Desert Is My Mother *(1994),* Delicious Hulabaloo
(1998), Fifty Below Zero *(1999), and* The Rainbow Tulip *(1999).
Her essays have been collected in* Nepantla: Essays from the Land
in the Middle *(1993), and she has written a memoir,* House of
Houses *(1997). This selection is taken from* Nepantla.

The enthusiasm and curiosity of young writers is a source of energy. In one
sense, we are all fledgling writers. With each new piece, we embark on the
mysterious process again, unsure if we can describe or evoke what is in our
minds and hearts. Sometimes it is difficult to convince those under thirty
that the struggle never ends, that art is not about formulas. Maybe that continuing risk lures us. Luckily, octogenarians such as movie director Akira
Kurosawa or Mexican painter Rufino Tamayo show us that we need never re-
tire, and that what we have to share near the end of our lives may be far
more lyrical than our early efforts in any art form. A sad truth about art is
that it is unlinked to virtue. Wretches can write well while saints produce
pedestrian passages.

I like to share what little I know, to encourage beginning writers. When
a friend asked if I'd give her thirteen-year-old daughter some advice, I
wrote her.

DEAR GABRIELLA,

4   Your mother tells me that you have begun writing poems and that you
wonder exactly how I do it. Do you perhaps wonder why I do it? Why would
anyone sit alone and write when she could be talking to friends on the telephone, eating mint chocolate chip ice cream in front of the TV, or buying a
new red sweater at the mall?

And, as you know, I like people. I like long, slow lunches with my
friends. I like to dance. I'm no hermit, and I'm not shy. So why do I sit with my
tablet and pen and mutter to myself?

There are many answers. I write because I'm a reader. I want to give to
others what writers have given me, a chance to hear the voices of people I
will never meet. Alone, in private. And even if I meet these authors, I wouldn't
hear what I hear alone with the page, words carefully chosen, woven into a
piece unlike any other, enjoyed by me in a way no other person will, in quite
the same way, enjoy them. I suppose I'm saying that I love the privateness of
writing and reading. It's delicious to curl into a book.

I write because I'm curious. I'm curious about me. Writing is a way of
finding out how I feel about anything and everything. Now that I've left the
desert where I grew up, for example, I'm discovering how it feels to walk on
spongy fall leaves and to watch snow drifting *up* on a strong wind. I notice

what's around me in a special way because I'm a writer, and then I talk to myself about it on paper. Writing is my way of saving my feelings.

8   I write because I believe that Mexican Americans need to take their rightful place in U.S. literature. We need to be published and to be studied in schools and colleges so that the stories and ideas of our people won't quietly disappear. Although I'm happy when I finish the draft of a poem or story, deep inside I always wish I wrote better, that I could bring more honor and attention to those like the *abuelitas,* grandmothers, I write about. That mix of sadness and pleasure occurs in life, doesn't it?

Although we don't discuss it often because it's depressing, our people have been and sometimes still are viewed as inferior. Maybe you have already felt hurt when someone by a remark or odd look said to you: you're not like us, you're not one of us, speaking Spanish is odd, your family looks funny.

Some of us decide we don't want to be different. We don't want to be part of a group that is often described as poor and uneducated. I remember feeling that way at your age. I spoke Spanish at home to my grandmother and aunt, but I didn't always want my friends at school to know that I spoke Spanish. I didn't like myself for feeling that way. I sensed it was wrong, but I didn't know why. Now, I know.

I know that the society we live in and that the movies, television programs, and commercials we see all affect us. It's not easy to learn to judge others fairly, not because of the car they drive, the house they live in, the church they attend, the color of their skin, the language they speak at home. It takes courage to face the fact that we all have ten toes, get sleepy at night, get scared in the dark. Some families, some cities, some states, and even some countries foolishly convince themselves that they are better than others. And then they teach their children this ugly lie. It's like a weed with burrs and stickers that pricks people.

12   How are young women who are African American, Asian American, American Indian, Latinas, or members of all the other ethnic groups supposed to feel about themselves? Some are proud of their cultural roots. But commercials are also busy trying to convince us that our car, clothes, and maybe even our family are not good enough. It's so hard today to be yourself, your many interesting selves, because billboards and magazines tell you that beautiful is being thin, maybe blonde, and rich, rich, rich. No wonder we don't always like ourselves when we look in the mirror.

There are no secrets to good writing. Read. Listen. Write. Read. Listen. Write. You learn to write well by reading wonderful writing and by letting those words and ideas become part of your blood and bones. But life is not all books. You become a better writer by listening—to yourself and to all the colors, shapes, and sounds around you. Listen with all of your senses. Listen to wrinkles on your *tia's,* your aunt's, face.

Writers write. They don't just talk about writing just as dancers don't just talk about dancing. They do it because they love it and because they want to get better and better. They practice and practice to loosen up just as you practiced and practiced when you were learning to talk. And because you practiced, you don't talk the way you did when you were three.

Do you know the quotation that says that learning to write is like learning to ice-skate? You must be willing to make a fool of yourself. Writers are willing to try what they can't do well so that one day they can write a strong poem or novel or children's book.

16   After a writer gains some confidence, she begins to spend more and more time revising, just as professional ice-skaters create and practice certain routines until they have developed their own, unique style. You probably don't like rewriting now. I didn't either until a few years ago.

How or why a book or poem starts varies. Sometimes I hear a story I want to save, sometimes it's a line or an idea. It would be as if you saw someone dance and you noticed a step or some special moves and for a few days you didn't actually try the steps, but off and on you thought about them. Maybe you even feel the moves inside you. And then one day you just can't stand it anymore and you turn on the music and begin to experiment. You don't succeed right away, but you're having fun even while you're working to get the rhythm right. And slowly you loosen up, and pretty soon you forget about your feet and arms, and you and the music are just moving together. Then the next day you try it again, and maybe alter it slightly.

My pen is like that music. Usually I like to start in a sunny spot with a yellow, lined tablet and a pen. I have a number of false starts like you did dancing. I'm working but having fun. Alone. The first line of a poem is sometimes a hard one because I want it to be an interesting line. It may be the only line a reader will glance at to decide whether to read the whole piece. I'm searching for the right beginning. I play a little game with myself. (This game works with any kind of writing.) I tell myself to write any line no matter how bad or dull, because I can later throw it away. If I sit waiting for the perfect line, I might never write the poem. I'm willing to make a fool of myself. So I start, usually slowly. I write a few lines, read them aloud, and often start again. I keep sections I like and discard the uninteresting parts. The next day I read my work and try to improve it. I'm trying to pull out of myself the poem or story that's deep inside. It's important not to fall in love with the words you write. Pick your words or phrases, and then stand back and look at your work. Read it out loud.

You and I are lucky to be writers. So many women in history and even today who could be much better writers than I am have not had that private pleasure of creating with words. Maybe their families think writing is a waste of time, maybe they don't believe in themselves, maybe they have to work hard all day and then have to cook and clean and take care of their children at night, maybe they've never been taught to read and write.

20   I hope that you develop pride in being Mexican American and that you discover what you have to say that no one else can say. I hope that you continue writing, Gabriella.

READER RESPONSE

Explain any insights you have gained from reading this essay that might help with your own writing.

QUESTIONS FOR DISCUSSION

1. Which, if any, of your own reasons for writing are the same as those that Mora gives for why she writes?
2. In paragraphs 10–14, Mora discusses the subject of image, beginning with the way in which many people view Mexican Americans. She writes, "How are young women who are African American, Asian American, American Indian, Latinas, or members of all the other ethnic groups supposed to feel about themselves?" (paragraph 12). How does this section relate to Mora's advice on writing?
3. Analyze the advice Mora gives for achieving good writing. What process does she follow when writing creatively? Do you find her advice useful? What other advice can you offer for producing good writing?
4. Mora's audience is only thirteen years old. What advice would you give a thirteen-year-old about writing?

The Silent Friendship of Men
Roger Rosenblatt

Roger Rosenblatt has been a contributing editor for Time, Life, Family Circle, The New Republic, Vanity Fair, *and* Men's Journal. *He has written and performed two one-man off-Broadway shows and won Peabody and Emmy awards for his essays on PBS's* The News Hour with Jim Lehrer. *His books include* The Man in the Water *(1994),* Coming Apart: A Memoir of the Harvard Wars of 1969 *(1997),* Rules for Aging *(2000), and* Where We Stand: 30 Reasons for Loving Our Country *(2002). "The Silent Friendship of Men" was first published as a* Time *essay on December 7, 1998.*

What I enjoyed most about my conversations with John Campbell was that they hardly existed. We spoke—at the post office, at the village store, whenever he pulled over to the curb on his bike—two, three times a month. But we said very little. In the still, blank autumn afternoons like these, our silence abetted the season. One of us would open with some typically male, moderately hearty greeting; the other would follow with an observation about essentially nothing, like the lowering sky; the other would grunt or nod; John would pedal away, and that would be that.

When he died some weeks ago, of leukemia at age 77, I didn't say much either—just bowed my head. I went over to see his wife Jane, and again said little. I asked John's daughter Frances if I might have a picture of him, so that I could recall his tight, sweet-tempered face. She gave me the choice of the dashing John as a fighter pilot in World War II, the one with the goggles dangling from his neck, or the older John I knew, who sold real estate. I took the more recent shot.

"I saw *Private Ryan*," Francie told me. "Funny to think that when the Army Air Force came to the rescue of Tom Hanks and his infantrymen, that was Dad. He never spoke about the war."

4   That made sense to me. The silence of men in general is over-talked about and overcriticized. To be sure, men never open up as much as women want them to, but there is a wordless understanding in which we function fairly well—especially in friendships. There are a dozen guys whom I count as friends and who do the same with me, yet months pass without our speaking, and even when we do, we don't

Old story: two women approach Calvin Coolidge. One says to the close-mouthed President, "Mr. Coolidge, I just bet my friend that I could get you to say three words." Says Coolidge: "You lose."

I believe, in fact, that most women would prefer a man to be glumly uncommunicative than to spill his guts at the drop of a hat. That (one recalls with a shudder) was the goal of the so-called men's movement of Robert Bly et al. in the 1980s and early '90s, which exhorted men to express their feelings. If anyone doubts the perils of men expressing feelings, he should watch *The McLaughlin Group* or Cable Monica.

This drum-beating, male-retreating, back-to-the-woods nonsense is still going on, by the way. Last February a hundred men retreated to a pine forest in Louisiana owned by Benedictine monks to acquire the ability to grieve. One reported that he had learned "to work my grief muscle." Thanks for sharing.

8   The push for men to express their feelings presumes that we have feelings, and we do have a few, but they remain submerged, and the airing of them often violates their authenticity. We are, as a gender, as dull as we seem. Contrary to the claptrap of the men's movement, men gain power through not talking. "The strength of the genie," said poet Richard Wilbur, "comes from being in a bottle." I'm no biologist, but my guess is that the male human animal was programmed for silence. One can make us talk counter to our genetic makeup, but it is like training kangaroos to box. It's mildly entertaining but pointless.

Older story: Wordsworth goes to visit Coleridge at his cottage, walks in, sits down and does not utter a word for three hours. Neither does Coleridge.

Wordsworth then rises and, as he leaves, thanks his friend for a perfect evening.

There's a deep, basically serene well of silence in most men, which, for better and worse, is where we live. I do not mean to start claptrapping myself, but I often think that all our acts of aggression and wanna-fight posturing arise from that well as forms of overcompensation or panic. Unlike women, men are not social creatures, not born administrators. It's nicely P.C. to think of God as female, but no woman would have thrown Lucifer out of heaven; she would have offered him a desk job. Had Lucifer been a woman, she would have dropped all that "myself am hell" business and taken it.

I would go so far as to argue that men were programmed to be isolated from one another and that aloneness is our natural state. Silence in male friendships is our way of being alone with each other. Once men have established a friendship, that itself is the word. The affection is obvious, at least to us. A main component of our silence is an appreciation of the obvious.

12   I may have spoken with my friend Campbell a total of a hundred times, yet I cannot recollect a single idea exchanged or the substance of a subject addressed. He knew that I wished him well, and I knew that he wished me the same. The day he died—before I learned that he had died—I called to him on his bike, mistaking a man of similar build and helmet for my friend. Later, when told of his death, I thought of that other man (I don't know why), and I pictured him pedaling away with a bright wave of the hand. See ya, John.

READER RESPONSE

If you are male, explore the degree to which your own friendships are like those Rosenblatt describes. If you are female, respond to Rosenblatt's statement in paragraph 6 that "most women would prefer a man to be glumly uncommunicative than to spill his guts at the drop of a hat."

QUESTIONS FOR DISCUSSION

1. To what extent do you agree or disagree with Rosenblatt's central point? How do the "old story" in paragraph 5 and the "older story" in paragraph 9 serve to illustrate his point?
2. What do you understand Rosenblatt to mean when he says in paragraph 4 that "months pass without our speaking, and even when we do, we don't"?
3. Locate passages in which Rosenblatt contrasts men with women. Do you agree with him on those points?

Woodstock's Message Is Still True

Steven Doloff

Steven Doloff is Associate Professor of English at Pratt Institute in New York City. His essays on culture and education have ap-peared in The New York Times, *the* Washington Post, *the* Philadel-phia Inquirer, *the* Boston Globe, *and* The Chronicle of Higher Education. *This essay appeared in the August 8, 1991, edition of the* Philadelphia Inquirer.

Eleven years ago, when I asked a class of New York City college students a question about the Woodstock music festival, no one had even heard of it. While the 20th anniversary celebration in Bethel, N.Y., two summers ago of this rock concert may have provided today's teenagers with the fact of the event, I doubt that the celebration's recycling of baby boomer nostalgia left us with the most historically accurate or useful grasp of the festival.

As Woodstock's practically ignored 22nd anniversary approaches (Aug. 15–17 [1991]), commentary on the event continues to omit its multiple con-nections to the Vietnam War and the social reform of the time. Perhaps this is because these issues still fester unresolved in the American psyche. Perhaps this is also because the conservative habit, now over a decade old, of "kicking the '60s" for all of today's social ills has reduced the festival to a symbol of sybaritic self-indulgence. However, if Woodstock is to be recorded as some kind of sociological watermark of an era, it will be best understood as a re-sponse to its context of civil unrest and, what's more, as a timely reaffirmation of a national ideal.

Despite its commercial aspects, Woodstock momentarily embodied the deeply characteristic American dream of a spiritual community, of an emotion-ally harmonious, all-inclusive sense of "us." Perhaps the most romantic concep-tion of this ideal was envisioned by the poet Walt Whitman 130 years ago, but its tradition reaches back to our Pilgrim beginnings. The novelty in the sum mer of 1969, however, was that this particular expression of the ideal became amplified and broadcast by the electronic media at unprecedented volume and speed to an already sensitized and self-conscious youth culture of un-precedented size.

4   In hindsight, the festival's sense of musical communion appears almost eerie. Rock-and-roll, itself derived from early black gospel music, became, not inappropriately, the emotionally unifying anthem for America's otherwise secu-larized youth. This may explain why Jimi Hendrix's Woodstock version of "The Star-Spangled Banner," as irony laden as it was, remains the most stirring rendi-tion many of those present have ever heard.

This '60s community of the young, like the reach of the music, owed much to the media's enhanced powers. The baby boomers since birth were made conscious of their collective echo on the radio and reflection on the television. The street chant at the tumultuous 1968 Democratic convention in Chicago, "The whole world is watching," was simply the first self-aware cry of Marshall McLuhan's global village children exercising their discovered political clout.

So why so great a protestation of youthful community in the summer of 1969? As domestic strife over the Vietnam War and racial issues intensified, many of the middle-class boomers, on the brink of entering, if not the Army itself, then the ranks of a deeply divided and distressed American adulthood, innocently tried to hold off that entry by a kind of collective ritual at Woodstock and at innumerable lesser Woodstocks all over the country.

The "No rain! No rain!" chant sung by the crowd at Woodstock to ward off the storm spoke metaphoric volumes. Many of us wanted to believe we could will things better by fervently affirming and savoring our sense of community.

8   This psychological "Woodstock Nation," while initially nurtured by the media's attention, remained all too dependent upon the media's support. When media pundits used the violent December 1969 Altamont concert in California to declare a neat end to the ephemeral "Woodstock era" of peace and love, the bright reflection of youthful community rapidly disintegrated.

The depressing spiral of the early '70s and the Vietnam denouement were upon us, and the myth of Woodstock, like the decade's earlier Camelot of the Kennedy presidency, began to pass into the shining realm of nostalgia. "Bye, bye, Miss American pie."

This is the Woodstock that 22 years later I find myself attempting to explain to students in the abstracted, anecdotal and generally distorted form that such myths take on in classrooms. The final irony, I suppose, is the exasperation among some of today's younger generation with the recycling of '60s nostalgia in magazines, books, movies, etc. They complain that their youth is somehow overshadowed by that of their parents. They resent being told that they "missed" Woodstock. It's a legitimate complaint.

But it is also true that today's young share in culture and outlook much more with their middle-aged boomer parents than did the boomers with their parents. So a full and honest appraisal of the boomers' youthful idealistic aspirations may have some genuine social utility yet.

12   The America of the '90s is a nation still painfully divided by issues of race, sex, poverty and morality. The Persian Gulf war has in no way alleviated the host of American social problems and anxieties so intimately associated with what has become loosely referred to as the "Vietnam syndrome."

Among today's youth the prospect of entering adulthood in our society may well elicit as much apprehension as it did two decades ago. A fuller understanding of Woodstock, certainly, will not solve these problems. But it might serve as a useful reminder of our national ideal of a compassionate community, of the all-inclusive "us." Who knows, it may even rekindle some enthusiasm for it among the disheartened of the boomer generation.

And how might reconsideration of a 22-year-old music festival serve today's youth, who while maybe more pragmatic and media savvy than their parents were, appear also more circumspect in their expectations of America? Perhaps, amid today's troubles, it will lead them to discover for themselves the need to dream Walt Whitman's, the Rev. Dr. Martin Luther King's and Woodie Guthrie's optimistic American dreams, and to find their own Woodstocks.

READER RESPONSE

Explore your response to Doloff's comment in paragraph 10 that today's younger generation is exasperated "with the recycling of '60s nostalgia in magazines, books, movies, etc." How do you respond to his statement in paragraph 11 that today's youth have much more in common with their parents than their parents did with their own parents?

QUESTIONS FOR DISCUSSION

1. According to Doloff, what did the twentieth anniversary celebration of the Woodstock Music Festival fail to acknowledge?
2. Explain what Doloff means when he writes: "Despite its commercial aspects, Woodstock momentarily embodied the deeply characteristic American dream of a spiritual community" (paragraph 3)? To what extent do you agree with his assessment of this aspect of the American character?
3. What role does Doloff believe the media played in perpetuating the image of "Woodstock Nation"? What image does the phrase "Woodstock Nation" evoke for you?
4. What useful connections does Doloff believe can be made between the Woodstock generation and today's generation of young people? That is, how does he answer the question he poses at the beginning of his final paragraph: "And how might a reconsideration of a 22-year-old music festival serve today's youth"?

Learning the Hard Way
Michael Denne

Michael Denne was an inmate at Folsom State Prison in Sacramento, California, serving a sentence of eight years for hit-and-run driving and driving while intoxicated, when wrote the following essay for the "My Turn" column of the November 23, 1998, issue of Newsweek *magazine.*

It was after midnight when the police came for me. I was standing in the kitchen, stunned, not sure what had just happened or what to do about it. But it all became surrealistically clear as I was led from my own house in handcuffs, bathed in flashing colored lights. Having gone only a few hundred yards on our way to the station, we came upon more flashing lights at the scene of the accident. "See that," the cop snapped at me. "You did that."

It's not easy being a menace to society, especially when you always thought you were one of the good guys. But that same society takes a particularly dim view of those of us who drink to excess, crash our cars and send innocent people to the emergency room with life-threatening injuries. So dim a view, in fact, that they send us to prison.

Before you despise me too much, though, I'd like to report that no one was crippled or killed as a result of my selfish stupidity. Two teenagers did, however, spend a few weeks in the hospital and several months recovering, as they both suffered head trauma from my Chevy Blazer's broadsiding their Mazda RX-7. Nine months after the crash, at my sentencing hearing, the victims appeared as two walking, talking, healthy-looking young adults. Their injuries lingered, though, in the form of a loss of hearing in one ear (for the girl), which may or may not come back, and memory loss (for the boy, who also broke his jaw and was semicomatose for a few weeks). Not quite as good as new, but awfully close and improving, considering their condition that first night in intensive care.

4 I offer no excuse because there isn't one. What I did was the height of irresponsibility. Like everyone else, I've seen hit-and-run accidents on television and in the newspapers and wondered how the drivers could leave the victims behind. Well, I did, and I still don't know. It's called hit and run, but I didn't run anywhere. I wasn't wearing a seat belt and I'd slammed my head into the windshield. I was shocked, and so close to home I thought that if I could just get to that sanctuary, I'd know what to do and everything would be all right. But somewhere in my beer-soaked brain must have been the fear that generated more concern for myself than for anyone I might have hurt. And I have to live with that.

I've been locked up for more than a year now and have had plenty of time to think. It seems to me that there's a price exacted for every lesson we learn in life, and the cost is rarely proportional to the relative simplicity or complexity of the idea. Consequently, what should have been a no-brainer is quite often the most expensive education we're ever likely to receive. What it cost me to ignore the most ubiquitous warning in the world (the one not to drink and drive) was merely everything: my license, my car, $30,000 in legal fees, a $50,000-a-year job I'd had for 10 years and my freedom are all casualties—with my house not far behind.

For far too many people this subject will forever be anathema, because the lives of their loved ones have been ruined or ended by some recreational inebriate just like me. To them and countless others I got exactly what I deserve, even though an excellent recovery and $530,000 of liability insurance appear to have left the victims in pretty good shape. I'll not portray myself as some drunken Robin Hood, because these people truly suffered, but they are not from wealthy families and now may well have opportunities they otherwise would never have had. And that's good; they deserve it.

I refuse to vilify the "demon" alcohol, because that's not what this is about. It's about responsibility. A few years ago, Miller Brewing Co. promoted an awareness campaign with the slogan "Think when you drink." That's good, but it doesn't go far enough, because we can't think when we drink. It's got to be "Think before you drink"—because as any substance-abuse professional will tell you, judgment is the first faculty that goes.

8   In his book of essays "Fates Worse Than Death," Kurt Vonnegut wrote, "Life without moments of intoxication is not worth a pitcher of spit." Included therein is intoxication from love or joy or the mystery of life itself, but so is, surely, a few belts at the corner bar. I'm no social scientist, but like anyone who's ever taken a college anthropology class, I learned that the society without a way to alter its perception is the exception to the rule. It is not aberrant behavior to celebrate, to alter one's consciousness, and to think that people will or should stop it is naive. But when it has a profoundly negative impact on the lives of others, it is totally unacceptable. In fact, it can be downright criminal.

My negligence was exactly that, though I am innocent of malice, of intent ever to hurt anyone. But it doesn't matter what you mean to do—it matters what you do. And few people know that better than I do.

The probation report said I'd led a respectable life but I should get six years in prison, anyway. The district attorney said I was a decent man and he felt sorry for me, but six years wasn't enough—I should do eight instead. And the judge agreed, but in his benevolence ruled that the extra two years could be served concurrently. There isn't space here to debate the deterrent value of a state prison sentence as opposed to alternative sentences, like making restitution to the injured through a work-furlough program or explaining the consequences of drinking and driving to high-school students, punishments that contain real value for the victims and the community.

That I deserve to be punished is clearer to me than it ever could be to anyone who hasn't lived it. Until you wake up in a jail cell, not knowing whether the people now in the hospital will be permanently disfigured (or will cease to be altogether) as a result of your recklessness, you can't imagine how it feels. The weight of it is oppressive.

12   I'm ashamed to have to lend my name to some of the most loathsome behavior known, but not so much so that it won't put forth a face and a fair warning to those who still choose to drink and drive: thinking it could never happen to you is your first mistake—and it only gets worse from there. For everyone.

READER RESPONSE

Do you feel any sympathy for Denne? Do you think he has received the punishment he deserves?

QUESTIONS FOR DISCUSSION

1. Denne writes in paragraph 10 that he does not have space "to debate the deterrent value of a state prison sentence as opposed to alternative sentences," but he does mention a couple of alternatives he would argue in such a debate. What do you think of the alternatives he suggests? Where would you position yourself in such a debate? Why?
2. Denne says that he does not blame alcohol for what he has done. What does he blame instead? Do you agree with him?
3. How do you think Denne wants readers to view him? Does he want your sympathy? Is he trying to excuse what he has done?
4. What has Denne "learn[ed] the hard way"?

Shooting an Elephant
George Orwell

George Orwell is the pseudonym of Eric Blair (1903–1950). Born in Bengal, India, he was brought up in England and educated at Eton. He served five years as a British policeman in Burma, with a growing disgust for the goals and values of British imperialism, before returning to England to become a writer. In 1936, he fought with the Loyalists in the Spanish Civil War. Orwell is best known for Animal Farm *(1945) and* 1984 *(1949), novels that reflect his hatred of totalitarianism and his sympathy for the oppressed. "Shooting an Elephant" is from* Shooting an Elephant and Other Essays *(1950).*

In Moulmein, in lower Burma, I was hated by large numbers of people—the only time in my life that I have been important enough for this to happen to me. I was subdivisional police officer of the town, and in an aimless, petty kind of way anti-European feeling was very bitter. No one had the guts to raise a riot, but if a European woman went through the bazaars alone somebody would probably spit betel juice over her dress. As a police officer I was an obvious target and was baited whenever it seemed safe to do so. When a nimble

Burman tripped me up on the football field and the referee (another Burman) looked the other way, the crowd yelled with hideous laughter. This happened more than once. In the end the sneering yellow faces of young men that met me everywhere, the insults hooted after me when I was at a safe distance, got badly on my nerves. The young Buddhist priests were the worst of all. There were several thousands of them in the town and none of them seemed to have anything to do except stand on street corners and jeer at Europeans.

All this was perplexing and upsetting. For at that time I had already made up my mind that imperialism was an evil thing and the sooner I chucked up my job and got out of there the better. Theoretically—and secretly, of course—I was all for the Burmese and all against their oppressors, the British. As for the job I was doing, I hated it more bitterly than I can perhaps make clear. In a job like that you see the dirty work of Empire at close quarters. The wretched prisoners huddling in the stinking cages of the lockups, the gray, cowed faces of the long-term convicts, the scarred buttocks of the men who had been flogged with bamboos—all these oppressed me with an intolerable sense of guilt. But I could get nothing into perspective. I was young and ill educated and I had had to think out my problems in the utter silence that is imposed on every Englishman in the East. I did not even know that the British Empire is dying, still less did I know that it is a great deal better than the younger empires that are going to supplant it. All I knew was that I was stuck between my hatred of the empire I served and my rage against the evil-spirited little beasts who tried to make my job impossible. With one part of my mind I thought of the British Raj as an unbreakable tyranny, as something clamped down, in *saecula saeculorum,* upon the will of prostrate peoples; with another part I thought that the greatest joy in the world would be to drive a bayonet into a Buddhist priest's guts. Feelings like these are the normal by-products of imperialism; ask any Anglo-Indian official, if you can catch him off duty.

One day something happened which in a roundabout way was enlightening. It was a tiny incident in itself; but it gave me a better glimpse than I had had before of the real nature of imperialism—the real motives for which despotic governments act. Early one morning the sub-inspector at a police station at the other end of the town rang me up on the 'phone and said that an elephant was ravaging the bazaar. Would I please come and do something about it? I did not know what I could do, but I wanted to see what was happening and I got on to a pony and started out. I took my rifle, an old .44 Winchester and much too small to kill an elephant, but I thought the noise might be useful *in terrorem.* Various Burmans stopped me on the way and told me about the elephant's doings. It was not, of course, a wild elephant, but a tame one which had gone "must." It had been chained up, as tame elephants always are when their attack of "must" is due, but on the previous night it had broken its chain and escaped. Its mahout, the only person who could manage it when it was in that state, had set out in pursuit, but had taken the wrong direction and was now twelve hours' journey away, and in the morning the elephant had suddenly reappeared in town. The Burmese population had no weapons and were quite helpless against it. It had already destroyed somebody's bamboo hut, killed a cow and raided some fruitstalls and devoured the stock; also it had met the municipal rubbish van and, when the driver jumped out and took to his heels, had turned the van over and inflicted violences upon it.

4   The Burmese sub-inspector and some Indian constables were waiting for me in the quarter where the elephant had been seen. It was a very poor quarter, a labyrinth of squalid bamboo huts, thatched with palm-leaf, winding all over a steep hillside. I remember that it was a cloudy, stuffy morning at the beginning of the rains. We began questioning the people as to where the elephant had gone and, as usual, failed to get any definite information. That is invariably the case in the East; a story always sounds clear enough at a distance, but the nearer you get to the scene of events the vaguer it becomes. Some of the people said that the elephant had gone in one direction, some said that he had gone in another, some professed not even to have heard of any elephant. I had almost made up my mind that the whole story was a pack of lies, when we heard yells a little distance away. There was a loud, scandalized cry of "Go away, child! Go away this instant!" and an old woman with a switch in her hand came round the corner of a hut, violently shooing away a crowd of naked children. Some more women followed, clicking their tongues and exclaiming; evidently there was something that the children ought not to have seen. I rounded the hut and saw a man's dead body sprawling in the mud. He was an Indian, a black Dravidian coolie, almost naked, and he could not have been dead many minutes. The people said that the elephant had come suddenly upon him round the corner of the hut, caught him with its trunk, put its foot on his back and ground him into the earth. This was the rainy season and the ground was soft, and his face had scored a trench a foot deep and a couple of yards long. He was lying on his belly with arms crucified and head sharply twisted on one side. His face was coated with mud, the eyes wide open, the teeth bared and grinning with an expression of unendurable agony. (Never tell me, by the way, that the dead look peaceful. Most of the corpses I have seen looked devilish.) The friction of the great beast's foot had stripped the skin from his back as neatly as one skins a rabbit. As soon as I saw the dead man I sent an orderly to a friend's house nearby to borrow an elephant rifle. I had already sent back the pony, not wanting it to go mad with fright and throw me if it smelt the elephant.

The orderly came back in a few minutes with a rifle and five cartridges, and meanwhile some Burmans had arrived and told us that the elephant was in the paddy fields below, only a few hundred yards away. As I started forward practically the whole population of the quarter flocked out of the houses and followed me. They had seen the rifle and were all shouting excitedly that I was going to shoot the elephant. They had not shown much interest in the elephant when he was merely ravaging their homes, but it was different now that he was going to be shot. It was a bit of fun to them, as it would be to an English crowd; besides they wanted the meat. It made me vaguely uneasy. I had no intention of shooting the elephant—I had merely sent for the rifle to defend myself if necessary—and it is always unnerving to have a crowd following you. I marched down the hill, looking and feeling a fool, with the rifle over my shoulder and an ever-growing army of people jostling at my heels. At the bottom, when you got away from the huts, there was a metalled road and beyond that a miry waste of paddy fields a thousand yards across, not yet ploughed but soggy from the first rains and dotted with coarse grass. The elephant was standing eight yards from the road, his left side toward us. He took not the slightest notice of the crowd's approach. He was tearing up bunches of grass, beating them against his knees to clean them, and stuffing them into his mouth.

I had halted on the road. As soon as I saw the elephant I knew with perfect certainty that I ought not to shoot him. It is a serious matter to shoot a working elephant—it is comparable to destroying a huge and costly piece of machinery—and obviously one ought not to do it if it can possibly be avoided. And at that distance, peacefully eating, the elephant looked no more dangerous than a cow. I thought then and I think now that his attack of "must" was already passing off; in which case he would merely wander harmlessly about until the mahout came back and caught him. Moreover, I did not in the least want to shoot him. I decided that I would watch him for a little while to make sure that he did not turn savage again, and then go home.

But at that moment I glanced round at the crowd that had followed me. It was an immense crowd, two thousand at the least and growing every minute. It blocked the road for a long distance on either side. I looked at the sea of yellow faces above the garish clothes—faces all happy and excited over this bit of fun, all certain that the elephant was going to be shot. They were watching me as they would watch a conjurer about to perform a trick. They did not like me, but with the magical rifle in my hands I was momentarily worth watching. And suddenly I realized that I should have to shoot the elephant after all. The people expected it of me and I had got to do it; I could feel their two thousand wills pressing me forward, irresistibly. And it was at this moment, as I stood there with the rifle in my hands, that I first grasped the hollowness, the futility of the white man's dominion in the East. Here was I, the white man with his gun, standing in front of the unarmed native crowd—seemingly the leading actor of the piece; but in reality I was only an absurd puppet pushed to and fro by the will of those yellow faces behind. I perceived in this moment that when the white man turns tyrant it is his own freedom that he destroys. He becomes a sort of hollow, posing dummy, the conventionalized figure of a sahib. For it is the condition of his rule that he shall spend his life in trying to impress the "natives," and so in every crisis he has got to do what the "natives" expect of him. He wears a mask, and his face grows to fit it. I had got to shoot the elephant. I had committed myself to doing it when I sent for the rifle. A sahib has got to act like a sahib; he has got to appear resolute, to know his own mind and do definite things. To come all that way, rifle in hand, with two thousand people marching at my heels, and then to trail feebly away, having done nothing—no, that was impossible. The crowd would laugh at me. And my whole life, every white man's life in the East, was one long struggle not to be laughed at.

8   But I did not want to shoot the elephant. I watched him beating his bunch of grass against his knees with that preoccupied grandmotherly air that elephants have. It seemed to me that it would be murder to shoot him. At that age I was not squeamish about killing animals, but I had never shot an elephant and never wanted to. (Somehow it always seems worse to kill a *large* animal.) Besides, there was the beast's owner to be considered. Alive, the elephant was worth at least a hundred pounds; dead, he would only be worth the value of his tusks, five pounds, possibly. But I had got to act quickly. I turned to some experienced-looking Burmans who had been there when we arrived, and asked them how the elephant had been behaving. They all said the same thing: he took no notice of you if you left him alone, but he might charge if you went too close to him.

It was perfectly clear to me what I ought to do. I ought to walk up to within, say, twenty-five yards of the elephant and test his behavior. If he charged, I could shoot; if he took no notice of me, it would be safe to leave him until the mahout came back. But also I knew that I was going to do no such thing. I was a poor shot with a rifle and the ground was soft mud into which one would sink at every step. If the elephant charged and I missed him, I should have about as much chance as a toad under a steamroller. But even then I was not thinking particularly of my own skin, only of the watchful yellow faces behind. For at that moment, with the crowd watching me, I was not afraid in the ordinary sense, as I would have been if I had been alone. A white man mustn't be frightened in front of "natives"; and so, in general, he isn't frightened. The sole thought in my mind was that if anything went wrong those two thousand Burmans would see me pursued, caught, trampled on, and reduced to a grinning corpse like that Indian up the hill. And if that happened it was quite probable that some of them would laugh. That would never do. There was only one alternative. I shoved the cartridges into the magazine and lay down on the road to get a better aim.

The crowd grew very still, and a deep, low, happy sigh, as of people who see the theater curtain go up at last, breathed from innumerable throats. They were going to have their bit of fun after all. The rifle was a beautiful German thing with cross-hair sights. I did not then know that in shooting an elephant one would shoot to cut an imaginary bar running from ear-hole to ear-hole. I ought, therefore, as the elephant was sideways on, to have aimed straight at his ear-hole; actually I aimed several inches in front of this, thinking the brain would be further forward.

When I pulled the trigger I did not hear the bang or feel the kick—one never does when a shot goes home—but I heard the devilish roar of glee that went up from the crowd. In that instant, in too short a time, one would have thought, even for the bullet to get there, a mysterious, terrible change had come over the elephant. He neither stirred, nor fell, but every line of his body had altered. He looked suddenly stricken, shrunken, immensely old, as though the frightful impact of the bullet had paralyzed him without knocking him down. At last, after what seemed a long time—it might have been five seconds, I dare say—he sagged flabbily to his knees. His mouth slobbered. An enormous senility seemed to have settled upon him. One could have imagined him thousands of years old. I fired again into the same spot. At the second shot he did not collapse but climbed with desperate slowness to his feet and stood weakly upright, with legs sagging and head drooping. I fired a third time. That was the shot that did for him. You could see the agony of it jolt his whole body and knock the last remnant of strength from his legs. But in falling he seemed for a moment to rise, for as his hind legs collapsed beneath him he seemed to tower upward like a huge rock toppling, his trunk reaching skyward like a tree. He trumpeted, for the first and only time. And then down he came, his belly toward me, with a crash that seemed to shake the ground even where I lay.

12   I got up. The Burmans were already racing past me across the mud. It was obvious that the elephant would never rise again, but he was not dead. He was breathing very rhythmically with long rattling gasps, his great mound of a side painfully rising and falling. His mouth was wide open—I could see far down into caverns of pale pink throat. I waited a long time for him to die, but his breathing did not weaken. Finally I fired my two remaining shots into the spot where I thought his heart must be. The thick blood welled out of him like red velvet, but still he did not die. His body did not even jerk when the shots hit him, the tortured breathing continued without a pause. He was dying, very slowly and in great agony, but in some world remote from me where not even a bullet could damage him further. I felt that I had got to put an end to that dreadful noise. It seemed dreadful to see the great beast lying there, powerless to move and yet powerless to die, and not even to be able to finish him. I sent back for my small rifle and poured shot after shot into his heart and down his throat. They seemed to make no impression. The tortured gasps continued as steadily as the ticking of a clock.

In the end I could not stand it any longer and went away. I heard later that it took him half an hour to die. Burmans were bringing dahs and baskets even before I left, and I was told they had stripped his body almost to the bones by the afternoon.

Afterward, of course, there were endless discussions about the shooting of the elephant. The owner was furious, but he was only an Indian and could do nothing. Besides, legally I had done the right thing, for a mad elephant has to be killed, like a mad dog, if its owner fails to control it. Among the Europeans opinion was divided. The older men said I was right, the younger men said it was a damn shame to shoot an elephant for killing a coolie, because an elephant was worth more than any damn Coringhee coolie. And afterward I was very glad that the coolie had been killed; it put me legally in the right and it gave me a sufficient pretext for shooting the elephant. I often wondered whether any of the others grasped that I had done it solely to avoid looking a fool.

READER RESPONSE

What do you think of Orwell's shooting the elephant simply to save face? Do you think you would have done the same under the circumstances?

QUESTIONS FOR DISCUSSION

1. This essay is written from the perspective of a mature writer looking back on something that happened to him many years before. What is Orwell's attitude toward what he did at age 19? Does he attempt to excuse his behavior? Is he sympathetic toward or critical of his "young and ill educated" self (paragraph 2)?
2. What was the British Raj (paragraph 2)? What does Orwell learn about "the nature of imperialism" (paragraph 3)? What evidence of its evils does Orwell give?
3. In paragraph 2, Orwell says that he has mixed feelings toward the Burmese. On the one hand, he "was all for the Burmese and all against their oppressors, the British." On the other hand, he "thought that the greatest joy in the world would be to drive a bayonet into a Buddhist priest's guts." Explain why he has these ambivalent feelings.
4. Orwell's essay contains some graphic descriptions of two deaths, the coolie's and the elephant's. To which death does Orwell devote more attention? Why? What does he mean in his concluding paragraph when he writes, "And afterward I was very glad that the coolie had been killed"?
5. Orwell says in paragraph 8 that he did not want to shoot the elephant. It seemed to him "that it would be murder to shoot him." Why, then, does Orwell shoot the elephant? Explain as fully as possible the dilemma of Orwell's situation.

The Story of an Hour
Kate Chopin

Kate Chopin (1851–1904) was born in St. Louis, the daughter of an Irish immigrant father who died in a train wreck when she was four. When she was eighteen, she visited New Orleans, where she met and two years later married Oscar Chopin. After her husband's death from swamp fever in 1882, Chopin and her six children returned to St. Louis, where she began writing fiction to support her family. Her first novel, At Fault *(1890), was followed by two collections of short stories,* Bayou Folk *(1894) and* A Night in Acadia *(1897). Although her previous work had been*

well received, her most famous novel, The Awakening *(1899),
was widely criticized and denounced as "immoral." Chopin's fiction often features women who attempt to balance personal
freedom with the demands of marriage, motherhood, and
society.*

Knowing that Mrs. Mallard was afflicted with a heart trouble, great care was
taken to break to her as gently as possible the news of her husband's death.

It was her sister Josephine who told her, in broken sentences; veiled
hints that revealed in half concealing. Her husband's friend Richards was
there, too, near her. It was he who had been in the newspaper office when intelligence of the railroad disaster was received, with Brently Mallard's name
leading the list of "killed." He had only taken the time to assure himself of its
truth by a second telegram, and had hastened to forestall any less careful, less
tender friend in bearing the sad message.

She did not hear the story as many women have heard the same, with a
paralyzed inability to accept its significance. She wept at once, with sudden,
wild abandonment, in her sister's arms. When the storm of grief had spent itself she went away to her room alone. She would have no one follow her.

There stood, facing the open window, a comfortable, roomy armchair.
Into this she sank, pressed down by a physical exhaustion that haunted her
body and seemed to reach into her soul.

She could see in the open square before her house the tops of trees that
were all aquiver with the new spring life. The delicious breath of rain was in
the air. In the street below a peddler was crying his wares. The notes of a distant song which some one was singing reached her faintly, and countless spar-
rows were twittering in the eaves.

There were patches of blue sky showing here and there through the
clouds that had met and piled one above the other in the west facing her
window.

She sat with her head thrown back upon the cushion of the chair, quite
motionless, except when a sob came up into her throat and shook her, as a
child who had cried itself to sleep continues to sob in its dreams.

She was young, with a fair, calm face, whose lines bespoke repression
and even a certain strength. But now there was a dull stare in her eyes, whose
gaze was fixed away off yonder on one of those patches of blue sky. It was not
a glance of reflection, but rather indicated a suspension of intelligent thought.

There was something coming to her and she was waiting for it, fearfully.
What was it? She did not know; it was too subtle and elusive to name. But she
felt it, creeping out of the sky, reaching toward her through the sounds, the
scents, the color that filled the air.

Now her bosom rose and fell tumultuously. She was beginning to recognize this thing that was approaching to possess her, and she was striving to
beat it back with her will—as powerless as her two white slender hands
would have been.

When she abandoned herself a little whispered word escaped her slightly parted lips. She said it over and over under her breath: "free, free, free!" The vacant stare and the look of terror that had followed it went from her eyes. They stayed keen and bright. Her pulses beat fast, and the coursing blood warmed and relaxed every inch of her body.

12   She did not stop to ask if it were or were not a monstrous joy that held her. A clear and exalted perception enabled her to dismiss the suggestion as trivial.

She knew that she would weep again when she saw the kind, tender hands folded in death; the face that had never looked save with love upon her, fixed and gray and dead. But she saw beyond that bitter moment a long procession of years to come that would belong to her absolutely. And she opened and spread her arms out to them in welcome.

There would be no one to live for her during those coming years: she would live for herself. There would be no powerful will bending hers in that blind persistence with which men and women believe they have a right to impose a private will upon a fellow-creature. A kind intention or a cruel intention made the act seem no less a crime as she looked upon it in that brief moment of illumination.

And yet she had loved him—sometimes. Often she had not. What did it matter! What could love, the unsolved mystery, count for in face of this possession of self-assertion which she suddenly recognized as the strongest impulse of her being!

16   "Free! Body and soul free!" she kept whispering.

Josephine was kneeling before the closed door with her lips to the keyhole, imploring for admission. "Louise, open the door! I beg; open the door— you will make yourself ill. What are you doing, Louise? For heaven's sake open the door."

"Go away. I am not making myself ill." No; she was drinking in a very elixir of life through that open window.

Her fancy was running riot along those days ahead of her. Spring days, and summer days, and all sorts of days that would be her own. She breathed a quick prayer that life might be long. It was only yesterday she had thought with a shudder that life might be long.

20   She arose at length and opened the door to her sister's importunities. There was a feverish triumph in her eyes, and she carried herself unwittingly like a goddess of Victory. She clasped her sister's waist, and together they descended the stairs. Richards stood waiting for them at the bottom.

Someone was opening the front door with a latchkey. It was Brently Mallard who entered, a little travel-stained, composedly carrying his gripsack and umbrella. He had been far from the scene of accident, and did not even know there had been one. He stood amazed at Josephine's piercing cry; at Richards' quick motion to screen him from the view of his wife.

But Richards was too late.

When the doctors came they said she had died of heart disease—of joy that kills.

READER RESPONSE

Freewrite for a few minutes about your initial response to this story. How do you feel about Louise Mallard's insights into her marriage and her feeling of liberation as she anticipates her future without her husband, especially in light of his "kind, tender hands folded in death" and his "face that had never looked save with love upon her" (paragraph 13)?

QUESTIONS FOR DISCUSSION

1. Find passages that describe Louise Mallard's character and that explain what kind of woman she is. Why does she feel "physical exhaustion" (paragraph 4)? What do you make of the information that her face "bespoke repression" (paragraph 8)? What has she been repressing?
2. What kind of man is Brently Mallard? What role do Josephine and Richards play? How are they like Brently Mallard?
3. Describe as fully as possible what you imagine Louise and Brently Mallard's marriage to have been like. What insights into her marriage does Louise have during the hour she spends alone in her room?
4. In what way is the doctors' conclusion that Louise Mallard "died of heart disease—of joy that kills" (paragraph 23) inaccurate? In what sense is it nonetheless correct? How do symbols and irony reinforce the central theme of the story?

ADDITIONAL SUGGESTIONS FOR WRITING ABOUT INSIGHTS

1. Tell about an occasion during which you experienced the "resolving kind of click" that Frank Conroy writes of in "Think About It: Ways We Know, and Don't."
2. Drawing on Frank Conroy's "Think About It" and your own experiences, define *education*.
3. If you have ever met someone famous, as Frank Conroy did, write an essay about the experience, including what you learned from that person.
4. Using Annie Dillard's technique of telling a story to illustrate a point, write an essay on what you think humans could learn from a particular animal or two.
5. With Pat Mora's "To Gabriella, a Young Writer" in mind, write a paper analyzing your own writing, including what you have learned about the writing process and how you apply it in your own work.
6. Write a letter to Michael Denne in which you respond to his essay, "Learning the Hard Way."
7. Explain a lesson you learned the hard way.

8. Give an account of your own experience, or that of someone you know, with drug use or abuse. Or, explain the effects of drug use or alcoholism on your own family or friends.

9. Analyze the degree to which alcohol or drug abuse is a problem in the high school you attended or in your community.

10. In the manner of George Orwell's "Shooting an Elephant," describe an event or incident that occurred many years ago and about which you have different feelings now. Tell what you did then, and explain your view of it now.

11. Narrate an incident in which you did something you thought was wrong because you did not want to look foolish or lose face in front of others. Describe not only what you did but also your feelings after the incident.

12. If you have ever made a decision to do something at a time when other people thought it was inappropriate, write an essay telling what the decision was, why you made it, and whether you now think it was the right thing to do.

13. Write a story based on Kate Chopin's "The Story of an Hour" in which your central character is the husband rather than the wife.

14. Write an analysis of Kate Chopin's "The Story of an Hour" in which you explore the insights it reveals about the nature of marriage and/or relationships.

15. Drawing on the insights of several selections in this chapter, define *insight* or *self-knowledge*. Illustrate your definition with a single extended example or several shorter ones.

16. Narrate an incident or event that taught you something about yourself, about another person (such as an authority figure, a parent, a relative, or a friend), or about an institution or organization (such as the police, a school, a church, or a club).

Chapter

5

SELF-PERCEPTION

Self-perception is a complicated matter, influenced by a number of factors. How we see ourselves is often strongly linked to the expectations others have of us rather than to a clear understanding or acceptance of ourselves. Indeed, we sometimes project an image that attempts to reflect what we think others see in us. The way we perceive ourselves often differs markedly from the way others see us. Thus, a discussion of self-perception must include consideration of self-knowledge and self-identity as well, for the way we see ourselves is strongly linked with how well we know ourselves. Many of the writers in this section discuss the relationship of other people's perceptions and pre-conceptions to individual self-image. If their perceptions are rooted in stereo types based on our ethnic or cultural background, socioeconomic level, difference from the norm, or physical ability, then we may have a tremendous struggle with self-image, as some of the writers suggest.

The first two essays focus on the effects of physical handicaps and how those features are compounded by other factors. In "You're Short, Besides!," Sucheng Chan explains the obstacles she has had to overcome because of both her physical handicap and her ethnic background. Nancy Mairs, in "On Being a Cripple," details the problems she faces in her daily struggle with a chronic debilitating illness. Writing frankly and honestly about their personal experiences with physical and psychological obstacles, both Chan and Mairs convey strong self-images and a clear understanding of who they are. Then, George Felton takes a humorous look at the matter of self-image in "The Twit Triumphant" by commenting on the ability of weight-loss champion Richard

Simmons to inspire hope and positive self-esteem in overweight people.

Next, two writers discuss the power of words to affect people's self-image. In "What's in a Name?," Lini S. Kadaba explores the subject of names, focusing on why people change their names. Names have enormous power, especially our family names. As Kadaba writes, "Names connect us to family. Names influence others' perception of us. Names mark us." Following Kadaba's essay, Rebecca Thomas Kirkendall protests the belittling of rural people in her commentary "Who's a Hillbilly?" As a person who grew up in the Ozarks, she objects to the unflattering stereotypes evoked by the term *hillbilly* and suggests that the current national interest in all things country does nothing to dispel the negative image of the word.

Noel Perrin, in "The Androgynous Male," describes his self-image in terms of how he does not meet traditional sex-role expectations for men in U.S. society. Secure in himself, he explains the positive benefits of the choices he has made and of the personal characteristics that, at times, draw surprised and even suspicious reactions from others. Certainly, Brent Staples, in "Just Walk on By: A Black Man Ponders His Power to Alter Public Space," is aware of the way in which people see him. Like Perrin, Staples addresses the matter of America's definition of manhood, but he is more interested in how his skin color alone affects the behavior of people around him.

The chapter ends with two excerpts from Sandra Cisneros's *House on Mango Street,* a series of short, interconnected vignettes based on her own experiences growing up. In "The House on Mango Street," which opens the collection, Cisneros introduces Esperanza, a poor, Latina adolescent who wants a room of her own and a house she can be proud of. The theme of self-identity continues with "My Name," in which Esperanza explores the variety of meanings associated with her name and its appropriateness to the way she sees herself.

1. Discuss the various reasons why people pierce their bodies.
2. Why do you think piercing and other forms of body modification are so popular among young people?

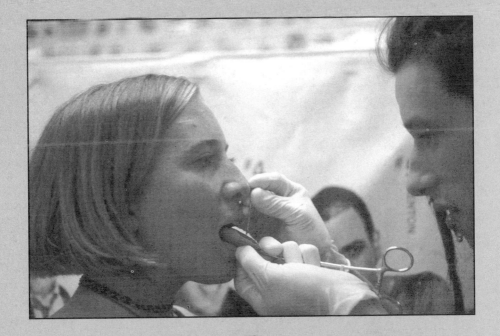

1. Looking at the photo of the man in the wheelchair race, what emotions do you imagine he is experiencing? How do you imagine he feels about himself?
2. What are some issues associated with being physically challenged, particularly in relation to of self-perception? What self-image issues might physically challenged and able-bodied persons have in common?

You're Short, Besides!

Sucheng Chan

*Sucheng Chang is Professor of Asian-American Studies and
Global Studies at the University of California, Santa Barbara.
She has published eleven books and won numerous awards for
her scholarship. She is the recipient of two distinguished teaching
awards and the founding editor of the Asian-American History
and Culture series published by Temple University Press. This
1989 essay is from* Making Waves: An Anthology of Writings by and
About Asian-American Women *(1989).*

When asked to write about being a physically handicapped Asian American
woman, I considered it an insult. After all, my accomplishments are many, yet I
was not asked to write about any of them. Is being handicapped the most
salient feature about me? The fact that it might be in the eyes of others made
me decide to write the essay as requested. I realized that the way I think
about myself may differ considerably from the way others perceive me. And
maybe that's what being physically handicapped is all about.

I was stricken simultaneously with pneumonia and polio at the age of
four. Uncertain whether I had polio of the lungs, seven of the eight doctors
who attended me—all practitioners of Western medicine—told my parents
they should not feel optimistic about my survival. A Chinese fortune teller my
mother consulted also gave a grim prognosis, but for an entirely different reason: I had been stricken because my name was offensive to the gods. My
grandmother had named me "grandchild of wisdom," a name that the fortune
teller said was too presumptuous for a girl. So he advised my parents to
change my name to "chaste virgin." All these pessimistic predictions notwith-
standing, I hung onto life, if only by a thread. For three years, my body was periodically pierced with electric shocks as the muscles of my legs atrophied.
Before my illness, I had been an active, rambunctious, precocious, and very curious child. Being confined to bed was thus a mental agony as great as my
physical pain. Living in war-torn China, I received little medical attention;
physical therapy was unheard of. But I was determined to walk. So one day,
when I was six or seven, I instructed my mother to set up two rows of chairs
to face each other so that I could use them as I would parallel bars. I attempted to walk by holding my body up and moving it forward with my arms
while dragging my legs along behind. Each time I fell, my mother gasped, but I
badgered her until she let me try again. After four nonambulatory years, I finally walked once more by pressing my hands against my thighs so my knees
wouldn't buckle.

My father had been away from home during most of those years because
of the war. When he returned, I had to confront the guilt he felt about my condition. In many East Asian cultures, there is a strong folk belief that a person's

physical state in this life is a reflection of how morally or sinfully he or she lived in previous lives. Furthermore, because of the tendency to view the family as a single unit, it is believed that the fate of one member can be caused by the behavior of another. Some of my father's relatives told him that my illness had doubtless been caused by the wild carousing he did in his youth. A well-meaning but somewhat simple man, my father believed them.

4   Throughout my childhood, he sometimes apologized to me for having to suffer retribution for his former bad behavior. This upset me; it was bad enough that I had to deal with the anguish of not being able to walk, but to have to assuage his guilt as well was a real burden! In other ways, my father was very good to me. He took me out often, carrying me on his shoulders or back, to give me fresh air and sunshine. He did this until I was too large and heavy for him to carry. And ever since I can remember, he has told me that I am pretty.

After getting over her anxieties about my constant falls, my mother decided to send me to school. I had already learned to read some words of Chinese at the age of three by asking my parents to teach me the sounds and meaning of various characters in the daily newspaper. But between the ages of four and eight, I received no education since just staying alive was a full-time job. Much to her chagrin, my mother found no school in Shanghai, where we lived at the time, which would accept me as a student. Finally, as a last resort, she approached the American School which agreed to enroll me only if my family kept an *amah* (a servant who takes care of children) by my side at all times. The tuition at the school was twenty U.S. dollars per month—a huge sum of money during those years of runaway inflation in China—and payable only in U.S. dollars. My family afforded the high cost of tuition and the expense of employing a full-time *amah* for less than a year.

We left China as the Communist forces swept across the country in victory. We found an apartment in Hong Kong across the street from a school run by Seventh-Day Adventists. By that time I could walk a little, so the principal was persuaded to accept me. An *amah* now had to take care of me only during recess when my classmates might easily knock me over as they ran about the playground.

After a year and a half in Hong Kong, we moved to Malaysia, where my father's family had lived for four generations. There I learned to swim in the lovely warm waters of the tropics and fell in love with the sea. On land I was a cripple; in the ocean I could move with the grace of a fish. I liked the freedom of being in the water so much that many years later, when I was a graduate student in Hawaii, I became greatly enamored with a man just because he called me a "Polynesian water nymph."

8   As my overall health improved, my mother became less anxious about all aspects of my life. She did everything possible to enable me to lead as normal a life as possible. I remember how once some of her colleagues in the high school where she taught criticized her for letting me wear short skirts. They

felt my legs should not be exposed to public view. My mother's response was, "All girls her age wear short skirts, so why shouldn't she?"

The years in Malaysia were the happiest of my childhood, even though I was constantly fending off children who ran after me calling, "*Baikah! Baikah!*" ("Cripple! Cripple!" in the Hokkien dialect commonly spoken in Malaysia). The taunts of children mattered little because I was a star pupil. I won one award after another for general scholarship as well as for art and public speaking. Whenever the school had important visitors my teacher always called on me to recite in front of the class.

A significant event that marked me indelibly occurred when I was twelve. That year my school held a music recital and I was one of the students chosen to play the piano. I managed to get up the steps to the stage without any problem, but as I walked across the stage, I fell. Out of the audience, a voice said loudly and clearly, "Ayah! A *baikah* shouldn't be allowed to perform in public." I got up before anyone could get on stage to help me and, with tears streaming uncontrollably down my face, I rushed to the piano and began to play. Beethoven's "Für Elise" had never been played so fiendishly fast before or since, but I managed to finish the whole piece. That I managed to do so made me feel really strong. I never again feared ridicule.

In later years I was reminded of this experience from time to time. During my fourth year as an assistant professor at the University of California at Berkeley, I won a distinguished teaching award. Some weeks later I ran into a former professor who congratulated me enthusiastically. But I said to him, "You know what? I became a distinguished teacher by *limping* across the stage of Dwinelle 155!" (Dwinelle 155 is a large, cold classroom that most colleagues of mine hate to teach in.) I was rude not because I lacked graciousness but because this man, who had told me that my dissertation was the finest piece of work he had read in fifteen years, had nevertheless advised me to eschew a teaching career.

12   "Why?" I asked.

"Your leg . . ." he responded.

"What about my leg?" I said, puzzled.

"Well, how would you feel standing in front of a large lecture class?"

16   "If it makes any difference, I want you to know I've won a number of speech contests in my life, and I am not the least bit self-conscious about speaking in front of large audiences. . . . Look, why don't you write me a letter of recommendation to tell people how brilliant I am, and let *me* worry about my leg!"

This incident is worth recounting only because it illustrates a dilemma that handicapped persons face frequently: those who care about us sometimes get so protective that they unwittingly limit our growth. This former professor of mine had been one of my greatest supporters for two decades. Time after time, he had written glowing letters of recommendation on my behalf. He had spoken as he did because he thought he had my best interests at heart; he thought that if I got a desk job rather than one that required me to be a visible, public person, I would be spared the misery of being stared at.

Americans, for the most part, do not believe as Asians do that physically handicapped persons are morally flawed. But they are equally inept at interacting with those of us who are not able-bodied. Cultural differences in the perception and treatment of handicapped people are most clearly expressed by adults. Children, regardless of where they are, tend to be openly curious about people who do not look "normal." Adults in Asia have no hesitation in asking visibly handicapped people what is wrong with them, often expressing their sympathy with looks of pity, whereas adults in the United States try desperately to be polite by pretending not to notice.

One interesting response I often elicited from people in Asia but have never encountered in America is the attempt to link my physical condition to the state of my soul. Many a time while living and traveling in Asia people would ask me what religion I belonged to. I would tell them that my mother is a devout Buddhist, that my father was baptized a Catholic but has never practiced Catholicism, and that I am an agnostic. Upon hearing this, people would try strenuously to convert me to their religion so that whichever God they believed in could bless me. If I would only attend this church or that temple regularly, they urged, I would surely get cured. Catholics and Buddhists alike have pressed religious medallions into my palm, telling me if I would wear these, the relevant deity or saint would make me well. Once while visiting the tomb of Muhammad Ali Jinnah in Karachi, Pakistan, an old Muslim, after finishing his evening prayers, spotted me, gestured toward my legs, raised his arms heavenward, and began a new round of prayers, apparently on my behalf.

20   In the United States adults who try to act "civilized" towards handicapped people by pretending they don't notice anything unusual sometimes end up ignoring handicapped people completely. In the first few months I lived in this country, I was struck by the fact that whenever children asked me what was the matter with my leg, their adult companions would hurriedly shush them up, furtively look at me, mumble apologies, and rush their children away. After a few months of such encounters, I decided it was my responsibility to educate these people. So I would say to the flustered adults, "It's okay, let the kid ask." Turning to the child, I would say, "When I was a little girl, no bigger than you are, I became sick with something called polio. The muscles in my leg shrank up and I couldn't walk very well. You're much luckier than I am because now you can get a vaccine to make sure you never get my disease. So don't cry when your mommy takes you to get a polio vaccine, okay?" Some adults and their little companions I talked to this way were glad to be rescued from embarrassment; others thought I was strange.

Americans have another way of covering up their uneasiness: they become jovially patronizing. Sometimes when people spot my crutch, they ask if I've had a skiing accident. When I answer that unfortunately it is something less glamorous than that, they say, "I bet you *could* ski if you put your mind to it!" Alternately, at parties where people dance, men who ask me to dance with them get almost belligerent when I decline their invitation. They say, "Of course you can dance if you want to!" Some have given me pep talks about how if I would only develop the right mental attitude, I would have more fun in life.

Different cultural attitudes toward handicapped persons came out clearly during my wedding. My father-in-law, as solid a representative of middle America as could be found, had no qualms about objecting to the marriage on racial grounds, but he could bring himself to comment on my handicap only indirectly. He wondered why his son, who had dated numerous high school and college beauty queens, couldn't marry one of them instead of me. My mother-in-law, a devout Christian, did not share her husband's prejudices, but she worried aloud about whether I could have children. Some Chinese friends of my parents, on the other hand, said that I was lucky to have found such a noble man, one who would marry me despite my handicap. I, for my part, appeared in church in a white lace wedding dress I had designed and made myself—a miniskirt!

How Asian Americans treat me with respect to my handicap tells me a great deal about their degree of acculturation. Recent immigrants behave just like Asians in Asia; those who have been here longer or who grew up in the United States behave more like their white counterparts. I have not encountered any distinctly Asian American pattern of response. What makes the experience of Asian American handicapped people unique is the duality of responses we elicit.

24   Regardless of racial or cultural background, most handicapped people have to learn to find a balance between the desire to attain physical independence and the need to take care of ourselves by not overtaxing our bodies. In my case, I've had to learn to accept the fact that leading an active life has its price. Between the ages of eight and eighteen, I walked without using crutches or braces but the effort caused my right leg to become badly misaligned. Soon after I came to the United States, I had a series of operations to straighten out the bones of my right leg; afterwards though my leg looked straighter and presumably better, I could no longer walk on my own. Initially my doctors fitted me with a brace, but I found wearing one cumbersome and soon gave it up. I could move around much more easily—and more important, faster—by using one crutch. One orthopedist after another warned me that using a single crutch was a bad practice. They were right. Over the years my spine developed a double-S curve and for the last twenty years I have suffered from severe, chronic back pains, which neither conventional physical therapy nor a lighter work load can eliminate.

The only thing that helps my backaches is a good massage, but the soothing effect lasts no more than a day or two. Massages are expensive, especially when one needs them three times a week. So I found a job that pays better, but at which I have to work longer hours, consequently increasing the physical strain on my body—a sort of vicious circle. When I was in my thirties, my doctors told me that if I kept leading the strenuous life I did, I would be in a wheelchair by the time I was forty. They were right on target: I bought myself a wheelchair when I was forty-one. But being the incorrigible character that I am, I use it only when I am *not* in a hurry!

It is a good thing, however, that I am too busy to think much about my handicap or my backaches because pain can physically debilitate as well as cause depression. And there are days when my spirits get rather low. What has helped me is realizing that being handicapped is akin to growing old at an accelerated rate. The contradiction I experience is that often my mind races along as though I'm only twenty while my body feels about sixty. But fifteen or twenty years hence, unlike my peers who will have to cope with aging for the first time, I shall be full of cheer because I will have already fought, and I hope won, that battle long ago.

Beyond learning how to be physically independent and, for some of us, living with chronic pain or other kinds of discomfort, the most difficult thing a handicapped person has to deal with, especially during puberty and early adulthood, is relating to potential sexual partners. Because American culture places so much emphasis on physical attractiveness, a person with a shriveled limb, or a tilt to the head, or the inability to speak clearly, experiences great uncertainty—indeed trauma—when interacting with someone to whom he or she is attracted. My problem was that I was not only physically handicapped, small, and short, but worse, I also wore glasses and was smarter than all the boys I knew! Alas, an insurmountable combination. Yet somehow I have managed to have intimate relationships, all of them with extraordinary men. Not surprisingly, there have also been countless men who broke my heart—men who enjoyed my company "as a friend," but who never found the courage to date or make love with me, although I am sure my experience in this regard is no different from that of many able-bodied persons.

28 The day came when my backaches got in the way of having an active sex life. Surprisingly that development was liberating because I stopped worrying about being attractive to men. No matter how headstrong I had been, I, like most women of my generation, had had the desire to be alluring to men ingrained into me. And that longing had always worked like a brake on my behavior. When what men think of me ceased to be compelling, I gained greater freedom to be myself.

I've often wondered if I would have been a different person had I not been physically handicapped. I really don't know, though there is no question that being handicapped has marked me. But at the same time I usually do not *feel* handicapped—and consequently, I do not *act* handicapped. People are therefore less likely to treat me as a handicapped person. There is no doubt, however, that the lives of my parents, sister, husband, other family members, and some close friends have been affected by my physical condition. They have had to learn not to hide me away at home, not to feel embarrassed by how I look or react to people who say silly things to me, and not to resent me for the extra demands my condition makes on them. Perhaps the hardest thing for those who live with handicapped people is to know when and how to offer help. There are no guidelines applicable to all situations. My advice is, when in doubt, ask, but ask in a way that does not smack of pity or embarrassment. Most important, please don't talk to us as though we are children.

So, has being physically handicapped been a handicap? It all depends on one's attitude. Some years ago, I told a friend that I had once said to an affirmative action compliance officer (somewhat sardonically since I do not believe in the head count approach to affirmative action) that the institution which employs me is triply lucky because it can count me as nonwhite, female and handicapped. He responded, "Why don't you tell them to count you four times? . . . Remember, you're short, besides!"

READER RESPONSE

In the opening paragraph, Chan writes, "I realized that the way I think about myself may differ considerably from the way others perceive me." How do you think others see you? Do you think that others see you differently from the way you see yourself? Explain your answer.

QUESTIONS FOR DISCUSSION

1. According to Chan, how do Eastern and Western beliefs, practices, and ways of viewing her differ?
2. Characterize Chan's attitude toward herself. What does the experience at the piano recital when Chan was twelve tell you about her?
3. Discuss the various obstacles Chan has faced. Which of them are directly related to her handicap? Which of them might anyone, handicapped or not, have to face? How do you think you might face such obstacles if Chan's circumstances were your own?

On Being a Cripple
Nancy Mairs

Nancy Mairs, a teacher and writer, holds a Ph.D. in English from the University of Arizona and has published an award-winning collection of poems, In All the Rooms of the Yellow House *(1984). Her essays have been collected in the following books:* Plaintext *(1986),* Remembering the Bone House: An Erotics of Place and Space *(1989),* Carnal Acts *(1990),* Ordinary Time: Cycles in Marriage, Faith, and Renewal *(1993),* Voice Lessons: On Becoming a (Woman) Writer *(1994), and* Waist-High in the World: A Life

Among the Non-Disabled *(1997). "On Being a Cripple" is taken from* Plaintext.

To escape is nothing. Not to escape is nothing.
LOUISE BOGAN

The other day I was thinking of writing an essay on being a cripple. I was thinking hard in one of the stalls of the women's room in my office building, as I was shoving my shirt into my jeans and tugging up my zipper. Preoccupied, I flushed, picked up my book bag, took my cane down from the hook, and unlatched the door. So many movements unbalanced me, and as I pulled the door open I fell over backward, landing fully clothed on the toilet seat with my legs splayed in front of me: the old beetle-on-its-back routine. Saturday afternoon, the building deserted, I was free to laugh aloud as I wriggled back to my feet, my voice bouncing off the yellowish tiles from all directions. Had anyone been there with me, I'd have been still and faint and hot with chagrin. I decided that it was high time to write the essay.

First, the matter of semantics. I am a cripple. I choose this word to name me. I choose from among several possibilities, the most common of which are "handicapped" and "disabled." I made the choice a number of years ago, without thinking, unaware of my motives for doing so. Even now, I'm not sure what those motives are, but I recognize that they are complex and not entirely flattering. People—crippled or not—wince at the word "cripple," as they do not at "handicapped" or "disabled." Perhaps I want them to wince. I want them to see me as a tough customer, one to whom the fates/gods/viruses have not been kind, but who can face the brutal truth of her existence squarely. As a cripple, I swagger.

But, to be fair to myself, a certain amount of honesty underlies my choice. "Cripple" seems to me a clean word, straightforward and precise. It has an honorable history, having made its first appearance in the Lindisfarne Gospel in the tenth century. As a lover of words, I like the accuracy with which it describes my condition: I have lost the full use of my limbs. "Disabled," by contrast, suggests any incapacity, physical or mental. And I certainly don't like "handicapped," which implies that I have deliberately been put at a disadvantage, by whom I can't imagine (my God is not a Handicapper General), in order to equalize chances in the great race of life. These words seem to me to be moving away from my condition, to be widening the gap between word and reality. Most remote is the recently coined euphemism "differently abled," which partakes of the same semantic hopefulness that transformed countries from "undeveloped" to "underdeveloped," then to "less developed," and finally to "developing" nations. People have continued to starve in those countries during the shift. Some realities do not obey the dictates of language.

4   Mine is one of them. Whatever you call me, I remain crippled. But I don't care what you call me, so long as it isn't "differently abled," which strikes me as pure verbal garbage designed, by its ability to describe anyone, to describe no one. I subscribe to George Orwell's thesis that "the slovenliness of our language makes it easier for us to have foolish thoughts." And I refuse to participate in the degeneration of the language to the extent that I deny that I have lost anything in the course of this calamitous disease; I refuse to pretend that the only differences between you and me are the various ordinary ones that distinguish any one person from another. But call me "disabled" or "handicapped" if you like. I have long since grown accustomed to them; and if they are vague, at least they hint at the truth. Moreover, I use them myself. Society is no readier to accept crippledness than to accept death, war, sex, sweat, or wrinkles. I would never refer to another person as a cripple. It is the word I use to name only myself.

I haven't always been crippled, a fact for which I am soundly grateful. To be whole of limb is, I know from experience, infinitely more pleasant and useful than to be crippled; and if that knowledge leaves me open to bitterness at my loss, the physical soundness I once enjoyed (though I did not enjoy it half enough) is well worth the occasional stab of regret. Though never any good at sports, I was a normally active child and young adult. I climbed trees, played hopscotch, jumped rope, skated, swam, rode my bicycle, sailed. I despised team sports, spending some of the wretchedest afternoons of my life, sweaty and humiliated, behind a field-hockey stick and under a basketball hoop. I tramped alone for miles along the bridle paths that webbed the woods behind the house I grew up in. I swayed through countless dim hours in the arms of one man or another under the scattered shot of light from mirrored balls, and gyrated through countless more as Tab Hunter and Johnny Mathis gave way to the Rolling Stones, Creedence Clearwater Revival, Cream. I walked down the aisle. I pushed baby carriages, changed tires in the rain, marched for peace.

When I was twenty-eight I started to trip and drop things. What at first seemed my natural clumsiness soon became too pronounced to shrug off. I consulted a neurologist, who told me that I had a brain tumor. A battery of tests, increasingly disagreeable, revealed no tumor. About a year and a half later I developed a blurred spot in one eye. I had, at last, the episodes "disseminated in space and time" requisite for a diagnosis: multiple sclerosis. I have never been sorry for the doctor's initial misdiagnosis, however. For almost a week, until the negative results of the tests were in, I thought that I was going to die right away. Every day for the past nearly ten years, then, has been a kind of gift. I accept all gifts.

Multiple sclerosis is a chronic degenerative disease of the central nervous system, in which the myelin that sheathes the nerves is somehow eaten away and scar tissue forms in its place, interrupting the nerves' signals. During its course, which is unpredictable and uncontrollable, one may lose vision, hearing, speech, the ability to walk, control of bladder and/or bowels, strength in any or all extremities, sensitivity to touch, vibration, and/or pain, potency, coordination of movements—the list of possibilities is lengthy and, yes, horrifying. One may also lose one's sense of humor. That's the easiest to lose and the hardest to survive without.

8   In the past ten years, I have sustained some of these losses. Characteristic of MS are sudden attacks, called exacerbations, followed by remissions, and these I have not had. Instead, my disease has been slowly progressive. My left leg is now so weak that I walk with the aid of a brace and a cane; and for distances I use an Amigo, a variation on the electric wheelchair that looks rather like an electrified kiddie car. I no longer have much use of my left hand. Now my right side is weakening as well. I still have the blurred spot in my right eye. Overall, though, I've been lucky so far. My world has, of necessity, been circumscribed by my losses, but the terrain left me has been ample enough for me to continue many of the activities that absorb me: writing, teaching, raising children and cats and plants and snakes, reading, speaking publicly about MS and depression, even playing bridge with people patient and honorable enough to let me scatter cards every which way without sneaking a peek.

Lest I begin to sound like Pollyanna, however, let me say that I don't like having MS. I hate it. My life holds realities—harsh ones, some of them—that no right-minded human being ought to accept without grumbling. One of them is fatigue. I know of no one with MS who does not complain of bone-weariness; in a disease that presents an astonishing variety of symptoms, fatigue seems to be a common factor. I wake up in the morning feeling the way most people do at the end of a bad day, and I take it from there. As a result, I spend a lot of time *in extremis* and, impatient with limitation, I tend to ignore my fatigue until my body breaks down in some way and forces rest. Then I miss picnics, dinner parties, poetry readings, the brief visits of old friends from out of town. The offspring of a puritanical tradition of exceptional venerability, I cannot view these lapses without shame. My life often seems a series of small failures to do as I ought.

I lead, on the whole, an ordinary life, probably rather like the one I would have led had I not had MS. I am lucky that my predilections were already solitary, sedentary, and bookish—unlike the world-famous French cellist I have read about, or the young woman I talked with one long afternoon who wanted only to be a jockey. I had just begun graduate school when I found out something was wrong with me, and I have remained, interminably, a graduate student. Perhaps I would not have if I'd thought I had the stamina to return to a full-time job as a technical editor; but I've enjoyed my studies.

In addition to studying, I teach writing courses. I also teach medical students how to give neurological examinations. I pick up freelance editing jobs here and there. I have raised a foster son and sent him into the world, where he has made me two grandbabies, and I am still escorting my daughter and son through adolescence. I go to Mass every Saturday. I am a superb, if messy, cook. I am also an enthusiastic laundress, capable of sorting a hamper full of clothes into five subtly differentiated piles, but a terrible housekeeper. I can do italic writing and, in an emergency, bathe an oil-soaked cat. I play a fiendish game of Scrabble. When I have the time and the money, I like to sit on my front steps with my husband, drinking Amaretto and smoking a cigar, as we imagine our counterparts in Leningrad and make sure that the sun gets down once more behind the sharp childish scrawl of the Tucson Mountains.

12   This lively plenty has its bleak complement, of course, in all the things I can no longer do. I will never run again, except in dreams, and one day I may have to write that I will never walk again. I like to go camping, but I can't follow George and the children along the trails that wander out of a campsite through the desert or into the mountains. In fact, even on the level I've learned never to check the weather or try to hold a coherent conversation: I need all my attention for my wayward feet. Of late, I have begun to catch myself wondering how people can propel themselves without canes. With only one usable hand, I have to select my clothing with care not so much for style as for ease of ingress and egress, and even so, dressing can be laborious. I can no longer do fine stitchery, pick up babies, play the piano, braid my hair. I am immobilized by acute attacks of depression, which may or may not be physiologically related to MS but are certainly its logical concomitant.

These two elements, the plenty and the privation, are never pure, nor are the delight and wretchedness that accompany them. Almost every pickle that I get into as a result of my weakness and clumsiness—and I get into plenty—is funny as well as maddening and sometimes painful. I recall one May afternoon when a friend and I were going out for a drink after finishing up at school. As we were climbing into opposite sides of my car, chatting, I tripped and fell, flat and hard, onto the asphalt parking lot, my abrupt departure interrupting him in mid-sentence. "Where'd you go?" he called as he came around the back of the car to find me hauling myself up by the door frame. "Are you all right?" Yes, I told him, I was fine, just a bit rattly, and we drove off to find a shady patio and some beer. When I got home an hour or so later, my daughter greeted me with "What have you done to yourself?" I looked down. One elbow of my white turtleneck with the green froggies, one knee of my white trousers, one white kneesock were bloodsoaked. We peeled off the clothes and inspected the damage, which was nasty enough but not alarming. That part wasn't funny: The abrasions took a long time to heal, and one got a little infected. Even so, when I think of my friend talking earnestly, suddenly, to the hot thin air while I dropped from his view as though through a trap door, I find the image as silly as something from a Marx Brothers movie.

I may find it easier than other cripples to amuse myself because I live propped by the acceptance and the assistance and, sometimes, the amusement of those around me. Grocery clerks tear my checks out of my checkbook for me, and sales clerks find chairs to put into dressing rooms when I want to try on clothes. The people I work with make sure I teach at times when I am least likely to be fatigued, in places I can get to, with the materials I need. My students, with one anonymous exception (in an end-of-the-semester evaluation), have been unperturbed by my disability. Some even like it. One was immensely cheered by the information that I paint my own finger-nails; she decided, she told me, that if I could go to such trouble over fine de-tails, she could keep on writing essays. I suppose I became some sort of bright-fingered muse. She wrote good essays, too.

The most important struts in the framework of my existence, of course, are my husband and children. Dismayingly few marriages survive the MS test, and why should they? Most twenty-two- and nineteen-year-olds, like George and me, can vow in clear conscience, after a childhood of chickenpox and summer colds, to keep one another in sickness and in health so long as they both shall live. Not many are equipped for catastrophe: the dismay, the depres-sion, the extra work, the boredom that a degenerative disease can insinuate into a relationship. And our society, with its emphasis on fun and its associa-tion of fun with physical performance, offers little encouragement for a whole spouse to stay with a crippled partner. Children experience similar stresses when faced with a crippled parent, and they are more helpless, since parents and children can't usually get divorced. They hate, of course, to be different from their peers, and the child whose mother is tacking down the aisle of a school auditorium packed with proud parents like a Cape Cod dinghy in a stiff breeze jolly well stands out in a crowd. Deprived of legal divorce, the child can at least deny the mother's disability, even her existence, forgetting to tell her about recitals and PTA meetings, refusing to accompany her to stores or church or the movies, never inviting friends to the house. Many do.

16   But I've been limping along for ten years now, and so far George and the children are still at my left elbow, holding tight. Anne and Matthew vacuum floors and dust furniture and haul trash and rake up dog droppings and but-ton my cuffs and bake lasagne and Toll House cookies with just enough grum-bling so I know that they don't have brain fever. And far from hiding me, they're forever dragging me by racks of fancy clothes or through teeming school corridors, or welcoming gaggles of friends while I'm wandering through the house in Anne's filmy pink babydoll pajamas. George generally calls before he brings someone home, but he does just as many dumb thank-less chores as the children. And they all yell at me, laugh at some of my jokes, write me funny letters when we're apart—in short, treat me as an ordinary human being for whom they have some use. I think they like me. Unless they're faking. . . .

Faking. There's the rub. Tugging at the fringes of my consciousness al-ways is the terror that people are kind to me only because I'm a cripple. My mother almost shattered me once, with that instinct mothers have—blind, I think, in this case, but unerring nonetheless—for striking blows along the fault-lines of their children's hearts, by telling me, in an attack on my selfish-ness, "We all have to make allowances for you, of course, because of the way you are." From the distance of a couple of years, I have to admit that I haven't any idea just what she meant, and I'm not sure that she knew either. She was awfully angry. But at the time, as the words thudded home, I felt my worst fear, suddenly realized. I could bear being called selfish: I am. But I couldn't bear the corroboration that those around me were doing in fact what I'd always suspected them of doing, professing fondness while silently putting up with me because of the way I am. A cripple. I've been a little cracked ever since.

Along with this fear that people are secretly accepting shoddy goods comes a relentless pressure to please—to prove myself worth the burdens I impose, I guess, or to build a substantial account of goodwill against which I may write drafts in times of need. Part of the pressure arises from social expectations. In our society, anyone who deviates from the norm had better find some way to compensate. Like fat people, who are expected to be jolly, cripples must bear their lot meekly and cheerfully. A grumpy cripple isn't playing by the rules. And much of the pressure is self-generated. Early on I vowed that, if I had to have MS, by God I was going to do it well. This is a class act, ladies and gentlemen. No tears, no recriminations, no faint-heartedness.

One way and another, then, I wind up feeling like Tiny Tim, peering over the edge of the table at the Christmas goose, waving my crutch, piping down God's blessing on us all. Only sometimes I don't want to play Tiny Tim. I'd rather be Caliban, a most scurvy monster. Fortunately, at home no one much cares whether I'm a good cripple or a bad cripple as long as I make vichyssoise with fair regularity. One evening several years ago, Anne was reading at the dining-room table while I cooked dinner. As I opened a can of tomatoes, the can slipped in my left hand and juice spattered me and the counter with bloody spots. Fatigued and infuriated, I bellowed, "I'm so sick of being crippled!" Anne glanced at me over the top of her book. "There now," she said, "do you feel better?" "Yes," I said, "yes, I do." She went back to her reading. I felt better. That's about all the attention my scurviness ever gets.

20   Because I hate being crippled, I sometimes hate myself for being a cripple. Over the years I have come to expect—even accept—attacks of violent self-loathing. Luckily, in general our society no longer connects deformity and disease directly with evil (though a charismatic once told me that I have MS because a devil is in me) and so I'm allowed to move largely at will, even among small children. But I'm not sure that this revision of attitude has been particularly helpful. Physical imperfection, even freed of moral disapprobation, still defies and violates the ideal, especially for women, whose confinement in their bodies as objects of desire is far from over. Each age, of course, has its ideal, and I doubt that ours is any better or worse than any other. Today's ideal woman, who lives on the glossy pages of dozens of magazines, seems to be between the ages of eighteen and twenty-five; her hair has body, her teeth flash white, her breath smells minty, her underarms are dry; she has a career but is still a fabulous cook, especially of meals that take less than twenty minutes to prepare; she does not ordinarily appear to have a husband or children; she is trim and deeply tanned; she jogs, swims, plays tennis, rides a bicycle, sails, but does not bowl; she travels widely, even to out-of-the-way places like Finland and Samoa, always in the company of the ideal man, who possesses a nearly identical set of characteristics. There are a few exceptions. Though usually white and often blonde, she may be black, Hispanic, Asian, or Native

American, so long as she is unusually sleek. She may be old, provided she is selling a laxative or is Lauren Bacall. If she is selling a detergent, she may be married and have a flock of strikingly messy children. But she is never a cripple.

Like many women I know, I have always had an uneasy relationship with my body. I was not a popular child, largely, I think now, because I was peculiar: intelligent, intense, moody, shy, given to unexpected actions and inexplicable notions and emotions. But as I entered adolescence, I believed myself unpopular because I was homely: my breasts too flat, my mouth too wide, my hips too narrow, my clothing never quite right in fit or style. I was not, in fact, particularly ugly, old photographs inform me, though I was well off the ideal; but I carried this sense of self-alienation with me into adulthood, where it regenerated in response to the depredations of MS. Even with my brace I walk with a limp so pronounced that, seeing myself on the videotape of a television program on the disabled, I couldn't believe that anything but an inchworm could make progress humping along like that. My shoulders droop and my pelvis thrusts forward as I try to balance myself upright, throwing my frame into a bony S. As a result of contractures, one shoulder is higher than the other and I carry one arm bent in front of me, the fingers curled into a claw. My left arm and leg have wasted into pipe-stems, and I try always to keep them covered. When I think about how my body must look to others, especially to men, to whom I have been trained to display myself, I feel ludicrous, even loathsome.

At my age, however, I don't spend much time thinking about my appearance. The burning egocentricity of adolescence, which assures one that all the world is looking all the time, has passed, thank God, and I'm generally too caught up in what I'm doing to step back, as I used to, and watch myself as though upon a stage. I'm also too old to believe in the accuracy of self-image. I know that I'm not a hideous crone, that in fact, when I'm rested, well dressed, and well made up, I look fine. The self-loathing I feel is neither physically nor intellectually substantial. What I hate is not me but a disease.

I am not a disease.

24   And a disease is not—at least not singlehandedly—going to determine who I am, though at first it seemed to be going to. Adjusting to a chronic incurble illness, I have moved through a process similar to that outlined by Elisabeth Kübler-Ross in *On Death and Dying*. The major difference—and it is far more significant than most people recognize—is that I can't be sure of the outcome, as the terminally ill cancer patient can. Research studies indicate that, with proper medical care, I may achieve a "normal" life span. And in our society, with its vision of death as the ultimate evil, worse even than decrepitude, the response to such news is, "Oh well, at least you're not going to *die*." Are there worse things than dying? I think that there may be.

I think of two women I know, both with MS, both enough older than I to have served me as models. One took to her bed several years ago and has been there ever since. Although she can sit in a high-backed wheelchair, because she is incontinent she refuses to go out at all, even though incontinence pants, which are readily available at any pharmacy, could protect her from embarrassment. Instead, she stays at home and insists that her husband, a small quiet man, a retired civil servant, stay there with her except for a quick weekly foray to the supermarket. The other woman, whose illness was diagnosed when she was eighteen, a nursing student engaged to a young doctor, finished her training, married her doctor, accompanied him to Germany when he was in the service, bore three sons and a daughter, now grown and gone. When she can, she travels with her husband; she plays bridge, embroiders, swims regularly; she works, like me, as a symptomatic-patient instructor of medical students in neurology. Guess which woman I hope to be.

At the beginning, I thought about having MS almost incessantly. And because of the unpredictable course of the disease, my thoughts were always terrified. Each night I'd get into bed wondering whether I'd get out again the next morning, whether I'd be able to see, to speak, to hold a pen between my fingers. Knowing that the day might come when I'd be physically incapable of killing myself, I thought perhaps I ought to do so right away, while I still had the strength. Gradually I came to understand that the Nancy who might one day lie inert under a bedsheet, arms and legs paralyzed, unable to feed or bathe herself, unable to reach out for a gun, a bottle of pills, was not the Nancy I was at present, and that I could not presume to make decisions for that future Nancy, who might well not want in the least to die. Now the only provision I've made for the future Nancy is that when the time comes—and it is likely to come in the form of pneumonia, friend to the weak and the old—I am not to be treated with machines and medications. If she is unable to communicate by then, I hope she will be satisfied with these terms.

Thinking all the time about having MS grew tiresome and intrusive, especially in the large and tragic mode in which I was accustomed to considering my plight. Months and even years went by without catastrophe (at least without one related to MS), and really I was awfully busy, what with George and children and snakes and students and poems, and I hadn't the time, let alone the inclination, to devote myself to being a disease. Too, the richer my life became, the funnier it seemed, as though there were some connection between largesse and laughter, and so my tragic stance began to waver until, even with the aid of a brace and a cane, I couldn't hold it for very long at a time.

28   After several years I was satisfied with my adjustment. I had suffered my grief and fury and terror, I thought, but now I was at ease with my lot. Then one summer day I set out with George and the children across the desert for a vacation in California. Part way to Yuma I became aware that my right leg felt funny. "I think I've had an exacerbation," I told George. "What shall we do?" he asked. "I think we'd better get the hell to California," I said, "because I don't know whether I'll ever make it again." So we went on to San Diego and then to Orange, up the Pacific Coast Highway to Santa Cruz, across to Yosemite, down to Sequoia and Joshua Tree, and so back over the desert to home. It was a fine two-week trip, filled with friends and fair weather, and I wouldn't have missed it for the world, though I did in fact make it back to California two years later. Nor would there have been any point in missing it, since in MS,

once the symptoms have appeared, the neurological damage has been done, and there's no way to predict or prevent that damage.

The incident spoiled my self-satisfaction, however. It renewed my grief and fury and terror, and I learned that one never finishes adjusting to MS. I don't know now why I thought one would. One does not, after all, finish adjusting to life, and MS is simply a fact of my life—not my favorite fact, of course—but as ordinary as my nose and my tropical fish and my yellow Mazda station wagon. It may at any time get worse, but no amount of worry or anticipation can prepare me for a new loss. My life is a lesson in losses. I learn one at a time.

And I had best be patient in the learning, since I'll have to do it like it or not. As any rock fan knows, you can't always get what you want. Particularly when you have MS. You can't, for example, get cured. In recent years researchers and the organizations that fund research have started to pay MS some attention even though it isn't fatal; perhaps they have begun to see that life is something other than a quantitative phenomenon, that one may be very much alive for a very long time in a life that isn't worth living. The researchers have made some progress toward understanding the mechanism of the disease: It may well be an autoimmune reaction triggered by a slow-acting virus. But they are nowhere near its prevention, control, or cure. And most of us want to be cured. Some, unable to accept incurability, grasp at one treatment after another, no matter how bizarre: megavitamin therapy, gluten-free diet, injections of cobra venom, hypothermal suits, lymphocytapheresis, hyperbaric chambers. Many treatments are probably harmless enough, but none are curative.

The absence of a cure often makes MS patients bitter toward their doctors. Doctors are, after all, the priests of modern society, the new shamans, whose business is to heal, and many an MS patient roves from one to another, searching for the "good" doctor who will make him well. Doctors too think of themselves as healers, and for this reason many have trouble dealing with MS patients, whose disease in its intransigence defeats their aims and mocks their skills. Too few doctors, it is true, treat their patients as whole human beings, but the reverse is also true. I have always tried to be gentle with my doctors, who often have more at stake in terms of ego than I do. I may be frustrated, maddened, depressed by the incurability of my disease, but I am not diminished by it, and they are. When I push myself up from my seat in the waiting room and stumble toward them, I incarnate the limitation of their powers. The least I can do is refuse to press on their tenderest spots.

32   This gentleness is part of the reason that I'm not sorry to be a cripple. I didn't have it before. Perhaps I'd have developed it anyway—how could I know such a thing?—and I wish I had more of it, but I'm glad of what I have. It has opened and enriched my life enormously, this sense that my frailty and need must be mirrored in others, that in searching for and shaping a stable core in a life wrenched by change and loss, change and loss, I must recognize the same process, under individual conditions, in the lives around me. I do not deprecate such knowledge, however I've come by it.

All the same, if a cure were found, would I take it? In a minute. I may be a cripple, but I'm only occasionally a loony and never a saint. Anyway, in my brand of theology God doesn't give bonus points for a limp. I'd take a cure; I just don't need one. A friend who also has MS startled me once by asking, "Do you ever say to yourself, 'Why me, Lord?' " "No, Michael, I don't," I told him, "because whenever I try, the only response I can think of is 'Why not?' " If I could make a cosmic deal, who would I put in my place? What in my life would I give up in exchange for sound limbs and a thrilling rush of energy? No one. Nothing. I might as well do the job myself. Now that I'm getting the hang of it.

READER RESPONSE

How do you think you would handle the kind of chronic debilitating illness that Mairs has?

QUESTIONS FOR DISCUSSION

1. Mairs begins by stating that her purpose is to write an essay "on being a cripple." What do you think she hoped to accomplish? How does the opening scene, which takes place in a public toilet, lead Mairs to decide "it was high time to write the essay" (paragraph 1)? How is that setting— both a very private and a public space—appropriate for introducing her essay?

2. Summarize the effects, both positive and negative, that Mairs's illness has had on her. Who are Caliban and Tiny Tim (paragraph 19)? Explain why she prefers to identify with Caliban.

3. Explain the connection Mairs draws between the image of "today's ideal woman" (paragraph 20) and her own self-concept.

4. To what extent do you agree with Mairs that women are "trained to display" themselves (paragraph 21)? Are men also trained to display themselves to others?

The Twit Triumphant

George Felton

George Felton is a professor of English at the Columbus College of Art & Design in Ohio, where he teaches writing and copywriting. He has published a textbook, Advertising: Concept and Copy *(1993), and his essays on pop culture, the media, and his own perplexities have appeared in* Newsweek, The New York Times,

Advertising Age, The Wall Street Journal, *and the* Los Angeles Times.
*He was educated at Duke University, DePauw University (B.A.,
psychology), and Ohio State University (M.A., English). This essay
first appeared in 1995 in* Wisconsin, *the Sunday magazine of*
The Milwaukee Journal.

I love Richard Simmons at last. Or to put it another way, I hate him less,
which amounts to the same thing with Richard. He invites my ridicule and
then co-opts it—so that hating him turns into loving the dogged absurdity of a
man on so relentless a mission, dressed for combat in only itsy-teensy nylon
shorts, that tank top, and those grandma Moses cardigans he throws over the
whole thing. I admire him now as he bounces from one TV studio to another,
emoting his way around America, crossing and uncrossing those unregenerate
thighs, thick as hams, pushing up his sweater sleeves, embracing the fatties, almost always women, and leading them in a good cry over what they are and
what they're trying to become.

Today Richard is appearing on something called "The Jerry Springer
Show," a Cincinnati-based talk show. Jerry, an earnest middle-aged fellow who
reminds you of your insurance agent, troops around the studio audience while
it investigates, badgers, sympathizes with, and acts out in front of that day's
dais of freaks. Right now it's three fat girls (ages 9 and 13) who come out,
drop their sprawl in swivel chairs, and recite their large, sad stories. The last of
them, sensibly enough, turns out to be Richard himself: Upon our return from
commercial, we find him quietly sitting among them.

Richard accepts their stories and tells us his: Almost 300 pounds as a
high school senior in a family of thin people, today he must eat no more than
1400 calories and exercise at least 1½ hours a day or he'll revert to that blub-
bering slob. He then gives us advice about how to lose weight ("Eat less fat.
Move your buns."), advice so staggeringly banal that I could get it off a soup
can, but I feel good about it anyway because what I can't get off the can is
Richard's power of commiseration, his sense of mission. Soon enough he, the
girls, and one of his "projects," a woman who's lost hundreds of pounds—
thanks to Richard and his phone calls—and has wobbled out to tell us about
it, are all bonding like crazy. Eyes lock and shine, voices quaver, it's sweaty and
moist. We tremble on the glistening lip of a breakdown.

4   Jerry intercedes: "This is this man's life, folks. He's not here selling tapes.
This is what he does for his existence. Everyone should go through life saving
other people." And indeed, while Richard mentions his tapes and wears a
"Sweatin' to the Oldies" sleeveless workout T underneath that crazy-quilt cardi-
gan, he doesn't overtly pitch. During a commercial break a slide—"1-800-541-
DIET Richard Simmons"—is put on the screen. I write it down.

Sitting here watching, I'm hungry for the tissue-fest of a good, slobbering
cry myself, the full floodtide of emotion that, with Richard and the fatties,
spills out into something like "We love who we might be and we're crying

about who we used to be and the pain of coming out of our closets and loving and hating ourselves in such a public way and I am you and you are me and we are all together." Hey, didn't the Beatles sing this 25 years ago? Yes, they did, but who says it can only work once?

Today, trapped between my pain and his, I appreciate Richard Simmons at last. I know why we need him: He forgives us, and what's more, he loves us. He's a feel-good faith healer for the transforming power of becoming thin. His Sweatin' to the Oldies videotapes become the hymns, his Deal-a-Meal cards the rosary beads, in an enactment of faith, with Richard the father confessor, the one who accepts our pain.

Like the best of the "here's the one thing that's killing you" people, able to distill the problems of lives-out-of-whack into one marketable principle, Richard locates our suffering in weight but sells the higher spiritual virtues along the way. An hour of him may be a little much, but one thing's for sure: We've seen the higher possibilities. Tomorrow *is* another day. Today is too—lunch itself, in fact—if we look at it right.

8   As the credits roll on "The Jerry Springer Show," Richard's leading the multitudes in the release of "Twist and Shout." Everybody's into it, even Springer, who's stripped off his jacket and is trying to get his spasms to simulate rhythm. After what we've been through, wandering in the wilderness of our overstuffed, underloved lives, we need this. It's uncannily like the close of a televangelist's service where we're invited to surrender our suffering to a higher power, deliver ourselves into the arms of salvation. As Richard raises his arms and lifts those mighty thighs, I see the same plea: "Out" yourselves, America. Accept that you are lost and come on down. It's powerful stuff.

Though I never do quite get off the bed, something inside me kicks free. I feel better about myself. Even though I'm not fat, I've got a plateful of problems, and I can generalize. My life's messes have been so tangled that it's taken a shrink years to unravel them, but one session with Richard, and life feels simple again, the day seems young. I *will* find that one dark spot. It may not be weight, but it's something, and I'll find it, I'll beat it, I'll turn my life around. That's no small gift, however illusory, to be handed before noon.

So I sing the praises of Richard Simmons. He is the twit triumphant, the apotheosis of the Great American boob: Gushy. Ridiculous. An I-Think-I-Can spirit struggling in a Tub o' Pudding body. Richard sells us hope in the form of sweat, self-esteem in the wash of our own tears. He even makes it easy on me. Since his gender is up for grabs—he's androgynous, the male as sweetmeat—I am relieved of the pressure to be a man's man. All I need to do is stand up, shake my bootie, and recite, "I'm a fatty, but I will be free." Though I weigh only 150, fat is where you find it, as Richard knows so well.

While I'm sure he's making plenty with his traveling circus of tapes, talks, diet plans, and infomercials, there's more, and I get a glimpse during the show. At one point, when the talking has stopped and we're going to commercial, the camera lingers on Richard laying his head on the shoulder of one of the girls in an act almost of supplication. He looks for one startling moment like a child at his mother's breast—he, the adult male, nestling up into the bulky neck of this girl—and I realize how much he is nourished by her. She feeds him her fat, and in that moment they are both transfigured.

READER RESPONSE

To what extent is your weight connected to your self-image? That is, do you worry about your weight? Are you happy with your weight? Has your weight ever been a concern to you?

QUESTIONS FOR DISCUSSION

1. In paragraph 7, Felton writes that Richard Simmons "sells the higher spiritual virtues" along with his ability to encourage overweight people to lose weight. What do you understand Felton to mean by "the higher spiritual values"?
2. Why do you think Felton refers to Richard Simmons as "the twit triumphant" (paragraph 10)? What qualities of Richard Simmons does Felton confess to admiring "even though [he's] not fat" himself (paragraph 9)?
3. Discuss the topic of weight in relation to self-image. What do you know about eating disorders and negative body-image issues? What role do you think Richard Simmons and others like him play in helping people to improve their self-esteem?

What's in a Name?
Lini S. Kadaba

Lini S. Kadaba writes for the Philadelphia Inquirer *not only on ethnic and immigration issues but also on health, the workplace, and lifestyle trends. She has published articles in* Technology Review, Woman's World, *and* Boston *magazine. This selection was first published in the December 7, 1997, issue of the* Philadelphia Inquirer.

In his homeland of Greece, the grandfather was a solid Papanastasiou—a name rooted in a centuries-old culture. But when he came to America in the early 1900s, his name, like his life, changed. The grandfather became Annas—a short, easy-to-say, straightforward name. *Annas,* surely that was a good American name.

It was good enough, too, for grandson Christopher Angelo Annas of South Philadelphia, until recently. The thirty-nine-year-old optometrist and second-generation Greek American, in large part, wanted to preserve—and re-claim—his heritage. In March, he legally switched his name to Christopher Angelo Anastasiou, almost all the way back to the original. "I could have changed it to Smith or Andrews—that would be easier to say—but I didn't want to do that," he said.

There was another reason Annas wanted to change his name. His grand-father, in his rush to Americanize his name, was unaware that, mispronounced, his new name sounded in English all too much like a certain part of anatomy. "I started to get a complex," said the grandson. He is now Dr. Anastasiou, though his diplomas on his office wall still bear his old identity. It is not a short name; it could span an ocean. It is not an easy name to say. Some patients call him Dr. Anesthesia now, but the grandson says he doesn't mind.

4   Like Anastasiou, other Americans are trading in their melting-pot names for a smorgasbord of ethnic appellations. In short, American names don't have to be white-bread names; they can be as ethnic as moussaka, tacos, or pita pockets, all of which have become, by some estimates, as American as apple pie. "We have gone from a general notion of assimilation and expunging of for-eignness to an identification and affirmation of it," said Edward Callary, editor of *Names: A Journal of Onomastics* and a professor of English at Northern Illinois University. "I'm Hungarian. I'm Polish. These are my roots. . . . We all like to look at ourselves as a continuation of some line." And so Annas be-comes Anastasiou, a name that embraces ethnicity but still offers a nod to the land of Yankee ingenuity. The original Papanastasiou—a wide load at thirteen letters—was too much for the grandson, and so he dropped *Pap*. Besides, he wanted to make sure his name still started with an *A,* because as a doctor, and no doubt a shrewd businessman, he wanted to remain first on the list of medical providers.

Jane Komarov, thirty-four, a composer who lives in Greenwich Village in New York, changed her name in 1991. She was Jane Komar*ow*. "It's only a change by one letter, but the pronunciation is remarkable. *Komurow*. It's very ambiguous. *Komarov*. It has a very distinctive Russian sound," she said with pride. According to family lore, the name was misspelled at Ellis Island. Her grandparents accepted the misnomer as their name. For Komarov, the return to the correct spelling—and pronunciation—connects her with a richer, more obvious ethnic heritage, she said, noting her name means mosquito. "It de-scribes me better," she said, "although I hope I'm not a mosquito."

The melting pot, it seems, has become more of a stew or goulash or curry as ethnic pride moves to the front burner and we discover our deep ethnic roots in many ways. We are studying our mother tongues. We are danc-ing to folk tunes. We are climbing our family trees.

Pediatrician Andres Valdes-Dapena, forty-five, of Media, Pennsylvania, re-cently completed a ten-week Spanish class at the Berlitz Language Center, in large part, he said, to affirm his heritage. "I have a name that reeks Spanish," he said. But Valdes-Dapena grew up in a "very American household," with little exposure to the language of his Cuban father. Now, the study of Spanish has become a family affair: His wife, though non-Spanish, also took a Berlitz class, and the couple's three children all study the language in school, with the eldest, a college student, planning to major in it.

8   At the Adam Mickiewicz Polish Language School in the Far Northeast, principal Debbie Majka said the forty students, ages four to fourteen, spend Saturday mornings learning the language, folk dances, and customs of Poland, another generation sustaining its history. "There's a value in knowing your heritage, who and what you are, where you come from," she said. The same surely holds true for Italian Americans or Jewish Americans.

Others celebrate their roots by tracing it generations back. According to a 1995 survey for *American Demographics* magazine, 42 million Americans have joined the genealogy hunt. But nothing, perhaps, heralds ethnicity more than a name.

"Names have more than simple label value," said biographer Justin Kaplan, coauthor with his wife, novelist Anne Bernays, of the 1997 *The Language of Names: What We Call Ourselves and Why It Matters*. "They carry the freight of historical association and personal association."

Names connect us to family. Names influence others' perception of us. Names mark us. In *The Language of Names,* Kaplan and Bernays write that "names are profoundly linked to identity and to private as well as public declarations of self and purpose; they have considerable affective power and, however unacknowledged in daily usage, a magical role as well, the power to change people's lives." Said Kaplan, "When you take away a person's name, it's a little like you're taking a person's soul."

12   Who can forget the scene from Alex Haley's *Roots* of the young slave Kunte Kinte refusing, even under the scourge of a whip, to give up his African name? He knew to do so would enslave him all the more. "I always felt an anger ever since I found out the history of America and slavery. That anger just melted away once I changed the name," said a fifty-year-old engineer who lives near Atlanta. It was the 1970s. "It was the great dashiki era," he said, when many blacks took African or Islamic names. The engineer had another impetus: He was expecting his first child.

After much consideration, he created a surname by perusing a map of Africa, picking Kenya as the heart of the continent and adding *ada,* a common ending for East African names. In 1975, he filed a petition in court to legally change his name to Richard Kenyada, citing his "cultural, ethnic and social heritage." Since then, he has never spoken or written his other name. At first, his relatives disliked the new name. "They thought it was a slight against the family." But Kenyada won them over. He named his son Kareem Kenyada. "He came up with a strong identity," the father said.

Lois Fernandez, a founder of the popular Odunde Festival, at times uses the name Omi Yori, her spiritual name given to her in 1994 when she was initiated into Yoruba, a religion and culture found in Nigeria. Earlier this year, the sixty-one-year-old South Philadelphian visited the African country and was given the title *Iyagbogbo Agbaye,* meaning "Chief Mother of the World." The African name grounds her, she said. "We did not come through Ellis Island," she said. "We came here involuntarily. We were stripped of our language, our culture, our names. We had to go back and fetch it."

For others, their names changed as they moved through Ellis Island's bureaucracy. By some accounts, many newcomers were rechristened with supposedly American names during the heyday of immigration at the turn of the century. Officials at the Ellis Island Immigration Museum, however, dispute such stories, blaming ship captains who routinely shortened or simplified names on manifests to ease passage through immigration.

16   Other changes occurred freely, a desire by the immigrant to fit the American mold, "right from your scalp to your toes, and that includes your name," Bernays said. In still other cases, it was a practical necessity in a country that didn't always welcome its newest arrivals with open arms. Whatever the reason, Yitzchak became Hitchcock; Harlampoulas, Harris; Warschawsky, Ward.

Smith, the most common American surname, serves as a linguistic catchall, taking in everything from Schmidt to McGowan, all of which, in their original language, mean someone who works with metal, according to *The Language of Names.* The case of Smith illustrates "the inexorable Americanization of foreign names . . . [that] yield their roughness and irregularity to the tidal wash of American convenience and usage." Pfoersching turns to Pershing; Huber, Hoover; Bjorkegren, Burke. "Often, all that survived of a surname was its initial letter," write Kaplan and Bernays.

By the 1960s, the pressure or desire to assimilate lessened. Take Hollywood—the mecca of name changes, once upon a time. These days, an actor or actress can gain fame with a name as ethnic as Arnold Schwarzenegger, John Travolta, or Richard Dreyfuss. Other well-known people began to take back their ethnic names. David, the son of Irving Wallace, the late best-selling author, discarded his surname in favor of the ethnic original, Wallechinsky.

The very notion of what it means to be American is changing. "American identity is increasingly defined by pluralism rather than by homogeneity," said Henry Giroux, a professor of education and cultural studies at Pennsylvania State University. That shift could lead to a national debate on ways to connect different ethnic groups, or it could create a tribalism, each hyphenated American out for himself. "I think it's a very dangerous time," he said.

20   While a new poll by Princeton Survey Research Associates showed a drop in anti-immigrant feelings since 1993, the nation still grapples with its ethnic melange, evidenced by rollbacks in affirmative action and calls to limit social services to immigrants. At the same time, none of us can escape our past or, apparently, want to. Whatever our race or ethnicity, we continue to dig for our roots and then, with great pride, proclaim the findings to all the world.

Tim Self, fifty-six, a retired carpenter who lives in Quail Valley in Southern California, is president of the Self Seekers, the Self Family Association, which has a Web site dedicated to genealogy. Self traced his name back to the

Viking name, Saewulf. In the mid-1980s, he started using the name Tim Seawolf, adopting the modern spelling. "Names get Americanized and shorter," he said. "I thought it would be nice to stretch it back out, give it more depth."

READER RESPONSE

What do you know of the origins or meaning of your own surname? How do you feel about your name?

QUESTIONS FOR DISCUSSION

1. What do you think of the reasons Kadaba cites for why people change their names? Can you add any other reasons to the list?
2. Explain paragraph 6. What is the "melting pot" Kadaba refers to? In what sense has it "become more of a stew or goulash or curry as ethnic pride moves to the front burner"?
3. Discuss the statements Kadaba makes about the meaning and power of names at the beginning of paragraph 11. In what ways do names "influence others' perception of us"? How do names "mark us"? Do you agree with Kadaba about the influence of names? What does your own name suggest about you and/or your ethnic background?
4. In paragraph 19, Kadaba writes, "The very notion of what it means to be American is changing." Explore your understanding of what she means by that and the extent to which you agree with her. What does Henry Giroux mean by his observation that "it's a very dangerous time" (paragraph 19)?

Who's a Hillbilly?

Rebecca Thomas Kirkendall

Rebecca Thomas Kirkendall was a doctoral student at the University of Missouri when she wrote this essay for the "My Turn" column of the November, 27, 1995, issue of Newsweek.

I once dated a boy who called me a hillbilly because my family has lived in the Ozarks in southern Missouri for several generations. I took offense, not realizing that as a foreigner to the United States he was unaware of the insult. He had meant it as a term of endearment. Nonetheless, it rankled. I started thinking about the implications of the term to me, my family and my community.

While growing up I was often surprised at the way television belittled "country" people. We weren't offended by the self-effacing humor of "The Andy Griffith Show" and "The Beverly Hillbillies" because, after all, Andy and Jed were the heroes of these shows, and through them we could comfortably laugh at ourselves. But as I learned about tolerance and discrimination in school, I wondered why stereotypes of our lifestyle went unexamined. Actors playing "country" people on TV were usually comic foils or objects of ridicule. Every sitcom seemed to have an episode where country cousins, wearing high-water britches and carrying patched suitcases, visited their city friends. And movies like "Deliverance" portrayed country people as backward and violent.

As a child I laughed at the exaggerated accents and dress, never imagining that viewers believed such nonsense. Li'l Abner and the folks on "Hee Haw" were amusing, but we on the farm knew that our work did not lend itself to bare feet, gingham bras and revealing cutoff jeans.

4   Although our nation professes a growing commitment to cultural egalitarianism, we consistently oversimplify and misunderstand our rural culture. Since the 1960s, minority groups in America have fought for acknowledgment, appreciation and, above all, respect. But in our increasingly urban society, rural Americans have been unable to escape from the hillbilly stigma, which is frequently accompanied by labels like "white trash," "redneck" and "hayseed." These negative stereotypes are as unmerciful as they are unfounded.

When I graduated from college, I traveled to a nearby city to find work. There I heard wisecracks about the uneducated rural folk who lived a few hours away. I also took some ribbing about the way I pronounced certain words, such as "tin" instead of "ten" and "agin" for "again." And my expressed desire to return to the country someday was usually met with scorn, bewilderment or genuine concern. Co-workers often asked, "But what is there to *do*?" Thoreau may have gone to Walden Pond, they argued, but he had no intention of staying there.

With the revival of country music in the early 1980s, hillbillyness was again marketable. Country is now big business. Traditional country symbols— Minnie Pearl's hat tag and Daisy Mae—have been eclipsed by the commercially successful Nashville Network, Country Music Television and music theaters in Branson, MO. Many "country" Americans turned the negative stereotype to their advantage and packaged the hillbilly legacy.

Yet with successful commercialization, the authentic elements of America's rural culture have been juxtaposed with the stylized. Country and Western bars are now chic. While I worked in the city, I watched with amazement as my Yuppie friends hurried from their corporate desks to catch the 6:30 line-dancing class at the edge of town. Donning Ralph Lauren jeans and ankle boots, they drove to the trendiest country bars, sat and danced together and poked fun at the local "hicks," who arrived in pickup trucks wearing Wrangler jeans and roper boots.

8   Every summer weekend in Missouri the freeways leading out of our cities are clogged with vacationers. Minivans and RVs edge toward a clear

river with a campground and canoe rental, a quiet lake resort or craft show in a remote Ozark town. Along these popular vacation routes, the rural hosts of convenience stores, gift shops and corner cafés accept condescension along with personal checks and credit cards. On a canoeing trip not long ago, I recall sitting on the transport bus and listening, heartbroken, as a group of tourists ridiculed our bus driver. They yelled, "Hey, plowboy, ain't ya got no ter-backer fer us?" They pointed at the young man's sweat-stained overalls as he, seemingly unaffected by their insults, singlehandedly carried their heavy aluminum canoes to the water's edge. That "plowboy" was one of my high school classmates. He greeted the tourists with a smile and tolerated their derision because he knew tourism brings dollars and jobs.

America is ambivalent when it comes to claiming its rural heritage. We may fantasize about Thomas Jefferson's agrarian vision, but there is no mistaking that ours is an increasingly urban culture. Despite their disdain for farm life—with its manure-caked boots, long hours and inherent financial difficulties—urbanites rush to imitate a sanitized version of this lifestyle. And the individuals who sell this rendition understand that the customer wants to experience hillbillyness without the embarrassment of being mistaken for one.

Through it all, we Ozarkians remind ourselves how fortunate we are to live in a region admired for its blue springs, rolling hills and geological wonders. In spite of the stereotypes, most of us are not uneducated. Nor are we stupid. We are not white supremacists, and we rarely marry our cousins. Our reasons for living in the hills are as complex and diverse as our population. We have a unique sense of community, strong family ties, a beautiful environment and a quiet place for retirement.

We have criminals and radicals, but they are the exception. Our public education system produces successful farmers, doctors, business professionals and educators. Country music is our favorite, but we also like rock and roll, jazz, blues and classical. We read Louis L'Amour, Maya Angelou and the *Wall Street Journal*. And in exchange for living here, many of us put up with a lower standard of living and the occasional gibe from those who persist in calling us "hillbillies."

READER RESPONSE

Explain your understanding of the word *hillbilly*. Do you think of people from the Ozarks and other parts of the rural South as "hillbillies"? Is there a stereotypical image of people from your geographical region?

QUESTIONS FOR DISCUSSION

1. Kirkendall says that certain television shows when she was growing up "belittled 'country' people" (paragraph 2). Does television still portray people from rural areas in a comic, stereotypical way?

2. Kirkendall asserts that Americans "consistently oversimplify and misunderstand our rural culture" (paragraph 4). Discuss the extent to which you agree with her.

3. In her introduction, Kirkendall says that she began "thinking about the implications of the term ['hillbilly']" to herself, her family, and her community. Summarize what the implications of the term are for her. What is her response to those implications?

4. Discuss what you think are the implications of such terms as not only *hillbilly* but also *white trash, redneck,* and *hayseed* for the people to whom those labels are applied. Then, extend your discussion to consider the nature of stereotypes and labels in general. For instance, where do they come from and what harm do they do?

The Androgynous Male
Noel Perrin

Noel Perrin, Adjunct Professor of Environmental Studies at Dartmouth College, has written more than a dozen books and essay collections. Among his books are the following: Amateur Sugar Maker (1972), Vermont: In All Weathers *(1973),* First Person Rural *(1978),* Second Person Rural *(1980),* Third Person Rural *(1983),* Reader's Delight *(1988),* Last Person Rural *(1991),* Solo: Life with an Electric Car *(1994), and* A Child's Delight *(1997). The essay reprinted here first appeared in the "On Men" column in the* New York Times Magazine *in 1984.*

The summer I was 16, I took a train from New York to Steamboat Springs, Colo., where I was going to be assistant horse wrangler at a camp. The trip took three days, and since I was much too shy to talk to strangers, I had quite a lot of time for reading. I read all of "Gone With the Wind." I read all the interesting articles in a couple of magazines I had, and then I went back and read all the dull stuff. I also took all the quizzes, a thing of which magazines were even fuller then than now.

The one that held my undivided attention was called "How Masculine/Feminine Are You?" It consisted of a large number of inkblots. The reader was supposed to decide which of four objects each blot most resembled. The choices might be a cloud, a steam engine, a caterpillar and a sofa.

When I finished the test, I was shocked to find that I was barely masculine at all. On a scale of 1 to 10, I was about 1.2. Me, the horse wrangler? (And not just wrangler, either. That summer, I had to skin a couple of horses that died—the camp owner wanted the hides.)

4   The results of that test were so terrifying to me that for the first time in
my life I did a piece of original analysis. Having unlimited time on the train, I
looked at the "masculine" answers over and over, trying to find what it was
that distinguished real men from people like me—and eventually I discovered
two very simple patterns. It was "masculine" to think the blots looked like
man-made objects, and "feminine" to think they looked like natural objects. It
was masculine to think they looked like things capable of causing harm, and
feminine to think of innocent things.

Even at 16, I had the sense to see that the compilers of the test were using rather limited criteria—maleness and femaleness are both more complicated than *that*—and I breathed a huge sigh of relief. I wasn't necessarily a
wimp, after all.

That the test did reveal something other than the superficiality of its
makers I realized only many years later. What it revealed was that there is a
large class of men and women both, to which I belong, who are essentially androgynous. That doesn't mean we're gay, or low in the appropriate hormones,
or uncomfortable performing the jobs traditionally assigned our sexes. (A few
years after that summer, I was leading troops in combat and, unfashionable as
it now is to admit this, having a very good time. War is exciting. What a pity
the 20th century went and spoiled it with high-tech weapons.)

What it does mean to be spiritually androgynous is a kind of freedom.
Men who are all-male, or he-man, or 100 percent red-blooded Americans, have
a little biological set that causes them to be attracted to physical power, and
probably also to dominance. Maybe even to watching football. I don't say this
to criticize them. Completely masculine men are quite often wonderful people: good husbands, good (though sometimes overwhelming) fathers, good
members of society. Furthermore, they are often so unself-consciously at ease
in the world that other men seek to imitate them. They just aren't as free as us
androgynes. They pretty nearly have to be what they are; we have a range of
choices open.

8   The sad part is that many of us never discover that. Men who are not
100 percent red-blooded Americans—say, those who are only 75 percent red-
blooded—often fail to notice their freedom. They are too busy trying to copy
the he-men ever to realize that men, like women, come in a wide variety of acceptable types. Why this frantic imitation? My answer is mere speculation, but
not casual. I have speculated on this for a long time.

Partly they're just envious of the he-man's unconscious ease. Mostly
they're terrified of finding that there may be something wrong with them
deep down, some weakness at the heart. To avoid discovering that, they spend
their lives acting out the role that the he-man naturally lives. Sad.

One thing that men owe to the women's movement is that this kind of
failure is less common than it used to be. In releasing themselves from the single ideal of the dependent woman, women have more or less incidentally released a lot of men from the single ideal of the dominant male. The one
mistake the feminists have made, I think, is in supposing that *all* men need

this release, or that the world would be a better place if all men achieved it. It wouldn't. It would just be duller.

So far I have been pretty vague about just what the freedom of the androgynous man is. Obviously, it varies with the case. In the case I know best, my own, I can be quite specific. It has freed me most as a parent. I am, among other things, a fairly good natural mother. I like the nurturing role. It makes me feel good to see a child eat—and it turns me to mush to see a 4-year-old holding a glass with both small hands, in order to drink. I even enjoyed sewing patches on the knees of my daughter Amy's Dr. Dentons when she was at the crawling stage. All that pleasure I would have lost if I had made myself stick to the notion of the paternal role that I started with.

12   Or take a smaller and rather ridiculous example. I feel free to kiss cats. Until recently it never occurred to me that I would want to, though my daughters have been doing it all their lives. But my elder daughter is now 22, and in London. Of course, I get to look after her cat while she is gone. He's a big, handsome farm cat named Petrushka, very unsentimental, though used from kittenhood to being kissed on the top of the head by Elizabeth. I've gotten very fond of him (he's the adventurous kind of cat who likes to climb hills with you), and one night I simply felt like kissing him on the top of the head, and did. Why did no one tell me sooner how silky cat fur is?

Then there's my relation to cars. I am completely unembarrassed by my inability to diagnose even minor problems in whatever object I happen to be driving, and don't have to make some insider's remark to mechanics to try to establish that I, too, am a "Man With His Machine."

The same ease extends to household maintenance. I do it, of course. Service people are expensive. But for the last decade my house has functioned better than it used to because I've had the aid of a volume called "Home Repairs Any Woman Can Do," which is pitched just right for people at my technical level. As a youth, I'd as soon have touched such a book as I would have become a transvestite. Even though common sense says there is really nothing sexual whatsoever about fixing sinks.

Or take public emotion. All my life I have easily been moved by certain kinds of voices. The actress Siobhan McKenna's, to take a notable case. Give her an emotional scene in a play, and within 10 words my eyes are full of tears. In boyhood, my great dread was that someone might notice. I struggled manfully, you might say, to suppress this weakness. Now, of course, I don't see it as a weakness at all, but as a kind of fulfillment. I even suspect that the true he-men feel the same way, or one kind of them does, at least, and it's only the poor imitators who have to struggle to repress themselves.

16   Let me come back to the inkblots, with their assumption that masculine equates with machinery and science, and feminine with art and nature. I have no idea whether the right pronoun for God is He, She or It. But this I'm pretty sure of. If God could somehow be induced to take that test, God would not come out macho, and not feminismo, either, but right in the middle. Fellow androgynes, it's a nice thought.

READER RESPONSE

To what extent are you and your friends "androgynous"? To what extent do you feel limited to or free from traditional sex-role expectations? How do you feel about men who are only "75 percent red-blooded" Americans (paragraph 8)?

QUESTIONS FOR DISCUSSION

1. To what extent do you agree with Perrin's definition of the purely masculine personality?
2. Perrin says that men who are not "100 percent red-blooded Americans" (paragraph 8) fail to notice their freedom because they are too busy trying to copy he-men. How does he account for this "frantic imitation" (paragraph 8)? Do you agree with him on this point?
3. Look at the examples of his own behavior that Perrin uses to define androgyny. Can you give other examples of "androgynous" behavior?
4. Summarize the point Perrin makes in his final paragraph, and discuss the extent to which you agree with him.
5. Perrin makes the statement that "there is a large class of men and women both . . . who are essentially androgynous" (paragraph 6). Given his definition of the androgynous male, how do you think he would define the androgynous female?

Just Walk on By: A Black Man Ponders His Power to Alter Public Space
Brent Staples

Brent Staples earned his Ph.D. in psychology from the University of Chicago and went on to hold several teaching positions before accepting a reporter's position at the Chicago Sun-Times. *He later joined the staff of* The New York Times, *where he serves on the editorial board, writing editorials on politics and culture. His memoir,* Parallel Time: Growing Up in Black and White, *was published in 1994. The essay reprinted here first appeared in* Ms. *magazine in 1986.*

My first victim was a woman—white, well dressed, probably in her early twenties. I came upon her late one evening on a deserted street in Hyde Park, a relatively affluent neighborhood in an otherwise mean, impoverished section of Chicago. As I swung onto the avenue behind her, there seemed to be a discreet, uninflammatory distance between us. Not so. She cast back a worried glance. To her, the youngish black man—a broad six feet two inches with a beard and billowing hair, both hands shoved into the pockets of a bulky military jacket—seemed menacingly close. After a few more quick glimpses, she picked up her pace and was soon running in earnest. Within seconds she disappeared into a cross street.

That was more than a decade ago. I was twenty-two years old, a graduate student newly arrived at the University of Chicago. It was in the echo of that terrified woman's footfalls that I first began to know the unwieldy inheritance I'd come into—the ability to alter public space in ugly ways. It was clear that she thought herself the quarry of a mugger, a rapist, or worse. Suffering a bout of insomnia, however, I was stalking sleep, not defenseless wayfarers. As a softy who is scarcely able to take a knife to a raw chicken—let alone hold it to a person's throat—I was surprised, embarrassed, and dismayed all at once. Her flight made me feel like an accomplice in tyranny. It also made it clear that I was indistinguishable from the muggers who occasionally seeped into the area from the surrounding ghetto. That first encounter, and those that followed, signified that a vast, unnerving gulf lay between nighttime pedestrians—particularly women—and me. And I soon gathered that being perceived as dangerous is a hazard in itself. I only needed to turn a corner into a dicey situation, or crowd some frightened, armed person in a foyer somewhere, or make an errant move after being pulled over by a policeman. Where fear and weapons meet—and they often do in urban America—there is always the possibility of death.

In that first year, my first away from my hometown, I was to become thoroughly familiar with the language of fear. At dark, shadowy intersections in Chicago, I could cross in front of a car stopped at a traffic light and elicit the *thunk, thunk, thunk, thunk* of the driver—black, white, male, or female— hammering down the door locks. On less traveled streets after dark, I grew accustomed to but never comfortable with people who crossed to the other side of the street rather than pass me. Then there were the standard unpleasantries with police, doormen, bouncers, cab drivers, and others whose business it is to screen out troublesome individuals *before* there is any nastiness.

4   I moved to New York nearly two years ago and I have remained an avid night walker. In central Manhattan, the near-constant crowd cover minimizes tense one-on-one street encounters. Elsewhere—visiting friends in SoHo, where sidewalks are narrow and tightly spaced buildings shut out the sky— things can get very taut indeed.

Black men have a firm place in New York mugging literature. Norman Podhoretz in his famed (or infamous) 1963 essay, "My Negro Problem—And Ours," recalls growing up in terror of black males; they "were tougher than we were, more ruthless," he writes—and as an adult on the Upper West Side of Manhattan, he continues, he cannot constrain his nervousness when he meets black men on certain streets. Similarly, a decade later, the essayist and novelist Edward Hoagland extols a New York where once "Negro bitterness bore down mainly on other Negroes." Where some see mere panhandlers, Hoagland sees "a mugger who is clearly screwing up his nerve to do more than just *ask* for money." But Hoagland has "the New Yorker's quick-hunch posture for broken-field maneuvering," and the bad guy swerves away.

I often witness that "hunch posture," from women after dark on the war-renlike streets of Brooklyn where I live. They seem to set their faces on neutral and, with their purse straps strung across their chests bandolier style, they forge ahead as though bracing themselves against being tackled. I understand, of course, that the danger they perceive is not a hallucination. Women are particularly vulnerable to street violence, and young black males are drastically overrepresented among the perpetrators of that violence. Yet these truths are no solace against the kind of alienation that comes of being ever the suspect, against being set apart, a fearsome entity with whom pedestrians avoid making eye contact.

It is not altogether clear to me how I reached the ripe old age of twenty-two without being conscious of the lethality nighttime pedestrians attributed to me. Perhaps it was because in Chester, Pennsylvania, the small, angry industrial town where I came of age in the 1960s, I was scarcely noticeable against a backdrop of gang warfare, street knifings, and murders. I grew up one of the good boys, had perhaps a half-dozen fist fights. In retrospect, my shyness of combat has clear sources.

8   Many things go into the making of a young thug. One of those things is the consummation of the male romance with the power to intimidate. An infant discovers that random flailings send the baby bottle flying out of the crib and crashing to the floor. Delighted, the joyful babe repeats those motions again and again, seeking to duplicate the feat. Just so, I recall the points at which some of my boyhood friends were finally seduced by the perception of themselves as tough guys. When a mark cowered and surrendered his money without resistance, myth and reality merged—and paid off. It is, after all, only manly to embrace the power to frighten and intimidate. We, as men, are not supposed to give an inch of our lane on the highway; we are to seize the fighter's edge in work and in play and even in love; we are to be valiant in the face of hostile forces.

Unfortunately, poor and powerless young men seem to take all this non-sense literally. As a boy, I saw countless tough guys locked away; I have since buried several, too. They were babies, really—a teenage cousin, a brother of twenty-two, a childhood friend in his mid-twenties—all gone down in episodes of bravado played out in the streets. I came to doubt the virtues of intimidation early on. I chose, perhaps even unconsciously, to remain a shadow—timid, but a survivor.

The fearsomeness mistakenly attributed to me in public places often has a perilous flavor. The most frightening of these confusions occurred in the late 1970s and early 1980s when I worked as a journalist in Chicago. One day, rushing into the office of a magazine I was writing for with a deadline story in hand, I was mistaken for a burglar. The office manager called security and, with an ad hoc posse, pursued me through the labyrinthine halls, nearly to my editor's door. I had no way of proving who I was. I could only move briskly toward the company of someone who knew me.

Another time I was on assignment for a local paper and killing time before an interview. I entered a jewelry store on the city's affluent Near North Side. The proprietor excused herself and returned with an enormous red Doberman pinscher straining at the end of a leash. She stood, the dog extended toward me, silent to my questions, her eyes bulging nearly out of her head. I took a cursory look around, nodded, and bade her good night. Relatively speaking, however, I never fared as badly as another black male journalist. He went to nearby Waukegan, Illinois, a couple of summers ago to work on a story about a murderer who was born there. Mistaking the reporter for the killer, police hauled him from his car at gunpoint and but for his press credentials would probably have tried to book him. Such episodes are not uncommon. Black men trade tales like this all the time.

12   In "My Negro Problem—And Ours," Podhoretz writes that the hatred he feels for blacks makes itself known to him through a variety of avenues—one being his discomfort with that "special brand of paranoid touchiness" to which he says blacks are prone. No doubt he is speaking here of black men. In time, I learned to smother the rage I felt at so often being taken for a criminal. Not to do so would surely have led to madness—via that special "paranoid touchiness" that so annoyed Podhoretz at the time he wrote the essay.

I began to take precautions to make myself less threatening. I move about with care, particularly late in the evening. I give a wide berth to nervous people on subway platforms during the wee hours, particularly when I have exchanged business clothes for jeans. If I happen to be entering a building behind some people who appear skittish, I may walk by, letting them clear the lobby before I return, so as not to seem to be following them. I have been calm and extremely congenial on those rare occasions when I've been pulled over by the police.

And on late-evening constitutionals along streets less traveled by, I employ what has proved to be an excellent tension-reducing measure: I whistle melodies from Beethoven and Vivaldi and the more popular classical composers. Even steely New Yorkers hunching toward nighttime destinations seem to relax, and occasionally they even join in the tune. Virtually everybody seems to sense that a mugger wouldn't be warbling bright, sunny selections from Vivaldi's Four Seasons. It is my equivalent of the cowbell that hikers wear when they know they are in bear country.

READER RESPONSE

How do you feel about Staples's decision to change his own behavior in public to accommodate other people's fear of him? Would you be willing to do the same? Why, or why not?

QUESTIONS FOR DISCUSSION

1. In what sense is the white woman in paragraph 1 a "victim"? Who else might be considered a victim? Is Staples himself a victim? Explain your answer.
2. What does Staples mean by "the language of fear" (paragraph 3). How does he feel about his effect on other people? Is he angry? Sympathetic? Outraged? Does he consider their fear to be unfair or irrational? Find specific passages to support your answer. Is his experience entirely a racial issue? If not, what else accounts for the fear he elicits from other people?
3. What is your response to the definition of manhood that Staples chose early in life not to embrace? To what degree do you agree with that definition?
4. What is Staples's image of himself? How does it differ from the image that others have of him?

The House on Mango Street
Sandra Cisneros

Sandra Cisneros, novelist, short-story writer, essayist, and poet, is one of the first Hispanic-American writers to achieve commercial success as well as praise from literary scholars and critics. Her most famous work, The House on Mango Street *(1983), is a series of interconnected vignettes or short pieces based on her own experiences growing up in America. As the only daughter among seven children, Cisneros felt pressured to assume a traditional female role. Furthermore, the family moved frequently between the United States and Mexico, leaving her feeling homeless and displaced. The character of Esperanza in* The House on Mango Street, *a poor, Latina adolescent who longs for a room of her own and a house of which she can be proud, articulates the conflicts, joys, and disappointments of Cisneros's own childhood. Cisneros's other works include* Woman Hollering Creek and Other Stories *(1991) and the poetry collection* Bad Boys and Loose Woman *(1994). She has also written a book for juveniles,* Pelitos *(1994). "The House on Mango Street" and "My Name" are the first and fourth vignettes, respectively, in* The House on Mango Street.

THE HOUSE ON MANGO STREET

We didn't always live on Mango Street. Before that we lived on Loomis on the third floor; and before that we lived on Keeler. Before Keeler it was Paulina, and before that I can't remember. But what I remember most is moving a lot. Each time it seemed there'd be one more of us. By the time we got to Mango Street we were six—Mama, Papa, Carlos, Kiki, my sister Nenny, and me.

The house on Mango Street is ours, and we don't have to pay rent to anybody, or share the yard with the people downstairs, or be careful not to make too much noise, and there isn't a landlord banging on the ceiling with a broom. But even so, it's not the house we'd thought we'd get.

We had to leave the flat on Loomis quick. The water pipes broke and the landlord wouldn't fix them because the house was too old. We had to leave fast. We were using the washroom next door and carrying water over in empty milk gallons. That's why Mama and Papa looked for a house, and that's why we moved into the house on Mango Street, far away, on the other side of town.

4   They always told us that one day we would move into a house, a real house that would be ours for always so we wouldn't have to move each year. And our house would have running water and pipes that worked. And inside it would have real stairs, not hallway stairs, but stairs inside like the houses on T.V. And we'd have a basement and at least three washrooms so when we took a bath we wouldn't have to tell everybody. Our house would be white with trees around it, a great big yard and grass growing without a fence. This was the house Papa talked about when he held a lottery ticket and this was the house Mama dreamed up in the stories she told us before we went to bed.

But the house on Mango Street is not the way they told it at all. It's small and red with tight steps in front and windows so small you'd think they were holding their breath. Bricks are crumbling in places and the front door is so swollen you have to push hard to get in. There is no front yard, only four little elms the city planted by the curb. Out back is a small garage for the car we don't own yet and a small yard that looks smaller between the two buildings on either side. There are stairs in our house, but they're ordinary hallway stairs, and the house has only one washroom. Everybody has to share a bed-room—Mama and Papa, Carlos and Kiki, me and Nenny.

Once when we were living on Loomis, a nun from my school passed by and saw me playing out front. The laundromat downstairs had been boarded up because it had been robbed two days before and the owner had painted on the wood YES WE'RE OPEN so as not to lose business.

Where do you live? she asked.

8   There, I said pointing up to the third floor.

You live *there?*

There. I had to look to where she pointed—the third floor, the paint peeling, wooden bars Papa had nailed on the windows so we wouldn't fall out. You live *there?* The way she said it made me feel like nothing. *There.* I lived *there.* I nodded.

I knew then I had to have a house. A real house. One I could point to. But this isn't it. The house on Mango Street isn't it. For the time being, Mama says. Temporary, says Papa. But I know how those things go.

MY NAME

12 In English my name means hope. In Spanish it means too many letters. It means sadness, it means waiting. It is like the number nine. A muddy color. It is the Mexican records my father plays on Sunday mornings when he is shaving, songs like sobbing.

It was my great-grandmother's name and now it is mine. She was a horse woman too, born like me in the Chinese year of the horse—which is supposed to be bad luck if you're born female—but I think this is a Chinese lie because the Chinese, like the Mexicans, don't like their women strong.

My great-grandmother. I would've liked to have known her, a wild, horse of a woman, so wild she wouldn't marry. Until my great-grandfather threw a sack over her head and carried her off. Just like that, as if she were a fancy chandelier. That's the way he did it.

And the story goes she never forgave him. She looked out the window her whole life, the way so many women sit their sadness on an elbow. I wonder if she made the best with what she got or was she sorry because she couldn't be all the things she wanted to be. Esperanza. I have inherited her name, but I don't want to inherit her place by the window.

16 At school they say my name funny as if the syllables were made out of tin and hurt the roof of your mouth. But in Spanish my name is made out of a softer something, like silver, not quite as thick as sister's name—Magdalena—which is uglier than mine. Magdalena who at least can come home and become Nenny. But I am always Esperanza.

I would like to baptize myself under a new name, a name more like the real me, the one nobody sees. Esperanza as Lisandra or Maritza or Zeze the X. Yes. Something like Zeze the X will do.

PERSONAL RESPONSE

Describe your feelings about the home you grew up in.

QUESTIONS FOR DISCUSSION

1. Do a character sketch of Esperanza based on details revealed in these two vignettes. What kind of girl do you think she is? How does she impress you?
2. What role do you think Esperanza's ethnic identity and socioeconomic level play in her self-image?
3. Discuss the importance of home to self-identity. What sorts of homes had Esperanza lived in before moving to Mango Street? What effect did the remark "You live *there*?" (paragraph 8) have on Esperanza? Why is the house on Mango Street disappointing to her?

4. Discuss Cisneros's language by looking at the way she uses metaphors. For instance, what do you think Esperanza means when she says that her name is a "muddy color" (paragraph 12)? In what way might syllables sound as if they were "made out of tin" (paragraph 16)?

ADDITIONAL SUGGESTIONS FOR DISCUSSION OR WRITING ABOUT SELF-PERCEPTION

1. Respond to this statement by Sucheng Chan in "You're Short, Besides!": "Perhaps the hardest thing for those who live with handicapped people is to know when and how to offer help."
2. Describe a person you know who has overcome or adjusted to a disability. Use very specific details to convey fully a sense of that person and the difficulties of the disability.
3. With Sucheng Chan's "You're Short, Besides!" and Nancy Mairs's "On Being a Cripple" in mind, write an essay on the use of euphemisms, such as those for dying, bodily functions, or certain occupations, citing examples and exploring possible reasons why people often prefer to use euphemisms. Relate your discussion of euphemisms to the subject of self-perception.
4. If you belong to a group that is often stereotyped, explore the implications of that stereotype for you personally as well as for your friends and family, as Rebecca Thomas Kirkendall does in "Who's a Hillbilly?"
5. Narrate a personal experience with being the victim of name-calling or other verbal abuse. What were the circumstances of the incident? How did you respond to it? How did you feel afterward?
6. In "Just Walk on By: A Black Man Ponders His Ability to Alter Public Space," Brent Staples writes from the point of view of a black man who is frightening to many people, particularly white women. Explore possible reasons for the apprehension of the woman in the first paragraph of his essay and for the actions she took in response to it. Or, if you have been in the position of the "victim" Staples describes, narrate that experience, and discuss reasons for your own behavior.
7. Write about an experience you have had that taught you something about yourself.
8. If you have undergone a change in self-image, contrast your image of yourself before with your image of yourself now. How do you account for the change?
9. Assess your own self-image. Are you content with the way you look? What, if anything, would you change about yourself? Why?
10. Narrate an incident from your childhood in which other children were cruel or bullying to you, and include your perception of the incident at the time and your perception of the incident now. Also include a discussion of how the incident affected your self-image. Can you account for

the other children's treatment of you? Do you feel differently about it now, looking back from the perspective of adulthood?

11. Explore the effects of a particular physical characteristic, such as a prominent birthmark, skin color, racial background, birth defect, or the like, on your own life or the life of someone you know.

12. Write about an experience in which you were very much aware of your difference—in skin color, political beliefs, religious beliefs, or some other noticeable way—from others around you. Explain the situation, how you differed from others, how you felt about yourself, and how you felt about the experience.

13. Drawing on relevant readings in this chapter, write an essay on the relationship between skin color and self-image.

14. With Lini S. Kadaba's "What's in a Name?" and Sandra Cisneros's "My Name" in mind, write an essay exploring the importance of one's name.

15. If you are latina or latino, relate your own experiences with those of Esperanza in "The House on Mango Street" and "My Name."

16. Explore the importance of family, neighborhood, or friends to one's self-image.

17. Explore the topic of the American standard of beauty as portrayed in popular culture and its effects on people who do not measure up to that standard.

18. What role does one's identity as masculine or feminine play in self-esteem? Discuss the extent to which you think that there is a "standard" of masculinity and femininity and the degree to which conforming to or differing from that standard affects both how people see themselves and how others see them.

Chapter

6

ROLE MODELS AND HEROES

Role models are people who serve as positive examples of admirable behavior or action and who provide hope, inspiration, or incentive to others. They may be heroes as well, for the terms *role model* and *hero* are often used interchangeably. Certainly, heroes can make excellent role models, and role models can be admired as heroes. People become heroes for feats of courage or nobility of purpose, such as in wartime, when heroism often involves a person sacrificing his or her life for the benefit of others. Heroes are also those who make special achievements or perform extraordinarily in their fields, such as scientists, entertainers, or athletes. They often become celebrities as well, widely known and admired for what they have done. Whether their fame is widespread or limited to family and community, whether they serve the greater good of society or benefit much smaller populations, role models or heroes are those outstanding individuals whose character we praise and after whom we would hope to pattern our own behavior or actions.

The readings in this chapter indicate the variety of ways in which people can serve as role models. Often, our first and most impression-making role models come from our family or neighborhood, for one need not be an entertainment personality or a professional to act heroically or remarkably. In addition to entertainers, sports stars, and public figures, employers and teachers are among the people who can influence others and act as good role models.

For a long time to come, the firefighters who responded to the attacks in New York and Washington, D.C., on September 11, 2001, will likely be among the first people who spring to mind when the word *hero* is mentioned. Former Mayor Rudolph W. Giuliani explains what it was about their actions that made them truly heroic in "A Call to Courage," an excerpt from the commencement address he delivered at Syracuse University in 2002.

Next, Bill Thompson, in "It's Too Bad We Don't Have Another Roy," notes the universal praise given to entertainer Roy Rogers on his death in 1998 and highlights Rogers's admirable traits, whereas the next two essays are tributes to inspirational teachers who had positive influences on their students. In "The Teacher Who Changed My Life," Nicholas Gage tells how one teacher inspired him to find his voice as a writer and to make journalism his career. In "I Became Her Target," Roger Wilkins narrates how his eighth-grade history teacher not only helped him to gain self-confidence but also, in one memorable incident, broke down the barriers between him and his classmates that ignorance and stereotypes had created. By contrast, in "Lessons from Two Ghosts," Scott Fisher narrates the effects of a bad teacher in an essay focused on two college friends who have influenced his life. Fisher explains how his friends, who were preparing to become teachers themselves, served as role models and continue to affect his own behavior as a teacher.

For a different perspective on heroes, Howard Zinn, in "Unsung Heroes," takes exception to the usual list of American national heroes, explains why he feels they should not be honored, and suggests instead a variety of "unsung heroes" whom he thinks we would do better to honor. Jedediah Purdy, in "Rebel Twilight," seems to be responding to Zinn's essay when he identifies the people he believes his generation's leaders will be.

The chapter ends with Bruce Catton's classic comparison/contrast essay "Grant and Lee: A Study in Contrasts," which examines what Ulysses S. Grant and Robert E. Lee represented to the soldiers who served under them and to the people for whom they were fighting. Catton identifies the differences and similarities between these two generals in charge of opposing armies during the American Civil War and makes clear why people revered them as both men and leaders.

1. How would you define bravery or courage?
2. Which volunteer jobs do you consider to be heroic? Why?
3. Thinking of the September 11, 2001, attacks on New York and Washington, D.C., who besides firefighters would you consider to be heroic?
4. Who are your role models and/or heroes?

A Call to Courage

Rudolph W. Giuliani

Rudolph Giuliani served two terms as mayor of New York City, a position he held at the time of the September 11, 2001, attacks against the World Trade Center towers. His strength as a leader during that time has been widely praised, earning him, among other awards, selection as Time *magazine's 2001 Person of the Year and a knighthood from Queen Elizabeth of England. He is author, with Ken Kurson, of* Leadership *(2002). The following piece is an excerpt from former mayor Giuliani's commencement address at Syracuse University on May 13, 2002.*

A lot of people are saying that America is more dangerous now than it was before September 11th. But the reality is that we're much stronger, emotionally and practically, than we were before.

I realized the reason for this an hour after the attack. I was out on the street trying to communicate with the people of New York, telling them to remain calm, that everything was being done that could be done, and to evacuate to the north. And as I was talking to the press, I kept looking around to see how people were reacting. What I saw was that they were doing exactly what I was asking them to do. They were fleeing, but they weren't panicking. They weren't running each other over or pushing each other aside. In fact, I could see people stopping and helping others, and being just as concerned for the safety of those around them as they were for their own.

I began to get a sense that something was happening that would overwhelm the viciousness of this attack. And later, as I thought about the enormity of the number of people we had lost—including close friends of mine, people I had loved and cared about and seen minutes before they died—as I was feeling the burden of that, I saw the photograph of the three firefighters who placed the American flag on top of six stories of fallen building. That photograph said to me right there that there's nothing stronger than the spirit of a free people. It was the first time I felt optimism and strength.

4   We were attacked because we're a country of beliefs. There is no American ethnic group; we're all ethnic groups. There is no American religion; we're all religions, or none. There is no American race; we're all races, and combinations of races. So what are we? We're people who believe in the same things, people who have a philosophy that we're proud of, that holds us together and gives us strength.

That was one of the things that brought out the firefighters and police officers and rescue workers and all of the others who saved thousands of lives, giving up their own, at the World Trade Center. When you think about what happened there, the evilness of the attack, stories of bravery and courage overwhelm it enormously.

I remember one particular firefighter. He'd gotten hurt the day before September 11th, and that morning, just after the doctor informed him that he couldn't go back to duty for several weeks, he heard about the attack. And instead of going home, he raced to a nearby firehouse. All the firefighters had gone to the World Trade Center, so he put on some gear and wrote a note explaining why he had taken it. Then he wrote, "Please tell my mother and father that I love them very much and that I owe everything to them."

I try to recreate in my mind what he did. He drove across the Brooklyn Bridge—and to drive across the Brooklyn Bridge on the morning of September 11th, you had to feel that you were driving into hell. You saw an inferno unlike anything I could possibly describe to you. He had every reason not to go. He was injured; he had been told not to report for duty—but he drove there. He went into one of the buildings and he saved people, twice, and then he went in again right before it collapsed, and he died.

8 Think of the courage that he had. It wasn't a lack of fear. Courage isn't a lack of fear. Courage is about being afraid, but being able to do what you have to do anyway. Courage is knowing you're going into the worst fire you'll ever face and that you may never return. But it's also understanding that you're a firefighter, that you can carry people down. Maybe I can't do that, maybe you can't do that, but he could do that. That's what his life was about; that's what he swore to do.

Every once in a while, when I would give a firefighter or a police officer an award for bravery, he would come up to the podium and be very nervous. His hands would shake, and he would be unable to speak. And it never ceased to amaze me. How could this man, who'd jumped into the East River and taken out a 10-year-old child and put his own life at risk, how could he be afraid to speak? I finally realized it was because he hadn't learned how to manage that fear.

That's what courage is about, managing your fears. You have to do that all your life. If you want to be happy, you need a belief, and you need courage. You need to know what you believe in and have the courage to act on those beliefs. If you have both those things, there's no way on earth you're not going to succeed.

PERSONAL RESPONSE

In the conclusion of this excerpt, Giuliani says that you "need to know what you believe in and have the courage to act on those beliefs." Do you know what you believe in? Do you have the courage to act on those beliefs?

QUESTIONS FOR DISCUSSION

1. Discuss the implications of this statement: "[T]here's nothing stronger than the spirit of a free people" (paragraph 3).

2. To what extent do you agree with the statements Giuliani makes about Americans in paragraph 4?
3. What, if anything, would you add to Giuliani's definition of courage? Do you know of an individual like the firefighter he mentions in paragraphs 6 and 7 who exemplifies courage?

It's Too Bad We Don't Have Another Roy
Bill Thompson

Bill Thompson began his newspaper career in 1967 as a sports reporter and feature writer at the Belleville, Illinois, News-Democrat. *In 1979 he became city editor of* The Times-Leader *in Wilkes-Barre, Pennsylvania. Thompson joined the* Fort Worth Star-Telegram *in 1986, and in September 1987 he began writing a column three times a week. This column appeared in the July 14, 1998, edition of the* Fort Worth Star-Telegram.

Here we are, several days after his death, and not a disparaging word has been spoken or written about Roy Rogers. Usually, two days is about all it takes for the typical movie star's ex-wives and estranged children to start hyping their soon-to-be-published books detailing what a jerk the guy was when the cameras shut down.

You'd have to figure that there would be a cynic or two in this cynical age who would feel compelled to find fault with Rogers's acting or his singing or maybe his decision to stuff ol'Trigger after the "smartest horse in the movies" went to the big corral in the sky.

Not a chance. Movie historians praise him as the greatest of moviedom's singing cowboys. Music critics write fondly of his early crooning with the Sons of the Pioneers and his solo singing later on.

4   President Clinton took a moment out from the demands of globetrotting and scandal-managing to appreciate what Rogers "stood for, the movies he made and the kind of values they embodied."

Onetime rival Gene Autry saluted his fellow singing cowboy as a "great humanitarian" and a "true Western hero."

Not one disparaging word.

Fort Worth Star-Telegram sports columnist Jim Reeves reminisced about his boyhood idol Tuesday and bemoaned the shortage of Rogers-like role models. "My greatest lament today," Reeves wrote, "is that my own sons, growing up in a far more complicated world, didn't have a Roy Rogers to emulate and learn from."

8 Which raises an interesting question. What would happen if Roy Rogers came along today? Would an adoring public make him a star, or would the skeptics scoff him out of show business? Would the critics dismiss his movies as corny and one-dimensional? Would Rogers's songs be shrugged off as trite and oversimplified? Would his sense of right and wrong be ridiculed as naive and uncompromising?

How ironic that Roy Rogers should leave this life as a focal point of universal approval at a time when just about everything he stood for and believed in seems to be under attack by a society that scorns the values he espoused.

Maybe he's being given his due because even those who no longer cherish his values just might suspect that the world was a better place when Roy Rogers reigned as King of the Cowboys.

More often than not, a celebrity obituary will include something negative. Frank Sinatra died, and even heartfelt tributes by Sinatra's devotees in the media included passing mention of his alleged mob connections and his penchant for slugging photographers. Robert Mitchum died, and every story dredged up a decades-old marijuana conviction.

12 It's as predictable as this year's "Titanic" Oscar binge. A show-business legend expires, and the obits are awash with tales of the late great's forays into barroom brawling, substance abuse, marital infidelity and who knows what other indiscretions. No matter how much the public reveres them, the rich and famous have a way of getting their names on a court docket—and the bad publicity follows them to the grave. We've seen so many celebrity "heroes" who turned out to be severely flawed individuals whose talent as performers might have been worthy of admiration but whose performance as human beings left much to be desired.

So the ubiquitous tributes to Roy Rogers, who died last week at age 86, are all the more remarkable for containing no hint of scandal or bad behavior by the movie-and-TV star who was known as "King of the Cowboys."

It's clear that Rogers was the same white-hat-wearing good guy in real life that he portrayed on screen. In a rare and gratifying cohesion of truth and fiction, the reel hero was a real hero. Rogers was devoted to his wife and family, treated his fans with respect and affection, and practiced in private the very same brand of Christianity that he preached in public. He never abused the position of trust awarded him by a public that treasured the image he conveyed as America's best-loved show-biz cowboy.

READER RESPONSE

Name a movie star or singer whom you admire, and explain what values you believe that person represents.

QUESTIONS FOR DISCUSSION

1. What do you understand Thompson to mean by "this cynical age" (paragraph 2). Discuss the extent to which you agree that this age is cynical.
2. Thompson quotes columnist Jim Reeves, who "bemoaned the shortage of Rogers-like role models" and laments that his sons do not have " 'a Roy Rogers to emulate and learn from' " (paragraph 6). What qualities did Rogers have that made people admire him? What values did he represent? Do you agree there are few—or no—people like him today?
3. Thompson wonders "what would happen if a Roy Rogers came along today" (paragraph 8). How would you answer the questions Thompson raises in paragraph 8? Do you agree that society "scorns the values [Rogers] espoused" (paragraph 9)?
4. Thompson refers to the many "celebrity 'heroes' who turned out to be severely flawed individuals" (paragraph 12). Can you supply additional examples to support this statement?

The Teacher Who Changed My Life
Nicholas Gage

Nicholas Gage wrote of the 1948 torture and murder of his mother by Communist guerrillas in Greece in his best-selling book Eleni *(1983). He is also author of* The Bourlotas Fortune *(1975);* Hellas, a Portrait of Greece *(1987); and* A Place for Us *(1989), in which he tells how he and his sisters adjusted to life in the United States. His most recent book is* Greece: Land of Light *(1998). This essay, adapted from that book, appeared in the December 17, 1989, issue of* Parade *magazine.*

The person who set the course of my life in the new land I entered as a young war refugee—who, in fact, nearly dragged me onto the path that would bring all the blessings I've received in America—was a salty-tongued, nononsense schoolteacher named Marjorie Hurd. When I entered her classroom in 1953, I had been to six schools in five years, starting in the Greek village where I was born in 1939.

When I stepped off a ship in New York Harbor on a gray March day in 1949, I was an undersized 9-year-old in short pants who had lost his mother and was coming to live with the father he didn't know. My mother, Eleni Gatzoyiannis, had been imprisoned, tortured and shot by Communist guerrillas for sending me and three of my four sisters to freedom. She died so that her children could go to their father in the United States.

The portly, bald, well-dressed man who met me and my sisters seemed a foreign, authoritarian figure. I secretly resented him for not getting the whole family out of Greece early enough to save my mother. Ultimately, I would grow to love him and appreciate how he dealt with becoming a single parent at the age of 56, but at first our relationship was prickly, full of hostility.

4   As Father drove us to our new home—a tenement in Worcester, Mass.— and pointed out the huge brick building that would be our first school in America, I clutched my Greek notebooks from the refugee camp, hoping that my few years of schooling would impress my teachers in this cold, crowded country. They didn't. When my father led me and my 11-year-old sister to Greendale Elementary School, the grim-faced Yankee principal put the two of us in a class for the mentally retarded. There was no facility in those days for non-English-speaking children.

By the time I met Marjorie Hurd four years later, I had learned English, been placed in a normal, graded class and had even been chosen for the college preparatory track in the Worcester public school system. I was 13 years old when our father moved us yet again, and I entered Chandler Junior High shortly after the beginning of seventh grade. I found myself surrounded by richer, smarter and better-dressed classmates who looked askance at my strange clothes and heavy accent. Shortly after I arrived, we were told to select a hobby to pursue during "club hour" on Fridays. The idea of hobbies and clubs made no sense to my immigrant ears, but I decided to follow the prettiest girl in my class—the blue-eyed daughter of the local Lutheran minister. She led me through the door marked "Newspaper Club" and into the presence of Miss Hurd, the newspaper adviser and English teacher who would become my mentor and my muse.

A formidable, solidly built woman with salt-and-pepper hair, a steely eye and a flat Boston accent, Miss Hurd had no patience with layabouts. "What are all you goof-offs doing here?" she bellowed at the would-be journalists. "This is the Newspaper Club! We're going to put out a *newspaper*. So if there's anybody in this room who doesn't like work, I suggest you go across to the Glee Club now, because you're going to work your tails off here!"

I was soon under Miss Hurd's spell. She did indeed teach us to put out a newspaper, skills I honed during my next 25 years as a journalist. Soon I asked the principal to transfer me to her English class as well. There, she drilled us on grammar until I finally began to understand the logic and structure of the English language. She assigned stories for us to read and discuss; not tales of heroes, like the Greek myths I knew, but stories of underdogs—poor people, even immigrants, who seemed ordinary until a crisis drove them to do something extraordinary. She also introduced us to the literary wealth of Greece— giving me a new perspective on my war-ravaged, impoverished homeland. I began to be proud of my origins.

8   One day, after discussing how writers should write about what they know, she assigned us to compose an essay from our own experience. Fixing me with a stern look, she added, "Nick, I want you to write about what

happened to your family in Greece." I had been trying to put those painful memories behind me and left the assignment until the last moment. Then, on a warm spring afternoon, I sat in my room with a yellow pad and pencil and stared out the window at the buds on the trees. I wrote that the coming of spring always reminded me of the last time I said goodbye to my mother on a green and gold day in 1948.

I kept writing, one line after another, telling how the Communist guerrillas occupied our village, took our home and food, how my mother started planning our escape when she learned that the children were to be sent to re-education camps behind the Iron Curtain and how, at the last moment, she couldn't escape with us because the guerrillas sent her with a group of women to thresh wheat in a distant village. She promised she would try to get away on her own, she told me to be brave and hung a silver cross around my neck, and then she kissed me. I watched the line of women being led down into the ravine and up the other side, until they disappeared around the bend—my mother a tiny brown figure at the end who stopped for an instant to raise her hand in one last farewell.

I wrote about our nighttime escape down the mountain, across the mine-fields and into the lines of the Nationalist soldiers, who sent us to a refugee camp. It was there that we learned of our mother's execution. I felt very lucky to have come to America, I concluded, but every year, the coming of spring made me feel sad because it reminded me of the last time I saw my mother.

I handed in the essay, hoping never to see it again, but Miss Hurd had it published in the school paper. This mortified me at first, until I saw that my classmates reacted with sympathy and tact to my family's story. Without telling me, Miss Hurd also submitted the essay to a contest sponsored by the Freedoms Foundation at Valley Forge, Pa., and it won a medal. The Worcester paper wrote about the award and quoted my essay at length. My father, by then a "five-and-dime-store chef," as the paper described him, was ecstatic with pride, and the Worcester Greek community celebrated the honor to one of its own.

12   For the first time I began to understand the power of the written word. A secret ambition took root in me. One day, I vowed, I would go back to Greece, find out the details of my mother's death and write about her life, so her grandchildren would know of her courage. Perhaps I would event track down the men who killed her and write of their crimes. Fulfilling that ambition would take me 30 years.

Meanwhile, I followed the literary path that Miss Hurd had so forcefully set me on. After junior high, I became the editor of my school paper at Classical High School and got a part-time job at the Worcester *Telegram and Gazette*. Although my father could only give me $50 and encouragement toward a college education, I managed to finance four years at Boston University with scholarships and part-time jobs in journalism. During my last year of college, an article I wrote about a friend who had died in the Philippines—the first person to lose his life working for the Peace Corps—led to my winning the Hearst Award for College Journalism. And the plaque was given to me in the White House by President John F. Kennedy.

For a refugee who had never seen a motorized vehicle or indoor plumbing until he was 9, this was an unimaginable honor. When the Worcester paper ran a picture of me standing next to President Kennedy, my father rushed out to buy a new suit in order to be properly dressed to receive the congratulations of the Worcester Greeks. He clipped out the photograph, had it laminated in plastic and carried it in his breast pocket for the rest of his life to show everyone he met. I found the much-worn photo in his pocket on the day he died 20 years later.

In our isolated Greek village, my mother had bribed a cousin to teach her to read, for girls were not supposed to attend school beyond a certain age. She had always dreamed of her children receiving an education. She couldn't be there when I graduated from Boston University, but the person who came with my father and shared our joy was my former teacher, Marjorie Hurd. We celebrated not only my bachelor's degree but also the scholarships that paid my way to Columbia's Graduate School of Journalism. There, I met the woman who would eventually become my wife. At our wedding and at the baptisms of our three children, Marjorie Hurd was always there, dancing alongside the Greeks.

16 By then, she was Mrs. Rabidou, for she had married a widower when she was in her early 40s. That didn't distract her from her vocation of introducing young minds to English literature, however. She taught for a total of 41 years and continually would make a "project" of some balky student in whom she spied a spark of potential. Often these were students from the most troubled homes, yet she would alternately bully and charm each one with her own special brand of tough love until the spark caught fire. She retired in 1981 at the age of 62 but still avidly follows the lives and careers of former students while overseeing her adult stepchildren and driving her husband on camping trips to New Hampshire.

Miss Hurd was one of the first to call me on Dec. 10, 1987, when President Reagan, in his television address after the summit meeting with Gorbachev, told the nation that Eleni Gatzoyiannis' dying cry, "My children!" had helped inspire him to seek an arms agreement "for all the children of the world."

"I can't imagine a better monument for your mother," Miss Hurd said with an uncharacteristic catch in her voice.

Although a bad hip makes it impossible for her to join in the Greek dancing, Marjorie Hurd Rabidou is still an honored and enthusiastic guest at all family celebrations, including my 50th birthday picnic last summer, where the shish kebab was cooked on spits, clarinets and *bouzoukis* wailed, and costumed dancers led the guests in a serpentine line around our Colonial farmhouse, only 20 minutes from my first home in Worcester.

20 My sisters and I felt an aching void because my father was not there to lead the line, balancing a glass of wine on his head while he danced, the way he did at every celebration during his 92 years. But Miss Hurd was there, surveying the scene with quiet satisfaction. Although my parents are gone, her presence was a consolation, because I owe her so much.

This is truly the land of opportunity, and I would have enjoyed its bounty even if I hadn't walked into Miss Hurd's classroom in 1953. But she was the one who directed my grief and pain into writing, and if it weren't for her I wouldn't have become an investigative reporter and foreign correspondent, recorded the story of my mother's life and death in *Eleni* and now my father's story in *A Place for Us,* which is also a testament to the country that took us in. She was the catalyst that sent me into journalism and indirectly caused all the good things that came after. But Miss Hurd would probably deny this emphatically.

A few years ago, I answered the telephone and heard my former teacher's voice telling me, in that won't-take-no-for-an-answer tone of hers, that she had decided I was to write and deliver the eulogy at her funeral. I agreed (she didn't leave me any choice), but that's one assignment I never want to do. I hope, Miss Hurd, that you'll accept this remembrance instead.

READER RESPONSE

Imagine that you are in Miss Hurd's English class and have been assigned to write about something from your own experience, perhaps something about which you have painful memories. What would you write about? What details would you include?

QUESTIONS FOR DISCUSSION

1. What strategies does Gage use to convey a clear chronology despite the fact that his narrative covers a number of years in a brief space?
2. Do you think that Gage successfully describes his teacher? How does he convey the closeness of their relationship since the time he was her pupil?
3. What was it about Miss Hurd's teaching that inspired Gage to become a writer? What did Gage learn from his writing assignment that sparked his determination to write the life story of his mother?
4. What details about his father does Gage's narrative reveal? How, for example, did his father feel about Gage's accomplishments as a writer?

I Became Her Target
Roger Wilkins

Roger Wilkins is a lawyer, writer, and educator. He has contributed to a variety of periodicals, including Esquire, Foreign Policy, Fortune, Mother Jones, The Nation, The New Yorker, *and* Village Voice, *and to newspapers, including the* Los Angeles Times,

The New York Times, *the* Washington Post, *and the* Washington
Star. *His autobiography,* A Man's Life: An Autobiography, *was published in 1982 and his book* Jefferson's Pillow *in 2001. Wilkins is
a senior fellow at the Institute for Policy Studies in Washington,
D.C., and has served on the Pulitzer Prize Board since 1979. This
essay first appeared in* Newsday, *September 9, 1987.*

My favorite teacher's name was "Dead-Eye" Bean. Her real name was Dorothy.
She taught American history to eighth graders in the junior high section of
Creston, the high school that served the north end of Grand Rapids, Mich. It
was the fall of 1944. Franklin D. Roosevelt was president; American troops
were battling their way across France; Joe DiMaggio was still in the service;
the Montgomery bus boycott was more than a decade away, and I was a 12-
year-old black newcomer in a school that was otherwise all white.

My mother, who had been a widow in New York, had married my stepfather, a Grand Rapids physician, the year before, and he had bought the best
house he could afford for his new family. The problem for our new neighbors
was that their neighborhood had previously been pristine (in their terms) and
they were ignorant about black people. The prevailing wisdom in the neighborhood was that we were spoiling it and that we ought to go back where we
belonged (or alternatively, ought not intrude where we were not wanted).
There was a lot of angry talk among the adults, but nothing much came of it.

But some of the kids, those first few weeks, were quite nasty. They threw
stones at me, chased me home when I was on foot and spat on my bike seat
when I was in class. For a time, I was a pretty lonely, friendless and sometimes
frightened kid. I was just transplanted from Harlem, and here in Grand Rapids,
the dominant culture was speaking to me insistently.

4   I can see now that those youngsters were bullying and culturally disadvantaged. I knew then that they were bigoted, but the culture spoke to me
more powerfully than my mind and I felt ashamed for being different—a non-
standard person

I now know that Dorothy Bean understood most of that and deplored it.
So things began to change when I walked into her classroom. She was a pleas-
ant-looking single woman, who looked old and wrinkled to me at the time,
but who was probably about 40.

Whereas my other teachers approached the problem of easing in their
new black pupil by ignoring him for the first few weeks, Miss Bean went right
at me. On the morning after having read our first assignment, she asked me
the first question. I later came to know that in Grand Rapids, she was viewed
as a very liberal person who believed, among other things, that Negroes were
equal.

I gulped and answered her question and the follow-up. They weren't
brilliant answers, but they did establish the facts that I had read the assignment and that I could speak English. Later in the hour, when one of my classmates had bungled an answer, Miss Bean came back to me with a question

that required me to clean up the girl's mess and established me as a smart person.

8   Thus, the teacher began to give me human dimensions, though not perfect ones for an eighth grader. It was somewhat better to be an incipient teachers' pet than merely a dark presence in the back of the room onto whose silent form my classmates could fit all the stereotypes they carried in their heads.

A few days later, Miss Bean became the first teacher ever to require me to think. She asked my opinion about something Jefferson had done. In those days, all my opinions were derivative. I was for Roosevelt because my parents were and I was for the Yankees because my older buddy from Harlem was a Yankee fan. Besides, we didn't have opinions about historical figures like Jefferson. Like our high school building or old Mayor Welch, he just was.

After I had stared at her for a few seconds, she said: "Well, should he have bought Louisiana or not?"

"I guess so," I replied tentatively.

12   "Why?" she shot back.

Why! What kind of question was that, I groused silently. But I ventured an answer. Day after day, she kept doing that to me, and my answers became stronger and more confident. She was the first teacher to give me the sense that thinking was part of education and that I could form opinions that had some value.

Her final service to me came on a day when my mind was wandering and I was idly digging my pencil into the writing surface on the arm of my chair. Miss Bean impulsively threw a hunk of gum eraser at me. By amazing chance, it hit my hand and sent the pencil flying. She gasped, and I crept mortified after my pencil as the class roared. That was the ice breaker.

Afterward, kids came up to me to laugh about "Old Dead-Eye Bean." The incident became a legend, and I, a part of that story, became a person to talk to.

16   So that's how I became just another kid in school and Dorothy Bean became "Old Dead-Eye."

READER RESPONSE

To what extent do you agree with Wilkins that prejudice comes, in part, from the stereotypes children are taught? Who teaches children stereotypes? What can be done to prevent or undo stereotyping?

QUESTIONS FOR DISCUSSION

1. What do you think Wilkins means when he says that "the dominant culture was speaking to [him] insistently" (paragraph 3). What effect did that insistent speaking have on the young Wilkins? How does Wilkins account for the reactions of the people in his new neighborhood to his family?

2. What do you think Wilkins means when he says that the youngsters who bullied him were "culturally disadvantaged" (paragraph 4)?

3. In what ways did Dorothy Bean give Wilkins "human dimensions" (paragraph 8)? What were those dimensions? Why does Wilkins call the eraser-throwing incident Miss Bean's "final service" (paragraph 14) to him?

4. Discuss the connection between prejudice and ignorance that Wilkins implies in his narrative. What can be done to dispel such ignorance? How might teachers and other professionals reduce the kind of ignorance that leads to prejudice?

Lessons from Two Ghosts
Scott Fisher

Scott Fisher teaches English at Rock Valley College, Rockford, Illinois. For many years he also taught vocational automotive and aircraft technology. His freelance work includes technical and training print and video publications for the automotive industry, two books on Iowa history, a dozen magazine and journal articles, and a dozen short fiction pieces. He has won writing awards in technical publications, short fiction, nonfiction historical narrative, and personal essay. "Lessons from Two Ghosts" was first published in the June 14, 1996, issue of The Chronicle of Higher Education.

I know many educators who, like me, spend scores of extra hours planning, developing, and evaluating ideas and materials for their courses. I admire my colleagues for being so dedicated to their students and their profession. I wish I could say my reasons for my long hours were as altruistic. In fact, I often wish I had more time to read for pleasure, hike in the mountains, or go to more baseball games.

The truth is that there are ghosts in my office that force me to stay there and work, even when I'd rather be somewhere else. Oh, they let me go home and get enough rest and nourishment to sustain my body. But they know I'll be back, and they're always waiting for me when I unlock the door to my office. As Poe would have asked: "You think me mad?" Maybe I am.

I've known these ghosts—there are two of them—for about 25 years. That's longer than I've been teaching, although they really only started haunting me on my first day as a student teacher. Every day since then, they've been standing right behind or on either side of me. Heck, I knew them before they were ghosts. They were young men once, as I was.

4   Their names are (were) Pritchard and Simplett. We were classmates—freshmen—in the late '60s at a teachers' college in the Midwest. Pritchard was the kicker on our football team. He could make field goals from any angle, off any surface, in any temperature, in rain, snow, or high winds. If the ball was inside the 30-yard line, Pritch could nail it dead center every time. He didn't miss a single field goal or extra point all season. I can testify to that, because I was his holder (I was too small and slow to start in any other position). We weren't a powerhouse team, by any means, but Pritchard's foot made the difference in some of our games.

Simplett and I were on the baseball team that year. He was an outstanding shortstop, with a rifle arm (excuse the cliché). He could go into the hole, drop to his knees, and fling a runner out at first base by two steps. I was a fourth-string catcher, used almost exclusively when the game was not in doubt and the coach didn't want to risk injury to any of his "good" players. That was also when Simp got his chance to pitch. He was magnificent—about one-third of the time. The other two-thirds, his blazing fastball had a mind of its own. Also, Simp had a little trouble reading his catcher's signs. He couldn't see too well from 60 feet away. That's why nobody wanted to catch for him. I tried everything—flashing the signs very slowly, wrapping white adhesive tape around my fingertips—but nothing worked. We finally agreed that he would just "throw 'em," and I'd try to "catch 'em," which worked out about as well as anything else. We didn't win many games, but we had fun.

Pritch, Simp, and I had a couple of other things in common besides sports. For one thing, we all liked to write. I liked research and writing historical narrative—essays on the Old West, sports teams of the 1930s, classic airplanes, that kind of thing.

Pritch was into fantasy. He could weave a wonderful tale, gripping readers with his spellbinding tales of planets and sorcerers, which he illustrated deftly with bizarre, intriguing drawings.

8   Simp was a poet. His mind worked in metaphor; even in the dugout he would call umpires the "traffic cops of the basepaths" and the pain of a batter's hands when the bat connected on a cold day "the sweet sting of spring." And he loved all kinds of music. He lived across the hall from me in the dorm, and on Thursday nights ("rave" nights, when it was okay to make a little more noise), he'd bring over his Country Joe McDonald records, and we'd sing along at the top of our offkey voices: "And it's one, two, three, what're we fightin' for? Don't ask me, I don't give a damn; next stop is Vietnam."

Just as I admired their athletic ability, I was in awe of my friends' talents and creativity, both in writing and in living. While I had to work for each ounce of strength, both on the athletic field and at the typewriter, Pritch and Simp had natural gifts. I was envious, but also proud to know them. Their talents inspired me to work harder to improve myself.

It may sound corny now, but those guys were preparing themselves to be skilled educators in every activity they pursued. They often helped out in the tutoring lab in the evenings and volunteered to coach elementary-school teams on weekends. They loved taking kids from the town on field trips to nearby farms or sporting events. I was amazed at how both of them could motivate even the shyest youngster. They were natural leaders and role models. Kids seemed to be drawn to them instinctively.

The only time all three of us were together regularly was in "Old Man" Rivers's (Professor Rivers, that is) English-composition class. Now, in retrospect, I can corroborate what we thought then: He was a complete jerk. He seemed to be about 160 years old, wore black suits, starched white shirts, bow ties, black wingtip shoes, and white socks. He was a fanatical Freudian and expected all our writing to reflect Freud's theories. Even though I did my best to work them into my narrative essays, short-story analyses, and research thesis, my papers always came back with a C, if I was lucky. Although I had been praised as a clear and insightful writer in high school, Old Man Rivers made it clear to me that I had no writing talent and that perhaps I should consider hiring a tutor or retaking the class in the summer.

12   I was too immature and unclear about my role as a future teacher to care all that much about what an eccentric English professor thought of me. But for Simp and Pritch it was different. They saw Professor Rivers for what he really was—a "scholarly bully," Simp called him. (Pritch's description was more profane, as I recall.) They often challenged (respectfully, at first) his weird interpretations of the stories, poems, and essays that we discussed in class. Of course, this did not please Rivers one bit, although their arguments made perfect sense to me.

Some of the more "intellectually needy" members of the class, including me, often tried to get some extra help from the old duffer, but he always was too busy to bother with "ignorant freshmen," especially if he was working on his latest textbook. He was particularly cool to us athletes, because he thought college sports were a waste of time and didn't like the fact that we had permission to miss classes when we had games at other colleges.

Most of us decided just to go with the flow, earn our solid C's, and get on with our lives. But Pritchard and Simplett were not about to go that route. They each spent hours preparing for the essays we had to write in class, looking up literary critical analysis that even doctoral candidates wouldn't want to read, just so they could prove their points with logic that Rivers couldn't refute. Yet Rivers was such a pedant that my two friends didn't stand a chance.

Those two guys spent all year—freshmen were stuck with Rivers for both semesters—trying to show him up. They each received D's the first semester, which threatened to put them on academic probation. By April, the situation had deteriorated to the point that they no longer even tried to suppress their snide comments in class. Pritch drew some hilarious, obscene sketches of Rivers expounding on Freudian aspects of fiction. And Simp concocted a tune about what a dirty old man Rivers was. Both of these creative scholarly works were published in the local forum—the men's bathroom in the athletic building.

16   Pritch and Simp each were called in by the dean at various times and told to knock it off. They were reminded that we "boys" were all 1-A in the eyes of Uncle Sam, and that without their educational deferments, they would quickly find themselves in the military.

But that wasn't enough of a threat for them, because they had very different ideas of what education was supposed to be. They continued to rebel against Old Man Rivers, and they continued to be reprimanded. In the end, they both failed Rivers's class the second semester and were placed on academic probation, with the understanding that they could make up the credits during summer session. But guess who taught all the summer composition classes?

There was a lot I didn't quite grasp back then. I couldn't understand how a teacher at the college to which we were paying such high tuition could be so aloof and arrogant. I also couldn't understand how a published author of English textbooks could fail to recognize the talents of two gifted writers, right under his own nose. But neither could I understand why two intelligent guys would keep trying to buck the system when they knew Rivers wasn't going to change. Didn't they get it? They could just get through the ⸲ class and pursue their own ideas after they graduated, with their own students.

But they just laughed in disgust at any notion of compromise. Each of them, separately, refused to take the summer-school makeup course from Rivers and decided to head back to their respective hometowns. They planned to take their chances with the draft, maybe start again at another college the following year or when they got out of the service, should they be drafted.

20   Within 18 months, Pritchard and Simplett were dead. Pritch was blown apart by a land mine during an infantry patrol. A few months later, the Army helicopter in which Simp was riding crashed and burned, leaving no survivors.

Of course, it's really not Old Man Rivers's fault that my friends died. It was just a cruel trick of timing. Still, I can't help thinking that by sticking around my office after hours, I might help some student stay on track. I feel the presence of my two old friends, and I see traits of theirs, such as their eagerness to ask challenging questions and explore opposing viewpoints, in a lot of my students. Some of them may go on to make a difference in young people's lives in a way in which my ghostly friends cannot. I hope they do. So I just keep plugging away, like a fourth-string catcher, giving extra help where I can. It's not because I'm a great humanitarian, or that I'm gifted or even dedicated.

I'm just haunted.

READER RESPONSE

Of the two responses to the arrogant and aloof Professor Rivers, which do you think is closer to the way you imagine yourself responding in a similar situation? Why?

QUESTIONS FOR DISCUSSION

1. What does Fisher most admire about his two friends? What about them especially haunts him?
2. Are you convinced by the details Fisher gives that Pritchard and Simplett were "natural leaders and role models" and that they were on their way to being "skilled educators" (paragraph 10)? Would you define "natural leader" and "role model" in the same way that Fisher does? What characteristics would you expect a skilled educator to have? Have you had such a teacher?
3. Fisher says that his friends often challenged Professor Rivers, at first respectfully and then with "snide comments in class" (paragraph 15). Discuss the appropriateness of such behavior. In what circumstances do you think it is appropriate to challenge teachers? Should it be done in class or privately?
4. Do you know people who keep trying to "buck the system" (paragraph 18) as Pritchard and Simplett did. Do you admire such people? Explain your answer.

Unsung Heroes
Howard Zinn

Historian, playwright, and professor emeritus of Boston University, Howard Zinn is author of more than sixty books of essays, plays, and articles. His articles and essays have appeared in such publications as Harper's, The Nation, The New Republic, *and* The Progressive. *He is perhaps best known for his revolutionary and controversial* A People's History of the United States *(1990). This essay was first published in the June 2000 issue of* The Progressive.

A high school student recently confronted me: "I read in your book *A People's History of the United States* about the massacres of Indians, the long

exordium

history of racism, the persistence of poverty in the richest country in the world, the senseless wars. How can I keep from being thoroughly alienated and depressed?"

It's a question I've heard many times before. Another question often put to me by students is: Don't we need our national idols? You are taking down all our national heroes—the Founding Fathers, Andrew Jackson, Abraham Lincoln, Theodore Roosevelt, Woodrow Wilson, John F. Kennedy.

Granted, it is good to have historical figures we can admire and emulate. But why hold up as models the fifty-five rich white men who drafted the Constitution as a way of establishing a government that would protect the interests of their class—slaveholders, merchants, bondholders, land speculators?

4   Why not recall the humanitarianism of William Penn, an early colonist who made peace with the Delaware Indians instead of warring on them, as other colonial leaders were doing?

Why not John Woolman, who, in the years before the Revolution, refused to pay taxes to support the British wars, and who spoke out against slavery?

Why not Captain Daniel Shays, veteran of the Revolutionary War, who led a revolt of poor farmers in Western Massachusetts against the oppressive taxes levied by the rich who controlled the Massachusetts legislature?

Why go along with the hero-worship, so universal in our history textbooks, of Andrew Jackson, the slave-owner, the killer of Indians? Jackson was the architect of the Trail of Tears, which resulted in the deaths of 4,000 of 16,000 Cherokees who were kicked off their land in Georgia and sent into exile in Oklahoma.

8   Why not replace him as national icon with John Ross, a Cherokee chief who resisted the dispossession of his people, and whose wife died on the Trail of Tears? Or the Seminole leader Osceola, imprisoned and finally killed for leading a guerrilla campaign against the removal of the Indians?

And while we're at it, should not the Lincoln Memorial be joined by a memorial to Frederick Douglass, who better represented the struggle against slavery? It was that crusade of black and white abolitionists, growing into a great national movement, that pushed a reluctant Lincoln into finally issuing a half-hearted Emancipation Proclamation, and persuaded Congress to pass the Thirteenth, Fourteenth, and Fifteenth amendments.

Take another Presidential hero, Theodore Roosevelt, who is always near the top of the tiresome lists of Our Greatest Presidents. There he is on Mount Rushmore, as a permanent reminder of our historical amnesia about his racism, his militarism, his love of war.

Why not replace him as hero—granted, removing him from Mount Rushmore will take some doing—with Mark Twain? Roosevelt, remember, had congratulated an American general who in 1906 ordered the massacre of 600 men, women, and children on a Philippine island. As vice president of the Anti-Imperialist League, Twain denounced this and continued to point out the cruelties committed in the Philippine war under the slogan "My country, right or wrong."

12   As for Woodrow Wilson, another honored figure in the pantheon of American liberalism, shouldn't we remind his admirers that he insisted on racial segregation in federal buildings, that he bombarded the Mexican coast, sent an occupation army into Haiti and the Dominican Republic, brought our country into the hell of World War I, and put anti-war protesters in prison?

Should we not bring forward as a national hero Emma Goldman, one of those Wilson sent to prison, or Helen Keller, who fearlessly spoke out against the war?

And enough worship of John F. Kennedy, a Cold Warrior who began the covert war in Indochina, went along with the planned invasion of Cuba, and was slow to act against racial segregation in the South.

Should we not replace the portraits of our Presidents, which too often take up all the space on our classroom walls, with the likenesses of grassroots heroes like Fannie Lou Hamer, the Mississippi sharecropper? Mrs. Hamer was evicted from her farm and tortured in prison after she joined the civil rights movement, but she became an eloquent voice for freedom. Or with Ella Baker, whose wise counsel and support guided the young black people in the Student Nonviolent Coordinating Committee, the militant edge of the civil rights movement in the Deep South?

16   In the year 1992, the quincentennial of the arrival of Columbus in this hemisphere, there were meetings all over the country to celebrate him, but also, for the first time, to challenge the customary exaltation of the Great Discoverer. I was at a symposium in New Jersey where I pointed to the terrible crimes against the indigenous people of Hispaniola committed by Columbus and his fellow Spaniards. Afterward, the other man on the platform, who was chairman of the New Jersey Columbus Day celebration, said to me: "You don't understand—we Italian Americans need our heroes." Yes, I understood the desire for heroes, I said, but why choose a murderer and kidnapper for such an honor? Why not choose Joe DiMaggio, or Toscanini, or Fiorello LaGuardia, or Sacco and Vanzetti? (The man was not persuaded.)

The same misguided values that have made slaveholders, Indian-killers, and militarists the heroes of our history books still operate today. We have heard Senator John McCain, Republican of Arizona, repeatedly referred to as a war hero. Yes, we must sympathize with McCain's ordeal as a war prisoner in Vietnam, where he endured cruelties. But must we call someone a hero who participated in the invasion of a far-off country and dropped bombs on men, women, and children?

I came across only one voice in the mainstream press daring to dissent from the general admiration for McCain—that of the poet, novelist, and *Boston Globe* columnist James Carroll. Carroll contrasted the heroism of McCain, the warrior, to that of Philip Berrigan, who has gone to prison dozens of times for protesting the war in Vietnam and the dangerous nuclear arsenal maintained by our government. Carroll wrote: "Berrigan, in jail, is the truly free man, while McCain remains imprisoned in an unexamined sense of martial honor."

Our country is full of heroic people who are not Presidents or military leaders or Wall Street wizards, but who are doing something to keep alive the spirit of resistance to injustice and war.

20   I think of Kathy Kelly and all those other people from Voices in the Wilderness who, in defiance of federal law, have traveled to Iraq more than a dozen times to bring food and medicine to people suffering under the U.S.-imposed sanctions.

I think also of the thousands of students on more than 100 college campuses across the country who are protesting their universities' connection with sweatshop-produced apparel.

I think of the four McDonald sisters in Minneapolis, all nuns, who have gone to jail repeatedly for protesting against the Alliant Corporation's production of land mines.

I think, too, of the thousands of people who have traveled to Fort Benning, Georgia, to demand the closing of the murderous School of the Americas.

24   I think of the West Coast Longshoremen who participated in an eight-hour work stoppage to protest the death sentence levied against Mumia Abu-Jamal.

And so many more.

Pevoratio We all know individuals—most of them unsung, unrecognized—who have, often in the most modest ways, spoken out or acted on their beliefs for a more egalitarian, more just, peace-loving society.

To ward off alienation and gloom, it is only necessary to remember the unremembered heroes of the past, and to look around us for the unnoticed heroes of the present.

PERSONAL RESPONSE

Zinn ends his essay by saying that "[w]e all know individuals—most of them unsung, unrecognized—who have, often in the most modest ways, spoken out or acted on their beliefs for a more egalitarian, more just, peace-loving society" (paragraph 26). Do you know of such individuals?

QUESTIONS FOR DISCUSSION

1. To what extent do you agree with Zinn that we are looking to the wrong people for heroes?
2. Do you agree with Zinn's position on "war heroes" and presidents?
3. Based on the reasons Zinn gives for why we should admire certain people rather than others, what values does Zinn admire?
4. Which of the names of the people Zinn suggests we should admire do you recognize? Share with the class what you know about those people.

Rebel Twilight

Jedediah Purdy

Jedediah Purdy is the author of For Common Things: Irony, Trust, and Commitment in America Today *(1999). At twenty-six years of age, he wrote this essay for the July/August 2002 issue of* Modern Maturity.

Someone asked to name the "generational leaders" of the turbulent '60s would have had no trouble listing a few candidates. Outspoken musicians like Bob Dylan and John Lennon. Abbie Hoffman, the celebrity radical who named his peers the "Woodstock Nation." Bobby Kennedy, the charismatic knight-errant who campaigned fearlessly in cities that threatened to burn themselves down.

In the '40s, the idea of "generational leaders" wouldn't have made much sense. A country at war may have cared intensely about its soldiers, but it wasn't looking to young people for guidance. America fell in line behind a more experienced set of politicians, generals, labor leaders, and journalists.

People now coming of age grew up in a skeptical and fragmented culture, without the unity of the World War II era or the pitched divisions of the '60s. Most of my contemporaries wouldn't want to roll back the clock, even if we could. But many of us are idealistic and are looking for places to express that idealism. We admire candor and quiet competence, and we can sight a huckster a block away. Our leaders will probably be less charismatic, less dramatic, and maybe even less youthful than earlier generations' headliners. They will make their names less with catchy words and images than with long-term work.

4   Most of us are ambivalent about rebellion, whether personal or social. Today's teens tend to follow rules, enjoy school, and respect professional success. But they are not just conformists: They say they want to improve the world, and they think that they will have the chance.

In their world, musical icons like Lennon or Dylan would be almost impossible. Pop music has split into a half-dozen genres, one for every adolescent mood. It also became more openly commercial, a source of products and postures, but not generational identity.

And politics is not about to produce another Bobby Kennedy. In 1968, the most important questions in America—civil rights at home and war abroad—were at the heart of politics, and RFK focused his campaign on the country's passions. Politics today is not charged or idealistic enough to become the core of a new generation's identity. Bill Clinton's self-indulgence and George W. Bush's diffidence are a much better fit for a time when politics is a sideshow to the stock market reports.

As for Abbie Hoffman, he was everything that today's young people want to avoid becoming. The tricks of self-promotion have gotten to be an everyday affair. Young people are invited to market themselves, like any other product, as "Brand You." When being a hustler is normal, the biggest hustler of all comes across as a tedious character.

8   So young people are looking for new models. What kind of leaders will they produce?

When I travel and talk to other young people, everyone agrees on one thing: The idea of a "generational spokesperson" is a fraud. American teens and twentysomethings know their experiences are so varied that no one can speak for them all. And they have already seen a series of briefly annointed smooth talkers, including myself, give it a try. Elizabeth Wurtzel's *Prozac Nation* was announced as the voice of a generation of chemical-soaked neurotics. Wendy Shalit's praise of chastity briefly convinced the country that a new modesty had arisen. On the publication of my own *For Common Things,* there was a rush to suggest that I might be the herald of a post-ironic age. The media's celebration of each new "representative" quickly fades, leaving everyone even more skeptical and disaffected.

Instead, leaders will arise gradually, not because they have attracted attention, but because they have done worthwhile things. Young people are often indifferent to electoral politics because they believe that politics—as W.H. Auden wrote of poetry—makes nothing happen. Administrations and Congresses come and go but the problems stay the same. So instead, young people work in tutoring programs and shelters. They build houses with Habitat for Humanity. They teach in charter schools. When Britain's Prince William spent time in a service program in Latin America, he was perfectly in tune with his cohort on both sides of the Atlantic.

So one kind of leader will be the person who, through this kind of direct service, learns enough to found a better charter school or design a better welfare-to-work program. There's no shortcut to this kind of leadership, whether it be showing up on the cover of *Rolling Stone* or being born into royalty. Doing things, unlike getting famous, takes time and effort. But anyone can achieve it.

12   As a student at Harvard and Yale over the past eight years, I have seen this kind of leadership every day. These campuses experienced dramatic divisions in the '60s. Yale was torn between new-blood radicalism and preppie conservatism, between Garry Trudeau and George W. Bush. Harvard's student radicals were among the most adamant in the country back then.

In my time, nothing at those schools was so black and white. Young Republicans and members of left-wing student-labor alliances might work in the same public-service programs. A graduate might spend a year or two at the McKinsey & Company consulting firm—one of the bastions of the Establishment—and then go on to work for an economic development program in Harlem. Young people want their work to have concrete results. Many do not care much about the ideological tags that other people attach to their projects.

These leaders may not become national figures. Many of them will be known only in the communities where they do their work. The civil rights era, although it produced a few national celebrities, also bequeathed the country a great many more local leaders, whose work lives on mainly among their neighbors, students, or parishioners. That is how movements and generations work, and one way to distinguish them from media events.

Another possibility is that the leaders of this generation will not be members of the generation. We have come a long way since students were warned not to trust anyone over 30. A generation that tends to respect its elders—and admires achievement more than hype—may choose leaders who are both inspiring and well-tested. Despite their deep political differences, both Bill Bradley and John McCain inspired bands of students and recent college graduates to join their campaigns. My friends who went to New Hampshire for these candidates didn't always agree with their politics, but were moved by the idea that their willingness to talk straight, campaign without scripts, and propose big changes in public life might make politics hopeful again.

16 Students also made up a good share of the crowds at Ralph Nader's rallies last fall. Despite Nader's dismal showing at the polls, attendance at some of his appearances topped 10,000, making them the largest events of the moribund presidential campaign. Nader is not known for his charisma, but he exuded the same appeal as McCain and Bradley: directness, candor, an eagerness to speak unpleasant truths. And, like Bradley and McCain, he is a man of undoubted accomplishment. The enthusiasm for all three suggests that this generation wants to follow its elders and is looking for adults who are worthy of their efforts.

This generation may also produce its own leaders from the politics currently brewing on college campuses. The most prominent is the anti-sweat-shop movement, a loose-knit, nationwide collection of students who object to companies manufacturing school sweatshirts and other goods in unsafe factories where workers earn poverty wages. These students have developed a distinctive blend of local and global politics: They pressure nearby university administrators in order to affect the policies of globalized companies. They have built coalitions of civic groups, labor organizations, and governments that are working to enforce standards in foreign factories. Along with students who work on environmental and human rights issues, they are shaping a civic spirit that is concerned with both the neighborhood and the planet.

Some of those activists will end up in Congress. More than previous generations, they will run the nonprofit organizations whose service, policy design, and political engagement make them more influential than ever before. The foreign policy of the Soros Foundation and the domestic work of the Bill and Melinda Gates Foundation can mean more than what any particular senator is after, and today's young idealists know that.

Leadership will look different in the rising generation. Leaders will cut their teeth in more kinds of work, they will proceed with more effort and less hype, and they will come from more than one generation. But one thing will not change: Leaders will be the ones who make the world young again.

PERSONAL RESPONSE

Purdy says of his generation that they are idealistic. Do you consider yourself idealistic?

QUESTIONS FOR DISCUSSION

1. Purdy says that "[t]oday's teens tend to follow rules, enjoy school, and respect professional success. But they are not conformists" (paragraph 4). Do your own observations of today's young people confirm or contradict this statement?
2. Explain, in your own words, the kinds of leaders that Purdy believes his generation will produce. Do you agree with him? Can you add any other kinds of leaders to the types that he identifies? Would you define *leadership* any differently than Purdy does?
3. Purdy mentions three people from an older generation whom he says young people admire: Ralph Nader, Bill Bradley, and John McCain. Discuss the qualities and ideals of each of these men. Do you agree with Purdy that they are admirable leaders?
4. How do the types of leaders that Purdy says his generation will produce differ from those of previous generations?

Grant and Lee: A Study in Contrasts
Bruce Catton

Bruce Catton (1899–1978) was born in Michigan and attended Oberlin College, but World War I interrupted his studies. After the war, Catton worked as a journalist and served as a public official for various government agencies. He was editor of American Heritage *magazine from 1954 until his death in 1978. A Civil War expert, he published many books on that subject, including* Mr. Lincoln's Army *(1951);* Glory Road *(1952);* A Stillness at Appomattox *(1953), for which he was awarded the Pulitzer Prize and a National Book Award;* This Hallowed Ground *(1956);* Terrible Swift Sword *(1963); and* Gettysburg: The Final Fury *(1974). This essay first appeared in a collection of historical essays,* The American Story *(1956).*

When Ulysses S. Grant and Robert E. Lee met in the parlor of a modest house at Appomattox Court House, Virginia, on April 9, 1865, to work out the terms for the surrender of Lee's Army of Northern Virginia, a great chapter in American life came to a close, and a great new chapter began.

These men were bringing the Civil War to its virtual finish. To be sure, other armies had yet to surrender, and for a few days the fugitive Confederate government would struggle desperately and vainly, trying to find some way to go on living now that its chief support was gone. But in effect it was all over when Grant and Lee signed the papers. And the little room where they wrote out the terms was the scene of one of the poignant, dramatic contrasts in American history.

They were two strong men, these oddly different generals, and they represented the strengths of two conflicting currents that, through them, had come into final collision.

4   Back of Robert E. Lee was the notion that the old aristocratic concept might somehow survive and be dominant in American life.

Lee was tidewater Virginia, and in his background were family, culture, and tradition . . . the age of chivalry transplanted to a New World which was making its own legends and its own myths. He embodied a way of life that had come down through the age of knighthood and the English country squire. America was a land that was beginning all over again, dedicated to nothing much more complicated than the rather hazy belief that all men had equal rights and should have an equal chance in the world. In such a land Lee stood for the feeling that it was somehow of advantage to human society to have pronounced inequality in the social structure. There should be a leisure class, backed by ownership of land; in turn, society itself should be keyed to the land as the chief source of wealth and influence. It would bring forth (according to this ideal) a class of men with a strong sense of obligation to the community; men who lived not to gain advantage for themselves, but to meet the solemn obligations which had been laid on them by the very fact that they were privileged. From them the country would get its leadership; to them it could look for the higher values—of thought, of conduct, of personal deportment—to give it strength and virtue.

Lee embodied the noblest elements of this aristocratic ideal. Through him, the landed nobility justified itself. For four years, the Southern states had fought a desperate war to uphold the ideals for which Lee stood. In the end, it almost seemed as if the Confederacy fought for Lee; as if he himself was the Confederacy . . . the best thing that the way of life for which the Confederacy stood could ever have to offer. He had passed into legend before Appomattox. Thousands of tired, underfed, poorly clothed Confederate soldiers, long since past the simple enthusiasm of the early days of the struggle, somehow considered Lee the symbol of everything for which they had been willing to die. But they could not quite put this feeling into words. If the Lost Cause, sanctified by so much heroism and so many deaths, had a living justification, its justification was General Lee.

Grant, the son of a tanner on the Western frontier, was everything Lee was not. He had come up the hard way and embodied nothing in particular

except the eternal toughness and sinewy fiber of the men who grew up beyond the mountains. He was one of a body of men who owed reverence and
obeisance to no one, who were self-reliant to a fault, who cared hardly anything for the past but who had a sharp eye for the future.

8   These frontier men were the precise opposites of the tidewater aristo-
crats. Back of them, in the great surge that had taken people over the Alleghe-
nies and into the opening Western country, there was a deep, implicit
dissatisfaction with a past that had settled into grooves. They stood for democracy, not from any reasoned conclusion about the proper ordering of human
society, but simply because they had grown up in the middle of democracy
and knew how it worked. Their society might have privileges, but they would
be privileges each man had won for himself. Forms and patterns meant nothing. No man was born to anything, except perhaps to a chance to show how
far he could rise. Life was competition.

Yet along with this feeling had come a deep sense of belonging to a national community. The Westerner who developed a farm, opened a shop, or set
up in business as a trader, could hope to prosper only as his own community
prospered—and his community ran from the Atlantic to the Pacific and from
Canada down to Mexico. If the land was settled, with towns and highways and
accessible markets, he could better himself. He saw his fate in terms of the nation's own destiny. As its horizons expanded, so did his. He had, in other
words, an acute dollars-and-cents stake in the continued growth and development of his country.

And that, perhaps, is where the contrast between Grant and Lee becomes most striking. The Virginia aristocrat, inevitably, saw himself in relation
to his own region. He lived in a static society which could endure almost anything except change. Instinctively, his first loyalty would go to the locality in
which that society existed. He would fight to the limit of endurance to defend
it, because in defending it he was defending everything that gave his own life
its deepest meaning.

The Westerner, on the other hand, would fight with an equal tenacity for
the broader concept of society. He fought so because everything he lived by
was tied to growth, expansion, and a constantly widening horizon. What he
lived by would survive or fall with the nation itself. He could not possibly
stand by unmoved in the face of an attempt to destroy the Union. He would
combat it with everything he had, because he could only see it as an effort to
cut the ground out from under his feet.

12   So Grant and Lee were in complete contrast, representing two diametri-
cally opposed elements in American life. Grant was the modern man emerging; beyond him, ready to come on the stage, was the great age of steel and
machinery, of crowded cities and a restless burgeoning vitality. Lee might have
ridden down from the old age of chivalry, lance in hand, silken banner fluttering over his head. Each man was the perfect champion of his cause, drawing
both his strengths and his weaknesses from the people he led.

Yet it was not all contrast, after all. Different as they were—in background, in personality, in underlying aspiration—these two great soldiers had much in common. Under everything else, they were marvelous fighters. Furthermore, their fighting qualities were really very much alike.

Each man had, to begin with, the great virtue of utter tenacity and fidelity. Grant fought his way down the Mississippi Valley in spite of acute personal discouragement and profound military handicaps. Lee hung on in the trenches at Petersburg after hope itself had died. In each man there was an indomitable quality . . . the born fighter's refusal to give up as long as he can still remain on his feet and lift his two fists.

Daring and resourcefulness they had, too; the ability to think faster and move faster than the enemy. These were the qualities which gave Lee the dazzling campaigns of Second Manassas and Chancellorsville and won Vicksburg for Grant.

16   Lastly, and perhaps greatest of all, there was the ability, at the end, to turn quickly from war to peace once the fighting was over. Out of the way these two men behaved at Appomattox came the possibility of a peace of reconciliation. It was a possibility not wholly realized, in the years to come, but which did, in the end, help the two sections to become one nation again . . . after a war whose bitterness might have seemed to make such a reunion wholly impossible. No part of either man's life became him more than the part he played in this brief meeting in the McLean house at Appomattox. Their behavior there put all succeeding generations of Americans in their debt. Two great Americans, Grant and Lee—very different, yet under everything very much alike. Their encounter at Appomattox was one of the great moments of U.S. history.

READER RESPONSE

In what ways has this essay expanded your understanding of the Civil War?

QUESTIONS FOR DISCUSSION

1. Explain, in your own words, how, according to Catton, Robert E. Lee represented aristocracy and Ulysses S. Grant represented the opposite. Do you think the United States still has the differences those two men represented?
2. State how Grant and Lee were similar, according to Catton.
3. Catton writes, "Each man was the perfect champion of his cause" (paragraph 12). In what ways was each man a hero?
4. What "debt" do "succeeding generations of Americans" owe Grant and Lee (paragraph 16)?

SUGGESTIONS FOR WRITING ABOUT
ROLE MODELS AND HEROES

1. Define the word *courage,* and illustrate that definition with at least one example of someone who performed a courageous act.

2. Write an essay focused on one particular group or individual whom you admire for acting heroically during or after the attacks on the World Trade Center and the Pentagon on September 11, 2001. Explain why you admire the group or person and how the group or person serves as a role model.

3. Taking into consideration selected readings from this chapter, define *role model.* Consider what common definitions of this term the writers share, whether you disagree with how any of them defines the term, and what you would add to the definition that emerges through these readings.

4. Roger Wilkins ("I Became Her Target") and Nicholas Gage ("The Teacher Who Changed My Life") describe colorful or remarkable people who had a strong influence on them. Taking their descriptive techniques as models, write an essay describing a person whom you find to be colorful and/or admirable, such as a parent, friend, relative, teacher, or coach. Try to convey the characteristics of that person and to explain, as precisely as possible, what you like and admire about her or him.

5. Bill Thompson, in "It's Too Bad We Don't Have Another Roy," notes that it is "a rare and gratifying cohesion of truth and fiction [that] the reel hero [Roy Rogers] was a real hero." Write an essay on another "reel hero" who is also a "real hero."

6. Nicholas Gage writes from his perspective as a Greek American and Roger Wilkins as an African American. Compare and contrast the views of these writers on the subject of American education or American culture. Include a statement about your own ethnic heritage and your position in relation to these writers on the subject of education or culture.

7. In "Lessons from Two Ghosts," Scott Fisher states his belief that his two friends were preparing to be skilled educators. Define *skilled educator,* and illustrate your definition by using examples of teachers you have had. You might consider comparing two teachers, one whom you believe to be skilled and the other unskilled.

8. Select one of the people Howard Zinn, in "Unsung Heroes," says that we should admire, find out more about him or her, and write a paper explaining whether you agree with Zinn that this person should be regarded as a hero.

9. Howard Zinn, in "Unsung Heroes," says that we all know individuals who have acted heroically but whose actions are not widely recognized or even known. Write an essay about a person you know who has done something heroic that others may not know about.

10. Using Bruce Catton's "Grant and Lee: A Study in Contrasts" as a model, compare and/or contrast two people who represent opposing views.

They could be people you know personally (friends, parents, or relatives), people you have read about (fictional characters or historic figures), or people you know through other means (performers, actors, or sports heroes).

11. Research either Grant's or Lee's life, and write an opinion essay on how you regard the man after learning more about him.

12. Write an essay on what defines nobility of character, and apply it to a person you know.

13. Argue in support of or against the statement that the United States no longer has heroes.

14. Argue in support of or against the statement that U.S. schools should teach about role models from minority groups.

15. Explain who your heroes are and why.

16. Explain how someone has had a strong effect on you, perhaps influencing you to see yourself differently, gain self-confidence, solve difficulties you were having, or determine goals for yourself.

17. Describe a person whom you admire for bravery or strength during a difficult time.

7

GENDERED RELATIONSHIPS

The readings in this chapter explore some of the issues related to relationships between men and women, including communication, friendship, love, and marriage. The topics discussed include ways to eliminate barriers between men and women, societal expectations regarding marriage, and the importance of commitment for making relationships work.

The chapter begins with a selection by Deborah Tannen, whose extensive research into the different communication styles of men and women has gained widespread national attention. "Sex, Lies, and Conversation" summarizes her findings about patterns of conversation between the sexes, notes the ways in which the different conversational styles of men and women affect relationships, and offers insights for overcoming those difficulties. Next, Deborah Blum, in "What's the Difference Between Boys and Girls?," considers the differences in behavior between boys and girls. She asks: "When is biology the primary influence? When does culture overtake it, and at what point, in the startling fluid landscape of human behavior, does one alter the other?" As you read Blum's essay, try to recall your early childhood—the toys you played with, the games you played, and your playmates.

Shifting the focus to love relationships between men and women, Carol Tavris, in "Love Story," argues for a vision of human love that differs from the one U.S. society seems to accept and support. Beginning and ending the selection with the love story of Annie Oakley and Frank Butler, Tavris maintains that if men and women would respect the differences and similarities between them, they could achieve an abiding intimacy and longlasting love. Similarly,

Wendell Berry, in "Men and Women in Search of Common Ground," is interested in improving the relationships between men and women. In this essay, written for a symposium on the subject of his title, he explores reasons why "relationships between men and women are now too often extremely tentative and temporary," and he suggests ways to make them "sound and permanent."

The next two essays respond to the dim view society takes of men older than forty who choose not to marry and of women in their early twenties who choose to marry. Ron Beathard, in "Over Forty and Unmarried," maintains that single men are widely misunderstood and even considered the suspect, although the discrimination against them is "benign and curious—and often amusing." Whereas Beathard's perspective is that of an older man who has chosen not to marry, Katherine Davis explores the dismay—and even hostility—that her decision to marry young created. In "I'm Not Sick, I'm Just in Love," Davis explains how her decision to marry at age twenty-three caused a furor among her friends.

The chapter ends with Julie Showalter's short story "Vows," which features a couple who marry despite having learned from previous failed marriages that love sometimes does not last and can even turn nasty and vindictive. The story explores the nature of commitment in light of that knowledge, and it affirms the possibilities for lasting love.

1. What is your view of relationships between the sexes? Do you find that you and/or your friends have successful relationships?
2. What makes a relationship work?
3. How can people break down barriers to good communication between the sexes?

DISCUSSION QUESTIONS/WRITING SUGGESTIONS

1. How would you define a successful marriage?
2. What benefits or drawbacks does marriage offer compared to remaining single?
3. To what extent does society privilege married people over single people? Do you feel pressured to marry?
4. Based on what you have experienced or observed, contrast the attitudes of men and women on dating, sex, commitment, and/or marriage.

Sex, Lies, and Conversation
Deborah Tannen

Deborah Tannen is professor of linguistics at Georgetown University. Her book, You Just Don't Understand: Women and Men in Conversation *(1990) was widely discussed on television, in print, and among couples across the nation. Tannen's other books include* That's Not What I Meant: How Conversational Style Makes or Breaks Relationships *(1986),* Talking from 9 to 5: Women and Men in the Workplace: Language, Sex, and Power *(1994),* Gender and Discourse *(1994), and* The Argument Culture: Moving from Debate to Dialogue *(1998). This article first appeared in the* Washington Post *on June 14, 1990, with the subtitle "Why Is It So Hard for Men and Women to Talk to Each Other?"*

I was addressing a small gathering in a suburban Virginia living room—a women's group that had invited men to join them. Throughout the evening, one man had been particularly talkative, frequently offering ideas and anecdotes, while his wife sat silently beside him on the couch. Toward the end of the evening, I commented that women frequently complain that their husbands don't talk to them. This man quickly concurred. He gestured toward his wife and said, "She's the talker in our family." The room burst into laughter; the man looked puzzled and hurt. "It's true," he explained. "When I come home from work I have nothing to say. If she didn't keep the conversation going, we'd spend the whole evening in silence."

This episode crystallizes the irony that although American men tend to talk more than women in public situations, they often talk less at home. And this pattern is wreaking havoc with marriage.

The pattern was observed by political scientist Andrew Hacker in the late '70s. Sociologist Catherine Kohler Riessman reports in her new book *Divorce Talk* that most of the women she interviewed—but only a few of the men—gave lack of communication as the reason for their divorces. Given the current divorce rate of nearly 50 percent, that amounts to millions of cases in the United States every year—a virtual epidemic of failed conversation.

4   In my own research, complaints from women about their husbands most often focused not on tangible inequities such as having given up the chance for a career to accompany a husband to his, or doing far more than their share of daily life-support work like cleaning, cooking, social arrangements and errands. Instead, they focused on communication: "He doesn't listen to me," "He doesn't talk to me." I found, as Hacker observed years before, that most wives ⟵ want their husbands to be, first and foremost, conversational partners, but few husbands share this expectation of their wives.

In short, the image that best represents the current crisis is the stereotypical cartoon scene of a man sitting at the breakfast table with a newspaper held up in front of his face while a woman glares at the back of it, wanting to talk.

LINGUISTIC BATTLE OF THE SEXES

How can women and men have such different impressions of communication in marriage? Why the widespread imbalance in their interests and expectations?

In the April [1990] issue of *American Psychologist,* Stanford University's Eleanor Macoby reports the results of her own and others' research showing that children's development is most influenced by the social structure of peer interactions. Boys and girls tend to play with children of their own gender, and their sex-separate groups have different organizational structures and interactive norms.

8   I believe these systematic differences in childhood socialization make talk between women and men like cross-cultural communication, heir to all the attraction and pitfalls of that enticing but difficult enterprise. My research on men's and women's conversations uncovered patterns similar to those described for children's groups.

For women, as for girls, intimacy is the fabric of relationships, and talk is the thread from which it is woven. Little girls create and maintain friendships by exchanging secrets; similarly, women regard conversation as the cornerstone of friendship. So a woman expects her husband to be a new and improved version of a best friend. What is important is not the individual subjects that are discussed but the sense of closeness, of a life shared, that emerges when people tell their thoughts, feelings, and impressions.

Bonds between boys can be as intense as girls', but they are based less on talking, more on doing things together. Since they don't assume talk is the cement that binds a relationship, men don't know what kind of talk women want, and they don't miss it when it isn't there.

Boys' groups are larger, more inclusive, and more hierarchical, so boys must struggle to avoid the subordinate position in the group. This may play a role in women's complaints that men don't listen to them. Some men really don't like to listen, because being the listener makes them feel one-down, like a child listening to adults or an employee to a boss.

12   But often when women tell men, "You aren't listening," and the men protest, "I am," the men are right. The impression of not listening results from misalignments in the mechanics of conversation. The misalignment begins as soon as a man and a woman take physical positions. This became clear when I studied videotapes made by psychologist Bruce Dorval of children and adults talking to their same-sex best friends. I found that at every age, the girls and women faced each other directly, their eyes anchored on each other's faces. At every age, the boys and men sat at angles to each other and looked elsewhere in the room, periodically glancing at each other. They were obviously attuned to each other, often mirroring each other's movements. But the tendency of

men to face away can give women the impression they aren't listening even when they are. A young woman in college was frustrated: Whenever she told her boyfriend she wanted to talk to him, he would lie down on the floor, close his eyes, and put his arm over his face. This signaled to her "He's taking a nap." But he insisted he was listening extra-hard. Normally, he looks around the room, so he is easily distracted. Lying down and covering his eyes helped him concentrate on what she was saying.

Analogous to the physical alignment that women and men take in conversation is their topical alignment. The girls in my study tended to talk at length about one topic, but the boys tended to jump from topic to topic. The second-grade girls exchanged stories about people they knew. The second-grade boys teased, told jokes, noticed things in the room and talked about finding games to play. The sixth-grade girls talked about problems with a mutual friend. The sixth-grade boys talked about 55 different topics, none of which extended over more than a few turns.

LISTENING TO BODY LANGUAGE

Switching topics is another habit that gives women the impression men aren't listening, especially if they switch to a topic about themselves. But the evidence of the 10th-grade boys in my study indicates otherwise. The 10th-grade boys sprawled across their chairs with bodies parallel and eyes straight ahead, rarely looking at each other. They looked as if they were riding in a car, staring out the windshield. But they were talking about their feelings. One boy was upset because a girl had told him he had a drinking problem, and the other was feeling alienated from all his friends.

Now, when a girl told a friend about a problem, the friend responded by asking probing questions and expressing agreement and understanding. But the boys dismissed each other's problems. Todd assured Richard that his drinking was "no big problem" because "sometimes you're funny when you're off your butt." And when Todd said he felt left out, Richard responded, "Why should you? You know more people than me."

16   Women perceive such responses as belittling and unsupportive. But the boys seemed satisfied with them. Whereas women reassure each other by implying, "You shouldn't feel bad because I've had similar experiences," men do so by implying, "You shouldn't feel bad because your problems aren't so bad."

There are even simpler reasons for women's impression that men don't listen. Linguist Lynette Hirschman found that women make more listener-noise, such as "mhm," "uhuh," and "yeah," to show "I'm with you." Men, she found, more often give silent attention. Women who expect a stream of listener-noise interpret silent attention as no attention at all.

Women's conversational habits are as frustrating to men as men's are to women. Men who expect silent attention interpret a stream of listener-noise as overreaction or impatience. Also, when women talk to each other in a close, comfortable setting, they often overlap, finish each other's sentences and anticipate what the other is about to say. This practice, which I call "participatory listenership," is often perceived by men as interruption, intrusion and lack of attention.

A parallel difference caused a man to complain about his wife, "She just wants to talk about her own point of view. If I show her another view, she gets mad at me." When most women talk to each other, they assume a conversationalist's job is to express agreement and support. But many men see their conversational duty as pointing out the other side of an argument. This is heard as disloyalty by women, and refusal to offer the requisite support. It is not that women don't want to see other points of view, but that they prefer them phrased as suggestions and inquiries rather than as direct challenges.

20   In his book *Fighting for Life,* Walter Ong points out that men use "agonistic" or warlike, oppositional formats to do almost anything; thus discussion becomes debate, and conversation a competitive sport. In contrast, women see conversation as a ritual means of establishing rapport. If Jane tells a problem and June says she has a similar one, they walk away feeling closer to each other. But this attempt at establishing rapport can backfire when used with men. Men take too literally women's ritual "troubles talk," just as women mistake men's ritual challenges for real attack.

THE SOUNDS OF SILENCE

These differences begin to clarify why women and men have such different expectations about communication in marriage. For women, talk creates intimacy. Marriage is an orgy of closeness: you can tell your feelings and thoughts, and still be loved. Their greatest fear is being pushed away. But men live in a hierarchical world, where talk maintains independence and status. They are on guard to protect themselves from being put down and pushed around.

This explains the paradox of the talkative man who said of his silent wife, "She's the talker." In the public setting of a guest lecture, he felt challenged to show his intelligence and display his understanding of the lecture. But at home, where he has nothing to prove and no one to defend against, he is free to remain silent. For his wife, being home means she is free from the worry that something she says might offend someone, or spark disagreement, or appear to be showing off; at home she is free to talk.

The communication problems that endanger marriage can't be fixed by mechanical engineering. They require a new conceptual framework about the role of talk in human relationships. Many of the psychological explanations that have become second nature may not be helpful, because they tend to blame either women (for not being assertive enough) or men (for not being in touch with their feelings). A sociolinguistic approach by which male-female conversation is seen as cross-cultural communication allows us to understand the problem and forge solutions without blaming either party.

24   Once the problem is understood, improvement comes naturally, as it did to the young woman and her boyfriend who seemed to go to sleep when she

wanted to talk. Previously, she had accused him of not listening, and he had refused to change his behavior, since that would be admitting fault. But then she
learned about and explained to him the differences in women's and men's ha-
bitual ways of aligning themselves in conversation. The next time she told him
she wanted to talk, he began, as usual, by lying down and covering his eyes.
When the familiar negative reaction bubbled up, she reassured herself that he
really was listening. But then he sat up and looked at her. Thrilled, she asked
why. He said, "You like me to look at you when we talk, so I'll try to do it."
Once he saw their differences as cross-cultural rather than right and wrong,
he independently altered his behavior.

are there 2 diff. cultures—male/female.

   Women who feel abandoned and deprived when their husband won't
listen to or report daily news may be happy to discover their husbands trying
to adapt once they understand the place of small talk in women's relationships. But if their husbands don't adapt, the women may still be comforted
that for men, this is not a failure of intimacy. Accepting the difference, the
wives may look to their friends or family for that kind of talk. And husbands
who can't provide it shouldn't feel their wives have made unreasonable demands. Some couples will still decide to divorce, but at least their decisions
will be based on realistic expectations.

how to bridge the gap?

   In these times of resurgent ethnic conflicts, the world desperately needs
cross-cultural understanding. Like charity, successful cross-cultural communication should begin at home.

READER RESPONSE

How accurately do Tannen's conclusions about the different conversational
styles of men and women reflect your own experiences?

QUESTIONS FOR DISCUSSION

1. What do you think of the evidence that Tannen gives to support her assertion in paragraph 2 that men's noncommunicativeness at home is
   "wreaking havoc with marriage"? How does Tannen account for the paradox in her opening paragraph about the talkative man who says his wife
   is "the talker"?
2. Can you offer your own answer to the questions Tannen poses in paragraph 6: "How can women and men have such different impressions of
   communication in marriage? Why the widespread imbalance in their interests and expectations?"
3. How do the differences Tannen has identified between men's and
   women's conversational styles cause frustration for both men and women
   when communicating with members of the other sex? Besides those Tannen mentions, what other differences in the conversational practices of
   men and women have you observed?

4. What do you think of the solution Tannen offers to the communication problems between men and women?

What's the Difference Between Boys and Girls?

Deborah Blum

Deborah Blum is a journalist and author of many works on ecology and environmental science. She received the Pulitzer Prize for her 1994 book Monkey Wars *and, more recently, has written* Sex on the Brain: The Biological Differences Between Men and Women *(1997) and* Love at Goon Park: Harry Harlow and the Science of Affection *(2002). This essay appeared in the July 1999 issue of* Life.

My four-year-old son asked for a Barbie this year. His blue eyes were hopeful, his small face angelic. His mother was suspicious.

Between this child and his older brother, our house is a Toys R Us warehouse of heavily muscled action figures, dinosaurs with jagged teeth, light-up swords, and leaking water pistols. Complaint is constant—Oh, Mom, you're no fun—over my refusal to buy more additions to the arsenal. My older son at one point began to see weapons in household objects the way adults dream up phallic symbols. "Shoot her with the toothbrush," he once shouted to a companion as they chased the cat around the house.

"Why do you want the Barbie, honey?" I asked.

4   "I wanna chop her head off."

There I was again, standing at the edge of the great gender divide, the place and the moment where one becomes absolutely sure that the opposite sex is, in fact, opposite. I know of no way for women of my generation, raised to believe in gender neutrality, to reach this edge faster than through trying to raise children.

"I did not do this," a friend insisted on the day her son started carefully biting his toast into the shape of a gun. "I think my daughter has a pink gene," a British journalist confided recently, as she confessed that her daughter has not only a Barbie collection but all the matched plastic purses and tiny high-heeled shoes. I don't think in pastels, myself. I think jungle-green, blood-red. Most of all, I think there's a reason—a reasonable biology—to the differences we see in little boys and girls, men and women, males and females.

We are, I hope, moving past the old politically correct notion that we are pure culture, that children are born blank slates to be influenced—or, worse, manipulated—by the adults around them. There's a straightforward reason why we are a male-female species: Reproductively, it works. We are all born with bodies designed to be the same (breathe, circulate blood) and to be different (produce sperm, produce eggs, produce milk, produce none). There's an internal biology—structural and behavioral—that supports those differences. It's not all of who we are, but it's a part. When is biology the primary influence? Where does culture overtake it, and at what point, in the startling fluid landscape of human behavior, does one alter the other?

8   One of my favorite illustrations of the way culture fine-tunes us for gender roles has to do with the Barbie versus Godzilla effect. It turns out that lots of little boys ask for dolls and other so-called girl toys. They aren't encouraged though; parents really hesitate to buy their children "gender inappropriate" toys. In a study involving almost 300 children, researchers found that if little boys asked for a soldier equipped with battle cannons for their birthday, they got it some 70 percent of the time. If they asked for a Barbie doll, or any of her plastic peers, the success rate was 40 percent or less. Can you think of a child who wouldn't figure out in, oh, a day, how to work that system?

Marc Breedlove, a neuroscientist at the University of California, Berkeley, points out that splitting apart biology and culture is analogous to splitting hairs. But scientists try to separate the strands anyway, exhaustively exploring early development. A few ambitious scientists have even looked for prebirth differences, arguing that it's difficult to slap too much cultural attitude onto a fetus. It turns out that boy fetuses are a little more active, more restless, than girl fetuses. And in the first year after birth, toy preferences already seem distinct: Boy infants rapidly engage with more mechanical or structural toys; little girls of a few months gravitate toward toys with faces, toys that can be cuddled.

The world of play—the toys we gravitate to, how we play with them, how we play in general—has now become serious business to scientists. Today's hottest theory of play is that it's a practice run at the challenges of adult life. Through games, the experts tell us, we learn the art of measuring the competition, how to win and lose gracefully (we hope), which leads pretty directly into how to build friendships. In scientific terms, we learn socialization.

"Play offers a non–life-threatening way of asserting yourself," says Christine Drea, a researcher. "By playing, you learn skills of managing competition and aggression." We are a social species. We find isolation destructive, and we establish patterns of childhood play that reflect adult social structures. In humans, our patterns tend to conform to our chemistry: Human males are likely to produce seven to ten times more testosterone, for example, than females. . . . And so, you would correctly predict, little boys tend to be more rough-and-tumble than little girls. That's true, in fact, for the entire realm of primates (monkey, apes, man).

12   Back in the late 1970s, Robert Goy, a psychologist at the University of Wisconsin, first documented that young male monkeys consistently played much more roughly than juvenile females. Goy then went on to show that if

you manipulate testosterone level—raising it in females, cutting it off in males—you reverse those effects, creating sweet little boy monkeys and rough-and-tumble girls. We don't experiment with human development this way, obviously. But there are naturally occurring genetic variations that make closely comparable points. As mentioned earlier, human males circulate higher levels of testosterone. There's a well-known exception, however, called congenital adrenal hyperplasia (CAH), in which a baby girl's adrenal gland inadvertently boosts testosterone levels. Researchers have found that CAH girls, in general, prefer trucks and cars and aggressive play. That doesn't mean they don't join in more traditional girl games with friends—but if left to choose, they prefer to play on the rowdy side of the street.

Higher testosterone levels are also responsible for another characteristic: competitiveness. In fact, testosterone is almost predictable in this regard. It shoots up before a competition; that's been measured in everything from chess matches to soccer games to courtroom battles to brawls. It stays up if you win, drops if you lose. Its role, scientists think, is to get you up and running and right on the competitive edge.

Even in preschool, boys and girls fall into very different play patterns. Boys tend to gather in larger, competitive groups. They play games that have clear winners and losers and bluster through them, boasting about their skills. Girls, early on, gather in small groups, playing theatrical games that don't feature hierarchy or winners. One study of children aged three to four found they were already resolving conflict in separate ways—boys resorting to threats, girls negotiating verbally and often reaching a compromise.

There are some provocative new insights into that verbal difference. Recently, researchers at Emory University have found that little female monkeys are much quicker to pick up "verbal" skills than little boy monkeys. Sound familiar? The small female monkeys do more contact calling (cooing affectionately) than their male counterparts. And it appears, again, that this is related to their mothers' prenatal hormones. Some very preliminary tests suggest that females exposed to androgens early in their fetal development become more like male monkeys: They are less likely to use language to express themselves.

16 In humans, too, we look for natural biological variations. In general, girls have sharper hearing than boys—the tiny hair cells that register sound waves vibrate more forcefully. These are ears tuned for intense communication. (The rare exception tends to be in boy-girl twin pairs. Those girls are more likely to have ears built a little more like their brothers'—less active hair cells, notched-down response. Researchers looking at this suspect a higher exposure to androgens in utero.) There's something about the biology of the egg-producing sex that seems to demand more acute communication abilities.

Of course, there's a whole range of personalities and behaviors that don't fall into any of the obvious stereotypes. What about tomboys, those exuberant girls who prefer softball to tea parties? What about the affectionate sweetness of little boys, who—away from the battle zone of their friends and brothers—turn out to be surprisingly cuddly and clingy? What about the female stiff, the chatty male, and so on, into infinity? The quick answer: Sex differences are group differences, overall patterns.

The complex of genes and hormones and neurotransmitters and internal chemistry that may influence our behaviors varies from person to person and is designed to be flexible. There's nothing in average, everyday biology that forbids either the truck-loving girl or the boy who likes to play house, the aggressive, competitive adult woman, or the nurturing, stay-at-home man. Human biology makes room for every possible type of personality and sexuality in the range between those stereotypes.

And finally, the way we behave can actually influence our biology. The link between testosterone and competition makes this point perfectly. Yes, corporate lawyers tend to have higher testosterone levels than ministers. But there's a chicken-or-egg aspect to this. Is the lawyer someone born with a high testosterone level? Or is it the profession that pushed it up? Or some combination of both? It's worth noting that the parallel works in men and in women; women in competitive jobs have more testosterone; men who stay home with their children have less.

20   Nothing in biology labels behaviors as right or wrong, normal or abnormal. Any stereotypes we impose on children—and, by extension, adults—are purely cultural, not biological. For example: Little boys are noisy and rambunctious; we tend to equate that with being emotionally tough. But what science actually tells us is the exact opposite. Little boys, we're learning, need a lot of emotional support. One revealing study of children of depressed and withdrawn mothers, done at U.C. Berkeley, found that a lack of affection actually lowered the IQ of little boys. Laura Allen, a neuroscientist at the University of California, Los Angeles, explains it like this: "I think boys need more one-on-one attention. I think affection may change the sex hormone level in the brain, which then affects brain development." Both the Berkeley study and a more recent federal daycare study find a different pattern in girls. They're emotionally sturdier—I think most of us have already figured this out—and their healthy development seems most harmed by being restricted. It's confinement that seems to drive down IQ in our daughters.

What's the real difference between boys and girls? More, and less, than we thought. With rare exceptions, the anatomy of gender is straightforward, separate. But the chemistry of gender is more complex. It's a continuum, I think, and we can each find a place within the wide band of "normal." What's more, we can change our place. And we can influence our children's places— not by force but by guidance.

And so, if you're wondering, I did not buy my son the doll. I'm too grown up these days to approve of dismembering pricey toys. I did let him pick out a scaled-down Barbie, instead of a toy car, in one of those fast-food kid's meal promotions. It turned out to be cream and gold in appearance, annoyingly indestructible, and he lost interest. These days, he likes to make books and draw pictures of blood-dripping dinosaurs. Me? I pass him the red crayons.

PERSONAL RESPONSE

In recalling your memories of early childhood, how much do you think your dress, your toys, the games you played, and even your behavior were influenced by your culture? Is it possible for you to determine how much those choices were biologically as opposed to culturally influenced?

QUESTIONS FOR DISCUSSION

1. What do you think Blum means by the phrases "gender neutrality" (paragraph 5) and "gender inappropriate" (paragraph 8)? What is your view of these concepts? That is, to what extent have you thought in terms of "neutrality" and "inappropriate" in relation to gender?
2. Based on your own experience and observations, discuss your response to the questions Blum asks in paragraph 7: "When is biology the primary influence? When does culture overtake it, and at what point . . . does one alter the other?"
3. What do you understand Blum to mean by "the Barbie versus Godzilla effect" (paragraph 8)? Can you give examples that either support or refute her point?
4. To what extent do your own experiences and observations support or contradict what various studies have concluded about the role of play in children's lives.

Love Story
Carol Tavris

Carol Tavris is a social psychologist, writer, and lecturer. She has written numerous articles and book reviews on many aspects of psychology for a wide variety of general interest magazines, such as Psychology Today, Discover, Harper's, New York, *and* Vogue. *Her books include* The Longest War: Sex Differences in Perspective *(1984) and* Psychology *(seventh ed., 2002), both coedited by Carole Wade;* Anger: The Misunderstood Emotion *(1989);* The Mismeasure of Woman *(1992), from which the following piece is excerpted; and* Invitation to Psychology *(2002).*

As a child, I was nuts about cowboys, guns, and Palomino ponies, and so when I first saw the musical *Annie Get Your Gun* I was in heaven. Annie Oakley was a woman who could ride, wear cowgirl outfits, and shoot. She became

my hero at once. She sang "Anything you can do, I can do better," and she out-
shot her rival, Frank Butler. I loved Annie Oakley so much that I entirely
blocked out the end of the musical, when she realizes that "You can't get a
man with a gun." Annie deliberately blows her next competition with Butler,
who of course then realizes he loves her after all. I couldn't understand why a
woman would give up being the world's best sharpshooter (even for Frank
Butler, who was definitely terrific), or why Frank Butler would love Annie only
if she gave up sharpshooting.

I wish I had known then what I know now: In the real-life story of Annie
Oakley and Frank Butler, she never had to make that choice. Annie did get her
man with a gun. In 1875, as a teenager, she defeated Frank Butler in an
arranged competition. "It was her first big match—my first defeat," wrote Butler. "The next day I came back to see the little girl who had beaten me, and it
was not long until we were married."[1] For the next fifty years they worked
and traveled together in Europe and America, Annie as featured sharpshooter
in the Buffalo Bill Wild West show and Frank as her manager. They remained
devoted, and Frank continued to express his affections for Annie in published
love poems and interviews with the press. They died, within eighteen days of
one another, in 1926.

"Why was the true love story of Annie Oakley and Frank Butler discarded as the basis for the musical?" asks writer Bonnie Kreps.[2] Because, she
argues, the real story was not romantic enough—which is to say, it did not fit
our myths of love. The strong silent hero does not rescue the poor weak lamb.
The woman does not have to trade love for competence; she's allowed to
have both. The man does not have to squeeze himself into some frozen mold
of masculinity, competing with the woman over who does what better. Instead, he speaks, in a human voice, of his love and admiration for the "little girl
who had beaten me." The true love story would never sell.

4   The feminization of love in America, the glorification of women's ways
of loving, is not about the love between autonomous individuals. It celebrates
a romantic, emotional love that promotes the myth of basic, essential differences between women and men. It supports the opposition of women's love
and men's work. In so doing, it derails women from thinking about their own
talents and aspirations, rewarding instead a narrowed focus on finding and
keeping Mr. Right.[3]

---

[1] Butler's memoirs cited in Bonnie Kreps (1990), *Subversive thoughts, authentic passions*
(San Francisco: Harper & Row, 1990), p. 78.

[2] Ibid., p. 79.

[3] See Dorothy C. Holland and Margaret A. Eisenhart (1991), *Educated in romance: Women,
achievement, and college culture* (Chicago: University of Chicago Press), who studied college
women at two southern schools over a period of several (recent) years. They found that peer
pressure and patriarchal culture are sharply curtailing the aspirations and expectations of young
women today. Many are entering college with high hopes and ambitions, and leaving with the
single goal of catching the right husband.

The stereotype of woman-as-love-expert blurs the similarity between the sexes in their human needs for love, intimacy, and attachment, *and* for autonomy and self-development.[4] It allows men's needs for attachment to remain covert and repressed, while women's needs become overt and exaggerated. It encourages women to overfocus on relationships and men to underfocus on them. As Francesca Cancian says, "When women are unhappy, they usually think they need more love; but the objective evidence suggests that they need more independence."[5] When men are unhappy, they usually think they need more success; but the objective evidence suggests that they need more time "to smell the flowers."

Women who live only for love will inevitably love too much. The need will become bottomless and unfillable, like the equally unquenchable thirst among some who live only for work, for more and more wealth. The trouble with romantic love, says Bonnie Kreps, is that it blinds women to the less charming realities of life with the Prince. Many women become what she calls a Reverse Sleeping Beauty: They kiss the Prince and promptly fall asleep. This is why so many of love's experts become, too easily, love's victims.

To move toward an alternative vision of human love, women and men would have to budge from their current certainty that their sex is the only one that knows how to love.

8   We would stop blaming women for everything that happens in the family and make men as accountable as women for the quality of family life. We would recognize that men's silences and absences have as deep and powerful an effect on the people around them as do the words and interventions of women.

We would value, as a society, the loving work that women and men do for one another. We would value, along with the ability to express feelings, productive work in the home and the physical care of others. We would acknowledge the ways men love, instead of assuming that they are helpless incompetents in the domains of feeling and the family.

We would break the polarity between the "male" model of stoicism and the "female" emotions it defends against. There is a place for stoicism. No one wants a firefighter to burst into tears at the sight of a fire, and in a crisis everyone should know how to behave without collapsing into puddles of anxiety.

---

[4] Studies of love, intimacy, grief, and attachment find no sex differences of any significance. Men and women are equally likely, for example, to have "secure" attachments or those marked by anxiety, ambivalence, and avoidance; see Phillip Shaver, Cindy Hazen, and Donna Bradshaw (1988), Love as attachment: The integration of three behavioral systems, in R. J. Sternberg and M. L. Barnes (Eds.), *The psychology of love* (New Haven, CT: Yale University Press). Paul Wright (1988) [Interpreting research on gender differences in friendship: A case for moderation and a plea for caution, *Journal of Social and Personal Relationships,* 5, 367–373] warns of the hazards of falsely dividing men and women into two exaggerated extremes, since the same kinds of experiences and exchanges take place to some degree in all close friendships.

[5] Francesca M. Cancian (1987), *Love in America: Gender and self-development* (Cambridge, England: Cambridge University Press), p. 81.

But there is also a place for feeling; empathy, remorse, regret, worry, sadness, and compassion are our links to other people and to the human condition.

None of this means, in my opinion, that women should try turning their husbands into their girlfriends, or that men should try to make their wives into one of the boys. Such efforts are bound to backfire, even when both participants know the other person's love language. One friend of mine told her lover, "Herb, I don't want you to do the male thing just now. I don't need advice. I've had a bad day, and I just want you to hold me and console me." He looked absolutely perplexed. "What good will that do?" he said.

12   Nor am I recommending some vague androgynous ideal, in which women have to give up their love of intimate chat and men have to give up teasing and kidding around. Instead, I am arguing for flexibility, the ability to speak both languages when required. I admit that narrow rules for a division of emotional labor are easier to follow. I think it will be as uncomfortable, even frightening, for women to modify their fondness for talk and risk independent action, when this is called for, as for men to modify their silences and risk vulnerability. It's much easier for women to focus on changing men, even if the results are few and puny, than to develop their own programs of self-development. It's much easier for men to withdraw into silence than to try to articulate the fears and losses that jeopardize masculine identity.

But perhaps we can begin by accepting the fact that neither sex has all the answers. Couples can regard each other as a source of charming anecdotes, a repository of a different kind of expertise, and a resource in emergencies. They can exchange help, knowledge, talents, stories, and experiences An abiding intimacy, in contrast to the fleeting intimacy of momentary emotions, does not require that partners be the same. It requires a reciprocity of affection, power, and respect for differences—the basis of a love between equals, the love between Annie Oakley and Frank Butler.

READER RESPONSE

To what degree does Tavris's analysis fit your personal view of men and women in love? If you are in love, how well does her analysis fit your relationship?

QUESTIONS FOR DISCUSSION

1. What are the "myths of love" that Tavris refers to in paragraph 3? How does the movie version of the Annie Oakley/Frank Butler relationship support Tavris's point about such myths? Can you provide other examples of movies that support her point?

2. What do you understand Tavris to mean by "the feminization of love" (paragraph 4)? Discuss the extent to which you agree with Tavris's point about its effects on male–female relationships.

3. Tavris calls for a "move toward an alternative vision of human love" (paragraph 7). State, in your own words, what Tavris believes we would have to do to achieve that alternative vision. Do you agree with her that such a vision of human love is achievable or even desirable?

Men and Women in Search of Common Ground
Wendell Berry

Wendell Berry is a poet, novelist, essayist, and farmer who has published more than a dozen books. His collections of essays include The Long-Legged Horse *(1969),* The Hidden Wound *(1970),* A Continuous Harmony *(1972),* The Unsettling of America *(1977),* The Gift of Good Land *(1981),* Standing by Woods *(1985),* A Continuous Harmony *(1988), and* Another Turn of the Crank *(1995). His book* What Are People For? *(1990) was issued on the twentieth anniversary of Earth Day and addresses his ongoing concern with the future of the human race and his belief that we must change the way we live to avoid destruction. "Men and Women in Search of Common Ground" is from Berry's 1987 collection of essays,* Home Economics.

The domestic joys, the daily housework or business,
the building of houses—they are not phantasms . . .
they have weight and form and location.

Walt Whitman, To Think of Time

I am not an authority on men or women or any of the possible connections between them. In sexual matters I am an amateur, in both the ordinary and the literal senses of that word. I speak about them only because I am concerned about them; I am concerned about them only because I am involved in them; I am involved in them, apparently, only because I am a human, a qualification for which I deserve no credit.

I do not believe, moreover, that any individual *can* be an authority on the present subject. The common ground between men and women can only be defined by community authority. Individually, we may desire it and think about it, but we are not going to occupy it if we do not arrive there together.

That we have not arrived there, that we apparently are not very near to doing so, is acknowledged by the title of this symposium ["Men and Women in Search of Common Ground," a symposium at the Jung Institute of San

Francisco]. And that a symposium so entitled should be held acknowledges implicitly that we are not happy in our exile. The specific cause of our unhappiness, I assume, is that relationships between men and women are now too often extremely tentative and temporary, whereas we would like them to be sound and permanent.

4   Apparently, it is in the nature of all human relationships to aspire to be permanent. To propose temporariness as a goal in such relationships is to bring them under the rule of aims and standards that prevent them from beginning. Neither marriage, nor kinship, nor friendship, nor neighborhood can exist with a life expectancy that is merely convenient.

To see that such connections aspire to permanence, we do not have to look farther than popular songs, in which people still speak of loving each other "forever." We now understand, of course, that in this circumstance the word "forever" is not to be trusted. It may mean only "for a few years" or "for a while" or even "until tomorrow morning." And we should not be surprised to realize that if the word "forever" cannot be trusted in this circumstance, then the word "love" cannot be trusted either.

This, as we know, was often true before our own time, though in our time it seems easier than before to say "I will love you forever" and to mean nothing by it. It is possible for such words to be used cynically—that is, they may be intended to mean nothing—but I doubt that they are often used with such simple hypocrisy. People continue to use them, I think, because they continue to try to mean them. They continue to express their sexual feelings with words such as "love" and "forever" because they want those feelings to have a transferable value, like good words or good money. They cannot bear for sex to be "just sex," any more than they can bear for family life to be just reproduction or for friendship to be just a mutually convenient exchange of goods and services.

The questions that I want to address here, then, are: Why are sexual and other human relationships now so impermanent? And under what conditions might they become permanent?

8   It cannot be without significance that this division is occurring at a time when division has become our characteristic mode of thinking and acting. Everywhere we look now, the axework of division is going on. We see ourselves more and more as divided from each other, from nature, and from what our traditions define as human nature. The world is now full of nations, races, interests, groups, and movements of all sorts, most of them unable to define their relations to each other except in terms of division and opposition. The poor human body itself has been conceptually hacked to pieces and parceled out like a bureaucracy. Brain and brawn, left brain and right brain, stomach, hands, heart, and genitals have all been set up in competition against each other, each supported by its standing army of advocates, press agents, and merchants. In such a time, it is not surprising that the stresses that naturally, and perhaps desirably, occur between the sexes should result in the same sort of division with the same sort of doctrinal justification.

This condition of division is one that we suffer from and complain about, yet it is a condition that we promote by our ambitions and desires and justify by our jargon of "self-fulfillment." Each of us, we say, is supposed to "realize his or her full potential as an individual." It is as if the whole two hundred million of us were saying with Coriolanus:

I'll never
Be such a gosling to obey instinct, but stand
As if a man were author of himself
And knew no other kin.

(V, iii, 34-37)

By "instinct" he means the love of family, community, and country. In Shakespeare's time, this "instinct" was understood to be the human norm—the definition of humanity, or a large part of that definition. When Coriolanus speaks these lines, he identifies himself, not as "odd," but as monstrous, a *danger* to family, community, and country. He identifies himself, that is, as an individual prepared to act alone and without the restraint of reverence, fidelity, or love. Shakespeare is at one with his tradition in understanding that such a person acted inevitably, not as the "author of himself," but as the author of tragic consequences both for himself and for other people.

The problem, of course, is that we are *not* the authors of ourselves. That we are not is a religious perception, but it is also a biological and a social one. Each of us has had many authors, and each of us is engaged, for better or worse, in that same authorship. We could say that the human race is a great coauthorship in which we are collaborating with God and nature in the making of ourselves and one another. From this there is no escape. We may collaborate either well or poorly, or we may refuse to collaborate, but even to refuse to collaborate is to exert an influence and to affect the quality of the product. This is only a way of saying that by ourselves we have no meaning and no dignity; by ourselves we are outside the human definition, outside our identity. "More and more," Mary Catharine Bateson wrote in *With a Daughter's Eye,* "it has seemed to me that the idea of an individual, the idea that there is someone to be known, separate from the relationships, is simply an error."

Some time ago I was with Wes Jackson, wandering among the experimental plots at his home and workplace, the Land Institute in Salina, Kansas. We stopped by one plot that had been planted in various densities of population. Wes pointed to a Maximilian sunflower growing alone, apart from the others, and said, "There is a plant that has 'realized its full potential as an individual.'"And clearly it had: It had grown very tall; it had put out many long branches heavily laden with blossoms—and the branches had broken off, for they had grown too long and too heavy. The plant had indeed realized its full potential as an individual, but it had failed as a Maximilian sunflower. We could say that its full potential as an individual *was* this failure. It had failed because it had lived outside an important part of its definition, which consists

of *both* its individuality and its community. A part of its properly realizable potential lay in its community, not in itself.

12   In making a metaphor of this sunflower, I do not mean to deny the value
or the virtue of a *proper* degree of independence in the character and economy of an individual, nor do I mean to deny the conflicts that occur between
individuals and communities. Those conflicts belong to our definition, too, and
are probably as necessary as they are troublesome. I do mean to say that the
conflicts are not everything, and that to make conflict—the so-called "jungle
law"—the basis of social or economic doctrine is extremely dangerous. A part
of our definition is our common ground, and a part of it is sharing and mutually enjoying our common ground. Undoubtedly, also, since we are humans, a
part of our definition is a recurring contest over the common ground: Who
shall describe its boundaries, occupy it, use it, or own it? But such contests obviously can be carried too far, so that they become destructive both of the
commonality of the common ground and of the ground itself.

The danger of the phrase "common ground" is that it is likely to be meant as
no more than a metaphor. I am not using it as a metaphor; I mean by it the actual ground that is shared by whatever group we may be talking about—the
human race, a nation, a community, or a household. If we use the term only as
a metaphor, then our thinking will not be robustly circumstantial and historical, as it needs to be, but only a weak, clear broth of ideas and feelings

          Marriage, for example, is talked about most of the time as if it were only
a "human relationship" between a wife and a husband. A good marriage is
likely to be explained as the result of mutually satisfactory adjustments of
thoughts and feelings—a "deep" and complicated mental condition. That is
surely true for some couples some of the time, but, as a general understanding
of marriage, it is inadequate and probably unworkable. It is far too much a
thing of the mind and, for that reason, is not to be trusted. "God guard me,"
Yeats wrote, "from those thoughts men think/In the mind alone . . ."

          Yeats, who took seriously the principle of incarnation, elaborated this
idea in his essay on the Japanese Noh plays, in which he says that "we only believe in those thoughts which have been conceived not in the brain but in the
whole body." But we need a broader concept yet, for a marriage involves more
than just the bodies and minds of a man and a woman. It involves locality, human circumstance, and duration. There is a strong possibility that the basic human sexual unit is composed of a man and a woman (bodies and minds), plus
their history together, plus their kin and descendants, plus their place in the
world with its economy and history, plus their natural neighborhood, plus
their human community with its memories, satisfactions, expectations, and
hopes.

16   By describing it in such a way, we begin to understand marriage as the
insistently practical union that it is. We begin to understand it, that is, as it is
represented in the traditional marriage ceremony, those vows being only a
more circumstantial and practical way of saying what the popular songs say

dreamily and easily: "I will love you forever"—a statement that, in this world, inescapably leads to practical requirements and consequences because it proposes survival as a goal. Indeed, marriage is a union much more than practical, for it looks both to our survival as a species and to the survival of our definition as human beings—that is, as creatures who make promises and keep them, who care devotedly and faithfully for one another, who care properly for the gifts of life in this world.

The business of humanity is undoubtedly survival in this complex sense—a necessary, difficult, and entirely fascinating job of work. We have in us deeply planted instructions—personal, cultural, and natural—to survive, and we do not need much experience to inform us that we cannot survive alone. The smallest possible "survival unit," indeed, appears to be the universe. At any rate, the ability of an organism to survive outside the universe has yet to be demonstrated. Inside it, everything happens *in concert;* not a breath is drawn but by the grace of an inconceivable series of vital connections joining an inconceivable multiplicity of created things in an inconceivable unity. But of course it is preposterous for a mere individual human to espouse the universe—a possibility that is purely mental, and productive of nothing but talk. On the other hand, it may be that our marriages, kinships, friendships, neighborhoods, and all our forms and acts of homemaking are the rites by which we solemnize and enact our union with the universe. These ways are practical, proper, available to everybody, and they can provide for the safekeeping of the small acreages of the universe that have been entrusted to us. Moreover, they give the word "love" its only chance to mean, for only they can give it a history, a community, and a place. Only in such ways can love become flesh and do its worldly work. For example, a marriage without a place, a household, has nothing to show for itself. Without a history of some length, it does not know what it means. Without a community to exert a shaping pressure around it, it may explode because of the pressure inside it.

These ways of marriage, kinship, friendship, and neighborhood surround us with forbiddings; they are forms of bondage, and involved in our humanity is always the wish to escape. We may be obliged to look on this wish as necessary, for, as I have just implied, these unions are partly shaped by internal pressure. But involved in our humanity also is the warning that we can escape only into loneliness and meaninglessness. Our choice may be between a small, human-sized meaning and a vast meaninglessness, or between the freedom of our virtues and the freedom of our vices. It is only in these bonds that our individuality has a use and a worth; it is only to the people who know us, love us, and depend on us that we are indispensable as the persons we uniquely are. In our industrial society, in which people insist so fervently on their value and their freedom "as individuals," individuals are seen more and more as "units" by their governments, employers, and suppliers. They live, that is, under the rule of the interchangeability of parts: What one person can do, another person can do just as well or a newer person can do better. Separate from the relationships, there is nobody to be known; people become, as they say and feel, nobodies.

It is plain that, under the rule of the industrial economy, humans, at least as individuals, are well advanced in a kind of obsolescence. Among those who have achieved even a modest success according to the industrial formula, the human body has been almost entirely replaced by machines and by a shrinking population of manual laborers. For enormous numbers of people now, the only physical activity that they cannot delegate to machines or menials, who will presumably do it more to their satisfaction, is sexual activity. For many, the only necessary physical labor is that of childbirth.

20   According to the industrial formula, the ideal human residence (from the Latin *residere,* "to sit back" or "remain sitting") is one in which the residers do not work. The house is built, equipped, decorated, and provisioned by other people, by strangers. In it, the married couple practice as few as possible of the disciplines of household or homestead. Their domestic labor consists principally of buying things, putting things away, and throwing things away, but it is understood that it is "best" to have even those jobs done by an "inferior" person, and the ultimate industrial ideal is a "home" in which *everything* would be done by pushing buttons. In such a "home," a married couple are mates, sexually, legally, and socially, but they are not helpmates; they do nothing useful either together or for each other. According to the ideal, work should be done *away* from home. When such spouses say to each other, "I will love you forever," the meaning of their words is seriously impaired by their circumstances; they are speaking in the presence of so little that they have done and made. Their history together is essentially placeless; it has no visible or tangible incarnation. They have only themselves in view.

In such a circumstance, the obsolescence of the body is inevitable, and this is implicitly acknowledged by the existence of the "physical fitness movement." Back in the era of the body, when women and men were physically useful as well as physically attractive to one another, physical fitness was simply a condition. Little conscious attention was given to it; it was a by-product of useful work. Now an obsessive attention has been fixed upon it. Physical fitness has become extremely mental; once free, it has become expensive, an industry— just as sexual attractiveness, once the result of physical vigor and useful work, has now become an industry. The history of "sexual liberation" has been a history of increasing bondage to corporations.

Now the human mind appears to be following the human body into obsolescence. Increasingly, jobs that once were done by the minds of individual humans are done by computers—and by governments and experts. Dr. William C. DeVries, the current superstar of industrial heart replacement, can blithely assure a reporter that "the general society is not very well informed to make those decisions [as to the imposition of restraints on medical experiments on human patients], and that's why the medical society or the government who has a wider range of view comes in to make those decisions" (Louisville

Courier-Journal, 3 Feb. 1985). Thus we may benefit from the "miracle" of modern medical science on the condition that we delegate all moral and critical authority in such matters to the doctors and the government. We may save our bodies by losing our minds, just as, according to another set of experts, we may save our minds by forsaking our bodies. Computer thought is exactly the sort that Yeats warned us against; it is made possible by the assumption that thought occurs "in the mind alone" and that the mind, therefore, is an excerptable and isolatable human function, which can be set aside from all else that is human, reduced to pure process, and so imitated by a machine. But in fact we know that the *human* mind is not distinguishable from what it knows and that what it knows comes from or is radically conditioned by its embodied life in this world. A machine, therefore, cannot be a mind or be like a mind; it can only replace a mind.

We know, too, that these mechanical substitutions are part of a long-established process. The industrial economy has made its way among us by a process of division, degradation, and then replacement. It is only after we have been divided against each other that work and the products of work can be degraded; it is only after work and its products have been degraded that workers can be replaced by machines. Only when thought has been degraded can a mind be replaced by a machine, or a society of experts, or a government.

24   It is true, furthermore, that, in this process of industrialization, what is free is invariably replaced by a substitute that is costly. Bodily health as the result of useful work, for instance, is or was free, whereas industrial medicine, which has flourished upon the uselessness of the body, is damagingly and heartlessly expensive. In the time of the usefulness of the body, when the body became useless it died, and death was understood as a kind of healing; industrial medicine looks upon death as a disease that calls for increasingly expensive cures.

Similarly, in preindustrial country towns and city neighborhoods, the people who needed each other lived close to each other. This proximity was free, and it provided many benefits that were either free or comparatively cheap. This simple proximity has been destroyed and replaced by communications and transportation industries that are, again, enormously expensive and destructive, as well as extremely vulnerable to disruption.

Insofar as we reside in the industrial economy, our obsolescence, both as individuals and as humankind, is fast growing upon us. But we cannot regret or, indeed, even know that this is true without knowing and naming those never-to-be-official institutions that alone have the power to reestablish us in our true estate and identity: marriage, family, household, friendship, neighborhood, community. For these to have an effective existence, they must be located in the world and in time. So located, they have the power to establish us in our human identity because they are not merely institutions in a public, abstract sense, like the organized institutions but are also private conditions.

They are the conditions in which a human is complete, body and mind, because completely necessary and needed.

When we live within these human enclosures, we escape the tyrannical doctrine of the interchangeability of parts; in these enclosures, we live as members, each in its own identity necessary to the others. When our spouse or child, friend or neighbor is in need or in trouble, we do not deal with them by means of a computer, for we know that, with them, we must not think without feeling. We do not help them by sending a machine, for we know that, with them, a machine cannot represent us. We know that, when they need us, we must go and offer ourselves, body and mind, as we are. As members, moreover, we are useless and worse than useless to each other if we do not care properly for the ground that is common to us.

28   It is only in these trying circumstances that human love is given its chance to have meaning, for it is only in these circumstances that it can be borne out in deeds through time—"even," to quote Shakespeare again, "to the edge of doom"—and thus prove itself true by fulfilling its true term.

In these circumstances, in place and in time, the sexes will find their common ground and be somewhat harmoniously rejoined, not by some resolution of conflict and power, but by proving indispensable to one another, as in fact they are.

READER RESPONSE

Do you believe, as Berry argues, that relationships between men and women now too often are only tentative and temporary, or have the relationships of people you know been permanent and committed? Explain your answer.

QUESTIONS FOR DISCUSSION

1. Why is Berry critical of the concept of "self-fulfillment" (paragraph 9)? In what ways are we not "the authors of ourselves" (paragraph 10)? Explain how the example of the Maximilian sunflower (paragraph 11) illustrates that statement.

2. Berry writes that "division has become our characteristic mode of thinking and acting" (paragraph 8). Explain what he means by that, and locate the examples he uses to illustrate it.

3. How does Berry's definition of marriage differ from the way it is often regarded? To what extent would you define marriage as Berry does?

4. Explain what Berry means when he says that the "smallest possible 'survival unit,' indeed, appears to be the universe" (paragraph 17). What is his point here? In what ways are human relationships forms of bondage, according to Berry? Do you agree with him?

5. Explain the extent to which you agree with Berry's comments regarding the impact of the industrial economy on humans. What does Berry think of the ideal human residence, according to "the industrial formula" (paragraph 20)?
6. What does Berry mean when he says in paragraph 21 that "the obsolescence of the body is inevitable"? Do you agree with him when he says that the human mind is "following the human body into obsolescence" (paragraph 22)?

Over 40 and Unmarried

Ron Beathard

Ron Beathard is a writer and columnist living in Harrison, Ohio. He wrote this essay for the "My Turn" column of the June 3, 1996, issue of Newsweek.

A few months ago, a major midwestern newspaper accepted an essay I had written on the topic of being over 40 and never married. The editor called and asked me to suggest a headline that would tie in with Valentine's Day, the date of publication. My subject, I explained, had nothing whatsoever to do with Valentine's Day, but since he had bought the column and paid for it, he could do with it as he pleased. And he did. The headline: MY AGING VALENTINE— ON AN OLDER MAN'S THOUGHTS NOT TURNING TO FANCY. Good Lord, I thought, that's me he's talking about. I was filled with woe.

The percentage of the population consisting of unmarried men over 40 has fluctuated between 3 and 6 percent over the years. No one knows why. Sociologists rarely study us, psychologists don't quiz us and politicians don't count us. For all we know, the fluctuation could be due to the length of the fur on autumn caterpillars. Or vice versa. We do know our numbers are increasing this decade and, according to forecasts, will continue to rise in the future. It is not for me to discuss why, but simply to explain who and what we are.

We are minority group, although we would never qualify for affirmative-action programs. The discrimination against us is benign and curious—and often amusing. ("Did you know he's never married?" "Is he gay?" "I don't think so." "There must be something wrong.") And: ("Have you ever tasted his lasagna?" "Delicious." "He'll make a great wife." Laughter.) Slightly suspect, we innocently create problems in a double-occupancy world. How does one divide an odd number into equal teams for golf, bridge or badminton? ("But I can't have five for dinner. It's not symmetrical." "Ask him to invite a friend." "What if he doesn't have any?")

4   Although a minority, we are accorded a high degree of social acceptability—higher than single women. We are bachelors; they are old maids. The men's magazines tell us we are forever young; the women's magazines tell them they are already old. The worst adjectives that are ever thrown at us are "confirmed" and "eccentric." Our biological clock has no hands. If we at the age of 60 sire a child, we are admired (snow on the roof but fire in the heart and all that); a mother at that age is tabloid material. Aside from wistful thoughts of a son to teach our secrets of throwing sliders or engaging the girls, the paternal urge lacks the urgency of the maternal one. Besides, nowadays cryogenic sex makes coupling unnecessary.

My peers and I are not much into Robert Bly's "Iron John" male thing. Let others sit cross-legged around a fire, outfitted in Pendleton plaid. Taking a journey into the mythopoetic spirit of the male wilderness is best left to men described by Somerset Maugham in "The Moon and Sixpence": "There are men whom a merciful Providence has undoubtedly ordained to a single life [but] have flown in the face of its decrees. There is no object more deserving of pity than the married bachelor."

Having heeded Providence, we aging singles lack an immediate companion with whom to share the good times of a winning lottery ticket or the beauty of a starry night. Social activities are haphazard and precarious. Without a built-in partner, a night out or an afternoon in requires coordination and planning. But sometimes we get seeds that drop from the feeder. ("I have an extra ticket for Saturday night." "Ask Ron. I'm sure he's not busy.")

We have learned to cope with our solitary state. It takes a confident man to dine alone. The less self-assured pretend they are on the road traveling from important client to important CEO, and read an important business journal as if they just don't have the time to eat and socialize simultaneously. They can order water and service for two, glance impatiently at their watches every two minutes, then sigh to the waiter, "I guess she got tied up in court."

8   Having less need of diversion than other men, we tend to take up solitary hobbies and pastimes—reading, collecting, building something in the basement, exploring rivers and mountains, and asking more "why" and "what if" questions than most people. We tend to be introspective. In our homes there is no one with whom to chit and chat about the weather and the elections. Without time-consuming and weekend-filling household chores, family pleasures and social responsibilities, we talk to ourselves a great deal because there is no one we know as well.

However, we are not hermits. Weighty introspection does not preclude an occasional encounter with contemporary cultural icons: Pearl Jam and Barney, rollerblading and line dancing, grungy and bungee. We do keep in touch. We try not to make stupid remarks like "I'm too old/mature for that." If we have to put limitations on ourselves, we'll do it tomorrow. Because there are few volleyball leagues, social clubs, newsletters or special days at the ballpark devoted exclusively to single men over 40, we are forced from our clique to enjoy the rewarding diversity of people.

Our married critics say that we are impractical and maintain a fantasy of perfection, that we shun family and parental involvement, that we are too self-centered to have children and—lowest of all—that we avoid commitment. Perhaps. We have many chances to get married; it's simply that we don't take any. But we understand the suspicions we arouse. We mention our mothers cautiously. We seem to raise Freudian eyebrows.

Contrary to popular opinion, the single life is not in direct opposition to family life. The two situations are not poles apart, not us-and-them or winners-and-losers. They are complementary. We make terrific uncles and great nice guys next door. We are serving and standing and waiting.

12   We aren't stylish, nor were we meant to be. Perhaps one brief day we will be in style, writing a best-selling confession or two, trotted out on talk shows, welcomed as the fifth dinner guest. Then after a few days we will go home quietly and continue to make our contributions to society.

READER RESPONSE

Beathard writes that most people view single men older than forty with surprise, curiosity, and humor. How did you view such men before reading this essay? Has your view changed?

QUESTIONS FOR DISCUSSION

1. Beathard says that he wants to explain "who and what [single men over forty] are" (paragraph 2). How successfully do you think he accomplishes this purpose? Do you now have a clearer understanding of Beathard and others like him?

2. Beathard devotes attention to the differences in how people perceive unmarried men and unmarried women. What contrasts in those perceptions does he identify? Do you agree with him? Can you add any other differences to those he names?

3. Beathard uses the terms *bachelor* and *old maid* in paragraph 4. What connotative values do those words have? Do people still use the phrase "old maid" to refer to unmarried women? At what age do men become "bachelors" and women "old maids"?

4. Discuss your understanding of the Somerset Maugham quotation that "'there is no object more deserving of pity than the married bachelor'" (paragraph 5).

I'm Not Sick, I'm Just in Love

Katherine Davis

Katherine Davis worked as an editorial assistant in New York City when she wrote this essay for the "My Turn" column of the July 24, 1996, issue of Newsweek.

A couple of months ago, I received a phone call from one of my college roommates. We hadn't spoken since our graduation from Barnard College a year ago, and we both had big news to share. Her boyfriend of five years had proposed. I was thrilled for her, but not surprised. Marriage seemed inevitable for two people who have been inseparable for as long as they have. I *was* surprised to hear that they won't be getting married for at least five years. She wants to concentrate on her career.

I, too, am engaged to be married. Unlike my friend, my big news included the start of wedding plans: designing a dress, invitations, menus, engagement parties and bridal showers. While I've probably picked up more copies of brides' magazines than *The Economist* lately, I also want to focus on my career. But since I decided to marry at the age of 23, I've been made to feel as if a career is no longer a viable option. Once I was viewed as a bright young woman with promise. Now I'm dismissed by acquaintances and strangers as being sentenced to an insignificant life. I *am* young, but no younger than women who married a generation ago. The distress and hostility I've encountered has more to do with changing attitudes toward the *role* of wife. When everyone is touting "family values," why does marriage have such a bad rap?

I certainly didn't plan on an early marriage. I didn't intend to get married, ever. I envisioned my future as a broadcast journalist, traveling, meeting international leaders and, more realistically, long days and deadlines—not a husband and kids. Friends predicted I'd be a real-life Murphy Brown: ambitious, self-serving and single.

4   My quest to become a reporter began at MTV News, where I interned during my last semester at college, and started working as a desk assistant upon graduation. That's where I met my fiancé. Eight years my senior, Wilson has spent most of his adult life abroad and is well versed in everything from Russian literature to motorcycle repair. We found common ground in our career ambitions and agreed to a get-together some night after work to discuss them. Then I avoided him. I convinced myself I was too busy with my senior thesis and job interviews. There was no room for another commitment.

Room *was* made. By the end of last year, we were in love—and engaged. At work, since we'd kept our relationship under wraps, the news of our engagement came as a shock. Wilson was treated to some pats on the back and a celebratory night on the town. Few congratulations were addressed to me, however. I received comments like "You're so young!" or "What about your career?" When I left MTV for print journalism, some coworkers assumed I'd quit to plan my wedding. Others made me feel, as a woman, I was ceding my place in the newsroom to Wilson. One suggested that I not mention my pending nuptials to prospective employers. It might suggest lack of motivation for hard work.

My plans also touched off panic among my girlfriends. It's a return of the domino theory and, to protect themselves, some have chosen not to sympathize with the enemy. I've been taunted that my days of "sowing my wild oats" are over and reproached for secretly wanting a baby right away. (There's even a bet I'll become pregnant by Jan. 31, 1998.) I've been accused of misrepresenting myself during college as someone trying to earn a MRS. degree rather than an education. When "feminist" friends hear that I am taking my husband's name, they act as if I'm forsaking "our" cause. One Saturday afternoon, a friend phoned and I admitted I was spending the day doing laundry—mine and his. Her voice resonated with such pity that I hung up.

New York City, where we live, breeds much of this antagonism toward marriage. I've read that half of Manhattan households consist of single people. Home to the worlds of "Friends" and "Seinfeld," marriage is sort of an anomaly here. One fifth of women in this town over the age of 45 have never been married. Manhattanites aren't exactly diving to catch the bouquet.

8   I've also experienced prejudice in my hometown in Colorado. At a local store's bridal registry, I walked in wearing a Columbia University sweatshirt and the consultant asked if I'd gone to school there. On hearing that I'd graduated 10 months earlier, she explained that she had a daughter my age. "But she is very involved in her career," she added, presuming that I, selecting a silverware pattern, was not.

Registering at another store brought my mother and me to tears. As I perused the housewares, my mom mistook my interest in cookware to be a sign of impending domesticity and wondered where she'd gone wrong. A former home-ec teacher, my mom always joked that my lowest grade in junior high was earned in her field of expertise. It's not funny when your careerbent daughter wants a Crockpot.

It's been difficult for my mom to watch her daughter choose a husband before establishing a career—as she once did. Throughout my education, she has seen the opportunities made available to me, some that weren't imaginable when she was young. She and my father strove to provide me with the skills to take advantage of these new avenues. In the process, she grew attached to the idea of my becoming a successful professional.

I have no intention of dropping my career goals for marriage. While I'm excited by the prospect of having children, motherhood will not necessarily be the defining feature of my life. And I'll be no worse a wife for having a career. My engagement has made me no less ambitious, hardworking—or a feminist.

12   During our conversation, my old roommate described her engagement ring, which sits in her jewelry box because she feels people treat her

differently when she wears it. I thought she was being a bit foolish. Now I understand her insecurities. Presented with an array of career options, young ~~thesis~~ women today are pressured to reject "traditional" roles.

Wilson and I are fortunate to have a relationship that allows us to be as committed to our professions as we are to each other. Soon I'll be his blushing bride. And my rosy complexion will be from exuberance—not embarrassment.

READER RESPONSE

If you are unmarried, what are your thoughts about when you will marry? How do you think marriage will affect your career? If you are married, write for a few minutes about how being married has changed your life.

QUESTIONS FOR DISCUSSION

1. Davis writes, "The distress and hostility I've encountered has more to do with changing attitudes toward the role of wife . . . [y]oung women today are pressured to reject 'traditional' roles" (paragraphs 2 and 12). In what ways have attitudes toward the role of wife changed? What is the "traditional" role of women? What sex-role expectations are there for young women today? Is the attitude toward the role of husband changing? Are men pressured to reject traditional roles?

2. Davis says that her friends predicted she would be "a real-life Murphy Brown" (paragraph 3). What other models of single women in key roles on television programs are there? Do they all fit the Murphy Brown pattern of being "ambitious, self-serving and single"?

3. Davis tells of the contrast in responses when her fiancé and she announced their engagement (paragraph 5). How does she account for those differences? Can you think of other reasons why the reactions of friends and coworkers would differ? Would the responses among your friends and coworkers be the same in similar circumstances?

4. Where do expectations about age of marriage for men and women come from? Is it unreasonable to think that a woman necessarily compromises her career by marrying young?

Vows

Julie Showalter

Julie Showalter (1945–1999) held a Ph.D. in English literature from Ball State University. A writer whose stories appeared in

Other Voices, *the* Chicago Sun-Times, *and the* Maryland Review, *she won a Glimmertrain new writer award in 1995 and the prestigious Pushcart Prize in 1998. She died in 1999 after a twenty-year battle with cancer. This story first appeared in the spring 1996 issue of* Other Voices, *a publication of the University of Illinois at Chicago.*

I was surprised that Adam wanted a wedding. He hadn't seemed to want to get married. But once we decided, he said of course there'll be a ceremony. Of course my parents will come. Of course your parents will come. Of course we'll invite our friends.

We'd lived together over two years, both damaged by previous divorces. Every few months he'd get angry and say, "Admit it, Jan, you really want to get married." My analyst said I should admit it because it was what I wanted, good girl from Missouri who didn't live with men unless she was married, no matter how many husbands she'd had. "Besides," he said, "the way Adam keeps bringing it up, I think he must want to get married too."

So, when he said it again, "Admit it. You're conventional. You want to get married," I said, "Yes, yes I am, yes I do."

4   We'd agreed from the start that he wasn't supposed to take care of me. I'd just come from a marriage where I'd been taken care of until I almost suffocated. And when Adam left his ex-wife, she said, "You promised to take care of me forever. I won't let you go so easy." So, we were agreed. We were independent people with independent lives, independent careers, and independent checkbooks. And now we were going to get married.

I thought we could just sneak into it, go to City Hall on a lunch hour, tell our friends and family sometime later. But he wanted a wedding, said there had to be a wedding. I thought people would laugh. Here I was, thirty-four years old, twice divorced, and acting like I thought I could be a bride; like my promise to love, honor, and cherish meant something; like I could make a lifetime commitment.

We found a minister who said, "About all anyone knows about Unitarians is that they'll marry anyone." After we laughed politely, he leaned forward, suddenly serious, assuming his spiritual-advisor role, "You two have to decide about your ceremony. I can't tell you what you want to promise each other. Only you can decide that."

Adam said, "We thought we'd go with the Dearly Beloved option."

8   The minister shook his head. "I don't do canned ceremonies. It has to come from your heart. You have to write it yourself."

As we left, Adam muttered, "Pompous asshole."

A small wedding in our home. Our parents, my daughter, a few close friends. Neither of us had met the other's parents. Twenty people at most. A simple service, a cake, coffee, some champagne. That's what we planned. Or what I planned, looking to him for approval.

Most of the time during the two months between our decision to marry and the wedding he seemed angry. When I suggested we call it off, he said no. "It's what you want," he said, "so we'll do it."

12   I wrote each invitation by hand. "Dear Ken and Bev, Please join us at our home for a celebration of our marriage," and so on. Then, two days after they were in the mail, I found a pebble in my left breast. I sat up in bed. "Feel this," I said, taking his hand. "What does this feel like to you?" Half asleep, he put his hand over my breast and squeezed. "No, here. Toward the top. There's something there."

He sat up and pushed me down, his hands suddenly doctor's hands, both moving lightly over my breast like a blind man reading Braille. "It feels like a lump," he said. "It's probably nothing. Give Joel a call tomorrow." Adam and Joel had been interns together; one of the invitations had gone to him. Now I had to call him about my breast.

We lay there a while. I said, "It's too bad I didn't find this last month."
"Why?"

16   "Well, you're more or less trapped into marrying me now."

"That's the stupidest thing you've ever said." He rolled over, presenting me with his back. We lay that way a long time, neither of us sleeping.

The next day I saw Joel who felt my breast and said, "I'm not impressed." Then he took me to see a surgeon—"best breast man in the city"—who said, "This is nothing. Don't worry. Come back in three weeks and I'll check it again." The follow-up appointment was scheduled for two days before the wedding.

When Adam got home from work, he said, "I'm glad things went well for you today. I know you were scared." He handed me a jewelry box—a gold watch. "It's a wedding gift, a little early." We didn't speak again of my fear, and we never mentioned his.

20   That night he held me while I slept. Twice I woke with a start. "There, there," he said, kissing my hair. "There, there."

His parents were due on Thursday before the wedding on Sunday. He'd arranged to get off early Thursday by scheduling patients until 9:00 Wednesday night. At 5:00 on Wednesday the phone rang. "This is your future mother-in-law. We can't find a parking place." I met them at the curb as they circled the block in their pickup. Adam's father didn't speak except to say, "I don't think this neighborhood looks safe."

With my ten-year-old daughter Rebecca, I tried to entertain them for the evening. It was difficult to find things to talk about because I didn't know how much they knew about me or how much Adam wanted them to know. I knew he didn't want them to know that he'd been involved with me while he was still married to Diane. I didn't think he wanted them to know I'd been married twice before. I settled on a position that made it look as if I'd sprung full-grown without a history into Adam's life about a year earlier. I hoped they wouldn't ask about Rebecca's father and that she wouldn't tell them she liked

Adam more than my last husband. His mother said, "You just have to understand that I'm going to slip and call you Diane. It's been Adam and Diane for so long, it will take me some time to adjust."

By the time Adam got home, they were ready for bed.

24   On Thursday, Adam and I both managed to get off early. We got home at 3:00 to find his parents were gone. Two washed coffee cups and a carefully refolded morning paper were the only signs they'd been there. "Maybe they left a note," I said, but there was no note. Adam mixed two gin and tonics without speaking.

At 5:00 the phone rang. Adam answered it. Just then, from our third floor window I saw my mother getting out of a cab. As she started up the walk, Adam slammed down the phone. "God damn them to hell!" he said. I helped Mother get her luggage up the stairs. When I came back, Adam had gone to our bedroom. After fifteen minutes, I went in. He was lying on the bed in the dark, his arm thrown over his eyes. "They're at a motel," he said. "My mother said my father was too upset to stay with us. I don't know if they'll be back for the wedding." He didn't move.

I went back to Mother. "Adam's upset," I explained. "Some problems with his folks." He didn't come out all evening. Mother kept saying, "I just know this has something to do with me. I'm sure if I weren't here, everything would be fine."

The next day was full. Prenuptial agreement in the morning, breast check in the afternoon. Adam met my mother at breakfast. He was gracious and charming. Apologized for being under the weather the night before. I wanted to kill him.

28   When we arrived at his lawyer's office, the attorney asked, "Didn't you bring your own lawyer? Do you understand what you're signing?"

"I think so," I said as I signed away all rights present and future to Adam's earnings. We both had a history of being taken in a divorce. My first husband stole my daughter. My second stole my car. Adam's ex-wife got all the money, all the furniture, and alimony besides. She even got the stereo his parents bought him as a graduation gift from medical school. The agreement I signed stated specifically that the stereo in our condo belonged to Adam.

In exchange for the prenuptial agreement, I asked that we discontinue our separate household financial accounts. I was tired of "you owe me $2.47 for half of the pound of corned beef I bought at the White Hen last week." For two years I had kept these accounts, a running balance of who owed what to whom. Twice a month I would present the list to Adam saying, "I owe you $10.50," or "Your paying for dinner last night balances us out." He always appeared to think he'd been cheated. He'd ask, "Did you divide the dry cleaning bill or charge it all to me?" I was tired of keeping the list, of the real or imagined suspicion.

I was ready to stop hedging my bets and keeping score, ready to start trusting again. That's why I signed the agreement. That's why I wanted to get married.

32   That afternoon, the surgeon patted my shoulder. "This is nothing. Hasn't changed a bit. I wouldn't worry." Then he said, "I can tell you're not going to be able to relax until we take a real look at it. We can do a biopsy to set your mind at rest."

     "Do you have any time available next Wednesday?" I asked. "My parents will be leaving on Tuesday. I'll just take one more vacation day."

Saturday afternoon my father arrived, bringing my nine-year-old niece with him. He thought adding Stephanie to the guest list would be a surprise for me and for Rebecca. My father, despite having three daughters, knew nothing about little girls and jealousy. As Rebecca announced, "I'm the bridesmaid. I'm the only bridesmaid. I get a bouquet," Stephanie kept saying, "I flew on the airplane with Grandpa. Just Grandpa and me." Over and over. Louder and louder.

     Adam's parents appeared mid-afternoon, as if nothing had happened, as if they hadn't just disappeared for two days. The two mothers exchanged stories about what foolish/clumsy/difficult children Adam and I had been. The two fathers sat in the den and didn't talk.

36   Sunday, July 20. Wedding day. Adam woke to say, "You're really not going to write my vows. I can't believe you're not going to write my vows." I had written the ceremony as the minister had required, passing it by Adam for approval lest it be promising more than he intended to promise, saying more than he wanted to say. But I had not written his vows.

     "Your vows are what you're promising to me," I said. "I can't write that."

     It was the hottest day of the summer. Our window air conditioner hummed ominously. When we bought the condo, we knew to check things like electrical wiring. We even had an independent inspector look things over. "That's a good breaker box," he'd said, looking at the giant box containing twenty-four circuit breakers. He was right, it was a good box. Unfortunately, only two circuits were wired. One controlled the dining room chandelier, the other the rest of the seven-room apartment. In the six months we'd been there, we accommodated to the electrical system's idiosyncrasies. We'd shout, "Don't use your hair dryer. I'm starting the microwave." Now we were running the air conditioner and the apartment was filling with people who thought they could just walk in a room and flip a light switch willy-nilly, with no regard for consequences. We kept losing power in the rest of the apartment while the dining room chandelier blazed on.

     People had been invited for 2:00. As each guest buzzed the buzzer, the two girls raced down the three flights of stairs. I had suggested that Rebecca introduce her cousin, hoping this official hostess role might make her feel special, make Stephanie feel like an honored guest. "This is my cousin Stephanie," she said to our friends. "She came unexpected."

40   The minister was late. His softball game had gone extra innings. Adam's father took Adam aside. "What kind of preacher plays baseball on Sunday?"

     The ceremony I had written thanked our friends for helping us make note of a gradual change in our relationship, a relationship which had evolved into a marriage and would continue to evolve. In other words, this is no big deal. In other words, ye gods of irony, bad timing and cruel jokes who have controlled my life thus far, don't pay any attention to what's going on here.

I had memorized my vows, planned to say them looking into Adam's eyes. But when the time came, I went blank. The artfully crafted lines with appropriate quotations from Donne and Shakespeare were gone. I looked at the floor, I looked at the ceiling, I looked at Adam. "I love you," I said finally, my voice quavering. "I want to spend my life with you." Adam put his arm around me and squeezed. Family and guests sighed and sniffled.

Then Adam took his vows from his pocket. He read them quickly, too quickly for me to remember. I know he said he loved me, but they seemed to focus more on what he wasn't promising than what he was. "I can't promise forever," he said, "because I can't know what will happen. I love you now." Later, when my mother asked for a copy of the service, Adam's vows had disappeared.

44   We cut the cake; I made the coffee; we opened the champagne. As we were serving, Adam's parents said, "We need to head back to Missouri." They left. It was 3:15. I asked for more champagne.

Joel took me aside and said, "Don't worry about the biopsy. It's nothing. It's really just to set your mind at rest."

"Fine, I won't worry," I said.

Cheryl, Joel's girlfriend, took me aside. "I hope you're not worried. I had a biopsy six months ago and it was nothing. I worried a lot for nothing."

48   "Fine," I said, "I'm not worried. I'll not give it another thought." I smiled. "Any more champagne?" I asked.

Guests started leaving:

Joel and Cheryl had a long drive.

The Chious had a family gathering.

52   The Jamisons begged off. He was tired from the radiation treatments for his brain tumor. We didn't know until the next week that she was divorcing him.

The Baileys, who were separated but had arrived together, looked as if they'd go the distance. Then Laura got sick from too much champagne and Dave had to take her home.

There were thirteen of us left. I had made no provision for dinner, unable to plan beyond the cake, the coffee, the champagne. "Let's go to Costa Brava," Adam suggested. We grabbed six bottles of burgundy and set off.

Later, as we straggled back to the apartment, the oppressive heat seemed on the verge of breaking. Lightning flashed over the lake. I walked with my father. "I may have had too much wine," I said.

56   "That's OK," he said. "You're entitled. This is your big day."

Adam used to say that sooner or later he ended up cleaning up the vomit of every woman he'd ever been involved with. He said, "I think it was a particular virus that made the rounds while I was in school. First symptom—

make a date with Adam Sherman; second symptom—mild nausea; third symptom—throw up where Adam has to clean it up." I always said that he'd never had to clean up after me and he never would. I could take care of myself.

On our wedding night, Adam held me while I threw up, helped me out of my wedding dress, and cleaned up the mess. In the living room the little girls explained to the remaining guests that ladies often got sick on their wedding nights. "It's part of the tradition," they said, those two little girls who would both end up pregnant and married, in that order, before they were eighteen.

I woke up the next morning wishing I could drop off the face of the earth. Surprisingly, no one was angry. "The heat," they said. "So much tension," they said. "Maybe a little too much wine," they said. "A combination," they said.

60   "How are you feeling, Hon Bun?" Adam asked. He was transformed. The angry, surly man I'd lived with the past two months was gone, and the loving, gentle fellow I'd fallen in love with had taken his place. It was as if he'd come through some terrible ordeal and was happy and surprised to be alive and in one piece.

On Wednesday, since it was no big deal, we agreed I'd just take a cab to the hospital. There was no reason to disrupt his day. I'd see him at home that evening.

I was in the waiting room trying to read when Adam appeared. "I finished rounds early and have a few minutes before I have to leave for outpatients. Thought I'd see how you were doing."

"I'm fine," I said. "I'm glad you came by, but don't mess up your schedule on my account."

64   "I have a few more minutes. I'll just get some work done here." We sat there, shoulders touching, both pretending to read. When they called my name, Adam said, "I'll wait around a little while longer. I don't have to leave until noon."

In the operating room, the surgeon joked with the nurses and with me. As he had promised, I felt some tugging, some pressure, but no pain. A tent of blue sheets kept me from seeing his face or what he was doing. We talked about Joel and other mutual friends as he worked.

He became silent. When he spoke again, we were no longer friends chatting. "How long have you had this?" he asked. His voice was flat.

"I noticed it three weeks ago," I said. "The night before I saw you the first time."

68   "Oh," he said.

There was no more banter in the room. Conversation was limited to commands like "Suction here" and replies like "Yes, Doctor."

Serious talk in serious voices.

Serious trouble.

72   I looked at the clock on the wall. It was 12:05. I said, "Could someone check to see if my husband's left yet? If he's still there, would you ask him to

stay for a few more minutes, tell him that I'd like to talk to him. Could some-one check right now. He may have already left."

A nurse went out. The clock flipped over to 12:07. He'd be gone. He was never late for his patients.

The nurse came back in. "He's here," she said. "He said not to worry. He said to tell you he'll be here. He promised."

READER RESPONSE

What do you think of the relationship between Adam and Jan, of their wed-ding vows, and of the likelihood that their marriage will work?

QUESTIONS FOR DISCUSSION

1. In what ways does Jan avoid committing to the marriage? When does she resolve her conflict about the marriage?
2. How does their knowledge that love sometimes does not last, that it can turn nasty and vindictive, affect Adam's and Jan's decision to marry and their willingness to trust one another?
3. Why does Jan sign a prenuptial agreement? How is that an act of trust?
4. What function do the man with the brain tumor and the wife who di-vorces him serve in relation to the matter of marriage and commitment? How does Jan's finding the lump relate to the central issue of the story? Is her cancer the central issue? If not, what is? Explain your answer.

ADDITIONAL SUGGESTIONS FOR WRITING ABOUT GENDERED RELATIONSHIPS

1. Do your own informal research on conversational patterns of men and women by observing conversations between men, between women, and between men and women. What conclusions can you draw? How do your conclusions relate to what Deborah Tannen writes in "Sex, Lies, and Conversation"?
2. Drawing on Deborah Tannen's "Sex, Lies, and Conversation," Wendell Berry's "Men and Women in Search of Common Ground," Carol Tavris's "Love Story," and/or Julie Showalter's "Vows," explore reasons for why couples divorce.
3. Explain what Carol Tavris, in "Love Story," means by the phrase "the fem-inization of love" and your own position on the subject of the roles men and women play in relationships. For instance, do you think men and women see love and marriage differently?

4. With Deborah Tannen's "Sex, Lies, and Conversation" and Carol Tavris's "Love Story" in mind, compare or contrast men and women in an area other than communication style.

5. Taking into consideration what Deborah Blum, in "What's the Difference Between Boys and Girls?" says about the role of play in childhood, explain the significance of your own choice of toys and games as a reflection of your gender.

6. Drawing on Ron Beathard's "Over 40 and Unmarried," Katherine Davis's "I'm Not Sick, I'm Just in Love," Carol Tavris's "Love Story," and Julie Showalter's "Vows," write an essay on cultural expectations for relationships between men and women. Explain whether your own view of relationships agrees with the commonly held, cultural view.

7. Analyze the extent to which you think messages from family, friends, or popular culture about relationships, marriage, and career limit or shape behavior. Have such influence affected your own behavior or plans for the future?

8. Drawing on Julie Showalter's "Vows" and other relevant readings in this chapter, define what you believe is a successful marriage. Support your generalizations with specific examples, using one or more married couples you know to illustrate what you mean.

9. Use humor or satire to comment on some aspect of relationships between the sexes, such as meeting someone new, dating, or maintaining a relationship.

10. Explain why a marriage or relationship you know of personally—your own, that of a friend, or even your parent's—did not last.

11. Explore the effects of divorce on the two people involved, on their family, and/or on their friends.

12. Write a reflective essay in which you explore your own concepts of masculinity and femininity (and, perhaps, androgyny) and how that concept has shaped the way you are today. Consider to what degree you think sex determines destiny.

13. Conduct your own investigative analysis of any of the following for their depiction of female and male sex roles: fairy tales, children's stories, advertising images, music videos, television programs, or film. Do you find stereotyped assumptions about masculinity and femininity? In what ways do you think the subject of your analysis reinforces or shapes cultural definitions of masculinity and femininity?

14. Explore ways in which you would like to see definitions of masculinity and femininity changed. How do you think relationships between the sexes would be affected if those changes were made?

15. Explain the degree to which you consider gender issues to be important. Do you think too much is made of gender? Does it matter whether definitions of masculinity and femininity are rigid?

Chapter

8

POPULAR CULTURE

Broadly speaking, popular culture refers to the music, literature, arts, and media of a particular society and the ways in which those things reflect its people's current tastes, interests, and talents. Thus, popular culture includes not only television, film, and music but also advertising, cartoons, newspapers, magazines, books, and virtually any other product you can think of that reveals something about people of a particular time and place. Because the subject covers such a wide range of topics, this chapter can only touch on some of the issues raised by several aspects of popular culture, in particular the role and influence of rock music, Hollywood and the movies, television, comic books, and advertising. The essays in this chapter reflect differing viewpoints or offer personal interpretations of several pervasive products of popular culture, and they will surely prompt you to reflect on other, related subjects encompassed by the broad subject of popular culture.

Music, of course, is an integral part of popular culture. All kinds of music enjoy popularity in American culture, but certain kinds, especially those that young people listen to, seem to draw the attention of cultural critics more than others do. For instance, rock-and-roll music, from its beginning in the 1950s, has been the object of heated critical debate, with arguments usually centering on its sexual content and the potential effect of such lyrics on audiences. In recent years, rap music has gained widespread public attention and prompted a host of opinions about its lyrics and musicians. Of particular concern to critics are rap music's violent lyrics, especially in the way they link sexuality with violence—not to mention the often-violent lives of rap musicians themselves. Tricia Rose, in "Rap Music and the Demonization of Young Black Males," expresses her concern about what she believes is unfair press given to rap music, especially the message that music sends about black males. Intriguingly, in the next essay, David Segal, in "Where's the Return Fire in Culture Wars?," observes that almost none of the usual critics of pop music lyrics is paying attention to rap or rock lyrics in 2002. His possible explanations for why that should be the case raise implications about the nature of music, especially its traditional association with rebelliousness, anti-authoritarianism, and nonconformity.

Hollywood has been subject to criticism from its earliest days. From the beginning of the film industry, discussion has focused on the relationship of movies to behavior. Do movies influence behavior, or do they merely reflect it? To what degree do filmmakers have a moral obligation to society? During the 1920s, concern over the possible negative influence of Hollywood films was so great that the Hays Office censorship code was developed to monitor their content. The current ratings system evolved out of that perceived need to block offensive content, especially material that might adversely affect young children. The PG-13 rating, for instance, came about because some movies with a PG rating were so violent they terrified young children. Although the issues keep reemerging and, at times, are subject to rather heated, widespread debate, they remain largely unresolved.

Several essays in this chapter comment on Hollywood and its impact on social norms and individual beliefs and behavior. Film critic Robert Roten, in "Is Hollywood Responsible for 9-11?" explores the question of Hollywood's role in the September 11, 2002, attacks on the World Trade Center and the Pentagon. The next two readings criticize those who would blame Hollywood for negatively influencing public morality and social mores. Christopher Sharrett, in "Movies, Morality, and Conservative Complaints," explains what he sees as weaknesses or generalizations in the views of conservatives and offers his own perspective on the issue. Richard Corliss, in "Bang, You're Dead," which was written shortly after the massacre of students at Columbine High School in Littleton, Colorado, responds to the tendency of dismayed parents and others to blame movies and television for such violence.

Almost all Americans either own television sets or have access to them and are quite familiar with television programming and the range of viewing options available. In addition to the major networks, hundreds of other stations exist, vying with one another for audiences and sponsors. Not surprisingly, television, like other components of popular culture with the potential for reaching vast numbers of people, has been subject to the scrutiny of critics from its inception. The readings in this chapter on television have been selected to suggest the kind of analysis that television programming gives rise to and the nature of criticism leveled against it.

John Davidson, in "Menace to Society," reviews the negative criticism regarding media images of sex and violence that occur, especially during election years, and suggests that the real menace when it comes to violent programming is not prime-time network shows but Saturday-morning children's shows. Similarly, objecting that complaints about sex and violence on prime-time network television are "beating a dead horse," Joe Saltzman argues, in "Beating the Same Old Dead Horse," that popular culture provides a host of sources other than television for graphic sex and violence.

Some critics believe that television reflects cultural values and attitudes. In this regard, David L. G. Arnold's "Cavalcade of Whimsey: Defending Springfield Against Itself" looks at the character of Sideshow Bob in the battle between high and low culture, between the intellectual elite and the moiling "mass," on *The Simpsons*. Arnold places his analysis in the context of mass-culture theorists from Matthew Arnold through the Frankfurt school, whose theories Arnold succinctly explains. Next, in "Do Ask, Do Tell," Joshua Gamson is particularly interested in talk shows that provide a forum for homosexuals to articulate their experiences and feelings. He explores the ways in which homosexual guests are treated by both talk-show hosts and audiences, and he assesses the implications of that treatment for both gay guests and gay viewers.

Turning to another popular-culture artifact, renowned comic-book author Gerard Jones argues that bloody videogames, gun-glorifying gangsta rap, and other forms of "creative violence," by giving kids a tool to master their rage, help far more children than they hurt. Using his own childhood as an example, Jones explains, in "Violent Media Is Good for Kids," how violence in various media can be a positive influence on children.

Finally, Alan Thein Durning, in "Can't Live Without It," analyzes the global reach of advertisements and assesses both the environmental and cultural impact of the advertising industry. He is concerned about "earth-threatening consumption levels" and the role the advertising industry plays in encouraging behaviors that are potentially deadly: resource depletion, environmental pollution, and habitat degradation.

1. What images of American culture do the Coke bottle and MTV logo represent?

2. To what extent do you think that the symbolic representations of the Coke and MTV icons are specifically American? That is, do you think they represent other things besides certain aspects of American culture? Explain your answer.

3. The photograph of the Coca-Cola billboard was taken in Managua, Nicaragua, in 1990. What contrasts does the photograph suggest between American culture and less-affluent cultures? What socioeconomic or cultural implications does the photograph imply?

4. What influence do you think American advertising has on other cultures?

Rap Music and the Demonization of Young Black Males

Tricia Rose

Tricia Rose is an assistant professor of history and African studies at New York University and author of Black Noise: Rap Music and Black Culture in Contemporary America *(1994). This essay first appeared in* USA Today Magazine *in May 1994.*

In these times, when media-crafted frenzies are the bread and butter of television news, entertainment programming, and tabloid journalism, street crime has become the coal that fires the crisis boiler. The notion that violent crime has swung out of control in this country is less a matter of fact and more a matter of perception constructed by law-and-order budget managers and ratings-hungry media executives. In fact, according to the FBI's National Crime Survey, burglary, homicides, and other violent crimes have decreased steadily since the mid 1970s.

Crime and violence have become the central focus of popular attention not because more and more people are the victims of crime, but because more Americans vicariously experience more violence through repetition of tabloid, televised news, and other reality-based programming. Street crime is sexy copy because, more than other equally pressing and even more urgent crises in American urban communities, it can be fitted into presentational formats crucial for mass media news consumption.

First, street crime lends itself to personal portraits of loss and horror; second, unlike corporate or economic crimes against people, it has clearly identifiable victims *and* villains, even when no villain is caught; third, it takes just one or two gruesome acts to terrorize viewers; and fourth, most street crime is committed by the least powerful members of society, those most easily villified. Other violent criminals with greater economic resources are less vulnerable to categorical public censure. Since reporting these sorts of crime appears to be a matter of public service, it creates the illusion that the terms of the discussion automatically are in the best interests of the public.

4   In this whirlwind of produced, heightened, and repeated anxieties, it is essential to take a step back and distinguish between criminal acts and the social language used to talk about crime and to define criminals. It is important not to lose sight of the fact that these are not one in the same. In other words, crimes taking place are not the same thing as the perception of these crimes nor are they equivalent to the process of counting, naming, categorizing, and labeling criminal activity and ultimately criminalizing populations. (Think for a moment about the media explosion of child abuse cases and its relationship to the history of child abuse.)

These distinctions are not merely a matter of semantics. Understanding them allows people to see how the way they talk about a problem determines the solutions they deem logical and necessary. In other words, the terms of the discussion on crime in the public arena are helping set the direction of public policy.

In a still profoundly segregated and racially hierarchical society, popular public images and descriptions of poor black and Latino communities as hotbeds of crime, drugs, and violent behavior appear to be "mere descriptions" of the people and environments where crime takes place. These stories and pictures are not simply descriptive, however. They describe *some* elements of life in poor communities with a particular set of assumptions and consistently leave out and obscure descriptions of other parts.

The stories that frame violent street crimes deliberately omit information that would draw attention away from the sense of crisis produced by the depiction of an overwhelmingly horrible incident. "What," the stories often cry out," would make a young person do such a thing?" Answers that might focus on the larger social picture—not flawed causal responses like poverty causes crime or there are more criminals so we need more prisons, but relational answers such as street crime is linked closely with unemployment and poverty—are deemed "excuses" by the logic of the story that surrounds it, not explanations.

8   The pity is that more information is not set forth about the conditions that foster such behaviors—the active municipal and corporate decisions that have exacerbated poverty, homelessness, and community instability. Relevant discourse could discourage current widespread public feelings of helplessness, bridge communities that do not currently see the similarities between them, and begin to lay the groundwork for a real examination of the vast and interdependent social forces and structures that have produced and transformed the face of street crime and destabilized the most fragile communities.

For all the public hue and cry about some categories of crime, rarely are Americans exposed to an informed exploration of the relationship between some kinds of crime and the extraordinary institutional violence done to the nation's poorest children of color. These include massive unemployment for them, their parents, and relatives; constant police harassment and violence against their peers, coupled with limited police efficacy against and in some cases complicity with the drug trade; routine arrests for "suspicious" behavior (anyone who is black and/or has lived in a poor black community knows that cops often equate suspicious behavior and black male bodies); appalling housing or none at all; limited access to legal or political redress; and dehumanizing state aid bureaucracies (such as demanding that welfare parents continually scour the listings for affordable apartments in order to keep their monthly rent coupons when the lowest market rentals cost two and three times more than their coupons can cover). This is topped off by economic shifts that have transformed the already bleak labor landscape in black urban communities into tenuous, low-pay, and dead-end service jobs.

Imagine how differently the same acts of violent street crime would read if they were coupled with stories that labeled these government-orchestrated institutional actions and neglects as acts of violence. What if these social policies that support the interests of the wealthy at the cruel expense of everyone else—especially the poor—were labeled acts of social violence? How then would Americans respond to the crime crisis? What policies would these criminal activities encourage?

Even more provocatively, what if we took a look at all crime (e.g., domestic violence, embezzlement, the savings and loan scandal, serial killers, real estate fraud, murder, arson, rape, etc.) and highlighted the most consistent common denominator—men—and decided that, to solve the problem, it was necessary somehow to change the behavior of men as a group regardless of race and class. How would this alter our understanding of the crime dilemma? Instead of exploring these relationships, we are treated to disproportionately high visibility of a relatively small number of violent offenders who are intended to inspire fear in us. Without any relationship between these aspects of so-called social order and behavior of society's least powerful, the "real" answer implied by the constructed irrationality of street crime or participation in the drug trade is already present in the story: These are not people; they are monsters.

MEDIA VILLIFICATION

12 The demonization of young black males in the popular media, by black and white leaders, and among law enforcement officials has been well-documented by a range of scholars and others. This portrayal of young black men as unhuman—or dangerously superhuman, like the police fantasies of Rodney King—is an important part of creating a moral justification for the perpetuation of brutal and dehumanizing state policies. The white American public, many of whom only tangentially know any young black men personally, has been inundated with images of young black men who appear fully invested in a life of violent crime, who have participated in drug-related gang shoot-outs and other acts of violence for "no apparent reason."

This last representation is crucial to the fear that current crime reporting encourages and to the work of demonizing. Such people are violent for no apparent reason; *they* are not like *us*. Isn't it reasonable to treat an animal like an animal? What rights and social obligations are extended to monsters?

Demonization is hard work. Making monsters out of a multitude of young people who struggle to survive under immense pressures involves drawing attention away from the difficulties they face, minimizing the abuses they suffer, and making their cultural activity seem a product or example of their status as dangerous creatures. "Representing" young black inner city males and "their ways" without considering black cultural literacy (especially hip hop) or devoting sufficient attention to larger structural forces and historical contextualization paves the way for readings of rap as the black monster's music. Adolescent and vernacular cultures always have tested the boundaries of acceptable speech, frequently exploring taboo and transgressive subjects. This is true of 18th-century English and Irish folk practices, the blues of the early 20th century, and rap today.

Most attacks on rap music offer profoundly shallow readings of its use of violent and sexist imagery and rely on a handful of provocative and clearly troubling songs or lyrics. Rarely is the genre described in ways that encompass the range of passionate, horrifying, and powerful storytelling in rap and gangsta rap. Few critics in the popular realm—there are some exceptions such as Robin D.G. Kelley, Maxine Waters (D.-Calif.), George Lipsitz, and Michael Dyson—have responded to rap's disturbing elements in a way that attempts to understand the logic and motivations behind these facets of its expressions.

16   The aesthetic complexity of some of the lyrics by prominent hardcore (some say gangsta) rappers such as Snoop Doggy Dog, Scarface from the Geto Boys, and Ice Cube and the genius of the best music that accompanies it almost always are overlooked completely in the attacks on rap, in part out of genuine ignorance (similar dismissals have clung to the reception of all black American music, jazz included), and in part because exploring these facets of rap's lure would damage the process of creating easily identifiable villains.

Basically, reality is more complicated than the current crime debate allows. Who would we blame, if not rappers and their fans? Rap music has become a lightning rod for those politicians and law and order officials who are hell-bent on scape-goating it as a major source of violence instead of attending to the much more difficult and complicated work of transforming the brutally unjust institutions that shape the lives of poor people. Attacking rap during this so-called crisis of crime and violence is a facile smokescreen that protects the real culprits and deludes the public into believing that public officials are taking a bite out of crime. In the face of daunting economic and social conditions that are felt most severely by the young people they represent, rappers are cast as the perpetrators.

Some hardcore rap no doubt is producing images and ideas that I, among many others, find troubling and saddening. This is not to be interpreted as a denial or defense of rap's problematic elements. At the same time and in equal amounts, many rappers are able to codify the everyday experiences of demonized young black men and bear witness to the experiences they face, never see explained from their perspective, but know are true. Many a gangsta rap tale chronicles the experience of wandering around all day, trying to make order out of a horizon of unemployment, gang cultural occupation, the threat of violence from police and rival teens, and fragile home relationships.

Given this complexity in rap's story telling, how is it that most Americans only know about the most extremely violent passages? What does it mean to villify rap in the face of the profound social and economic dispossession that consumes poor communities today? How can a black leader like Rev. Calvin Butts make his media name on attacking a cultural form he exhibits so little knowledge about? How can black representatives, such as Rep. Cardiss Collins (D.-Ill.) and Sen. Carol Moseley-Braun (D.-Ill.), hold a series of Congressional and Senatorial hearings on gangsta rap under the Sub-committees on Commerce and Consumer Protection and Youth and Urban Crime, respectively, when life and death matters of social and political justice that face Chicago's black teens remain unscheduled for public scrutiny? These hearings are a form of empty moral grandstanding, a shameful attempt by politicians to earn political favors and ride the wave of public frenzy about crime while at the same time remaining unable and often unwilling to tackle the real problems that plague America's cities and their poorest black children.

20   Hip hop culture and rap music have become the cultural emblem for America's young black city kids, only a small percentage of which participate in street crimes. The more public opinion, political leaders, and policymakers criminalize hip hop as the cultural example of a criminal way of thinking, the more imaginary black monsters will surface. In this fearful fantasy, hip hop style (or whatever style young black men create and adopt) becomes a code for criminal behavior, and censuring the music begins to look more and more like fighting crime.

READER RESPONSE

What do you think of Rose's charges against those who criticize rap music? For instance, look again at the series of questions she asks in paragraph 19 and her allegation that congressional and senatorial hearings on rap music are "empty moral grandstanding." What is your response to what she says there and elsewhere about the unfair press given to rap music?

QUESTIONS FOR DISCUSSION

1. Explain the extent to which you agree with Rose's position on the subject of rap lyrics.
2. Discuss Rose's use of language to convey her position. For instance, look at the opening paragraph, and consider her use of such phrases as "media-crafted frenzies," "the bread and butter of television news," "the coal that fires the crisis boiler," and "ratings-hungry media executives." What do they tell you about her stance on the subject and her opinion of the media? Locate other words and phrases that you think convey Rose's position particularly well.
3. What do you think of the reasons Rose gives to explain why "street crime is sexy copy" (paragraph 2) and of the distinction she believes must be made "between criminal acts and the social language used to talk about crime and to define criminals" (paragraph 4). Do you support the changes Rose would like to see in the media's representation of street crime and in the discussions about rap music?

4. How does Rose define *demonization?* Does she convince you that popular media demonize young black males?

5. Evaluate the strengths and weaknesses of Rose's argument. Does she provide convincing evidence? Does she support generalizations? Does she develop her argument logically and reasonably? Is she fair in her attacks on the media and others?

Where's the Return Fire in Culture Wars?
David Segal

David Segal worked at The Monthly *as an editor from 1993 to 1994 and is currently a music critic for* The Washington Post. *This essay was first published in the July 2, 2002, edition of* The Washington Post.

Where, oh where, is the outrage?

The Billboard charts are crammed full of the vulgar and violent these days, with lyrics celebrating every pathology under the sun, plus a couple of pathologies that apparently were hiding under bridges. Among the best-selling: the new Korn album, "Untouchables," which is a carnival of high dudgeon and hate, and the third album by Cam'ron, a rapper who's scored big with "Come Home With Me," a thoroughly vile depiction of whores, drugs and venereal disease.

Most notably there's Eminem, whose latest, is a potty-mouthed soap opera of dysfunction and hostility. It's also witty and hugely entertaining, but never mind that for a moment. There was a time when an album that imagined diabolical ways to poison women with anthrax would stir a little protest. Not long ago, records about stalking women, deriding gays and snorting cocaine in front of children might be expected to get a rise from *someone*—especially if that album became a sales phenomenon, as "Show" has become, spending five straight weeks at the No. 1 spot and selling more than 3 million copies. Detroit's dye-job rapper, born Marshall Mathers, is now the most popular artist in the country, and the bulk of his audience is kids under 18.

4   But from the nation's culture commentators, not a peep has been heard. Nobody is organizing a boycott or picketing radio stations or even thundering in editorials. There's been, in fact, a resounding silence from Eminem's critics, even those who rose to condemn his previous release, "The Marshall Mathers LP," two years ago. One of the most reliable fonts of umbrage wasn't even aware that Eminem had a new album out.

"I haven't heard it yet, but I'm certainly going to go get it now," said C. DeLores Tucker, chair of the National Congress of Black Women, and for years a vocal scold of record labels that release gangsta rap.

"I heard one of his songs on the way to work today," said David Smith, spokesman for the Human Rights Campaign, a gay rights group that has been critical of Eminem's gay-bashing lyrics. "We're not exercised enough about him to run out and buy it and check every syllable."

Even Lynne Cheney has been low-key, despite being baited by name on "Show." "Mrs. Cheney has no response because, as she sees it, the issue is larger," explained the Second Lady's press spokeswoman, Natalie Rule. "Namely, Mr. Mathers's repeated glorification of violence against women and gay people. That deserves to be widely condemned."

8   But a wide condemnation has yet to materialize. Which raises a question: Why not? Whatever happened to the age-old culture spaz-out that's been a staple of pop since Elvis learned to undulate in the '50s? The tango between stars and their exasperated detractors has followed a clear pattern: The artists allegedly push the boundaries of taste and the critics splutter, usually to the benefit of the artists, who get tagged as controversial, which invariably stirs sales. Billy Joel, for example, has long claimed that "Only the Good Die Young," from 1977's "The Stranger," would have slid into oblivion if Catholic groups hadn't denounced it. After protests helped it catch on, he joked recently, he nearly asked the clergy to inveigh against other singles.

Maybe we simply have no goat left to get. Or perhaps the wire for outrage is now so high that nobody, not even Eminem, can trip it. It makes sense, demographically speaking. Most parents these days were raised on rock and they remember how silly their own dads seemed getting spooked by people like Alice Cooper.

Or maybe the commentariat has more pressing matters on its collective mind. William Bennett, one of the most prominent of the culture critics and a director of Empower America, a conservative think tank, says the silence from his side is the result of a reprioritizing of issues forced by national traumas in the past year.

"I'm interested in what's on the radio and TV, but I'm more interested in whether my country is going to survive," he says. "We had the luxury of talking about the culture a couple years ago because we weren't at war. It would be great if the culture were better, but we've got to say, that's about entertainment. Now we've got to make sure our institutions work—the presidency, the military, schools, the church."

12   A culture *Kampf* might, it turns out, be a sign of relative peace, not turmoil. ("A Shattered Nation Longs to Care About Stupid [Stuff] Again," read an Onion headline in October.) Perhaps we'll know we've returned to genuine tranquillity when the words to a song ruffle some feathers. Or the current truce could signify that the lyrics wars of yesteryear weren't real wars.

"It was always a phony problem," says Steve Gottlieb, president of TVT Records, the New York label that has released albums by Nine Inch Nails and Naughty by Nature. "It was always a political issue that played well in the media during a time of peace and prosperity. Thinking people never thought there was a correlation between rock lyrics and violence, any more than there is a correlation between gospel music and good behavior."

We've got real problems now, he adds, like terrorism and multibillion-dollar corporate scandals, which make arguing about lyrics seem silly. Stories that linked crime to music, Gottlieb says, "weren't competing for the front pages with substantive evil, and now that we have substantive evil—whether in the Middle East or in the boardroom—we know it's not caused by lyrics."

What's funny is that nobody seems to have told Eminem, or any of the other supposedly objectionable rappers and rockers, that the combat is over and they have triumphed. On "Show," Eminem anticipates all the turmoil he'll cause and all the fits he'll give assorted "haters." But as much as Em loves playing the oppressed underdog, that tag is now ridiculous. He's rich, he's popular, and nobody is complaining about him anymore.

16   "They've won," says Bennett. "They can't stand to have won, but it's over and they've won. They get to say and do anything and make billions and castigate us in the process."

Maybe it's all a brilliant bit of counter-strategy. Attacking music has never worked in the past. We're about to find out if ignoring it works any better.

READER RESPONSE

Do your personal observations support Segal's assertion that no one cares today about the lyrics in rock and rap music?

QUESTIONS FOR DISCUSSION

1. Segal asks in paragraph 8: "Whatever happened to the age-old culture spaz-out that's been a staple of pop since Elvis learned to undulate in the '50s?" Explain, in your own words, what you understand him to mean by that question. What is "the age-old culture spaz-out" that he's referring to?
2. Discuss the extent to which you agree with Segal that the controversy over lyrics in popular music is a dead issue. Can you provide examples of songs that either support or refute his central idea?
3. Segal offers a number of reasons to explain what he sees as the current lack of interest in violent or vulgar song lyrics. Assuming that Segal is at least to some extent correct in his thesis, explore your views on the possible explanations he proposes. Which, if any, seem to be plausible?
4. Respond to or comment on this statement by William Bennett: "'They've won. They can't stand to have won, but it's over and they've won. They get to say and do anything and make billions and castigate us in the process.'" (paragraph 16).

Is Hollywood Responsible for 9-11?

Robert Roten

*Robert Roten is a Laramie, Wyoming, film critic and member of
the Online Film Critics Society. This essay was published in the
April 15, 2002, edition of* Laramie Movie Scope, *an online series
of movie reviews, news, links and commentary on the film industry located at http://www.lariat.org/AtTheMovies/*

Robert Altman, a renowned Hollywood director, says Hollywood is to blame
for the attacks of September 11. Altman, director of such classics as
"Nashville," "MASH," "McCabe and Mrs. Miller," "The Player," "Short Cuts,"
"Cookie's Fortune" and many other films, including a recent Academy Award
contender, "Gosford Park," is not just some average film director. He is a highly
acclaimed director. His words carry a lot of weight.

Altman was quoted as saying in an Associated Press story, "The movies
set the pattern, and these people have copied the movies . . . Nobody would
have thought to commit an atrocity like that (the attack on the World Trade
Centers) unless they'd seen it in a movie." He was also quoted in same article
as saying, "How dare we continue to show this kind of mass destruction in
movies? . . . I just believe we created this atmosphere and taught them how
to do it."

While I subscribe to the theory that violence in the mass media results
in more violent behavior in society, I have trouble with Altman's contention.
First of all, I don't remember ever seeing a film in which hijackers crash
planes into buildings. In the case of 9-11, the artistic precedent for that attack
was not a movie, but a book, Tom Clancy's "Debt of Honor" in which the pilot
of a jetliner crashes his aircraft into the Capitol building in Washington, D.C.,
wiping out most of this nation's elected officials in the process. The pilot's suicide attack was meant to avenge his son's death at the hands of U.S. troops in
a war. There was also a similar story in the pilot episode of Fox television's
short-lived *X-Files* spinoff series, *The Lone Gunmen,* in which the gunmen
thwart a plot to crash a remotely-piloted jetliner into the World Trade Centers.

4   Films like "Independence Day," "Deep Impact," "Armageddon," and just
about every James Bond movie ever made are examples of films that celebrate, and profit from, the depiction of destruction on a grand scale. These are
the types of films that Altman is probably referring to. The final scene in "Fight
Club," for instance, is a spectacular vision of apocalyptic destruction, in which
large financial institutions are brought down by explosives in the name of anarchy. It is a scene hauntingly similar to the fall of the World Trade Centers.
When the World Trade Centers were attacked, many eyewitnesses remarked
the surreal scene was "just like a movie." It should be noted that some of Altman's own films, including "Nashville," "Short Cuts" and "Gosford Park," include
scenes of graphic violence, but on a very small scale. Apparently that makes a
difference. Murder is acceptable, but mass murder is not.

Perhaps more important than Altman's allegation is the underlying assumptions it reveals. It means that in Altman's mind, violence in movies does have an impact on the behavior of people in the real world. This is at odds with the apologists for movie violence, like award-winning critic Roger Ebert. He argues movies simply reflect the violence in society, and that they don't really cause violence. The opposite view is that of media critics like myself and Neal Gabler. In Gabler's book, "Life, the Movie: How Entertainment Conquered Reality," he argues that entertainment has become a dominant force in everyday life. He argues that we live our lives by the rules laid down in the movies. We think of our lives through the filter of television and film. Although most films do not represent reality, they *seem* like reality, and they produce real emotions, and tangible emotional responses, such as laughing and crying, in the audience. This creates a powerful illusion of reality which becomes part of the emotional experience of each audience member. This emotional legacy becomes, in a sense, indistinguishable from the legacy of real life experiences. In other words, film does not merely reflect reality as Ebert argues, it changes reality by interacting with the minds of the viewers.

I don't quite buy Altman's exact argument that Hollywood is to blame for the September 11 terrorist attacks because it gave the terrorists the idea. I think you have to give the terrorists some credit for being able to come up with their own ideas about how to attack America. The hijacking of four jets at once to attack New York and Washington simultaneously went well beyond even the lurid imagination of Hollywood screenwriters.

I do think that Hollywood films had an indirect role in the attacks, however. As some film critics have pointed out, Hollywood films ("American Beauty," for instance) show America in a very bad light. The image of America projected overseas in films is perfectly suited to the purposes of Islamic extremists who want to stir up hatred against the U.S. We are depicted as a dangerous, violent, vengeful, corrupt people, preoccupied with sex, violence and money. We are seldom depicted as spiritual, religious, generous, loving, family-oriented, giving or caring people. In other words, most American films are perfectly suited for religious extremists who want to demonize us. These extremists could not have done a better job making us look evil had they made the films themselves.

8   Altman's statement was, in a sense, wishful thinking on his part. He hoped against hope to influence Hollywood, and filmgoers, to support movies that are more character-driven and thought-provoking (like "In the Bedroom"), rather than big, mindless action movies (like "Collateral Damage"). Altman was quoted as saying, "Maybe there's a chance to get back to . . . grown-up films . . . Anything that uses humor and dramatic values to deal with human emotions and gets down to what people are to people." Those are the kinds of films that Altman likes to make. However, those aren't the kinds of films that make money in foreign markets. The movies that translate well across different cultures are . . . you guessed it, movies that are short on dialogue and long on spectacle: big, mindless action movies. Foreign markets make up a big percentage of the profit made on films nowadays. In many cases, foreign box office

receipts are greater than domestic box office totals, even for American-made films. It's not an art, it isn't even about reality, it is a business, and it is all about the money.

So be careful what films you support with your money. If you'll go see any old teen sex comedy, no matter how bad it is, then that is just what Hollywood will produce in the future. Think about how movies depict Americans as a people. Is this who we really are? Besides, you never know who else is watching this stuff and what they are thinking, and how they might use it for their own purposes.

READER RESPONSE

Roten ends his essay by saying, "So be careful what films you support with your money." What films do you like to view? Explore for a few minutes what appeals to you about those films. Are there movies that you refuse to spend your money on? Explain your answer.

QUESTIONS FOR DISCUSSION

1. Discuss your response to Robert Altman's statement that movies are responsible for the September 11, 2001, terrorist attacks on the World Trade Center and the Pentagon.
2. What is the central controversy over the effect of violent Hollywood films on behavior? What is your position on that controversy?
3. In paragraph 7, Roten discusses the images of America in Hollywood films that he says are projected to viewers all over the world. State, in your own words, what that image is. Can you give examples of films that illustrate Roten's viewpoint? Can you supply examples that refute his statement?
4. Roten also says that films seldom portray Americans as "spiritual, religious, generous, loving, family-oriented, giving or caring people" (paragraph 7). Can you give examples of films that support that statement? What about examples that refute the statement?

Movies, Morality, and Conservative Complaints
Christopher Sharrett

Christopher Sharrett is an associate professor of communications at Seton Hall University, Associate Mass Media Editor of USA Today, *and Editorial Board Member of* Cinema Journal. *His books include* Crisis Cinema: The Apocalyptic Idea in Postmodern Narrative Film *(1992) and* Mythologies of Violence in Postmodern Media *(1999). This essay appeared in the September 1993 issue of* USA Today Magazine.

There has been renewed discourse lately about Hollywood's moral obligations to the public and the extent to which the sex and violence of feature films does violence to existing social morés. The most notable feature of the largely unremarkable debate is its lack of timeliness. Had it occurred at the heyday of Reaganism, when Jerry Falwell, Jimmy Swaggart, and their ilk were riding high in the media spectacle (and the nation was enjoying a bizarre somnambulism), these condemnations would be of a piece with the reaction of the 1980s. Neoconservative culture has not left the scene with the closing of the Reagan/Bush era, but the recent complaints about Hollywood's sins, particularly given the forward-looking Clinton moment, seem hopelessly anachronistic.

The renewed hand-wringing about movie morality has at its base a theory of communication enunciated more than 50 years ago by Harold Lasswell, who suggested a "hypodermic" notion of media, wherein communication processes are seen as something an individual or agency does to someone else. Like "impact" theories of art, this idea proceeds on the assumption that the public is a kind of *tabula rasa* (clean slate) upon which is inscribed all social, cultural, economic, political, and moral ideas. Such theories pay little attention to the role media have in reflecting ideas already circulating in society. According to this notion, "Hill Street Blues" and "Miami Vice" were different from "Dragnet" not because 1980s television necessarily reflected 1980s culture, but because TV producers decided to sabotage the time-honored and unshakable style and ideology of Jack Webb.

When John Hinckley shot Ronald Reagan, a few critics immediately seized on the assailant's preoccupation with the film "Taxi Driver." Such a focus exempts us from a more complex discourse about the root causes of violence or other anti-social conduct. When Ted Bundy blamed horror movies and pornography for his crimes, the New Right jumped on a bandwagon that a sociopath and pathological liar propped up for them, failing to notice that horror films and porn were rather tame when Bundy began his murderous career, and those things that impact a sociopath, abused from childhood, might have negligible effect on the rest of society.

4   The conservative criticism of cinema is and always has been involved in the pursuit of scapegoats. This criticism is little interested in systemic issues that very well may be involved in both the dominant ideology and moral code, as well as their built-in self-destruction. These critiques also look back to a halcyon, innocent age, a common inclination these days given the amount of nostalgia for the 1950s that saturates cultural production. Yearning for the innocence of childhood, always a cultural fixation, may be particularly difficult

to overcome when our view of this golden age of serene suburban households constantly is returned to us through the prisms of the media, through
"Father Knows Best" and the whipped-cream image of America in which Hollywood specialized during its overly sentimentalized studio system epoch.

Very often, criticism of the films Hollywood produces is combined with
that of the behavior of its producers. A large bluenose alarmist faction became
very upset in the 1920s with the Fatty Arbuckle scandal and similar tales of
Hollywood Babylon, which had almost as much to do with the effectuation of
the Hays Office censorship code as did the actual content of movies. Although
we continue to thrive on scandal more than we revile it, similar processes occur in our reception of cultural products. Madonna's success as sex goddess,
heir to Marilyn Monroe, etc., is as much involved in the minute off-screen
chronicling of her antics and the promotion of various books, CDs, videos, and
films. The quality, even the shock value, of these products is almost uniformly
mediocre, leading to some very essential questions: If the show biz world is so
out of step with American values and if, in fact, Hollywood is conspiring to rot
our moral fiber, why do we keep buying? If the image of sexuality in "Basic Instinct" and "Body of Evidence" is so distant from audiences' tastes, why do they
keep coming back for more?

I would agree with the neoconservatives that we could do with far
fewer films along the lines of "Basic Instinct," although my position is that they
simply are bad art with a retrograde view of gender relations; far too absurd,
in my judgment, to have much consequence for human behavior. Hollywood,
like the rest of our cultural outlets, feeds us rancid bowls of Froot Loops because it is easy and safe to do so since we have become accustomed to such
junk food and have failed, for a century or more, to ask anything else of our
culture.

If the cinema is to be accused of anything, it is anesthetizing us, but here
again, the blame lies squarely and solely with the consumer. It is not in the interest of the commercial media to do anything but move product in the quick-
est and most efficient way possible. Consequently, everything that might be
termed "art" thoroughly is marginalized and moved to venues off the average
consumer's beaten path. If Hollywood product seems more nihilistic and
amoral, we might take note that Vietnam, Watergate, the Reagan/Bush years,
and the relegation of the U.S. to debtor status with the collapse of its economy have given this nation a considerably more jaded palate than it had, say,
in the 1950s. Accordingly, the culture mills must add more hot sauce, horserad-
ish, and red pepper to such overcooked, leftover stews. It's time to look for
new recipes, rather than lynch the woebegone, ignorant chef.

READER RESPONSE

Do you share Sharrett's view that Hollywood, as well as the rest of popular
culture, feeds the public "junk food"? Explain your answer.

QUESTIONS FOR DISCUSSION

1. To what extent do you agree with Sharrett's criticism of conservatives's attacks on the movie industry?
2. Respond to this question: "If the show biz world is so out of step with American values and if, in fact, Hollywood is conspiring to rot our moral fiber, why do we keep buying?" (paragraph 5).
3. Respond to this statement: "Hollywood, like the rest of our cultural outlets, feeds us rancid bowls of Froot Loops because it is easy and safe to do so since we have become accustomed to such junk food and have failed, for a century or more, to ask anything else of our culture" (paragraph 6). Make sure you consider all aspects of the statement.
4. Discuss Sharrett's comment in his concluding paragraph that "everything that might be termed 'art' thoroughly is marginalized and moved to venues off the average consumer's beaten path."

Bang, You're Dead

Richard Corliss

Richard Corliss is a senior writer at Time *magazine, writing about movies, show business, and sports. Before joining* Time *in 1980, he was a film critic for several publications. He served as film editor for* Comment *magazine from 1970 to 1990. His books* Talking Pictures, *a study of Hollywood screenwriters, and* Greta Garbo *were both published in 1974. This selection first appeared in the May 3, 1999, issue of* Time.

The young and the older always eye one another across a gaping chasm. Gray heads shake in perplexity, even in a week of mourning [for the Columbine school shooting], even over the mildest expressions of teen taste. Fashion, for example. Here are these nice kids from suburban Denver, heroically documenting the tragedy for TV, and they all seem to belong to the Church of Wearing Your Cap Backward. A day later, as the teens grieve en masse, oldsters ask, "When we were kids, would we have worn sweats and jeans to a memorial service for our friends?" And of course the trench-coat killers had their own distinctive clothing: Johnny Cash by way of Quentin Tarantino. Should we blame the Columbine massacre on haberdashery?

No, but many Americans want to pin the blame for this and other agonizing splatter fests on pop culture. Adults look at the revenge fantasies their kids see in the 'plexes, listen (finally) to the more extreme music, glance over their kids' shoulders at Druid websites and think, "Seems repulsive to me. Maybe pop culture pulled the trigger."

Who wouldn't want to blame self-proclaimed Antichrist superstar Marilyn Manson? Listen to *Lunchbox,* and get the creeps: "The big bully try to stick his finger in my chest/Try to tell me, tell me he's the best/But I don't really give a good goddamn cause/I got my lunchbox and I'm armed real well . . . / Next motherf_____ gonna get my metal/ . . . Pow pow pow." Not quite *Stardust.*

4   Sift through teen movies of the past 10 years, and you could create a hindsight game plan for Littleton. Peruse *Heathers* (1989), in which a charming sociopath engineers the death of jocks and princesses. Study carefully, as one of the Columbine murderers reportedly did, *Natural Born Killers* (1994), in which two crazy kids cut a carnage swath through the Southwest as the media ferociously dog their trail. Sample *The Basketball Diaries* (1995), in which druggy high schooler Leonardo DiCaprio daydreams of strutting into his homeroom in a long black coat and gunning down his hated teacher and half the kids. *The Rage: Carrie 2* (now in theaters) has jocks viciously taunting outsiders until one girl kills herself by jumping off the high school roof and another wreaks righteous revenge by using her telekinetic powers to pulverize a couple dozen kids.

Grownups can act out revenge fantasies too. In *Payback,* Mel Gibson dishes it out (pulls a ring out of a punk's nose, shoots his rival's face off through a pillow) and takes it (gets punched, switch-bladed, shot and, ick, toe-hammered). *The Matrix,* the first 1999 film to hit $100 million at the box office, has more kung fu than gun fu but still brandishes an arsenal of firepower in its tale of outsiders against the Internet droids.

In Littleton's wake, the culture industry has gone cautious. CBS pulled an episode of *Promised Land* because of a plot about a shooting in front of a Denver school. The WB has postponed a *Buffy the Vampire Slayer* episode with a schoolyard-massacre motif. Movie-studio honchos, who furiously resist labeling some serious adult films FOR ADULTS ONLY, went mum last week when asked to comment on any connection between violent movies and violent teen behavior. That leaves us to explain things.

Revenge dramas are as old as *Medea* (she tore her sons to pieces), as hallowed as *Hamlet* (seven murders), as familiar as *The Godfather*. High drama is about the conflict between shades of good and evil, often within the same person. But it's easier to dream up a scenario of slavering evil and imperishable good. This is the moral and commercial equation of melodrama: the greater the outrage suffered, the greater the justification for revenge. You grind me down at first; I grind you up at last. This time it's personal.

8   Fifty years ago, movies were homogenous, meant to appeal to the whole family. Now pop culture has been Balkanized; it is full of niches, with different groups watching and playing their own things. And big movies, the ones that grab $20 million on their first weekend, are guy stuff. Young males consume

violent movies, in part, for the same reason they groove to outlaw music: because their parents can't understand it—or stand it. To kids, an R rating for violence is like the Parental Advisory on CDs: a Good Housebreaking Seal of Approval.

The cultural gap, though, is not just between old and young. It is between the haves and the self-perceived have-nots of teen America. Recent teen films, whether romance or horror, are really about class warfare. In each movie, the cafeteria is like a tiny former Yugoslavia, with each clique its own faction: the Serbian jocks, Bosnian bikers, Kosovar rebels, etc. And the horror movies are a microcosm of ethnic cleansing.

Movies may glamorize mayhem while serving as a fantasy safety valve. A steady diet of megaviolence may coarsen the young psyche—but some films may instruct it. *Heathers* and *Natural Born Killers* are crystal-clear satires on psychopathy, and *The Basketball Diaries* is a mordant portrait of drug addiction. *Payback* is a grimly synoptic parody of all gangster films. In three weeks, 15 million people have seen *The Matrix* and not gone berserk. And *Carrie 2* is a crappy remake of a 1976 hit that led to no murders.

Flash: movies don't kill people. Guns kill people. "What's more troubling," asks Steve Tisch, producer of *Forrest Gump* and *American History X,* "a kid with a sawed-off shotgun or a kid with a cassette of *The Basketball Diaries*? It's not just movies. Lots of other wires have to short before a kid goes out and does something like this. It's a piece of a much bigger, more complex puzzle."

12   Some images in recent films are both repellent and (the tricky part) exciting. Some song lyrics express a rage that's not easy to take as irony. And, yes, a movie or song or TV show *may* inspire some sick twist to earn satanic stardom with a gun. But most kids deserve the respect their parents wanted when they were kids: to be able to consume bits of pop culture and decide on their own whether it's poetry, entertainment or junk.

There is a lapse in parental logic that goes from "I don't get it" to "It must be evil," and from that to "It makes kids evil." Today, moms and dads gaze at the withdrawn souls across the kitchen table chasm. They see what their kids wear; they may know what their kids see. But, in another Manson lyric, they "fail to see the anguish in my eyes." Parents should try looking into their kids' eyes. If they do, and do more, they might even "see the tragic/Turnin' into magic."

READER RESPONSE

Respond to Corliss's statement in paragraph 8 that "to kids, an R rating for violence is like the Parental Advisory on CDs: a Good Housebreaking Seal of Approval."

QUESTIONS FOR DISCUSSION

1. To what extent do you think Corliss's tone is appropriate? Do you think that he trivializes a very real concern?
2. In paragraph 4, Corliss writes, "Sift through teen movies of the past 10 years, and you could create a hindsight game plan for Littleton." In the next paragraph, he writes, "Grownups can act out revenge fantasies too." If you have seen any of the movies Corliss mentions as examples, comment on your impressions of them. Can you name other films that "could create a hindsight game plan" for school shootings?
3. Discuss this statement in paragraph 9: "The cultural gap, though, is not just between old and young. It is between the haves and the self-perceived have-nots of teen America."
4. Discuss the extent to which you agree with Corliss's observation: "Flash: movies don't kill people. Guns kill people" (paragraph 11).
5. Discuss the language Corliss uses in the final paragraph. What are the implications of "withdrawn souls," "kitchen-table chasm," " 'the anguish in my eyes,' " and " 'the tragic . . . into magic' "?

Menace to Society
John Davidson

John Davidson is a writer living in Austin, Texas. He wrote this essay for the February 22, 1996, issue of Rolling Stone.

With three-quarters of Americans surveyed convinced that movies, television and music spur young people to violence, and politicians on the left and right blasting the entertainment industry for irresponsibility, the debate over violence in popular culture is likely to be a key issue in the presidential campaign.

Republican presidential front-runner Bob Dole, conservative guru William Bennett, black activist C. DeLores Tucker and liberal Democrat Sen. Paul Simon all have attacked portrayals of violence, treating the link between art and reality as gospel truth. They've found support for their claims from the American Psychological Association and the American Psychiatric Association, which have both issued reports stating that television violence causes aggression.

And a new controversy surrounding video games has been sparked by Lt. Col. Dave Grossman, a psychologist and Army Ranger. In his book *On*

Killing, he claims that these games function like firing ranges, using the same type of conditioning employed to overcome soldiers' built-in inhibition to killing in the Vietnam War.

4   The research, however, is less clear. Most experts who have studied the issue believe there is *some* link—indirect, perhaps—between seeing violence and committing it, but there is no agreement on how strong that link is or how to measure it. What's more, even those who argue most persuasively that there is a case to be made for connecting violence and culture agree that the biggest problem may not be teenagers seeing *Natural Born Killers* or listening to the Geto Boys but small children watching Saturday morning cartoons.

For the last 40 years, social scientists have attempted to measure how media violence affects people, with the bulk of the research focused on television. One of the most influential studies was directed by George Gerbner. Beginning in 1967, Gerbner, who at that time was dean of the Annenberg School for Communication at the University of Pennsylvania, and his colleagues created a violence index that is still used to measure the percentage of network programs that have violence, the number of violent acts, the percentage of characters involved in violence and the percentage involved in killing. Their index doesn't reflect the increased amount of violent material made available through cable television and VCRs. (That count, according to the National Coalition on Television Violence, is that children in homes with cable TV and/or a VCR will see about 32,000 murders and 40,000 attempted murders by the time they're 18.)

Gerbner's group concluded that television acts as an electronic melting pot, which creates a national culture. Part of that culture is "the mean-world syndrome," which leads people to believe that they are more likely to be victims of violence than they are in reality. "People who watch the most television are usually the ones who have fewer options, less money and less education," says Nancy Signorielli, a professor of communication at the University of Delaware who worked on the Gerbner study. "Their views of the world reflect what they see on television, and they overestimate their chances of being involved in violence." Like the man in Louisiana who in 1992 shot and killed a Japanese exchange student looking for a Halloween party, people overreact to perceived threats and act violently.

Remarkably, Gerbner found that the indexes have remained relatively constant during the past two decades. Nonetheless, he's been accused of exaggerating the amount of violence by not taking context into consideration. A poke in the eye, as far as he's concerned, is basically a poke in the eye; his group counts *The Three Stooges* and Road Runner cartoons as violent programming.

8   A landmark study funded by the four major networks in response to congressional pressure and released this past fall attempted to correct that deficiency and qualify different types of violence by looking at time slot, parental advisory, duration, explicitness, relation to the story and

consequences. Researchers at the Center for Communication Policy at the University of California at Los Angeles confirmed that context is crucial. In other words, a TV program that shows kids beating up a fellow student with impunity could have a more harmful effect than one that shows a couple of murderers who end up in jail. Even Signorielli acknowledges that context is important: "What we have in the U.S. is happy violence. In Japan, violence is much more graphic and much more realistic," she says. "There, television violence may actually work as a deterrent. But here, if someone's shot we don't see the wound. There's not much bleeding on U.S. television."

Leonard Eron, a research scientist at the University of Michigan, has taken another approach. He began by studying how aggression develops in children, never considering television to be important. "I thought television was just another version of the sort of things children were exposed to in the past—fairy tales, stories and movies," says Eron. "But television is different, if in no other way than [that programs are] repeated over and over again."

Eron and his colleagues tested 875 third-graders in New York's Columbia County and interviewed about 80 percent of their parents. To relieve tension in the interviews, Eron threw in a question about television viewing. What surprised him was the correlation between aggression and viewing habits. Children whose parents said they watched a lot of violent television turned out to be aggressive in school, and 10 years later, in the first of the follow-up studies, Eron discovered that what a child watched at 8 years old was "one of the best predictors" of adult aggression—more important than the parents' child-rearing habits or socioeconomic factors. "I could compare children over time," says Eron. "At 8, if the less aggressive of two children was watching more television violence, at 18, he would be the more aggressive of the two."

Eron's findings correspond with what psychologists believe about child development: Children are most vulnerable to television from ages 2 to about 8, when they become more capable of distinguishing what they see on the screen from reality. The conclusions also conform to what we know about the development of a child's moral sense: It is developed by age 9 at the latest.

12   Just how children learn from the media is the subject of competing theories. According to the simplest, the viewing of aggressive material triggers aggressive thoughts that influence subsequent actions. Kids imitate what they see, just as adults emulate styles of dress and behavior observed in movies and TV shows.

The theory is fine as far as it goes but doesn't take into account the child's expectations and comprehension—nor does it explain the cumulative effects of watching violence. Educators theorize that a child's response depends upon five variables: the child's intellectual achievement, social popularity, identification with television characters, belief in the realism of the violence and the amount of fantasizing about aggression. If a child identifies with the characters, for instance, then he tends to internalize "scripts" for future aggressive behavior. As a child becomes more aggressive, he becomes less popular and more troublesome in school. The more trouble he has with teachers and friends, the more likely it is he will turn to aggressive television for affirmation, thus establishing a vicious cycle.

What turned out to be the most startling result of Eron's study, however, was that a child's viewing beyond the age of 8 seems to have virtually *no* effect on his level of aggression: Once an 8-year-old's level of aggression is established, it tends to remain stable. If this is true, then most of the attacks on media are far off base. Children under the age of 8 are exposed to feature films but even with VCRs and cable, Hollywood movies are not staples in children's media diets in the same way that *Mighty Morphin Power Rangers* or *Teenage Mutant Ninja Turtles* are. In fact, the UCLA study singled out seven Saturday morning network shows including *Power Rangers* and *Ninja Turtles* for containing "sinister combat violence" or "violence for the sake of violence." The report warned that "the dark overtones and unrelenting combat in these shows constitute a fairly recent trend, which appears to be on the rise."

Of course, Eron's work is the subject of controversy. There are experts who warn against linking culture and violence at all. Jonathan Freedman, a psychology professor at the University of Toronto, says that after thoroughly reviewing all the existing studies on television and violence, he had to conclude that there was no convincing evidence that the media have an influence on real violence. "You always hear that there are 3,000 studies that prove that television contributes to violence," says Freedman, "but that's absolutely false. There are maybe 200 pertinent studies, and almost no one has read the literature. It sounds plausible that television causes violence, and everyone takes the word of the so-called experts. I was amazed at how different the studies were from what was being said about them."

16   Of those 200 studies, Freedman says, about 160 are lab studies, which he dismisses as "not totally irrelevant but not very meaningful." In typical lab studies, subjects are shown violent films, and then an attempt is made to measure their response. In one study, increased aggression was measured by showing children a balloon and asking if it would be fun to break it. In others, children were given plastic Bobo dolls that are designed to be hit. Freedman says that most experimenters get positive results because violent programs are simply more arousing than neutral programs and because children respond in the way they think the researchers expect them to. "All that these experiments show is potential effect," says Freedman. "But what is the real effect? In lab experiments they expose children to one kind of media, but in the real world no one watches just violence. You watch lots of different kinds of television. There's lots of different mediating stimuli."

Freedman finds the field studies equally disappointing. He thinks that Eron and his colleagues are true believers because they've devoted their careers to and built their reputations on the damaging effects of television violence. "Most people don't have the statistical and methodological expertise to

read and evaluate the studies," Freedman explains. "Since [these study] com-
mittees all base their conclusions on the words of those few experts, naturally
. . . they all conclude that television violence is harmful.

"People say that children are more aggressive," Freedman continues.
"More aggressive than when? Not more than 1880. Somalia and Bosnia are
worse than here, and Somalia doesn't have television."

The research on video games and rap music is even more inconclusive. A
1993 study of 357 seventh- and eighth-graders, for instance, found that 32 percent said fantasy violence was their favorite game category, while 17 percent
chose human violence. But the study is small and doesn't draw conclusions
between the games and aggression. As for rap, Peter Christiansen, a professor
of communication at Lewis and Clark College, in Portland, Ore., says, "Seventy-
six percent of rap is purchased by middle-class kids. For them, rap is a kind of
cultural tourism. . . . They aren't turned on by the explicit lyrics."

20   Poverty, the easy accessibility of guns, domestic abuse, social instability
and the like may all contribute more than the media do to the level of violence. Even researchers like Signorielli warn against drawing cause-and-effect
conclusions. "You can't just blame TV for the problems of society," she says.
"Television contributes to children's aggressiveness, but it's only one of the
factors."

Unfortunately, the political debate tends to ignore the nuances and uncertain-
ties contained in the research. In reaction to the wave of political pressure,
Time Warner sold its interest in Interscope, which distributed some of rap's
most inflammatory artists, and Time Warner Chairman Gerald Levin agreed to
develop standards for the distribution and labeling of potentially objectionable music. Meanwhile, Jack Valenti, the president of the Motion Picture Association of America, has commented that the entertainment industry "must . . .
act as if TV is indeed a factor in anti-social behavior," adding that the industry
"has to be more responsible." Valenti, however, still questions the link between
media and violence. A sociopath could be triggered by reading a Bible verse as
easily as by watching a film. As Valenti says, "We can't create movies that are
safe for deviants. Anything can set them off. We can't function at their level."

Fortunately, even the most fervent critics, like William Bennett, still shy
away from advocating legislative remedies; Bennett declares he hopes to
"shame" the industry into taking a more responsible stand. Meanwhile, the
Democrats are still pushing for a federal law that will create a ratings system
for all programs and require new TVs to have a V chip, which gives parents
the power to shut off certain pornographic or violent channels.

With the presidential race heating up, however, the rhetorical battle isn't
likely to cool down any time soon. Dole is demanding in his campaign ads
that "Hollywood stop corrupting our children." He has said on the Senate
floor: "Those who continue to deny that cultural messages can and do bore
deep into the hearts and minds of our young people are deceiving themselves
and ignoring reality."

24   Yet if Saturday morning cartoons are more a problem than Hollywood blockbusters or rap music, who's ignoring reality?

READER RESPONSE

List the names of Saturday morning cartoons you remember watching as a child. Which of them do you recall as being violent? What forms did the violence take? Do you think the violence in cartoons shaped you or affected your behavior in any way?

QUESTIONS FOR DISCUSSION

1. What is the "menace to society" to which the title refers?
2. What is it about media images of sex and violence that makes them particularly likely targets of politicians during election years? What is your opinion of such attacks? Do you think there are other, more pressing issues that politicians ought to address?
3. Summarize, in your own words, the debate over the link between the media and violence. Does Davidson seem to lean toward one side? Explain your answer. Where do you position yourself in that debate?
4. Davidson mentions the push to get a federal law requiring new television sets to have a V chip that would allow parents to prevent their children from viewing programs they feel are too explicitly sexual or violent (paragraph 22). Discuss how effective you think such a chip would be.

Beating the Same Old Dead Horse
Joe Saltzman

Joe Saltzman is Associate Mass Media Editor of USA Today *and is a professor of journalism in the University of Southern California School of Journalism in Los Angeles. This essay appeared on the "Words & Images" page of the November 1993 issue of* USA Today Magazine.

Whenever everything looks the bleakest and there seems to be no political way out of the severe social and economic problems facing the nation, Congress always can be counted on to come up with a crusade against sex and violence on television. It has happened repeatedly for the last 40 years and undoubtedly will again in the future. It's a safe and popular subject, one that doesn't involve taking away benefits from voters or increasing taxes. It's fool-proof, especially when wrapped in a patriotic campaign to save children. Everyone wants to do something good for the kids, to protect them from the evils that men and women do and no one but adults seem to know about.

Nobody seems to want violence or sex on television except the viewers. Humanists and moralists abhor violence because they say it inures young viewers to the pain and suffering of others, and they abhor sex because they say it promotes promiscuity and, in the age of AIDs, a dangerous lifestyle. Femi-nists say they hate both because they feel all of it is anti-female. Ministers and educators say they hate both because they believe TV should provide healthy, life-affirming experiences to the young, not sordid, vicious experiences. Pub-licly, Congressmen and women don't want sex or violence on TV for all of these reasons. Privately, they adore it because, for four decades, it has given them a safe port free from the real horrors—government taxes and spending, the deficit, health care, gun control, and crime prevention.

The latest wrinkle, labeling violent programming—and undoubtedly sex-ual programming in the future—is as absurd as the debate itself. All any kid who *really* wants to see sex and violence has to do is turn to cable, run down to the video store, or go to the movies.

4   Watching a female police officer being attacked by a burglar on TV be-fore she shoots him in the face is nothing compared to monsters murdering everyone in sight with axes, chain saws, butcher knives, sawed-off shotguns, and explosives. If you want real violence, take a look at the biggest-grossing action films: "Lethal Weapon" (and all of its sequels) or any Arnold Schwarzenegger, Sylvester Stallone, or Chuck Norris pectoral extravaganza. Want to really be grossed out? Take a look at any in the "Alien" or "Robocop" or "Terminator" series; those martial-arts films with soundtracks guaranteed to catch every breaking bone and body in sight; "Halloween" or Freddy Krueger in any of his vicious incarnations; or almost anything from Stephen King.

Watching a soap opera discreetly showing two naked bodies making love is nothing compared to the soft-core porn available on the big screen or late-night cable. Most movies have gone beyond a roll in the hay. Take a look at "Basic Instinct" or "Body of Evidence." They offer cleverly choreographed sex-ual violence, designed to titillate.

The debate over TV violence would be meaningless if it didn't distract legislators, entertainers, and the public from more serious issues at hand that can't be blown away with publicity and grandstanding. TV producers worry once again that a rating system labeling violence (and sex is sure to be next) will have a chilling effect on their creativity and provocative programming. That will only come about if television executives panic and kick some of their highest-rated programs off the air. But that won't happen. There may be more editing of violent and sexy theatrical films shown on TV, more blue pen-ciling of strong violence or rough sexual behavior and language, but that too will pass. Maybe concerned producers even will hire writers to beef up story and character, and not rely on special effects and raunchy sex, but that too will pass because network executives want to keep their constituents happy.

Sex and violence always are good targets because, at first blush, everyone, publicly at least, wants them off TV. Privately, it's a different matter. Just look at the ratings. Many of the most popular programs of the past and present, whether they be "Hunter" or "Miami Vice," "Hill Street Blues" or "St. Elsewhere," "L.A. Law" or "Married . . . with Children" were and are popular because they pour(ed) on lots of action—physical or verbal violence or sex, or both. Sex and violence have been an intricate part of art and entertainment since recorded history because sex and violence involve the deepest and most absorbing parts of our being and history.

8   Reality programs and newsmagazines now dominate the networks' prime time as the genre of the day. They tell the same stories their fictional counterparts do, but cover them with the cloaks of actuality and authenticity. Like entertainment docudramas, most of the time these programs skillfully blend fact and fiction, but they're popular because they sell real sex and real violence perpetrated by real people. "Real" always has been more attractive than fiction. By focusing on the underbelly of the U.S., "America's Most Wanted," "Cops," and other reality shows offer the kind of programming young and old Americans always have liked best—stories involving violent and sometimes sexual events.

Isn't it time for responsible adults to quit beating a dead horse and get on with the important things in life? The human body always will be involved in some form of grappling, sexual or otherwise. Let it go at that. Turn off those programs you don't want your kids to watch. Don't let them go to the movies without your permission. Supervise what they read. And let the rest of us get on with our busy and sometimes desperate lives, where all that seems to make sense at the end of a hard day is to come home, kick off our shoes, grab a beer, and watch two gorgeous people making love or bashing each other into pulp. Freedom of choice—it's the American way.

READER RESPONSE

Saltzman makes the point several times that "nobody seems to want violence or sex on television except the viewers" (paragraph 2). Do you agree with him?

QUESTIONS FOR DISCUSSION

1. To what extent do you agree with Saltzman's complaints about critics of television programming?

2. Why does Saltzman think that complaining about sex and violence on television is "beating a dead horse" (paragraph 9)? Do you find his reasoning sound?

3. Saltzman calls the proposal to label violent television programs "absurd" (paragraph 3). Do you agree with the reasons he gives for doubting the effectiveness of such a labeling system? What is your position on labeling television programs?
4. What do you think of the alternatives to crusading against sex and violence on television that Saltzman suggests in his last paragraph?

Calvacade of Whimsey: Defending Springfield Against Itself

David L. G. Arnold

David L. G. Arnold is an Assistant Professor of English at the University of Wisconsin–Stevens Point. He has published previously on The Simpsons, *his article "And the Rest Writes Itself: Roland Barthes Watches* The Simpsons" *appearing in* The Simpsons and Philosophy *(2001). Other research interests include modern literature, the works of William Faulkner, as well as film and television criticism. He is also an aspiring novelist and screenwriter. This selection is excerpted from a longer essay, titled " 'Use a Pen, Sideshow Bob': The Simpsons and the Threat of High Culture," published originally in* Leaving Springfield: The Simpsons and the Possibilities of Oppositional Culture, *edited by John Alberti (Wayne State University Press, 2003).*

We can learn a lot about ourselves by watching the Simpsons watch TV. This television family spends a lot of time consuming television, and their habits reveal a great deal about how our society uses culture. The opening sequence in an episode entitled "Marge on the Lam," for instance, raises several interesting questions about their relationship with television and culture. In it find them seated as usual on the sofa and watching a public television fund-drive. The host resembles radio personality and writer Garrison Keillor and reads a monologue in the "Prairie Home Companion" vein. The TV audience laughs politely at the gentle, homespun humor, but the Simpsons are baffled. "What the hell's so funny about that," Homer asks. "Maybe it's the TV," Bart suggests. Homer gets up and whacks the TV, scolding it: "Stupid TV! Be more funny!"[1]

Later Homer is horrified when Marge contributes $30 to the public TV telethon, but he seems appeased when she says she'll receive two tickets to the ballet. "The ballet!" he says, "Woohoo!" "You like the ballet?" Marge asks,

---

[1] "Marge on the Lam" (episode 1F03), original airdate 11-04-93.

incredulous. "Marjorie please, I enjoy all the meats of our cultural stew. Ah, ballet," Homer retorts, and we see that he is imagining a bear in a fez driving a little Shriners car around in circles under a circus big top.[2]

This scene raises questions about perceived differences between high and low culture and about how we and the Simpson family respond to both. Homer's conception of ballet is a good index of the family's relationship to culture. He clearly has no idea what ballet is all about, but he knows that it represents high culture, and that high culture is somehow a value. Furthermore, his comparison of cultural diversity to a stew, while bathetic, nonetheless reveals an awareness that culture can function on different levels. The family's response to the Garrison Keillor sequence is also illuminating inasmuch as it suggests that they have no real idea where cultural artifacts come from or how they are produced. Subtle humor like this has little meaning for them, and it interrupts their access to television and to forms of entertainment they find more meaningful. Nonetheless, despite the profound mystery surrounding its sources, Homer at least imagines an interactive relationship with his culture, one in which he can alter currents of media taste and production by the simple, direct expedient of scolding his television set.

For Homer, though, and for the rest of the family (except perhaps the precocious Lisa), culture functions at a very low level. They have acquired this minimally functional culture, the show suggests, as a result of a slipshod educational system, an all-encompassing environment of consumerism and commodification, careless and misguided parenting, and, of course, television. If this evacuated, smilingly ignorant and militantly banal sense of culture seems familiar, it is because literary and cultural critics have been warning us about it for generations. In *The Simpsons* we find, digested and realized, the worst fears of mass culture theorists from Matthew Arnold to the Frankfurt School and beyond. In general these theorists decry the effects of democratization, urbanization, and industrialization on culture, arguing that if common people are allowed to define culture, it becomes common. People with more refined taste and sensibilities, they argue, must assume stewardship of culture before it is lost in the moil of popular music, trashy romance novels, and TV sitcoms.

My subject in this essay is the perceived struggle enacted in *The Simpsons* between self-appointed defenders of culture and the entropic forces of consumerism, degeneration of community, and intellectual sloth. At the center of this struggle stands Sideshow Bob, a second-string TV clown with an Ivy-League education and a passionate, indeed murderous desire to elevate culture in Springfield. In the rhetoric of the show he stands in opposition to Bart, proud underachiever and product of a mass-culture upbringing. For the most part Bob's portrayal on the show invites us to label him simply as a bad guy, as Bart's nemesis. But in an examination of cultural conflict, assessing Bob's character becomes more complicated. How does such a figure, a crusader for high-cultural values, function in an animated television sitcom? Is Bob a

---

[2] Ibid.

laughable snob or an emblem of the possibility that an institution like network television can give rise to truly oppositional culture?

Before assessing the threat Bob poses, we need to get a sense of how
cultural theorists of this century and the last have set up the differences between high, low, and mass culture, and what kinds of social and political
forces they see underlying the creation of a mass society.

* * *

In *Culture and Anarchy* Matthew Arnold defines culture as a process of
distillation and education. Being cultured, he stipulates, amounts to a "pursuit
of our total perfection by means of getting to know, on all the matters which
most concern us, the best which has been thought and said in the world."[3] He
argues that "the difficulty for democracy is, how to find and keep high ideals,"
and voices the need for a state-ordained cultural hierarchy to ensure that English culture will not suffer what he calls "Americanization," the situation that
comes from "the multitude being in power, with no adequate ideal to elevate
or guide the multitude."[4] Maintaining a focus on "the best which has been
thought and said," in other words, requires that the elite assume stewardship
of culture.

8   By the early 20th century what Arnold had expressed as a mild concern
was becoming (high-) cultural hysteria as literary critics and cultural theorists
responded against the perceived deadening of culture brought on by industrialism and urbanization. F. R. Leavis, for example, envisions an organic society
run by a natural oligarchy as a cure for the cultural desiccation brought on by
the shift to an industrial society. While he insists, like Arnold, on the centrality
of democracy in an enlightened society, he decries the attendant decline in
cultural standards. He argues that "In any period it is upon a very small minority that the discerning appreciation of art and literature depends: it is . . . only
a few who are capable of unprompted, first-hand judgment."[5] He asserts the
need for a cultural elite to guide society, and condemns the suggestion that his
argument promotes his own class interests.

Leavis is suggesting that appreciation of literature and art itself com-
prises culture, where for Arnold this was merely a step toward a harmonious,
"cultured" existence. An advocate, though guardedly, of democratized education, Arnold also suggested that everyone should have access to culture, where
Leavis seems to contend that it is the purview only of an elite, discerning
minority.

Similarly, Q. D. Leavis suggests that for an intellectual and cultural elite
determined to stem the tide of ignorance, "all that can be done . . . must take

---

[3] Matthew Arnold, *Culture and Anarchy* (Cambridge: Cambridge University Press, 1932), 6.

[4] Matthew Arnold, "Democracy." Introduction to "The Popular Education of France" in *The
Complete Prose Works of Matthew Arnold*. R. H. Super, ed. 12 volumes. Vol. 2 (Ann Arbor: University of Michigan Press, 1962), 17, 18.

[5] F. R. Leavis, *Education and the University* (London: Chatto and Windus, 1961), 143.

the form of resistance by an armed and conscious minority." Education, though not the kind Arnold envisioned, is central to Q. D. Leavis's plan of attack, specifically "the training of a picked few who would go into the world equipped for the work of forming and organising a conscious minority," a cadre of guerillas, it seems, who would then undertake an ambitious "training of taste."[6] The Leavises, like Arnold, see literature and art as an expression of ethical and cultural values, but as an expression in particular of the universal values for which they and their university-trained colleagues speak. They view academics and intellectuals as an embattled minority whose responsibility it is to take charge of the cultural well-being of the masses.

The Leavises and theorists like them worked on the premise that the rise of urban industrialism and of mass media was engendering a new, atomized, homogenized social class, one less burdened by the necessity of constant work but still bound by taste, education, and predilection to the lower classes. While the masses had, arguably, only limited access to the resources of "high" culture, neither had they any longer a connection with the organic or "folk" culture associated with older, more cohesive, agrarian societies. Where before a "natural" distinction had existed between high and low or folk culture, now only an amorphous "mass" culture obtained. Arguing that part of the effect of mass culture is the regrettable effacement of the distinction between high and low culture, Dwight MacDonald suggests that:

> Like nineteenth-century capitalism, Mass Culture is a dynamic, revolutionary force, breaking down the old barriers of class, tradition, taste, and dissolving all cultural distinctions. It mixes and scrambles everything together, producing what might be called homogenized culture. . . . It thus destroys all values, since value judgments imply discrimination. Mass culture is very, very democratic: it absolutely refuses to discriminate against, or between, anything or anybody. All is grist to its mill, and all comes out finely ground indeed.[7]

For MacDonald the democratization of culture is a threat, an indication that society is in danger of losing sight of its highest cultural traditions.

12   More serious than this is the dangerous influence of mass production and mass media on the collective consciousness. In a shrill condemnation of mass culture MacDonald suggests that capitalism and industrialism are not only to blame for the degeneration of culture, but that this degeneration is a conscious attempt on the part of the producers of culture to enforce class domination.

We hear these same fears echoing in the work of Frankfurt School social theorists like Theodor Adorno and Max Horkheimer, who suggest, in their conception of the "Culture Industry," that cultural commodities are imposed on

---

[6] Q. D. Leavis, *Fiction and the Reading Public* (London: Chatto and Windus, 1932), 270–271.

[7] Dwight MacDonald, "A Theory of Mass Culture." In *Mass Culture: The Popular Arts in America,* ed. Bernard Rosenberg and David Manning White (Glencoe: The Free Press, 1957), 62.

society by forces of production, and that consumers are passive recipients of these cultural suggestions. According to Adorno,

> The culture industry . . . forces together the spheres of high and low art, separated for thousands of years. The seriousness of high art is destroyed in the speculation about its efficacy; the seriousness of the lower perishes with the civilizational constraints imposed on the rebellious resistance inherent within it as long as social control was not yet total. Thus, although the culture industry undeniably speculates on the conscious and unconscious state of the millions towards which it is directed, the masses are not primary but secondary, they are an object of calculation, an appendage of the machinery.[8]

Note that here as well we see a "top-down" stratification of culture and consumption, in which class hierarchy has been functionally supplanted by commercial hierarchy. Through the mechanism of the culture industry the shape of culture is wholly determined by market forces, by the profit-motivated decisions of industry and media leaders.

As Adorno suggests above we can see mass media not only as a product of the culture industry, but as its chief tool, a pervasive, powerfully suggestive voice with which to *create and fulfill* consumer/cultural needs. In this way producers can use mass media to set up the *illusion* of freedom and choice while in reality limiting the development of individual cultural expression.

Arguing along similar lines, Bernard Rosenberg suggests that the goal of mass media is to take over society, arguing that "at its worst, mass culture threatens not only to cretinize our taste, but to brutalize our senses while paving the way to totalitarianism."[9]

16   This brief and incomplete survey of ideas about mass culture demonstrates that over the course of many years cultural theorists and critics have experienced a growing sense of panic. In these sound bites we hear a self-conscious elegy for high culture and also an unmistakable strain of intolerance. The members of mass-cultural society are either to be pitied because they are the passive dupes of political and commercial forces they can't understand, or reviled because their torpor contributes to the deracination of culture. In a society thus cheerfully committed to cultural decline, what place is left for the intellectual? Of what use can taste, refinement, and an expensive education be?

* * *

It is with these kinds of questions in mind that we can begin our examination of Sideshow Bob, the role he plays in Springfield society, and the kind

---

[8] Theodor Adorno, *The Culture Industry* (London: Routledge, 1991), 85.
[9] Ibid., 9.

of society Springfield represents. Bob is by profession a clown, a secondary figure on Krusty the Clown's TV show. Krusty himself is an esteemed figure in the world of Springfield culture, and his status as an "artist" says a fair amount about the state of culture in Springfield. Bob's frustration at playing second fiddle and his sense of himself as an embattled intellectual, is first highlighted in "Krusty Gets Busted." [10] Like many others in the *Simpsons* canon, this episode foregrounds the power of television in shaping a society's attitudes, but here we see an especially articulate distinction between high and low culture, a distinction that mounts into a lethal struggle. In this episode Sideshow Bob frames Krusty in a holdup of the Kwik-E-Mart so he can take over Krusty's TV show and broadcast what may be Springfield's first glimpse of high culture.

Springfield society accords Krusty's show a profound respect. Bart expresses his devotion plainly: in response to a scene in the show in which Krusty fires Sideshow Bob out of a cannon, Bart reverently intones "Comedy, thy name is Krusty." Later the role of the show and of television in general in the formation of Bart's intellect becomes clear when he says, "I've based my whole life on Krusty's teachings."

This is an obvious jab at the quality of television in general and at the level of culture to be found in Springfield: how much can we expect when a TV clown represents any kind of artistic pinnacle? In this context Sideshow Bob's efforts to elevate his society's culture appear plainly as the struggle of high against low, of refinement besieged by encroaching crudity. Frustrated at his role as a "sideshow," as a stooge in Krusty's cheap gags, Bob stages a kind of media/cultural coup and usurps Krusty's role as don of Springfield's cultural life.

20   Interestingly, despite his self-serving motives in deposing Krusty, Bob seems genuinely committed to a program of artistic and intellectual enlightenment. He changes the name of the show to "Sideshow Bob's Cavalcade of Whimsy" and replaces the traditional clown show shenanigans with readings from classic literature, Cole Porter tunes, and segments that examine issues of social and emotional importance to pre-teens.

By all accounts, except perhaps Bart's, Sideshow Bob's elevated approach to entertainment is a success. The kids in the audience cheer just as loudly for Bob, and even Lisa comments that he's "much less condescending" than Krusty. Chatting with producers about marketing rights, Bob comments, "I'm glad we finally dispelled the myth that I'm too 'uptown' for the tots." Bob sees Krusty's brand of culture as "lowbrow," and assumes that children, that people in general, will respond positively to more sophisticated fare. Exposure to high culture, he believes, will enhance the lives of his audience. In this stance he splits the difference between Arnold and the Leavises: he becomes the embattled intellectual fighting to preserve society's values.

---

[10] "Krusty Gets Busted" (episode 7G12), original airdate 4-29-90.

The paradox, of course, is that despite what Matthew Arnold might say about the salubrious effects of "the best that has been thought and said," Bob's own conscience and morality are clearly unaffected by the high culture he represents. In addition to being an armed robber and a snob, he is, as subsequent episodes reveal, a multiple-attempted-murderer, a terrorist, an election fixer, a Republican, and other heinous things. Furthermore, in his attempt to gain control of the media and impose his values on the masses, he sets himself up as an intolerant and ruthless opponent of their culture.

The difference here of course has to do with motives. Rather than a least-common-denominator sales pitch, Bob seems to offer something substantial: entertainment that actually stimulates reflective appreciation of the "finer things." In his aggressive play to get the word out, though, he exposes a darker side to the proselytizing of culture. He is not merely a snob, but a murderous snob, and he gives high culture a dangerous name.

24   The grudge against Bart that begins in "Krusty Gets Busted" develops through subsequent episodes. In "Black Widower,"[11] for instance, Bob plots to marry Aunt Selma and murder her as a way of exacting revenge on Bart. In "Cape Feare,"[12] which parodies the Martin Scorsese remake of "Cape Fear" released in 1991, Sideshow Bob plays the parolee who terrorizes the family and ultimately tries to kill Bart and thwart the gradual evacuation of culture Bart represents. Both of these episodes focus on Bob's role as an intellectual in society and highlight the explicit threat posed by his cultural campaign. Bob's conception of the social function of intellectuals recalls Q. D. Leavis's call for "resistance by an armed and conscious minority" against the incursions of mass culture. This becomes especially apparent in episodes like "Sideshow Bob Roberts" and "Sideshow Bob's Last Gleaming," in both of which Bob focuses directly on his own and his culture's use of television. It's not only his chief enemy, but his chief weapon.

These episodes and Bob's career in general suggest that the push to elevate culture and redefine society to reflect "natural" social hierarchies is inherently dangerous. If we see Bart as a representative of mass cultural interests, this threat is specific and lethal: Sideshow Bob wants to kill Bart. This may be because Bart can consistently thwart him, or simply because Bart represents all that he sees as wrong with society, the threat of creeping mass culture hegemony, a kind of cartoon Snopesism that threatens his more refined vision of the world.

* * *

What do Bob's efforts, and his failures, to enhance Springfielders' appreciation of the finer things, tell us about Springfield and about the show's comment on high and low culture? The most overt message is that this society mistrusts high culture, regarding it at best as a laughable eccentricity, at worst

---

[11] "Black Widower" (episode 8F20), original airdate 4-8-92.
[12] "Cape Feare" (episode 9F22), original airdate 10-7-93.

as a dangerous threat. Clearly, however, this amounts more to a critique of Springfield society than of Bob.

In the end we must balance the show's mistreatment of Bob against its straightforward condemnation of television and its effects on mass culture. The main message of *The Simpsons* has always been that intellectual, social, and family values suffer when television replaces quality parenting and when it supersedes reasoned public debate. Its influence on society is so pervasive, so fundamental, that it is often represented on the show as a kind of heavy industry: in one instance we see a factory, complete with belching smokestacks, as the site of television production; in another we see cartoons being produced by row upon row of hunched workers in a sweatshop. These and other images suggest the sinister and damaging collusion of industry and culture identified by members of the Frankfurt School.

28   But whatever our opinions about television, or for that matter about Cole Porter, Dumas, or Gilbert and Sullivan, it is clear that Sideshow Bob is a crank. By employing him as this kind of structure the writers of *The Simpsons* seem cheerfully to disdain the puffery and snobbishness of high culture without degenerating into a simple celebration of LCD working class society: the show's bottom line remains an excoriation of lowbrow thoughtlessness and the dominance of TV. But if we see in Homer and in Bart the depths to which democracy and the deterioration of high cultural values will allow us to degenerate if we let them, in Sideshow Bob we get a vision of high culture that makes degeneracy look pretty good.

WORKS CITED

Adorno, Theodor. *The Culture Industry*. London: Routledge, 1991.

Arnold, Matthew. "Democracy." Introduction to "The Popular Education of France" in *The Complete Prose Works of Matthew Arnold*. R. H. Super, ed. 12 volumes. Vol. 2. Ann Arbor: University of Michigan Press, 1962.

—. *Culture and Anarchy*. Cambridge: Cambridge University Press, 1932.

Leavis, F. R. *Education and the University*. London: Chatto and Windus, 1961.

Leavis, Q. D. *Fiction and the Reading Public*. London: Chatto and Windus, 1932.

MacDonald, Dwight. "A Theory of Mass Culture." In *Mass Culture: The Popular Arts in America,* ed. Bernard Rosenberg and David Manning White. Glencoe: The Free Press, 1957.

EPISODES CITED

Note: information about episodes of *The Simpsons*, including title, number, and original airdate, is drawn from The Simpsons: episode guide website, located at *http://www.snpp.com/guides/ep.guide.html*

"Black Widower," airdate 4-8-92 (episode 8F20). Writer: Jon Vitti. Director: David Silverman.

"Cape Feare," airdate 10-7-93 (episode 9F22). Writer: Jon Vitti. Director: Rich Moore.

"Krusty Gets Busted," airdate 4-29-90 (episode 7G12). Writers: Jay Kogen and Wallace Wolodarsky. Director: Brad Bird.

"Marge on the Lam," airdate 11-4-93 (episode 1F03). Writer: Bill Canterbury. Director: Mark Kirkland.

"Sideshow Bob's Last Gleaming," airdate 11-26-95 (episode 3F08). Writer: Spike Ferenstein. Director: Dominic Polcino.

"Sideshow Bob Roberts," airdate 10-9-94 (episode 2F02). Writers: Bill Oakley and Josh Weinstein. Director: Mark Kirkland.

READER RESPONSE

Are you a regular viewer of *The Simpsons*? Explain what appeals to you—or what doesn't—about the program.

QUESTIONS FOR DISCUSSION

1. Explain, in your own words, how Matthew Arnold's definition of the concept of "culture" differs from F. R. Leavis's. How do you define *culture?*
2. According to cultural theorists like Dwight MacDonald, how have industrialization and urbanization affected culture?
3. Most scholars and historians agree that William Shakespeare wrote for a popular audience and regarded his plays primarily as works of entertainment. How might this change the way we understand the relationship between culture and "entertainment" like television shows?
4. In what sense can we think of a television show as "culture"?
5. Do you see any problems or paradoxes inherent in a television show criticizing and satirizing the television industry and the effects of television on American society?

Do Ask, Do Tell

Joshua Gamson

Joshua Gamson is associate professor of sociology at Yale University and the author of Claims to Fame: Celebrity in Contemporary America *(1994) and* Freaks Talk Back: Tabloid Talk Shows and

Sexual Nonconformity *(1998). This essay appeared in the Fall
1995 issue of* The American Prospect.

At the end of his 22 years, when Pedro Zamora lost his capacity to speak, all
sorts of people stepped into the silence created by the AIDS-related brain disease that shut him up. MTV began running a marathon of *The Real World,* its
seven-kids-in-an-apartment-with-the-cameras-running show on which Pedro
Zamora starred as Pedro Zamora, a version of himself: openly gay, Miami
Cuban, HIV-positive, youth activist. MTV offered the marathon as a tribute to
Zamora, which it was, and as a way to raise funds, especially crucial since
Zamora, like so many people with HIV, did not have private insurance. Yet, of
course, MTV was also paying tribute to itself, capitalizing on Pedro's death
without quite seeming as monstrous as all that.

President Clinton and Florida governor Lawton Chiles made public statements and publicized phone calls to the hospital room, praising Zamora as a
heroic point of light rather than as a routinely outspoken critic of their own
HIV and AIDS policies. The Clinton administration, in the midst of its clamp-
down on Cuban immigration, even granted visas to Zamora's three brothers
and a sister in Cuba—a kindly if cynical act, given the realities of people with
AIDS awaiting visas and health care in Guantánamo Bay.

Thus, according to *People* magazine, did Zamora reach a bittersweet ending. He was unable to see, hear, or speak, yet with his family reunited, "his
dream had come true." Behind the scenes, one who was there for Zamora's
last weeks told me, the family actually separated Zamora from his boyfriend—
quite out of keeping with the "dreams" of Pedro's life. When Pedro had his
own voice, he had spoken powerfully of how anti-gay ideology and policy, typically framed as "pro-family," contributed to teen suicides and the spread of
HIV; when he died, those who spoke for him emphasized individual heroism
and the triumph of the heterosexual family.

4   That others appropriated Zamora on his deathbed hardly tarnishes his
accomplishment. As an MTV star, he had probably reduced suffering among
lesbian and gay teenagers more, and affected their thinking more deeply, than
a zillion social service programs. He spoke publicly to millions in his own
words and with the backing of a reputable media institution, and he did not
just tell them to wear condoms, or that AIDS is an equal-opportunity de-
stroyer. Nor did he simply fill in the sexual blanks left by prudish government
prevention campaigns. He also told them and showed them: Here is me loving
my boyfriend; here is what a self-possessed gay man looks like hanging out
with his roommates; here is what my Cuban family might have to say about
my bringing home a black man; here is me at an AIDS demonstration, getting
medical news, exchanging love vows.

To speak for and about yourself as a gay man or a lesbian on television,
to break silences that are systematically and ubiquitously enforced in public
life, is profoundly political. "Don't tell" is more than a U.S. military policy; it

remains U.S. public policy, formally and informally, on sex and gender nonconformity. Sex and gender outsiders—gay men, transsexuals, lesbians, bisexuals—
are constantly invited to lose their voices, or suffer the consequences (job
loss, baseball bats) of using them. Outside of the occasional opening on MTV
or sporadic coverage of a demonstration or a parade, if one is not Melissa
Etheridge or David Geffen, opportunities to speak as a nonheterosexual, or to
listen to one, are few and far between. Even if the cameras soon turn elsewhere, these moments are big breakthroughs, and they are irresistible, giddy
moments for the shut up.

Yet, in a media culture, holding the microphone and the spotlight is a
complicated sort of power, not just because people grab them back from you
but because they are never really yours. If you speak, you must be prepared to
be used. The voice that comes out is not quite yours: It is like listening to
yourself on tape (a bit deeper, or more clipped) or to a version dubbed by
your twin. It is you and it is not you. Zamora's trick, until his voice was taken,
was to walk the line between talking and being dubbed. The troubling question, for the silenced and the heard alike, is whether the line is indeed walka-
ble. Perhaps the best place to turn for answers is the main public space in
which the edict to shut up is reversed: daytime television talk shows.

For lesbians, gay men, bisexuals, drag queens, transsexuals—and combinations thereof—watching daytime television has got to be spooky. Suddenly,
there are renditions of you, chattering away in a system that otherwise ignores
or steals your voice at every turn. Sally Jessy Raphael wants to know what it's
like to pass as a different sex, Phil Donahue wants to support you in your battle against gay bashing, Ricki Lake wants to get you a date, Oprah Winfrey
wants you to love without lying. Most of all, they all want you to talk about it
publicly, just at a time when everyone else wants you not to. They are interested, if not precisely in "reality," at least not in fictional accounts. For people
whose desires and identities go against the norm, this is the only spot in mainstream media culture to speak on their own terms or to hear others speaking
for themselves. The fact that talk shows are so much maligned, and for so
many good reasons, does not close the case.

8   The other day, I happened to tune into the *Ricki Lake Show*, the fastest-
rising talk show ever. The topic: "I don't want gays around my kids." I caught
the last 20 minutes of what amounted to a pro-gay screamfest. Ricki and her
audience explicitly attacked a large woman who was denying visitation rights
to her gay ex-husband ("I had to explain to a 9-year-old what 'gay' means"; "My
child started having nightmares after he visited his father"). And they went at
a young couple who believed in keeping children away from gay people on
the grounds that the Bible says "homosexuals should die." The gay guests and
their supporters had the last word, brought on to argue, to much audience
whooping, that loving gays are a positive influence and hateful heterosexuals
should stay away from children. The anti-gay guests were denounced on any
number of grounds, by host, other guests, and numerous audience members:
They are denying children loving influences, they are bigots, they are

misinformed, they read the Bible incorrectly, they sound like Mormons, they are resentful that they have put on more weight than their exes. One suburban-looking audience member angrily addressed each "child protector" in turn, along the way coming up with a possible new pageant theme: "And as for you, Miss Homophobia . . ."

The show was a typical mess, with guests yelling and audiences hooting at the best one-liners about bigotry or body weight, but the virulence with which homophobia was attacked is both typical of these shows and stunning. When Lake cut off a long-sideburned man's argument that "it's a fact that the easiest way to get AIDS is by homosexual sex" ("That is not a fact, sir, that is not correct"), I found myself ready to start the chant of "Go, Ricki! Go, Ricki!" that apparently wraps each taping. Even such elementary corrections, and even such a weird form of visibility and support, stands out sharply. Here, the homophobe is the deviant, the freak.

Lake's show is among the new breed of rowdy youth-oriented programs, celebrated as "rock and roll television" by veteran Geraldo Rivera and denigrated as "exploitalk" by cultural critic Neal Gabler. Their sibling show, the older, tamer "service" programs such as *Oprah* and *Donahue,* support "alternative" sexualities and genders in quieter, but not weaker, ways. Peruse last year's *Donahue:* two teenage lesbian lovers ("Young, courageous people like yourself are blazing the way for other people," says Donahue), a gay construction worker suing his gay boss for harassment ("There's only eight states that protect sexual persuasion," his attorney reports), a bisexual minister, a black lesbian activist, and two members of the African-American theater group Pomo Afro Homos ("We're about trying to build a black gay community," says one), the stars of the gender-crossing *Priscilla, Queen of the Desert* ("I have a lot of friends that are transsexuals," declares an audience member, "and they're the neatest people"), heterosexuals whose best friends are gay, lesbians starting families, gay teens, gay cops, gay men reuniting with their high school sweethearts, a gay talk show. This is a more diverse, self-possessed, and politically outspoken group of nonheterosexuals than I might find, say, at the gay bar around the corner. I can only imagine what this means for people experiencing sexual difference where none is locally visible.

Certainly *Donahue* makes moves to counter its "liberal" reputation, inviting right-wing black preachers and the widely discredited "psychologist" Paul Cameron, who argues that cross-dressing preceded the fall of Rome, that people with AIDS should be quarantined, and that sexuality "is going to get us." But more often than not, Donahue himself is making statements about how "homophobia is global" and "respects no nation," how "we're beating up homosexual people, calling them names, throwing them out of apartments, jobs." The "we" being asserted is an "intolerant" population that needs to get over itself. We are, he says at times, "medieval." In fact, Donahue regularly asserts that "for an advanced, so-called industrialized nation, I think we're the worst."

12   Oprah Winfrey, the industry leader, is less concerned with the political treatment of difference; she is overwhelmingly oriented toward "honesty" and "openness," especially in interpersonal relationships. As on Lake's show,

lesbians and gays are routinely included without incident in more general themes (meeting people through personal ads, fools for love, sons and daughters you never knew), and bigotry is routinely attacked. But Winfrey's distinctive mark is an attack on lies, and thus the closet comes under attack—especially the gay male closet—not just for the damage it does to those in it, but for the betrayals of women it engenders.

On a recent program in which a man revealed his "orientation" after 19 years of marriage, for example, both Winfrey and her audience were concerned not that Steve is gay, but that he was not honest with his wife. As Winfrey put it, "For me, always the issue is how you can be more truthful in your life." One of Steve's two supportive sons echoes Winfrey ("I want people to be able to be who they are"), as does his ex-wife, whose anger is widely supported by the audience ("It makes me feel like my life has been a sham"), and the requisite psychologist ("The main thing underneath all of this is the importance of loving ourselves and being honest and authentic and real in our lives"). Being truthful, revealing secrets, learning to love oneself: These are the staples of Winfrey-style talk shows. Gay and bisexual guests find a place to speak as gays and bisexuals, and the pathology becomes not sexual "deviance" but the socially imposed closet.

All of this, however, should not be mistaken for dedicated friendship. Even when ideological commitments to truth and freedom are at work, the primary commitment of talk shows is, of course, to money. What makes these such inviting spots for nonconforming sex and gender identities has mostly to do with the niche talk shows have carved out for ratings. The shows are about talk; the more silence there has been on a subject, the more not-telling, the better a talk topic it is. On talk shows, as media scholar Wayne Munson points out in his book *All Talk* (Temple University Press, 1993), "differences are no longer repressed" but "become the talk show's emphasis," as the shows confront "boredom and channel clutter with constant, intensified novelty and 'reality.'" Indeed, according to Munson, Richard Mincer, *Donahue*'s executive producer, encourages prospective guests "to be especially unique or different, to take advantage of rather than repress difference."

While they highlight different sex and gender identities, expressions, and practices, the talk shows can be a dangerous place to speak and a difficult place to get heard. With around 20 syndicated talk shows competing for audiences, shows that trade in confrontation and surprise (*Ricki Lake, Jenny Jones, Jerry Springer*) are edging out the milder, topical programs (*Oprah, Donahue*).

16 As a former *Jane Whitney Show* producer told *TV Guide*, "When you're booking guests, you're thinking, 'How much confrontation can this person provide me?' The more confrontation, the better. You want people just this side of a fistfight."

For members of groups already subject to violence, the visibility of television can prompt more than just a fistfight, as last year's *Jenny Jones* murder underlined. In March, when Scott Amedure appeared on a "secret admirer" episode of the *Jenny Jones Show,* the admired Jon Schmitz was apparently expecting a female admirer. Schmitz, not warming to Amedure's fantasy of tying him up in a hammock and spraying whipped cream and champagne on his body, declared himself "100 percent heterosexual." Later, back in Michigan, he punctuated this claim by shooting Amedure with a 12-gauge shotgun, telling police that the embarrassment from the program had "eaten away" at him. Or, as he reportedly put it in his 911 call, Amedure "fucked me on national TV."

Critics were quick to point out that programming that creates conflict tends to exacerbate it. "The producers made professions of regret," Neal Gabler wrote in the *Los Angeles Times* after the Amedure murder, "but one suspects what they really regretted was the killer's indecency of not having pulled out his rifle and committed the crime before their cameras." In the wake of the murder, talk show producers were likened over and over to drug dealers: Publicist Ken Maley told the *San Francisco Chronicle* that "they've got people strung out on an adrenaline rush," and "they keep raising the dosage;" sociologist Vicki Abt told *People* that "TV allows us to mainline deviance;" Michelangelo Signorile argued in *Out* that some talk show producers "are like crack dealers scouring trailer park America." True enough. Entering the unruly talk show world, one is apt to become, at best, a source of adrenaline rush, and at worst a target of violence.

What most reporting tended to ignore, however, was that most anti-gay violence does not require a talk show "ambush" to trigger it. Like the Oakland County, Michigan, prosecutor who argued that "*Jenny Jones*'s producers' cynical pursuit of ratings and total insensitivity to what could occur here left one person dead and Mr. Schmitz now facing life in prison," many critics focused on the "humiliating" surprise attack on Schmitz with the news that he was desired by another man. As in the image of the "straight" soldier being ogled in the shower, in this logic the revelation of same-sex desire is treated as the danger, and the desired as a victim. The talk show critics thus played to the same "don't tell" logic that makes talk shows such a necessary, if uncomfortable, refuge for some of us.

20 Although producers' pursuit of ratings is indeed, unsurprisingly, cynical and insensitive, the talk show environment is one of the very few in which the declaration of same-sex desire (and, to a lesser degree, atypical gender identity) is common, heartily defended, and often even incidental. Although they overlook this in their haste to hate trash, the critics of exploitative talk shows help illuminate the odd sort of opportunity these cacophonous settings provide. Same-sex desires become "normal" on these programs not so much because different sorts of lives become clearly visible, but because they get sucked into the spectacular whirlpool of relationship conflicts. They offer a particular kind of visibility and voice. On a recent *Ricki Lake,* it was the voice of an aggressive, screechy gay man who continually reminded viewers, between laughs at his own nasty comments, that he was a regular guy. On other days, it's the take-your-hands-off-my-woman lesbian, or the I'm-more-of-a-woman-than-you'll-ever-be transsexual. The vicious voice—shouting that we

gay people can be as mean, or petty, or just plain loud, as anybody else—is the first voice talk shows promote. It's one price of entry into mainstream public visibility.

The guests on the talk shows seem to march in what psychologist Jeanne Heaton, co-author of *Tuning in Trouble* (Jossey-Bass, 1995), calls a "parade of pathology." Many talk shows have more than a passing resemblance to freak shows. Neal Gabler, for example, argues that guests are invited to exhibit "their deformities for attention" in a "ritual of debasement" aimed primarily at reassuring the audience of its superiority. Indeed, the evidence of dehumanization is all over the place, especially when it comes to gender crossing, as in the titles of various recent *Geraldo* programs; the calls of sideshow barkers echo in "Star-Crossed Cross-Dressers: Bizarre Stories of Transvestites and Their Lovers" and "Outrageous Impersonators and Flamboyant Drag Queens" and "When Your Husband Wears the Dress in the Family." As long as talk shows make their bids by being, in Gabler's words, "a psychological freak show," sex and gender outsiders arguably reinforce perceptions of themselves as freaks by entering a discourse in which they may be portrayed as bizarre, outrageous, flamboyant curiosities. (Often, for example, they must relinquish their right to defend themselves to the ubiquitous talk show "experts.")

Talk shows do indeed trade on voyeurism, and it is no secret that those who break with sex and gender norms and fight with each other on camera help the shows win higher ratings. But there is more to the picture: the place where "freaks" talk back. It is a place where Conrad, born and living in a female body, can assert against Sally Jessy Raphael's claims that he "used and betrayed" women in order to have sex with them that women fall in love with him as a man because he considers himself a man; where months later, in a program on "our most outrageous former guests" (all gender crossers), Conrad can reappear, declare himself to have started hormone treatment, and report that the woman he allegedly "used and betrayed" has stood by him. This is a narrow opening, but an opening nonetheless, for the second voice promoted by the talk show: the proud voice of the "freak," even if the freak refuses that term. The fact that talk shows are exploitative spectacles does not negate the fact that they are also opportunities; as Munson points out, they are both spectacle and conversation. They give voice to the systematically silenced, albeit under conditions out of the speaker's control, and in tones that come out tinny, scratched, distant.

These voices, even when they are discounted, sometimes do more than just assert themselves. Whatever their motivations, people sometimes wind up doing more than just pulling up a chair at a noisy, crowded table. Every so often they wind up messing with sexual categories in a way that goes beyond a simple expansion of them. In addition to affirming both homosexuality and heterosexuality as normal and natural, talk show producers often make entertainment by mining the in-between: finding guests who are interesting exactly because they don't fit existing notions of "gay" and "straight" and "man" and

"woman," raising the provocative suggestion that the categories are not quite
working.

24   The last time I visited the *Maury Povich Show,* for instance, I found myself distracted by Jason and Tiffanie. Jason, a large 18-year-old from a small
town in Ohio, was in love with Calvin. Calvin was having an affair with Jamie
(Jason's twin sister, also the mother of a three-month-old), who was interested
in Scott, who had sex with, as I recall, both Calvin and Tiffanie. Tiffanie, who
walked on stage holding Jamie's hand, had pretty much had sex with everyone except Jamie. During group sex, Tiffanie explained, she and Jamie did not
touch each other. "We're not lesbians," she loudly asserted, against the noisy
protestations of some audience members.

The studio audience, in fact, was quick to condemn the kids, who were
living together in a one-bedroom apartment with Jamie's baby. Their response
was predictably accusatory: You are freaks, some people said; immoral, said
others; pathetically bored and in need of a hobby, others asserted. Still other
aspects of the "discussion" assumed the validity and normality of homosexuality. Jason, who had recently attempted suicide, was told he needed therapy to
help him come to terms with his sexuality, and the other boys were told they
too needed to "figure themselves out." Yet much talk also struggled to attach
sexual labels to an array of partnerships anarchic enough to throw all labels
into disarray. "If you are not lesbians, why were you holding hands?" one
women asked Tiffanie. "If you are not gay," another audience member asked
Calvin, "how is it you came to have oral sex with two young men?"

This mix was typically contradictory: condemnation of "immoral sex" but
not so much of homosexuality per se, openly gay and bisexual teenagers
speaking for themselves while their partners in homosexual activities declare
heterosexual identities, a situation in which sexual categories are both assumed and up for grabs. I expect the young guests were mainly in it for the
free trip to New York, and the studio audience was mainly in it for the brush
with television. Yet the discussion they created, the unsettling of categorical
assumptions about genders and desires, if only for a few moments in the midst
of judgment and laughter, is found almost nowhere else this side of fiction.

The importance of these conversations, both for those who for safety
must shut up about their sexual and gender identities and for those who
never think about them, is certainly underestimated. The level of exploitation
is certainly not. Like Pedro Zamora, one can keep one's voice for a little while,
one finger on the commercial megaphone, until others inevitably step in to
claim it for their own purposes. Or one can talk for show, as freak, or expert,
or rowdy—limits set by production strategies within the talk show genre.

28   Those limits, not the talk shows themselves, are really the point. The
story here is not about commercial exploitation, but about just how effective
the prohibition on asking and telling is in the United States, how stiff the
penalties are, how unsafe this place is for people of atypical sexual and gender
identities. You know you're in trouble when Sally Jessy Raphael (strained smile
and forced tear behind red glasses) seems like your best bet for being heard,

understood, respected, and protected. That for some of us the loopy, hollow light of talk shows seems a safe haven should give us all pause.

READER RESPONSE

What is your opinion of talk shows in general? Do you watch them? Why, or why not?

QUESTIONS FOR DISCUSSION

1. Explain how Gamson's title reflects his central purpose. What function does the opening example of Pedro Zamora serve? How does it relate to Gamson's discussion of "voice"?
2. Gamson notes that "the primary commitment of talk shows is, of course, to money. . . . the more silence there has been on a subject, the more not-telling, the better a talk topic it is" (paragraph 14). Do you think limits should be placed on the topics television talk shows should be allowed to air, or should any subject be fair game as long as guests are willing to appear on the programs?
3. Explain what you understand Gamson to mean when he writes that "talk shows can be a dangerous place to speak and a difficult place to get heard" (paragraph 15).
4. Gamson suggests that "[t]he fact that talk shows are exploitative spectacles does not negate the fact that they are also opportunities . . . they are both spectacle and conversation" (paragraph 22). Discuss the merits and drawbacks of television talk shows, including those that intentionally court controversy and encourage heated confrontation and the tamer, more conservative talk shows. What value, besides entertainment, do such programs have?

Violent Media Is Good for Kids
Gerard Jones

Gerard Jones is a veteran writer of comics, cartoons, and screen-plays, including "Batman," "Spider-Man," "Ultraforce," and the forthcoming "Pokémon" newspaper comic strip and the Web strip The Haunted Man. *He is the author of several books, including* Honey I'm Home: Sitcoms Selling the American Dream *(1992). This essay appeared in the June 28, 2000, issue of* MotherJones.com.

Mother Jones *was the first general-interest magazine in the country to offer its content online (November 1993).* Mother Jones Interactive *morphed into the* MoJo Wire *in 1995 and into* MotherJones.com *in March 2001.*

At 13 I was alone and afraid. Taught by my well-meaning, progressive, English-teacher parents that violence was wrong, that rage was something to be overcome and cooperation was always better than conflict, I suffocated my deepest fears and desires under a nice-boy persona. Placed in a small, experimental school that was wrong for me, afraid to join my peers in their bumptious rush into adolescent boyhood, I withdrew into passivity and loneliness. My parents, not trusting the violent world of the late 1960s, built a wall between me and the crudest elements of American pop culture.

Then the Incredible Hulk smashed through it.

One of my mother's students convinced her that Marvel Comics, despite their apparent juvenility and violence, were in fact devoted to lofty messages of pacifism and tolerance. My mother borrowed some, thinking they'd be good for me. And so they were. But not because they preached lofty messages of benevolence. They were good for me because they were juvenile. And violent.

4 The character who caught me, and freed me, was the Hulk: overgendered and undersocialized, half-naked and half-witted, raging against a frightened world that misunderstood and persecuted him. Suddenly I had a fantasy self to carry my stifled rage and buried desire for power. I had a fantasy self who was a self: unafraid of his desires and the world's disapproval, unhesitating and effective in action. "Puny boy follow Hulk!" roared my fantasy self, and I followed.

I followed him to new friends—other sensitive geeks chasing their own inner brutes—and I followed him to the arrogant, self-exposing, self-assertive, superheroic decision to become a writer. Eventually, I left him behind, followed more sophisticated heroes, and finally my own lead along a twisting path to a career and an identity. In my 30s, I found myself writing action movies and comic books. I wrote some Hulk stories, and met the geek-geniuses who created him. I saw my own creations turned into action figures, cartoons, and computer games. I talked to the kids who read my stories. Across generations, genders, and ethnicities I kept seeing the same story: people pulling themselves out of emotional traps by immersing themselves in violent stories. People integrating the scariest, most fervently denied fragments of their psyches into fuller senses of selfhood through fantasies of superhuman combat and destruction.

I have watched my son living the same story—transforming himself into a bloodthirsty dinosaur to embolden himself for the plunge into preschool, a Power Ranger to muscle through a social competition in kindergarten. In the first grade, his friends started climbing a tree at school. But he was afraid: of falling, of the centipedes crawling on the trunk, of sharp branches, of his friends' derision. I took my cue from his own fantasies and read him old Tarzan comics, rich in combat and bright with flashing knives. For two weeks he lived in them. Then he put them aside. And he climbed the tree.

But all the while, especially in the wake of the recent burst of school shootings, I heard pop psychologists insisting that violent stories are harmful to kids, heard teachers begging parents to keep their kids away from "junk culture," heard a guilt-stricken friend with a son who loved Pokémon lament, "I've turned into the bad mom who lets her kid eat sugary cereal and watch cartoons!"

8   That's when I started the research.

"Fear, greed, power-hunger, rage: these are aspects of our selves that we try not to experience in our lives but often want, even need, to experience vicariously through stories of others," writes Melanie Moore, Ph.D., a psychologist who works with urban teens. "Children need violent entertainment in order to explore the inescapable feelings that they've been taught to deny, and to reintegrate those feelings into a more whole, more complex, more resilient selfhood."

Moore consults to public schools and local governments, and is also raising a daughter. For the past three years she and I have been studying the ways in which children use violent stories to meet their emotional and developmental needs—and the ways in which adults can help them use those stories healthily. With her help I developed Power Play, a program for helping young people improve their self-knowledge and sense of potency through heroic, combative storytelling.

We've found that every aspect of even the trashiest pop-culture story can have its own developmental function. Pretending to have superhuman powers helps children conquer the feelings of powerlessness that inevitably come with being so young and small. The dual-identity concept at the heart of many superhero stories helps kids negotiate the conflicts between the inner self and the public self as they work through the early stages of socialization. Identification with a rebellious, even destructive, hero helps children learn to push back against a modern culture that cultivates fear and teaches dependency.

12   At its most fundamental level, what we call "creative violence"—head-bonking cartoons, bloody videogames, playground karate, toy guns—gives children a tool to master their rage. Children will feel rage. Even the sweetest and most civilized of them, even those whose parents read the better class of literary magazines, will feel rage. The world is uncontrollable and incomprehensible; mastering it is a terrifying, enraging task. Rage can be an energizing emotion, a shot of courage to push us to resist greater threats, take more control, than we ever thought we could. But rage is also the emotion our culture distrusts the most. Most of us are taught early on to fear our own. Through immersion in imaginary combat and identification with a violent protagonist, children engage the rage they've stifled, come to fear it less, and become more capable of utilizing it against life's challenges.

I knew one little girl who went around exploding with fantasies so violent that other moms would draw her mother aside to whisper, "I think you should know something about Emily. . . ." Her parents were separating, and she was small, an only child, a tomboy at an age when her classmates were dividing sharply along gender lines. On the playground she acted out "Sailor Moon" fights, and in the classroom she wrote stories about people being stabbed with knives. The more adults tried to control her stories, the more she acted out the roles of her angry heroes: breaking rules, testing limits, roaring threats.

Then her mother and I started helping her tell her stories. She wrote them, performed them, drew them like comics: sometimes bloody, sometimes tender, always blending the images of pop culture with her own most private fantasies. She came out of it just as fiery and strong, but more self-controlled and socially competent: a leader among her peers, the one student in her class who could truly pull boys and girls together.

I worked with an older girl, a middle-class "nice girl," who held herself together through a chaotic family situation and a tumultuous adolescence with gangsta rap. In the mythologized street violence of Ice T, the rage and strutting of his music and lyrics, she found a theater of the mind in which she could be powerful, ruthless, invulnerable. She avoided the heavy drug use that sank many of her peers, and flowered in college as a writer and political activist.

16   I'm not going to argue that violent entertainment is harmless. I think it has helped inspire some people to real-life violence. I am going to argue that it's helped hundreds of people for every one it's hurt, and that it can help far more if we learn to use it well. I am going to argue that our fear of "youth violence" isn't well-founded on reality, and that the fear can do more harm than the reality. We act as though our highest priority is to prevent our children from growing up into murderous thugs—but modern kids are far more likely to grow up too passive, too distrustful of themselves, too easily manipulated.

We send the message to our children in a hundred ways that their craving for imaginary gun battles and symbolic killings is wrong, or at least dangerous. Even when we don't call for censorship or forbid "Mortal Kombat," we moan to other parents within our kids' earshot about the "awful violence" in the entertainment they love. We tell our kids that it isn't nice to play-fight, or we steer them from some monstrous action figure to a pro-social doll. Even in the most progressive households, where we make such a point of letting children feel what they feel, we rush to substitute an enlightened discussion for the raw material of rageful fantasy. In the process, we risk confusing them about their natural aggression in the same way the Victorians confused their children about their sexuality. When we try to protect our children from their own feelings and fantasies, we shelter them not against violence but against power and selfhood.

READER RESPONSE

Describe a figure, character, recurring daydream, or escapist fantasy that gave you comfort or strength when you were growing up.

QUESTIONS FOR DISCUSSION

1. What do you think of Jones's basic premise? Have you observed "people pulling themselves out of emotional traps by immersing themselves in violent stories" (paragraph 5).
2. Have your own observations or experiences confirmed or contradicted the belief of many people that "violent stories are harmful to kids" (paragraph 7)?
3. Jones says that he and his colleague have found that "every aspect of even the trashiest pop-culture story can have its own developmental function" (paragraph 11). Besides the examples he gives, can you think of other ways in which that statement is valid?
4. To what extent do you find Jones's conclusions about the role of violent images in children's lives convincing? Are you swayed by his argument? Explain your answer.
5. To what extent do you agree with Jones when he says that "modern kids are . . . too passive, too distrustful of themselves, too easily manipulated" (paragraph 16)?

Can't Live Without It

Alan Thein Durning

Alan Thein Durning is a senior researcher at Worldwatch Institute and author of How Much Is Enough?: The Consumer Society and the Future of the World *(1992),* The Car and the City: 24 Steps to Safe Streets and Healthy Communities *(1993),* This Place on Earth: Home and the Practice of Permanence *(1996),* Building on Success: The Age of Energy Efficiency *(1998), and* Green Collar Jobs: Working in the New Northwest *(1999). This essay was written for the May/June 1993 issue of* World Watch. *You can contact the Worldwatch Institute at their website, www.worldwatch.org*

Last January a single message was broadcast simultaneously in every inhabited part of the globe. The message was not "love thy neighbor" or "thou shalt not kill." It was "Drink Coke."

This first global advertisement was, on the face of it, simply a piece of technical showmanship—an inevitable one, considering the pace of change in telecommunications. On a symbolic level, however, it was something more. It was a neat encapsulation of the main trend in human communications world-wide: commercialization.

For better or for worse, almost all of humanity's 5.5 billion individuals, divided among 6,000 distinct cultures, are now soaking in the same gentle bath of advertising. The unctuous voices of the marketplace are insinuating themselves into ever more remote quarters of the globe and ever more private realms of human life.

4   Advertising has become one of the world's most premier cultural forces. Almost every living person knew the word "Coke," for example, long before the global ad. Two years ago, the trade journal *Adweek* published a two-page spread depicting Hitler, Lenin, Napoleon, and a Coke bottle. "Only one," read the caption, "launched a campaign that conquered the world. How did Coke succeed where history's most ambitious leaders failed? By choosing the right weapon. Advertising."

Aside from the arrogance of that statement, what is disturbing about it is its truth. Owing to a skillful and persistent marketing, Coke is sold in virtually every place people live. Go to the end of a rural road on any Third World continent, walk a day up a donkey trail to a hardscrabble village, and ask for a Coke. Odds are, you'll get one. This state of affairs—development workers call it "Coca Colonization"—means that Coke's secret formula has probably reached more villages and slums than has clean drinking water or oral rehydration formula.

The point here is not to single out Coca-Cola—others would have circumadvertised the globe soon if the soft drink empire hadn't—but rather to question whether advertising has outgrown its legitimate role in human affairs. Advertisers maintain that their craft, far from being too widely practiced, is just beginning to achieve its destiny: to stimulate business growth, create jobs, and to unify humanity by eroding the ancient hatreds that divide us and joining us together in the universal fellowship of a Coke.

But from the perspective of the Earth's long-term health, the advertising industry looks somewhat different. Stripped to its essentials, contemporary advertising has three salient characteristics. It preys on the weaknesses of its host. It creates an insatiable hunger. And it leads to debilitating over-consumption. In the biological realm, things of that nature are called parasites.

8   If that rather pointed metaphor is apt, we are left with the sticky problem doctors face in treating any parasite: finding a medicine and a dosage that will kill the worm without poisoning the patient. How can we restrain the excesses of advertising without resorting to poisonous state censorship or curtailing the flow of information in society? Actions that are too heavy-handed, for example, could bankrupt the free—but advertising-dependent—press.

THE MANUFACTURE OF NEEDS

The purpose of advertising, according to orthodox economic theory, is to provide us with information about the goods and services offered in the marketplace. Without that stream of information we consumers won't make informed choices, and Adam Smith's invisible hand will be not only invisible but also blind. We won't know when a better frozen dinner comes along, nor will we know where to get the best deal on a new car.

The contents of marketing messages themselves, however, show the simple-mindedness of that explanation. Classified ads and yellow page telephone directories would suffer if advertising were only about telling people who already want something where to get it and what it costs. Rather, advertising is intended to expand the pool of desires, awakening wants that would lie dormant otherwise—or, as critics say, manufacturing wants that would not otherwise exist.

Entire industries have manufactured a need for themselves. Writes one advertising executive, ads can serve "to make [people] self-conscious about matter of course things such as enlarged nose pores [and] bad breath." Historically, advertisers have especially targeted women, playing on personal insecurities and self-doubt by projecting impossible ideals of feminine beauty.

12   As B. Earl Puckett, then head of the department store chain Allied Stores Corporation, put it 40 years ago, "It is our job to make women unhappy with what they have." Thus for those born with short, skinny eyelashes, the message mongers offer hope. For those whose hair is too straight, or too curly, or grows in the wrong places, for those whose skin is too dark or too light, for those whose body weight is distributed in anything but this year's fashion, advertising assures that synthetic salvation is close at hand.

Ads are stitched together from the eternal cravings of the human psyche. Their ingredients are images of sexual virility [*sic*], eternal youth, social belonging, individual freedom, and existential fulfillment. Advertisers sell not artifacts but lifestyles, attitudes, and fantasies, hitching their wares to the infinite yearnings of the soul.

They also exploit the desire individuals in mass societies feel to define a distinctive identity. Peter Kim, director of research and consumer behavior for the advertising agency J. Walter Thompson, says the role of brands in consumer society is "much akin to the role of myth in traditional societies. Choosing a brand becomes a way for one group of consumers to differentiate themselves from another."

Advertisers are extraordinarily sophisticated in the pursuit of these ends. The most finely wrought ads are masterpieces—combining stunning imagery, bracing speed, and compelling language to touch our innermost fears and fancies. Prime-time television commercials in the industrial countries pack more suggestion into a minute than anything previously devised.

16   From an anthropological perspective, ads are among the supreme creations of this era, standing in relation to our technological, consumer culture as the pyramids did to the ancients and the Gothic cathedrals to the

medievals. Those structures embodied faith in the transcendent, acted out a quest for immortality, and manifested hierarchical social rankings. Advertisements, like our age, are mercurial, hedonistic, image-laden, and fashion-driven; they glorify the individual, idealize consumption as the route to personal fulfillment, and affirm technological progress as the motive force of density.

ADVERTISING AND THE EARTH

Of course, advertising is not the only force to promote consumption in today's world. That point is amply evident in the recent history of Eastern Europe. There where most advertising was illegal under the communist regimes of the past, popular desires for the Western consumer lifestyle were pervasive—indeed, they were among the forces that overthrew socialism. Communism had failed to deliver the goods.

Other forces driving the earth-threatening consumption levels of the world's affluent societies include everything from human nature's acquisitive streak to the erosion of informal, neighborhood sharing networks that has accompanied the rising mobility of our time. They include social pressures to keep up with the Joneses, the proliferation of "convenience" goods to meet the time-crunch created by rising working hours, national economic policies that favor consumption over savings and raw materials production over efficiency and recycling, and the prevailing trend in urban design—away from compact, human-scale cities toward anonymous, auto-scale malls and sprawl.

All these things—plus the weight of sheer purchasing power—define one of the world's most pressing environmental challenges: to trim resource consumption in industrial countries. Citizens of these nations typically consume 10 times as much energy as their developing country counterparts, along with 10 times the timber, 13 times the iron and steel, 14 times the paper, 18 times the synthetic chemicals, and 19 times the aluminum.

20   The consumer societies take the lion's share of the output of the world's mines, logging operations, petroleum refineries, metal smelters, paper mills, and other high-impact industrial plants. These enterprises, in turn, account for a disproportionate share of the resource depletion, environmental pollution, and habitat degradation that humans have caused worldwide. A world full of consumer societies is an ecological impossibility.

And even if advertising is not the sole force driving up consumption, it is an important one. It is a powerful champion of the consumer lifestyle, and is spreading its influence widely.

COMMERCIALIZING THE GLOBE

"Fifty years ago," wrote philosopher Ivan Illich in 1977, "most of the words an American heard were personally spoken to him as an individual, or to someone standing nearby." That certainly isn't true today. Most of the words an American—or a citizen of any industrial country—hears are sales pitches broadcast over the airwaves to us as members of a mass market. The text we read, the images we see, and the public places we visit are all dominated by commercial messages.

Take the example of commercial television, long the premier medium. Aside from sleeping and working, watching television is the leading activity in most consumer societies, from the United States and the United Kingdom to Japan and Singapore.

24   Commercial TV is advancing around the world, and everywhere it has proved exceptionally effective at stimulating buying urges. As Anthony J. F. Reilly, chief executive of the food conglomerate H. J. Heinz, told *Fortune* magazine, "Once television is there, people of whatever shade, culture, or origin want roughly the same things." Harnessed as an educational tool, TV can be powerful and effective, as in India and Africa, where lessons are beamed to teacherless villages. But the overwhelming trend in broadcasting almost everywhere is commercialization.

In 1985, the International Advertising Association rhapsodized: "The magical marketing tool of television has been bound with the chains of laws and regulations in much of the world, and it has not been free to exercise more than a tiny fraction of its potential as a conduit of the consumer information and economic stimulation provided by advertising. Those chains are at last being chiseled off."

During the 1980s, governments deregulated or privatized television programming in most of Western Europe. Public broadcasting monopolies splintered in Belgium, France, Italy, Germany, Norway, Portugal, Spain, and Switzerland—allowing advertising on a scale previously witnessed only in the United States. As the European Community became both a single market and a common broadcasting region this year, advertising time on European TV became a hot commodity, providing access to the region's 330 million consumers and $4 trillion of disposable income.

Meanwhile, commercial television is quickly spreading outside the industrial countries. In India, declares Gurcharan Das, chairman of Procter & Gamble India, "an advertiser can reach 200 million people every night" through television. India has gone from 3 million TVs in 1983 to more than 14 million today. Latin America has built or imported 60 million sets, almost one per family, since the early 1950s. All told, perhaps half the world's people have access to commercial television broadcasts.

28   The commercialization of television is just one part of the general expansion that includes magazines and newspapers, billboards and displays, catalogs, and other media. The overall growth stands out starkly in historical trends.

Total global advertising expenditures multiplied nearly sevenfold from 1950 to 1990; they grew one-third faster than the world economy and three times faster than the world population. They rose—in real, inflation-adjusted terms—from $39 billion in 1950 to $256 billion in 1990. (For comparison, the gross national product of India, the world's second most populous state, was just $256 billion that year.) In 1950, advertisers spent $16 for each person on the planet, in 1970 they spent $27, and in 1990, $48.

Americans are the most advertised-to people on earth. U.S. marketers account for nearly half of the world's budget, according to the International Advertising Association in New York, spending $468 per American in 1991. Among the industrial countries, Japan is second in the advertising league, dedicating more than $300 per citizen to sales pitches each year. Western Europe is close behind. A typical European is the target of more than $200 worth of ads a year. The latest boom is under way in Eastern Europe, a region that John Lindquist of the Boston Consulting Group calls "an advertising executive's dream—people actually remember advertisements."

Advertising is growing fast in developing countries as well, though it remains small-scale by Western standards. South Korea's advertising industry grew 35 to 40 percent annually in the late 1980s, and yearly ad billings in India jumped fivefold in the 1980s, surpassing one dollar per person for the first time.

AD-ING LIFE

32   The sheer magnitude of the advertising barrage in consumer societies has some ironic results. For one thing, the clamor for people's attention means relatively few advertisements stick. Typical Americans are exposed to some 3,000 commercial messages a day, according to *Business Week*. Amid such a din, who notices what any one ad says?

To lend their messages greater influence, marketers are forced to deliver even higher-quality pitches—to seek new places to make them. They are constantly on the lookout for new routes into people's consciousness.

With the advent of the remote control, the mute button, and the video cassette recorder during the 1980s, people could easily avoid TV commercials, and advertisers had to seek out consumers elsewhere. Expanding on the traditional print and broadcast media, advertisers began piping messages into classrooms and doctors' offices, weaving them into the plots of feature films, posting them on chair-lift poles, printing them on postage stamps and board games, stitching them on Boy Scout merit badges and professional athletes' jerseys, mounting them in bathroom stalls, and playing them back between rings on public phones.

Marketers hired telephone solicitors, both human and computerized, to call people directly in their homes. They commissioned essays from well-known authors, packaged them between full-page ads fore and aft, and mailed them to opinion leaders to polish the sponsors' images. And they created ad-packed television programming for use at airports, bus stops, subway stations, exercise clubs, ski resorts, and supermarket checkout lines.

36   This creeping commercialization of life has a certain inevitability to it. As the novelty of each medium wears off, advertisers invent another one, relentlessly expanding the share of our collective attention span that they occupy with sales spiels.

Next, they will meet us at the mall, follow us to the dinner table, and shine down on us from the heavens. In shopping centers, they have begun erecting wall-sized video screens to heighten the frenzy of the shopping experience. Food engineers are turning the food supply into an advertising medium. The Viskase company of Chicago prints edible ad slogans on hot dogs, and Eggverts International is using a similar technique to advertise on thousands of eggs in Israel. Lighting engineers are hard at work on featherweight ways to turn blimps into giant airborne neon signs, and, demonstrating that not even the sky is the limit, Coca-Cola convinced orbiting Soviet cosmonauts to sip their soda on camera a couple of years ago.

The main outcome of this deadening commercialization is to sell not particular products, but consumerism itself. The implicit message of all advertising is the idea that there is a product to solve each of life's problems. Every commercial teaches that existence would be satisfying and complete if only we bought the right things. As religious historian Robert Bellah put it, "That happiness is to be attained through limitless material acquisition is denied by every religion and philosophy known to humankind, but is preached incessantly by every American television set."

GET 'EM WHILE THEY'RE YOUNG

The commercialization of space and time has been accompanied by the commercialization of youth. Marketers are increasingly targeting the young. One specialist in marketing to children told the *Wall Street Journal,* "Even two-year-olds are concerned about their brand of clothes, and by the age of six are full-out consumers." American children and teenagers sit through about three hours of television commercials each week—20,000 ads a year, translating to 360,000 by the time they graduate from high school.

40   The children's market in the United States is so valuable—topping $75 billion in 1990—that American companies spent $500 million marketing to kids in 1990, five times more than they spent a decade earlier. They started cartoons centered around toys and began direct-mail marketing to youngsters enrolled in their company-sponsored "clubs."

Such saturation advertising has allowed some firms to stake huge claims in the children's market. Mattel vice president Meryl Friedman brags, "Mattel has achieved a stunning 95 percent penetration with Barbie [dolls] among girls 3 to 11 in the United States."

Predictably, major retailers have opened Barbie departments to compete for the loyalty of doll-doting future consumers, and marketers pay premium prices to employ the dolls as an advertising medium. Barbies come equipped with Reebok shoes and Benetton clothes.

MADISON AVENUE'S PAPER TRAIL

Advertising's main ecological danger may be the consumption it inspires, but it also consumes heavily itself. Advertisers use a substantial share of the world's paper, particularly its heavily processed high-quality paper. Paper production involves not only forest damage but also large energy inputs and pollution outputs.

44   Ads pack the daily mail: 14 billion glossy, difficult-to-recycle mail-order catalogs plus 38 billion other assorted ads clog the post office each year in the United States. Most of those items go straight into the trash—including 98 percent of advertising letters sent in direct-mail campaigns, according to the marketing journal *American Demographics*.

Ads fill periodicals: most American magazines reserve 60 percent of their pages for advertising, and some devote far more. *Bride's* was so proud of its February/March 1990 edition that it submitted the issue to the *Guinness Book of World Records* and boasted in *Advertising Age,* "The Biggest Magazine in History. . . . It contains 1,040 pages—including 798 advertising pages."

Newspapers are no different; in the United States, they typically contain 65 percent, up from 40 percent half a century ago. Every year, Canada cuts 42,000 acres of its primeval forests—an area the size of the District of Columbia—just to provide American dailies with newsprint on which to run advertisements.

For big and immediate paper savings, newspapers could shift classified advertising—and telephone companies their directories—onto pay-per-use electronic databases accessible through phone lines. Still, advertising remains heavy in non-classified sections of newspapers. Trim out all the ads and most of the text would fit in a single section.

48   The problem in reducing the scale of advertising in the print media is that the financial viability of newspapers and magazines is linked to the number of advertising pages they sell. In the past two years of economic recession, for example, advertising pages have been harder to sell, and many periodicals have been forced to publish fewer articles. That is not good for the flow of information in democratic societies. To get less-commercialized information sources, subscribers may have to accept higher prices, as have the readers of *Ms.,* which dropped advertising three years ago.

THE INDUSTRY OF NEEDS

The needs industry—advertising—defends itself, ultimately, by claiming that advertising, whatever its social and cultural demerits, is an indispensable component of a healthy economy. As one Madison Avenue axiom counsels, "A terrible thing happens when you don't advertise. Nothing." Advertising, in this view, isn't the trim on the industrial economy, it's the fuel. Take out the ads, and the economy sputters to a halt; put in more ads, and the economy zooms. More ads equal more wants, more wants make more spending, and more spending makes more jobs.

Some promoters even call for governments to foster more advertising. The American Advertising Federation took out a full page in *Time* magazine last March to write, "Dear Mr. President . . . We respectfully remind you of advertising's role as an engine of economic growth. It raises capital, creates jobs,

and spurs production. . . . It increases government revenues since jobs produce taxable income, and greater sales increase sales taxes. . . . Incentives to
advertise are incentives for growth."

The validity of such claims is dubious, of course, but they cut to the heart
of a critical issue. Even if advertising does promote growth, the question remains as to what kind of growth. Growth in numbers of second mortgages and
third cars and fourth televisions may increase the money flowing around the
economy without making us one bit happier. If much advertising is an exercise
in generating dissatisfaction so that people will spend more and work harder,
the entire process appears morally questionable. Several generations ago,
Catholic theologian John Ryan dubbed this treadmill "squirrel cage progress."

52   Many of the areas in which the world needs growth most desperately—
environmental literacy, racial and sexual equality, and political participation,
for example—are not the stuff of advertising campaigns. "Civilization, in the
real sense of the term," advised Gandhi, "consists not in the multiplication, but
in the deliberate and voluntary reduction of wants."

RECHANELLING ADVERTISING

What legitimate role is there for advertising, then? In a substainable society,
how much advertising would there be?

None! say some, as E. F. Schumacher commented in 1979: "What is the
great bulk of advertising other than the stimulation of greed, envy and avarice
. . . at least three of the deadly sins?" More succinctly, reader Charlotte Bur-
rowes of Penacook, New Hampshire, wrote to *World Weekly* a year ago,
"There'll be a special hell for advertisers."

In fairness, though, some advertising does provide useful information
about products and services. The task for democratic societies struggling to restore balance between themselves and their ecosystems is to decide how
much advertising to tolerate, and while respecting the right of individuals to
speak their minds, to place appropriate limits on marketing.

56   The precise limits cannot yet be identified, but it may help define the issue
to consider whether there are spaces that should be free of advertising.
Churches? Schools? Hospitals? Funeral homes? Parks? Homes? Workplaces?
Books? Public libraries? Public swimming pools? Public buildings? Public buses?
Public streets? Mail boxes? Newspapers? Television broadcasts? What about times
of day, days of the week, and times of life? Early morning? Sundays? Childhood?

Restraining the excesses of marketers and limiting commercials to their
legitimate role of informing consumers would require fundamental reforms in
the industry, changes that will not come about without a well-organized grassroots movement. The advertising industry is a formidable foe on the march
around the world, and advertisers are masters at the slippery art of public relations. Madison Avenue can buy the best talents available to counter and circumvent reformers' campaigns, unless those campaigns are carefully focused
and begin with the industry's vulnerabilities.

Advertising's Achilles heel is its willingness to push products demonstrably dangerous to human health, and this is the area where activists have been most successful and best organized. Tobacco ads are or soon will be banished from television throughout the Western democracies, and alcohol commercials are under attack as never before.

Another ready target for advertising-reform activists is the assault that marketers make on children. Public sentiment runs strongly against marketing campaigns that prey on youngsters. Action for Children's Television, a citizens' group based in Boston, won a victory in late 1990 when the U.S. Congress limited television commercials aimed at children. The same year, public interest organizations in the European Community pushed through standards for European television that will put strict limits on some types of ads.

60   The Australian Consumers' Association is attacking junk food ads, calling for a ban or tough restrictions on hawking unhealthful fare to youngsters. Of food ads aired during children's television programs, the association's research shows that 80 percent are for high-fat, high-salt, excessively packaged snacks. The American Academy of Pediatrics is similarly concerned. Noting the high proportion of advertisements for products that violate nutrition guidelines, the organization is urging Congress to ban food ads that target the young.

Alternatively, consumers could take aim at trumped-up corporate environmental claims. Since 1989, marketers have been painting their products "green" in an attempt to defuse citizen anger at corporate ecological transgressions. In 1990, for example, the oil company Texaco offered Americans "free" tree seedlings to plant for the good of the environment; to qualify, a customer had to buy eight or more gallons of gasoline. Unmentioned in the marketing literature was the fact that it takes a typical tree about four years to restore as much carbon dioxide as is released in refining and burning eight gallons of fuel, and that most tree seedlings planted by amateurs promptly die.

In the United States, one-fourth of all new household products introduced in 1990 advertised themselves as "ozone-friendly," "biodegradable," "recyclable," "compostable," or something similar—claims that half of all Americans recognize as "gimmickry." Environmentalists in The Netherlands and France have attempted to cut away such misinformation by introducing a 12-point environmental advertising code in their national legislatures. Ten state attorneys general are pushing for similar national standards in the United States. Meanwhile, official and unofficial organizations throughout Europe, North America, and Japan have initiated "green labeling" programs, aiming to steer consumers to environmentally preferable products.

Efforts to restrict advertising of tobacco and alcohol, to curtail advertising to children, and to regulate environmental claims of marketers are part of a broader agenda. The nonprofit Center for the Study of Commercialism in Washington, D.C., is calling for an end to brand-name plugs in feature films, for schools to declare themselves advertising-free zones, and for revision of the tax code so that money spent on advertising is taxable.

64   Just as the expanding reach of advertising is not going unchallenged, small networks of citizens everywhere are beginning to confront commercial television. In Vancouver, British Columbia, English teacher Michael Maser gets secondary students to study television production so they will be able to recognize techniques used to manipulate viewers' sentiments. Millions of young people could benefit from such a course, considering how many products are pitched to them on TV. Along the same lines as Maser's teaching, the Center for Media and Values in Los Angeles has been promoting media literacy since 1989, by furnishing parents throughout North America with tips on teaching their children to watch with a critical eye.

More boldly, some attempt to fight fire with fire. The Vancouver-based Media Foundation is building a movement aimed at using the same cleverness and humor evident in much commercial advertising to promote substainable ends. Local groups raise funds to show the group's products on commercial television and in commercial magazines. TV spots have run in California, Ontario, and a half-dozen other states and provinces. Their "Tube Head" series of ads tell [*sic*] viewers to shut off the set. In one magazine ad, above a photo of a dark, sleek sports car, a caption purrs, "At this price, it will surely take your breath away." And below: "$250,000." In fine print, it explains, "U.S. sticker price based on individual share of social costs associated with automobiles in U.S. over average car life of 10 years. Does not include . . . oil spills at sea and on land; acid rain from auto emissions . . . environmental and health costs from global warming."

The premier spot in the Media Foundation's "High on the Hog" campaign shows a gigantic animated pig frolicking on a map of North America while a narrator intones: "Five percent of the people in the world consume *one-third* of the planet's resources. . . . Those people are us." The pig belches.

Imagine a message like *that* broadcast simultaneously to every inhabited part of the globe!

READER RESPONSE

Durning says that the advertising industry creates consumerism. Are you and your friends driven to consume? Do you buy for the sake of buying, or do you buy only because of genuine need? To what extent do you think you are influenced by advertisements?

QUESTIONS FOR DISCUSSION

1. How do advertisers manipulate their audiences? Why do you think that "advertisers have especially targeted women" (paragraph 11)? Why do you think markets are increasingly targeting children?

2. To what extent do you agree with Durning's assessment of our age as "mercurial, hedonistic, image-laden, and fashion-driven" (paragraph 16).
3. According to Durning, why is advertising ecologically threatening? What aspects of advertising does Durning find morally questionable? Do you agree with him?
4. What "new routes into people's consciousness" (paragraph 33) have advertisers used?
5. How does Durning answer the questions he poses in paragraph 53? How would you answer those questions?

ADDITIONAL SUGGESTIONS FOR WRITING ABOUT POPULAR CULTURE

1. Argue for or against extending the First Amendment's guarantee of freedom of speech to include violent lyrics in rap or rock music. Consider how far you think the First Amendment's protection of free speech should be allowed to go.
2. Select a passage from Tricia Rose's "Rap Music and the Demonization of Young Black Males," and explore its significance in relation to rap music.
3. Write your own commentary on the subject of sexism and/or misogyny in rap lyrics.
4. Argue your own position on the subject of imitative responses to media images. Do you think that violence in films cause violence in society?
5. In "Movies, Morality, and Conservative Complaints," Christopher Sharrett's position on such films as *Basic Instinct* and *Body of Evidence* is that "they simply are bad art with a retrograde view of gender relations." If you have seen either film—or one with a similar theme and similar depiction of sexuality—and have an opinion on its artistic quality and view of gender relations, write an essay explaining your views.
6. Examine selected movies in terms of whether good triumphs over evil, or vice versa.
7. View several current Hollywood films, and analyze them in terms of their message about religion, ethics, morality, or values. What values do the movies project?
8. Explain your position on the topic of Hollywood's moral obligation to the public.
9. Select a statement from Richard Corliss's "Bang, You're Dead," and support or refute it with evidence from current films or popular music.
10. Drawing on Alan Thein Durning's "Can't Live Without It," select several advertisements in any medium, and analyze them in terms of the dreams they sell or the values they promote and whether you consider their tactics to be ethical.

11. Drawing from the lyrics of selected popular rock songs, support or argue against the contention that such lyrics legitimize and even promote violence against women.

12. Analyze the content of several MTV videos that depict violence of any sort. What messages do they send?

13. With John Davidson's "Menace to Society" in mind, watch Saturday morning children's programs on television for several hours, paying particular attention to their violent content. Then write an analysis of the shows you watched. One approach to this assignment is to address your comments to a particular audience: parents of young children, the president of one of the major television networks, or the producers or sponsors of the programs you watched. If you find the violent component to be negligible, focus on other aspects of the programs that you either liked or disliked, explaining why by citing examples from the programs.

14. Select several daytime talk shows such as those mentioned in Joshua Gamson's "Do Ask, Do Tell," and analyze the programs in terms of subject matter, audience reaction to the guests, behavior of the guests, and attitude of the hosts toward the subject, the guests, and the audience. What conclusions can you draw from your brief survey of daytime talk shows?

15. Joe Saltzman, in "Beating the Same Old Dead Horse," maintains that critics of television sex and violence should stop complaining because of the easy availability of movies that are much more violent or sexually explicit. Write an essay in which you explain your stand on this issue. Do you agree with Saltzman or with critics of television, or do you have an entirely different perspective on the subject?

16. Argue in support of or against a federal law requiring new television sets to have a V chip that would allow parents to prevent their children from viewing programs they feel are too explicitly sexual or violent.

17. Explain your own perspective on some aspect of popular culture, taking into account the views expressed by any of the writers in this chapter. Focus on a specific issue about which you have formed an opinion after reading their views, refer to the other writers as a way of providing the context for your own essay, and then explain in detail your own position. For instance, examine one form of popular entertainment, such as rock videos, popular music, television shows, advertising, or movies, for the ways in which it promotes or fosters an acceptance of violence.

Chapter

9

PREJUDICE AND DISCRIMINATION

Despite civil rights struggles and the contemporary women's movement, despite legislation to ensure equal treatment under the law and the creation of agencies to monitor and punish discriminatory practices, prejudice and discrimination remain problems in American society. Many people, particularly young adults, believe that the problems faced by women and minorities in the past have been eradicated and that such matters are no longer issues. However, statistics demonstrate that women and minorities have not achieved equity with white males, nor has discrimination on the basis of sex, race, or ethnicity disappeared. Indeed, as some of the selections in this chapter demonstrate, prejudice and discrimination are still very much a part of the American fabric.

The first essay, Michel Wieviorka's "The Ruses of Racism," examines the conditions under which racial violence as a means of oppression is encouraged to grow. Next, writing from personal experience, Mary Crow Dog, in "A Woman from He-Dog," tells of her involvement in the 1970s conflict between Native Americans and federal troops at Wounded Knee. This selection is the first chapter of her autobiography, *Lakota Woman* (1990). According to her publisher, the book documents "a story of death, of determination against all odds, and of the cruelties perpetrated against American Indians during the last several decades. It is also a deeply moving account of a woman's triumphant struggle to survive in a hostile world."

The next essay addresses the subject of affirmative action, or equitable treatment regardless of sex or race. Stephen Steinberg explains, in "The

Affirmative Action Debate," how affirmative action policies were developed and why he believes they are still needed. Following Steinberg's essay, Patricia J. Williams, in "Racial Privacy," raises a number of points related to affirmative action, racial profiling, and discrimination in her argument against a new initiative in California to prevent public agencies from classifying people on the basis of race, ethnicity, color, or national origin. While these two essays alone are not enough to do justice to the complexity of the affirmative action issue or the problem of racial discrimination, they provide starting points for further research and inquiry into a number of topics related to those issues.

One interesting trend resulting from our nation's collective examination of and sensitivity to prejudice and discrimination has been the "political correctness" movement. The term *political correctness,* or *P.C.,* was developed to describe the views of those opposed to speech, writing, and behavior that smack of racism, sexism, ageism, or other "-isms" that have the potential to demean selected groups. In their efforts to make American culture more inclusive and to eradicate discrimination, for instance, feminists, Blacks, Hispanics, Asians, gays and lesbians, disabled people, and similar groups object to language that excludes, belittles, or demeans them. Their attempts to monitor both written and spoken words have led some people to criticize them for being overly sensitive and extreme in their recommendations for change. This controversy has engendered heated debate between those who favor politically correct language and their critics, who find them silly and even obnoxious.

This chapter includes essays by two writers who are critical of political correctness. Writing for a monthly feature of *USA Today Magazine* called "Parting Thoughts," Gerald F. Kreyche, in "Have We Lost Our Sense of Humor?," maintains that "political correctness is making cowards of almost everyone" and that "people have become thin-skinned, touchy, overly sensitive." He provides many examples of jokes to illustrate his belief that virtually any group is subject to being joked about and that such humor is harmless. Michiko Kakutani takes exception to political correctness as well. In "The Word Police," she explains her objections to "the methods and fervor of the self-appointed language police." As you read their reasons for opposing political correctness, consider the extent to which you agree with Kreyche and Kakutani. Are all their reasons persuasive? Do you take exception to any of their statements?

Next is William Raspberry's "Symbolic Arguments." Raspberry raises an intriguing question: To what extent are the symbols of the old South—the Confederate flag, General Robert E. Lee, and the song "Dixie"—innocent, nostalgic icons of the culture and heritage of a former way of life, and to what extent are they evidence of present-day racism? In light of the other readings in this chapter, Raspberry's commentary should lead to some lively classroom discussion.

Finally, Toni Cade Bambara's short story "The Lesson," which is told from the viewpoint of a street-tough, inner-city, African-American girl, focuses on insights several children have about the disparity between the rich and the poor as a result of a field trip to a very expensive New York City Fifth Avenue toy store. This understanding of the chasm between what her family and friends can afford and what the rich parents of wealthy children can afford also leads the narrator to discover something important about herself. Implicit in the story is the suggestion that a connection exists between skin color and poverty.

1. Under what circumstances, if any, do you think that civil protest, picketing, and similar activities are called for?
2. If you have witnessed or been party to discrimination on any basis, describe the experience.
3. Where do stereotypes come from? Why do you think some people are prejudiced against others with a different skin color, religion, nationality, or ethnic identity? How can you personally work against stereotyping and prejudice?
4. Explore the personality of bigots. Are there particular characteristics, such as income, education, or geographical location, that bigots have in common? Under what circumstances does personal preference or opinion become prejudice?
5. Offer one possible solution to the problem of racism or ethnoviolence in America.

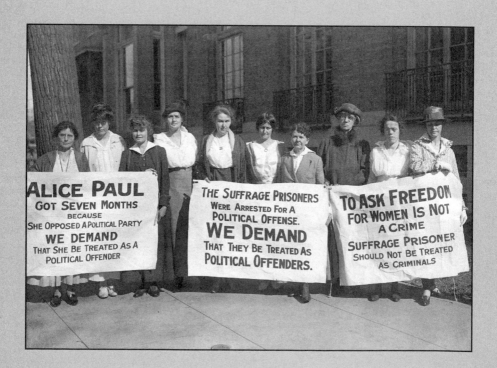

The Ruses of Racism

Michel Wieviorka

Michel Wieviorka is a French sociologist, a lecturer at the University of Paris–Dauphine, and director of the Centre d'Analyse et d'Intervention Sociologiques in Paris. He is coauthor, with Dominique Wolton, of Terrorisme à la une *(1987) and author of* Sociétiés et Terrorisme *(1988),* The Making of Terrorism *(1993), and* The Arena of Racism: Theory, Culture and Society *(1995). This essay is reprinted from the February 1993 issue of* The UNESCO Courier.

Racism is not always overtly, brutally violent—it does not always kill. Racial discrimination, expressions of prejudice and racist tracts can all carry ominous overtones of violence, but they cannot be ranked alongside the physical violence perpetrated in pogroms, lynchings, immigrant-bashing, murders and other types of assault, which is what I wish to discuss.

What is more, the most violent forms of racism do not necessarily grow out of other varieties of racism. Contrary to popular belief, prejudice does not invariably and inevitably lead on to acts of violence. Deep-seated racism may be widespread in societies where there is no outward sign of naked violence.

For racist violence to erupt, a certain set of conditions must exist. One conditioning factor is the attitude of those in authority: what they are willing and able to do in order to deal with those who engage in racist acts. When a government is weak or remote, or even tinged with racism itself, it encourages political groups and forces wishing to turn their message of hatred, contempt, subordination and rejection into deeds. It may even become actively racist itself or manipulate racist violence, as happened in the Russian Empire at the turn of the century, where the Czarist regime was largely instrumental in setting off the pogroms.

4   But there are other factors. Some institutions—particularly the legal system and the police—may use methods which, although not deliberately or explicitly racist in themselves, nevertheless contribute to the spread of serious outbreaks of violence. Many official enquiries have found that when police behaviour has exacerbated ethnic and social tensions instead of defusing them, it has often led to an escalation of violence in which racism occupies a prominent place.

Yet another factor is the existence of political forces capable of providing racist violence with an organized structure and an ideological foundation. As long as such forces do not exist or are relegated to the sidelines of society, violence is always possible and sometimes erupts, but it crops up in the form of sudden outbursts and short-lived explosions, in other words of acts which, numerous though they may be, are not linked by any apparent unifying principle.

When such forces do gain a political foothold, however, the violence for which they provide a structure, even if it is not directly organized by them, nonetheless becomes more cold-blooded, methodical, and active. It becomes a matter of schemes and strategies; it channels popular feelings of hatred and hostility towards the group marked out as a racial target, but does not allow them to be expressed spontaneously. It may even prevent them from being expressed at all, on the political grounds that any act of violence should be consistent with the aims and thinking of the party or organization.

This is why the emergence of a political force with a racist ideology and plans does not necessarily mean that there will be an immediate increase in violence, for violence may actually be detrimental to its attempts to achieve legitimate political status. Violence may create an image of disorder and accordingly be played down until the movement achieves power, when it will be able to indulge in violence in its most extreme forms. Conversely, there may be an increase in violence when the power of a racist force or party is on the wane, because some of its members may take a harder line if they feel they have no political future. The end of apartheid in South Africa is providing scope not for more racism but for more racial violence.

8   Since the beginning of the modern era, racism has been linked to patterns of domination, especially those of colonialism set against the background of empire-building. But it has also informed trends in thinking which, from the nineteenth century onwards, influenced aspects of physical anthropology and other doctrinaire intellectual movements. When the term "racism" emerged in the period between the two World Wars, some of the theories from the past were refurbished. Above all, racist attitudes spread all over the world in the wake of the social upheavals that are at the root of various forms of racial violence.

Racial violence is no longer only the crude expression of colonial-type domination. It may also stem from an economic crisis, in which a deprived group, threatened with a decline in social status or exclusion from the mainstream, turns against another group in an attempt to oust it, on racial grounds, from a shrinking job market. The racism of the poor whites, which led to the lynching of blacks in the southern United States in the first half of the twentieth century, came about when the whites saw their black neighbours as dangerous competitors on the industrial job market.

But racial violence may also occur among more affluent classes, which want to maintain the gap separating them from the less privileged. The method they use is a combination of social and racial segregation, which may in fact lead to more cold-blooded and calculated forms of violence. At the beginning of the century, well-to-do white citizens in the southern United States organized lynching parties to punish black men accused of raping white women or theft.

However, racist violence does not always stem solely or directly from social factors. It may originate in a real or imagined threat to the identity of a group, or it may accompany the expansion of a state or religion, sometimes claiming to represent universal values, as often happened during the colonial period.

12   The urge to uphold a particular identity can lead to unlimited violence, fuelled either by an obsessive fear of "racial intermingling" or by reference to an absolute difference that prohibits all social intercourse and all contact between races except in war. Such forms of racism are intended to keep others at bay, to ensure that they are segregated or even expelled or destroyed. The aim is not so much to establish the inferior status of a group on the grounds of its physical attributes as to ensure that a community remains homogeneous or a nation remains pure, or to justify their unimpeded expansion.

Identity-related racism and the violence that goes with it can have three quite distinct motivations.

In some cases, this form of racism is founded on the affirmation of an identity that claims to be universal and seeks to crush everything that opposes it. The history of colonialism contains many instances of this phenomenon. Conversely, it may be based on the resistance of a nation or community to the modern world, in which case the chosen target is a group that is seen as the incarnation of evil, intrusion, or the corruption of culture or traditional values. The Jews have long been denounced and attacked as representatives of a hated modernity. The explosive violence of the pogroms and the more methodical violence of the gas chambers largely grew out of criticisms, phantasms and rumours that reproached the Jews on the grounds of their cosmopolitanism, wealth, political power and influence in the media.

Thirdly, this identity-related racism may flare up as a result of a clash between two or more communities within the same political entity or multiracial or multicultural society. In such cases, violence results from strained relations between communities, from a process of interaction in which one group's real or imagined attempt to assert itself prompts reactions from other groups and triggers off a spiralling power struggle that may end in an outburst of violence and political chaos. The civil war in Lebanon and the breakup of Yugoslavia are recent examples of conflicts where overt or implied references to race can be sensed behind rhetorical appeals to the nation or to the cultural, confessional and historical community.

16   When violence is associated with racism, therefore, it is governed by various conditions that dictate the course it takes and is rooted in a wide range of social and identity-related factors. But the important thing about violence is that it compresses into a single action factors that may be not only different but contradictory. Perpetrators of racist violence may wish, for example, to exclude a specific group from their society so as to exploit it. This happens frequently in industrialized countries, where immigrants are employed to do low-grade jobs and rejected on account of their culture. Or to take another case, in Czarist Russia and central Europe at the beginning of the present century, it was the rich, assimilated Jew, symbol of modernity, who was regarded as an intolerable threat, yet the victims of the pogroms were the culturally conspicuous and poverty-stricken Jewish masses.

This is the paradox of violence: not only is it unembarrassed by its inherent contradictions, it also creates its own logic and its own dynamics, so that in the end it alters the conditions that allowed it to emerge in the first place.

READER RESPONSE

Wieviorka offers a number of reasons, from a sociological perspective, to account for the emergence and growth of racial violence. What are your personal thoughts on the subject?

QUESTIONS FOR DISCUSSION

1. Looking at each factor Wieviorka says is necessary for racial violence to erupt, comment on the extent to which you agree with him.
2. Explain, in your own words, what Wieviorka means when he says that when a political force with a racist ideology emerges, there is not necessarily an immediate increase in racial violence (paragraph 7). When is a racist force or party likely to increase its use of violence, according to Wieviorka?
3. Summarize the sociological causes of racial violence that Wieviorka identifies. Can you cite other examples of such violence besides those that he gives?
4. State, in your own words, what you understand Wieviorka to mean by identity-related racial violence, and then summarize the three distinct motivations for identity-related racism that he identifies.
5. Explain the title.

A Woman from He-Dog
Mary Crow Dog

Mary Crow Dog grew up on a South Dakota reservation in a one-room cabin without running water or electricity. She became active in the Native-American tribal pride movement in the 1960s and 1970s and married the movement's chief medicine man. "A Woman from He-Dog" is the first chapter of Mary Crow Dog's autobiography Lakota Woman *(written with Richard Erdoes and published in 1990).*

A nation is not conquered until
the hearts of its women are on the ground.
Then it is done, no matter

how brave its warriors
nor how strong their weapons.

Cheyenne Proverb

I am Mary Brave Bird. After I had my baby during the siege of Wounded Knee they gave me a special name—Ohitika Win, Brave Woman, and fastened an eagle plume in my hair, singing brave-heart songs for me. I am a woman of the Red Nation, a Sioux woman. That is not easy.

I had my first baby during a firefight, with the bullets crashing through one wall and coming through the other. When my newborn son was only a day old and the marshals really opened up on us, I wrapped him up in a blanket and ran for it. We had to hit the dirt a couple of times, I shielding the baby with my body, praying, "It's all right if I die, but please let him live."

When I came out of Wounded Knee I was not even healed up, but they put me in jail at Pine Ridge and took my baby away. I could not nurse. My breasts swelled up and grew hard as rocks, hurting badly. In 1975 the feds put the muzzles of their M-16s against my head, threatening to blow me away. It's hard being an Indian woman.

4   My best friend was Annie Mae Aquash, a young, strong-hearted woman from the Micmac Tribe with beautiful children. It is not always wise for an Indian woman to come on too strong. Annie Mae was found dead in the snow at the bottom of a ravine on the Pine Ridge Reservation. The police said that she had died of exposure, but there was a .38-caliber slug in her head. The FBI cut off her hands and sent them to Washington for fingerprint identification, hands that had helped my baby come into the world.

My sister-in-law, Delphine, a good woman who had lived a hard life, was also found dead in the snow, the tears frozen on her face. A drunken man had beaten her, breaking one of her arms and legs, leaving her helpless in a blizzard to die.

My sister Barbara went to the government hospital in Rosebud to have her baby and when she came out of anesthesia found that she had been sterilized against her will. The baby lived only for two hours, and she had wanted so much to have children. No, it isn't easy.

When I was a small girl at the St. Francis Boarding School, the Catholic sisters would take a buggy whip to us for what they called "disobedience." At age ten I could drink and hold a pint of whiskey. At age twelve the nuns beat me for "being too free with my body." All I had been doing was holding hands with a boy. At age fifteen I was raped. If you plan to be born, make sure you are born white and male.

8   It is not the big, dramatic things so much that get us down, but just being Indian, trying to hang on to our way of life, language, and values while being surrounded by an alien, more powerful culture. It is being an iyeska, a half-blood, being looked down upon by whites and full-bloods alike. It is being a backwoods girl living in a city, having to rip off stores to survive. Most of all

it is being a woman. Among Plains tribes, some men think that all a woman is good for is to crawl into the sack with them and mind the children. It compensates for what white society had done to them. They were famous warriors and hunters once, but the buffalo is [*sic*] gone and there is not much rep in putting a can of spam or an occasional rabbit on the table.

As for being warriors, the only way some men can count coup nowadays is knocking out another skin's teeth during a barroom fight. In the old days a man made a name for himself by being generous and wise, but now he has nothing to be generous with, no jobs, no money; and as far as our traditional wisdom is concerned, our men are being told by the white missionaries, teachers, and employers that it is merely savage superstition they should get rid of if they want to make it in this world. Men are forced to live away from their children, so that the family can get ADC—Aid to Dependent Children. So some warriors come home drunk and beat up their old ladies in order to work off their frustration. I know where they are coming from. I feel sorry for them, but I feel even sorrier for their women.

To start from the beginning, I am a Sioux from the Rosebud Reservation in South Dakota. I belong to the "Burned Thigh," the Brule Tribe, the Sicangu in our language. Long ago, so the legend goes, a small band of Sioux was surrounded by enemies who set fire to their tipis and the grass around them. They fought their way out of the trap but got their legs burned and in this way acquired their name. The Brules are part of the Seven Scared Campfires, the seven tribes of the Western Sioux known collectively as Lakota. The Eastern Sioux are called Dakota. The difference between them is their language. It is the same except that where we Lakota pronounce an L, the Dakota pronounce a D. They cannot pronounce L at all. In our tribe we have this joke: "What is a flat tire in Dakota?" Answer: "Bdowout."

The Brule, like the Sioux, were a horse people, fierce riders and raiders, great warriors. Between 1870 and 1880 all Sioux were driven into reservations, fenced in and forced to give up everything that had given meaning to their life—their horses, their hunting, their arms, everything. But under the long snows of despair the little spark of our ancient beliefs and pride kept glowing, just barely sometimes, waiting for a warm wind to blow that spark into a flame again.

12 My family was settled on the reservation in a small place called He-Dog, after a famous chief. There are still some He-Dogs living. One, an old lady I knew, lived to be over a hundred years old. Nobody knew when she had been born. She herself had no idea, except that when she came into the world there was no census yet, and Indians had not yet been given Christian first names. Her name was just He-Dog, nothing else. She always told me, "You should have seen me eighty years ago when I was pretty." I have never forgotten her face—nothing but deep cracks and gullies, but beautiful in its own way. At any rate very impressive.

On the Indian side my family was related to the Brave Birds and Fool Bulls. Old Grandpa Fool Bull was the last man to make flutes and play them, the old-style flutes in the shape of a bird's head which had the elk power, the power to lure a young girl into a man's blanket. Fool Bull lived a whole long century, dying in 1976, whittling his flutes almost until his last day. He took me to my first peyote meeting while I was still a kid.

He still remembered the first Wounded Knee, the massacre. He was a young boy at that time, traveling with his father, a well-known medicine man. They had gone to a place near Wounded Knee to take part in a Ghost Dance. They had on their painted ghost shirts which were supposed to make them bulletproof. When they got near Pine Ridge they were stopped by white soldiers, some of them from the Seventh Cavalry, George Custer's old regiment, who were hoping to kill themselves some Indians. The Fool Bull band had to give up their few old muzzle-loaders, bows, arrows, and even knives. They had to put up their tipis in a tight circle, all bunched up, with the wagons on the outside and the soldiers surrounding their camp, watching them closely. It was cold, so cold that the trees were crackling with a loud noise as the frost was splitting their trunks. The people made a fire the following morning to warm themselves and make some coffee and then they noticed a sound beyond the crackling of the trees: rifle fire, salvos making a noise like the ripping apart of a giant blanket; the boom of cannon and the rattling of quick-firing Hotchkiss guns. Fool Bull remembered the grown-ups bursting into tears, the women keening: "They are killing our people, they are butchering them!" It was only two miles or so from where Grandfather Fool Bull stood that almost three hundred Sioux men, women, and children were slaughtered. Later grandpa saw the bodies of the slain, all frozen in ghostly attitudes, thrown into a ditch like dogs. And he saw a tiny baby sucking at his dead mother's breast.

I wish I could tell about the big deeds of some ancestors of mine who fought at the Little Big Horn, or the Rosebud, counting coup during the Grattan or Fetterman battle, but little is known of my family's history before 1880. I hope some of my great-grandfathers counted coup on Custer's men, I like to imagine it, but I just do not know. Our Rosebud people did not play a big part in the battles against generals Crook or Custer. This was due to the policy of Spotted Tail, the all-powerful chief at the time. Spotted Tail had earned his eagle feathers as a warrior, but had been taken East as a prisoner and put in jail. Coming back years later, he said that he had seen the cities of the whites and that a single one of them contained more people than could be found in all the Plains tribes put together, and that every one of the wasičuns' factories could turn out more rifles and bullets in one day than were owned by all the Indians in the country. It was useless, he said, to try to resist the wasičuns. During the critical year of 1876 he had his Indian people keep most of the young men on the reservation, preventing them from joining Sitting Bull, Gall, and Crazy Horse. Some of the young bucks, a few Brave Birds among them, managed to sneak out trying to get to Montana, but nothing much is known. After having been forced into reservations, it was not thought wise to recall such things. It might mean no rations, or worse. For the same reason many in my family turned Christian, letting themselves be "whitemanized." It took many years to reverse this process.

16   My sister Barbara, who is four years older than me, says she remembers the day when I was born. It was late at night and raining hard amid thunder and lightning. We had no electricity then, just the old-style kerosene lamps with the big reflectors. No bathrooms, no tap water, no car. Only a few white teachers had cars. There was one phone in He-Dog, at the trading post. This was not so very long ago, come to think of it. Like most Sioux at that time my mother was supposed to give birth at home, I think, but something went wrong, I was pointing the wrong way, feet first or stuck sideways. My mother was in great pain, laboring for hours, until finally someone ran to the trading post and called the ambulance. They took her—us—to Rosebud, but the hospital there was not yet equipped to handle a complicated birth, I don't think they had surgery then, so they had to drive my mother all the way to Pine Ridge, some ninety miles distant, because there the tribal hospital was bigger. So it happened that I was born among Crazy Horse's people. After my sister Sandra was born the doctors there performed a hysterectomy on my mother, in fact sterilizing her without her permission, which was common at the time, and up to just a few years ago, so that it is hardly worth mentioning. In the opinion of some people, the fewer Indians there are, the better. As Colonel Chivington said to his soldiers: "Kill 'em all, big and small, nits make lice!"

I don't know whether I am a louse under the white man's skin. I hope I am. At any rate I survived the long hours of my mother's labor, the stormy drive to Pine Ridge, and the neglect of doctors. I am an iyeska, a breed, that's what the white kids used to call me. When I grew bigger they stopped calling me that, because it would get them a bloody nose. I am a small woman, not much over five feet tall, but I can hold my own in a fight, and in a free-for-all with honkies I can become rather ornery and do real damage. I have white blood in me. Often I have wished to be able to purge it out of me. As a young girl I used to look at myself in the mirror, trying to find a clue as to who and what I was. My face is very Indian, and so are my eyes and my hair, but my skin is very light. Always I waited for the summer, for the prairie sun, the Badlands sun, to tan me and make me into a real skin.

The Crow Dogs, the members of my husband's family, have no such problems of identity. They don't need the sun to tan them, they are fullbloods—the Sioux of the Sioux. Some Crow Dog men have faces which make the portrait on the buffalo Indian nickel look like a washed-out white man. They have no shortage of legends. Every Crow Dog seems to be legend in himself, including the women. They became outcasts in their stronghold at Grass Mountain rather than being whitemanized. They could not be tamed, made to wear a necktie or go to a Christian church. All during the long years when practicing Indian beliefs was forbidden and could be punished with jail, they went right on having their ceremonies, their sweat baths and sacred dances. Whenever a Crow Dog got together with some relatives, such as those equally untamed, unregenerated Iron Shells, Good Lances, Two Strikes, Picket Pins, or Hollow Horn Bears, then you could hear the sound of the can gleska, the drum, telling all the world that a Sioux ceremony was in the making. It took courage and suffering to keep the flame alive, the little spark under the snow.

The first Crow Dog was a well-known chief. On his shield was the design of two circles and two arrowheads for wounds received in battle—two white man's bullets and two Pawnee arrow points. When this first Crow Dog was lying wounded in the snow, a coyote came to warm him and a crow flew ahead of him to show him the way home. His name should be Crow Coyote, but the white interpreter misunderstood it and so they became Crow Dogs. This Crow Dog of old became famous for killing a rival chief, the result of a feud over tribal politics, then driving voluntarily over a hundred miles to get himself hanged at Deadwood, his wife sitting beside him in his buggy; famous also for finding on his arrival that the Supreme Court had ordered him to be freed because the federal government had no jurisdiction over Indian reservations and also because it was no crime for one Indian to kill another. Later, Crow Dog became a leader of the Ghost Dancers, holding out for months in the frozen caves and ravines of the Badlands. So, if my own family lacks history, that of my husband more than makes up for it.

20   Our land itself is a legend, especially the area around Grass Mountain where I am living now. The fight for our land is at the core of our existence, as it has been for the last two hundred years. Once the land is gone, then we are gone too. The Sioux used to keep winter counts, picture writings on buffalo skin, which told our people's story from year to year. Well, the whole country is one vast winter count. You can't walk a mile without coming to some family's sacred vision hill, to an ancient Sun Dance circle, an old battleground, a place where something worth remembering happened. Mostly a death, a proud death or a drunken death. We are a great people for dying. "It's a good day to die!" that's our old battle cry. But the land with its tarpaper shacks and outdoor privies, not one of them straight, but all leaning this way or that way, is also a land to live on, a land for good times and telling jokes and talking of great deeds done in the past. But you can't live forever off the deeds of Sitting Bull or Crazy Horse. You can't wear their eagle feathers, freeload off their legends. You have to make your own legends now. It isn't easy.

READER RESPONSE

What do you know about the 1890 confrontation at Wounded Knee? Were you aware of the 1970s conflict that Mary Crow Dog writes about here? Do you have any new insights or perspectives on the experience of Native Americans as a result of reading this selection?

QUESTIONS FOR DISCUSSION

1. Are you convinced by Mary Crow Dog's story that, as she asserts, it is not easy being an Indian woman? What does this selection tell you about life today for Indian men?

2. What does Crow Dog mean when she refers to things "it was not thought wise to recall" (paragraph 15).
3. In paragraph 17, Crow Dog says that she used to look into the mirror as a young girl to try to "find a clue as to who and what [she] was." What does this selection tell you about who she is? What aspects of her character does she reveal?
4. What contrasts does Crow Dog draw between how Native Americans live now and how they once lived? In what ways do Crow Dog and other Native Americans keep alive "the little spark of [their] ancient beliefs and pride" (paragraph 11)?

The Affirmative Action Debate
Stephen Steinberg

Stephen Steinberg, a sociologist, is a professor in the Urban Studies Department at Queens College and at the Graduate School and University Center of the City University of New York. His book The Ethnic Myth *(1989) is widely recognized as one of the leading critical interpretations of race, ethnicity, and class in America. Other books include* The Academic Melting Pot *and* The Tenacity of Prejudice *(1977) and* Turning Back: The Retreat from Racial Justice in American Thought and Policy *(1995). He is also the editor of* Race and Ethnicity in the United States *(2000). This selection is from the March 1996 issue of* The UNESCO Courier.

The civil rights revolution in the United States was primarily a struggle for liberty, not equality. It sought to dismantle the system of official segregation that had been erected in the aftermath of slavery and to secure full rights of citizenship for African Americans. The abiding faith of the movement was that once the walls of segregation came tumbling down, blacks would be free to assume their rightful place in American society.

No sooner were the historic Civil Rights Acts of 1964 and 1965 passed, however, than it became clear that legislation alone would not address the deep-seated inequalities that were the legacy of two centuries of slavery and another century of Jim Crow. This was acknowledged by President Lyndon Johnson in a commencement address at Howard University in Washington, D.C., in June 1965, the very month that the Voting Rights Act received Congressional approval. As he told the graduating class:

Freedom is not enough. You do not wipe away the scars of centuries by saying: "Now you are free to go where you want, do as you desire, choose the leaders you please."You do not take a person who for years has been hobbled by chains and liberate him, bring him to the starting line and then say,"You are free to compete with all the others," and still justly believe that you have been completely fair.We seek not just freedom but opportunity, not just equality as a right and a theory but equality as a fact and as a result.

PASSIVE AND ACTIVE POLICIES

4   Johnson's oratory was punctuated by the outbreak of racial violence in the Watts section of Los Angeles only two months later. In the ensuing years there were scores of other "riots" that threw American society into a deep political crisis, one that forced the nation to confront the issue of equality as well as liberty.This is the historical context in which affirmative action evolved as national policy.

Affirmative action has never been formulated as a coherent policy, but evolved incrementally through a series of presidential executive orders, administrative policies and court decisions. Partly for this reason, the term itself is so fraught with ambiguity that it is not always clear what advocates and opponents are squabbling about. Let us therefore make several crucial distinctions.

First, affirmative action must be distinguished from policies of non-discrimination.Although both seek racial justice in the workplace, policies of non-discrimination merely enjoin employers not to practice discrimination in the recruitment, hiring and promotion of workers. It is essentially a passive injunction not to discriminate.Affirmative action, on the other hand, commits employers to go a decisive step beyond non-discrimination and to *actively* seek out protected groups in employment. In this form—essentially "outreach" programmes reliant on the good faith efforts of employers—affirmative action arouses little or no opposition.

There is another form of affirmative action, however, that goes a decisive step beyond outreach and involves granting "preference" to minority applicants in order to guarantee the desired result.This is where controversy begins. For example, in his confirmation hearings to the Supreme Court in 1991, Clarence Thomas spoke passionately of his support for outreach programmes to extend opportunity to women and minorities, but he was equally adamant in his opposition to affirmative action programmes that involve preference.

8   These three forms of anti-discrimination are not mere abstractions, but are anchored in history. Let us briefly review how social policy evolved from non-discrimination, to outreach, to preference.

OCCUPATIONAL APARTHEID

Africans were originally imported to the United States to provide labour in the South's evolving plantation economy. In the century after slavery, when tens of millions of immigrants from Europe were rapidly absorbed into the

North's burgeoning industries, a colour line excluded blacks from employment in the entire industrial sector, with the exception of a few menial and low-paying jobs. When the Southern economy finally underwent modernization, blacks were still confined to "negro jobs"—servile and undesirable jobs that were reminiscent of slavery itself. As late as the 1960s, even as the civil rights movement reached its triumphant climax, the United States had, in effect, a system of occupational apartheid that excluded blacks from entire job sectors. Most black men worked as unskilled labourers; most black women as low-level service workers, especially domestics.

This racial division of labour went virtually unchallenged until the Second World War, when the black union leader A. Philip Randolph threatened a march on Washington unless blacks were given access to jobs in defence industries. This also led to the establishment of a Fair Employment Practices Committee [FEPC]. Even though the FEPC had few resources and virtually no power to enforce non-discrimination, it was quickly engulfed in controversy and disbanded as soon as the war was over. Here was an early sign that attempts to enforce compliance with non-discriminatory policies would encounter enormous resistance.

In the 1940s and 1950s a second FEPC, along with other federal and state agencies, preached non-discrimination, but with meagre results at best. Indeed, this is precisely what eventually led to a shift from non-discrimination to affirmative action. A major turning point occurred in 1961 when President John F Kennedy, again in response to rising protest from the black community, issued Executive Order 10925, which required federal contractors to take "affirmative action" to desegregate their work force. Unlike similar declarations in the past, the presidential edict established specific sanctions, including termination of contract, to be applied against contractors who were not in compliance. Three years later Title VII of the 1964 Civil Rights Act proscribed employment discrimination on the basis of race, colour, religion, sex or national origin. A year later President Johnson issued Executive Order 11246 that put further teeth into affirmative action by requiring federal contractors to develop specific goals and timetables for increasing the employment of women and minorities.

CORPORATE INERTIA

12   One might think that these developments would have dealt a fatal blow to America's system of occupational apartheid. This was hardly the case. In 1973—nine years after the passage of the 1964 Civil Rights Act—a telephone company which was the nation's largest corporate employer and a major government contractor still had a highly segregated workforce. The company employed 165,000 persons in low-paying operator classifications—99.9 percent of whom were female. Of 190,000 higher-paying craft workers, 99 percent were male. Virtually no women were in management positions, and even supervisory personnel in "female" departments were male.

The company, furthermore, could boast of "equal opportunity" policies that had increased black employment from 2.5 percent in 1960 to 10 percent in 1970, but this mainly reflected the hiring of black women as operators to replace white women who were experiencing a high rate of turnover. There were virtually no black males in craft jobs and even fewer in management. This was the context in which the Federal Communications Commission opposed a rate increase on the grounds of the company's discriminatory employment practices.

Eventually this resulted in a landmark consent decree with the Equal Employment Opportunity Commission (EEOC), the Department of Justice, and the Department of Labor in which the company paid monetary damages to aggrieved classes and agreed to change its employment policies and meet employment targets for women and minorities. According to a study on the impact of the consent decree, the programme got off to a poor start but by 1976, 99 percent of its short-term targets had been reached. Furthermore, these gains occurred in the context of a declining labour force due to the impact of new technology.

WHAT'S AT STAKE

As this case illustrates, good-faith efforts to increase minority representation were generally ineffective until they were backed up by specific "goals and timetables" that, in effect, gave preference to minority applicants who met basic qualifications but might not have been hired or promoted without affirmative action mandates. Critics, of course, complain that this amounts to a system of de facto quotas. Like Clarence Thomas, they raise no objection to affirmative action so long as it involves "outreach," but reject affirmative action as soon as it involves "preference."

16   What these critics overlook, however, is that decades of preaching non-discrimination produced little or no change in the system of occupational apartheid. Indeed, this is why affirmative policy shifted from outreach to preference in the first place.

Unfortunately, no systematic body of evidence exists that would permit a precise accounting of what has been achieved under affirmative action. This much is clear, however: the occupational spheres where blacks have made the most notable progress—in government service, in major blue-collar occupations, in corporate management, and in the professions—are all areas where vigorous affirmative action programmes have been in place over the past two decades. Before affirmative action, the black middle class consisted of a small number of professionals and businessmen anchored in the ghetto economy. Most of the progress that we celebrate—particularly the emergence of a large black middle class with roots in mainstream economic structures—is a direct product of affirmative action.

Thus, much is at stake in the current debate over the future of affirmative action. In recent years there has been a rising chorus of criticism against affirmative action programmes, and it has not come only from whites who feel that they are being asked to pay the price for crimes that they did not commit. Criticism also has been levelled by legal scholars who challenge the constitutionality of affirmative action and see it as betraying the cardinal principle of the civil rights movement itself: a color-blind society. A new genre of black conservatives have denounced affirmative action as patronizing to blacks and subversive of black self-esteem. Even some liberals who say they support affirmative action in principle have concluded that it is self-defeating because it triggers a popular backlash that only serves their political enemies.

These are powerful arguments, based as they are on legal and moral principles as well as on political pragmatism. However, they fail to recognize the lesson of history: that even laws proscribing discrimination and well-intentioned efforts to increase minority representation were never effective until they were backed up with specific affirmative action mandates.

20 Thus, the problem is stated falsely when it is suggested that we must choose between merit or preference, or between the rights of individuals and the rights of groups, or between a color-blind or a color-conscious society. Rather, the paramount choice is between racial progress or returning to the status quo ante: the period before affirmative action when we salved our national conscience with laws on the books that did little or nothing to reverse centuries of occupational apartheid.

READER RESPONSE

What is your opinion of affirmative action?

QUESTIONS FOR DISCUSSION

1. Explain, in your own words, how affirmative action and policies on nondiscrimination differ. What led to the development of affirmative action policies?
2. What do you understand Steinberg to mean by "occupational apartheid"?
3. Summarize the arguments in support of and against affirmative action. Where do you position yourself in the debate?

Racial Privacy

Patricia J. Williams

Patricia J. Williams, a professor of law at Columbia University and member of the State Bar of California and the Federal

Court of Appeals for the 9th Circuit, writes The Nation *column
"Diary of a Mad Law Professor." Her books include* The Alchemy
of Race & Rights *(1993),* The Rooster's Egg *(1995) and* Seeing a
Color-Blind Future:The Paradox of Race *(1997). This column ran
in the June 17, 2002, issue of* The Nation.

Ward Connerly, figurehead for California's anti-affirmative action Proposition
209, is up to more mischief.This time it's a push to prevent California's public
agencies from classifying "any individual by race, ethnicity, color or national
origin in the operation of public education, public contracting or public employment." Classification is defined as any "act of separating, sorting or organizing by race, ethnicity, color or national origin including, but not limited to,
inquiring, profiling, or collecting such data on government forms."

Shrewdly titled the Racial Privacy Initiative, it sounds like a plan to protect us from the manipulative purview of Big Brother, or perhaps an act to
prohibit police profiling or to protect medical records from being misused or
to prevent consumer credit and employment histories from being revealed in
ways that discriminate against minorities."Racial privacy" beguiles with the
promise of removing race and all its contentiousness from public view, keeping its secrets in a vault for only the rightful owner to know.A kind of "don't
ask, don't tell" stance of racial revelation.

In fact, the proposed enactment contains a series of crucial exceptions
that quickly turn such rosily "color-blind" expectations completely upside
down. First, in a blatant concession to Big Brother writ large, there is an exemption for police. Sociologists Troy Duster and Andy Barlow have worried
that this exemption will allow police alone to collect racial data:"What about
the concern of many citizens that police practices need to be monitored for
racial profiling? The racial privacy initiative would not allow such data to be
kept."

4   Similarly, while permitting racial and ethnic classification of "medical research subjects and patients," the initiative bars the collection of data for
population-based surveys that are the cornerstone of public health administra-
tion.And while there is a superficially charitable exemption for the Department of Fair Employment and Housing, that much of a given is rather severely
constrained in that the department "shall not impute a race, color, ethnicity or
national origin to any individual." In any event, this particular exemption "shall
expire ten years after the effective date of this measure." In fact, the Racial Privacy Initiative is not about protecting data from being misused; instead it effectively eliminates data collection at all. If enacted, it would continue a trend
begun by Ronald Reagan and pursued by every Republican administration
since: limiting the accountability of public institutions by making vital public
information unavailable. In such a world, there can be no easy way to know
whether Native American women are being sterilized at higher rates in public
hospitals than other groups. One would not be able to determine whether

public schools were tracking black students into remedial classes and white students into advanced placement. Documentation of ghettoization and other patterns of residential segregation would be magically wiped from census data.

With no impartial public archive of such data, the burden of compiling such statistics would fall either upon independent academics who would have to find funding for their studies on a project-by-project basis; or upon a cacophony of competing interest groups—a competition that no doubt will be more than skewed by better-funded conservative think tanks like the Manhattan Institute and the American Enterprise Institute.

Indeed, this initiative is not about "privacy" as most laypeople think of it. It is actually about privatizing racially based behavior. And privatized racism has been a dream of the far right since the first whites-only private schools sprang up in the wake of *Brown v. Board of Education*. Segregation is "private choice," a "social" problem, not a legal one, according to this logic. You can't force people to love you. Suing over discrimination is victimology. As long as the government doesn't force you to drink out of a separate water fountain or go to a separate school, then that is the limit of equal opportunity.

Eliminating official knowledge of race and ethnicity in the public sphere at first sounds like part of the same enterprise as eliminating Jim Crow laws. (Indeed, many California voters seem as confused about the meaning of the initiative as they were about Prop 209, which sounded to many as though it would lead to more inclusion rather than less.) In fact, however, "racial privacy" accomplishes little more than institutionalizing an official stance of denial and, in the process, eviscerates essential civil rights enforcement mechanisms. Californians may as well put those three little moral idiots, Hear-no-evil, See-no-evil and Speak-no-evil, in charge of remediation for discrimination. In what has been one of the most effective maneuvers of the right in recent years, defenders of the initiative have co-opted a good deal of the vocabulary of the civil rights community in a blizzard of definitional inversions. Ward Connerly insists that this measure will keep the state from "profiling" its citizens. If one accepts that to most Americans "profiling" connotes the unethical use of data to discriminate (as in Driving While Black), this conflation with the neutral act of data collection itself is tremendously misleading. By the same token, the name of Connerly's group, the American Civil Rights Coalition, would seem to imply a greater measure of protection for civil rights rather than lesser. I do worry that such studied reversals of terms will come to overtake the discourse as much as the term "quota" has displaced any public understanding of the actual meaning of affirmative action.

8   The publicly collected statistics we take for granted today show undisputed racial and ethnic disparities in every realm of American life. Any proposition that this gap is either not worth documenting—or, even more insidiously, is aggravated by the gathering of such knowledge—consigns us to a world in which "intelligence" is the exclusive preserve of unrestrained police surveillance. The collective ignorance with which we will be left will quite literally keep us from ever speaking truth to power.

PERSONAL RESPONSE

What is your view on the subject of same-sex or same-race schools?

QUESTIONS FOR DISCUSSION

1. Are you persuaded by the arguments that Williams makes against the initiative in California to prevent classifying on the basis of race, ethnicity, color, or national origin? For each of William's major points, explain whether you agree with her and why.
2. Explain each of the following references: Big Brother (paragraph 2), *Brown v. Board of Education* (paragraph 6), and Jim Crow laws (paragraph 7). If you are not familiar with these terms, do some research, and share your findings with the class.
3. Williams attacks Republicans and the far right in several places. Do you think that she is fair in the charges she makes against them? How would you counter her on those points?
4. Williams raises the issue of racial profiling and refers to the dangers of "unrestrained police surveillance" (paragraph 8). Comment on the implications of these practices.

Have We Lost Our Sense of Humor?
Gerald F. Kreyche

Gerald F. Kreyche, emeritus professor of philosophy at DePaul University in Chicago and American Thought Editor of USA Today Magazine, *is the author of two books:* Thirteen Thinkers—Plus: A Sample of Great Philosophers *(1984) and* Visions of the American West *(1989). This commentary appeared in the "Parting Thoughts" column of the May 1994 issue of* USA Today Magazine.

Philosophers claim that only humans are risible, meaning that we can laugh at a joke or a funny situation and appreciate the comical. In short, humor is a peculiarly human trait requiring insight and intelligence. Often, it gives us perspective and helps get us through crisis situations. Our tendency always is to get overly serious, and humor puts a helpful brake on this. It is a truism that the person who can laugh at himself has a firm grip on his world.

Seeming to acknowledge the importance of humor in our country, the U.S. Post Office put out a series of stamps honoring comedians such as Jack

Benny, Red Skelton, Sid Caesar, and even ventriloquist Edgar Bergen's dummy, Charlie McCarthy. Talk show hosts such as Jay Leno and David Letterman try to keep up the tradition. However, all is not well with humor in America.

Actress-comedienne Whoopi Goldberg recently charged that the nation is losing its sense of humor, as she was criticized for a "blackface" skit she wrote for Ted Danson, former star of "Cheers" and her boyfriend at the time. The occasion was a "roasting" of Goldberg at the Friars Club in New York. While it unquestionably was an example of poor taste, the resulting furor proved again that political correctness is making cowards of almost everyone.

4   People have become thin-skinned, touchy, overly sensitive—"underhumored," as one commentator put it. Foremost among those killing a sense of humor are the deadly serious feminists. The fact is that *they* just don't get it! Everyone is on edge today, ready to charge bias, a lack of respect, or harassment of some imagined type or another. Ethnic jokes used to abound, and the ethnic group itself enjoyed them more than anyone. Jews, for instance, delighted in telling jokes on and about themselves, usually connected with business, Jewish mothers, or one-upmanship. Now, anyone uttering a joke about Jews is deemed anti-Semitic.

For years, there have been a rash of so-called "Polish" jokes (in different parts of the country, other nationalities are the butt). For instance, Chicago is the largest Polish city outside of Warsaw. It seems that the Polish aldermen there were getting fed up with Polish jokes and decided to send an entourage to Washington to protest to Congress. They all got on a plane and landed in . . . Seattle! Now how can one take umbrage at that? Everyone knows that Poland has a rich intellectual and musical heritage, producing a Copernicus, a Chopin, a Pope John Paul II, and a Paderewski. Nevertheless, such jokes have become taboo, and the world is worse off for it.

It is interesting that jokes often seem to have national traits. Take the story of an Englishman, German, and Frenchman being put into a library and told to write about the elephant. After a while, the Englishman came out with a slim treatise, entitled *The Elephant and the Queen.* The Frenchman emerged with his book, *The Sex Life of the Elephant.* The German then revealed his *opus magnus* of six volumes, *Introduction to the Study on the Elephant.*

As a rule, English humor tends to be cryptic and clever. It is not so much what is said, but the *way* it is said that matters. For example: One Englishman was talking to another and mentioned, "I say, I passed your house last night." Replied the other, "Thank you." Again, one Englishman was visiting another in the latter's new home and declared, "I thought your house was bigger than it is." The reply came, "How could it be?" Obviously, these are intellectual in genre and require quick-wittedness.

8   Gallic humor shares the wittiness of English. Apocryphally, the story is told that, when Charles DeGaulle was preparing for his death, he visited the undertaker to make final arrangements. When asked what size mausoleum the famous general would desire to mark his resting place, DeGaulle shrugged his shoulders and replied, "None, Monsieur. After all, it will be for only three days."

A little laughter goes a long way in today's world. There are clever, often caustic, "one-liners" that also serve as "put-downs." Examples: He kept up his end of the conversation to the point of being perpendicular. Or, consider Mark Twain's remark: "He was a good man—in the worst sense of the term."

Surely "cornball" must be another category. Did you hear about the modern man who turned on the radio and thought he went blind? Or about the chameleon who landed on a Scotch plaid blanket and blew up? Then there were two doctors who made an incision into a patient's stomach. When a bunch of butterflies flew out, one surgeon said to the other, "What do you know? He was right!"

Animal jokes make up a very large category. A billy goat got loose in a Hollywood film studio and ate a reel of "Gone with the Wind." Another goat asked him how he liked it. Replied the first: "I thought the book was better." Then there was the farmer who mated a cow with an octopus. Asked what the result was, the farmer replied: "I don't know, but it is able to milk itself."

12   Many jokes revolve around a play on words. Punsters, such as Lou Rukeyser of "Wall Street Week," would appreciate the following: A contest between two southern debaters ended in a drawl. A male Christmas shopper was looking for a gift for his beloved and asked the saleswoman, "Do you have any notions?" "Yes," she answered, "but we're not allowed to express them during business hours." When a dinghy came to rescue two men who had fallen into the water, the rescuer said he only could pick up one at a time. He asked the one still in the water, "Can you float alone?" "Yes," was the response, "but this is no time to talk business!"

Although trite, the old adage still is true. "Laugh and the world laughs with you. Cry and you cry alone."

READER RESPONSE

What do you think people should do when they hear a joke they believe is offensive for whatever reason? What do you do in such situations, especially if no one but you seems to be bothered by it?

QUESTIONS FOR DISCUSSION

1. Explain whether you agree or disagree with Kreyche's observations that "political correctness is making cowards of almost everyone" (paragraph 3) and that "[p]eople have become thin-skinned, touchy, overly sensitive" (paragraph 4).
2. Do you think that the examples Kreyche gives adequately support his central purpose?
3. Discuss the question of how to distinguish between what is funny and what is in poor taste.

4. Share a joke you have heard about a particular group of people, and examine it in terms of the political correctness issue. Is the joke offensive?
Is it funny? Should you repeat the joke? What do you think is a tactful way
to handle a situation in which someone has told an offensive joke?

The Word Police
Michiko Kakutani

Michiko Kakutani, the leading daily book reviewer for The New
York Times, *won a Pulitzer Prize for Distinguished Criticism in
1998.* "The Word Police" *was first published in the January 31,
1993, issue of* The New York Times. *The reference to "this month's
inaugural festivities" that begins the essay is to the 1993 inauguration of President Clinton.*

 This month's inaugural festivities, with their celebration, in Maya Angelou's
words, of "humankind"—"the Asian, the Hispanic, the Jew/The African, the Native American, the Sioux,/The Catholic, the Muslim, the French, the Greek/The
Irish, the Rabbi, the Priest, the Sheik,/The Gay, the Straight, the Preacher,/The
privileged, the homeless, the Teacher"—constituted a kind of official embrace
of multiculturalism and a new politics of inclusion.

The mood of political correctness, however, has already made firm in-
roads into popular culture. Washington boasts a store called Politically Correct
that sells pro-whale, anti-meat, ban-the-bomb T-shirts, bumper stickers and buttons, as well as a local cable television show called "Politically Correct Cooking" that features interviews in the kitchen with representatives from groups
like People for the Ethical Treatment of Animals.

The Coppertone suntan lotion people are planning to give their long-
time cover girl, Little Miss (Ms?) Coppertone, a male equivalent, Little Mr. Coppertone. And even Superman (Superperson?) is rumored to be returning this
spring, reincarnated as four ethnically diverse clones: an African-American, an
Asian, a Caucasian and a Latino.

4   Nowhere is this P.C. mood more striking than in the increasingly noisy
debate over language that has moved from university campuses to the country at large—a development that both underscores Americans' puritanical zeal
for reform and their unwavering faith in the talismanic power of words.

Certainly no decent person can quarrel with the underlying impulse behind political correctness: a vision of a more just, inclusive society in which
racism, sexism and prejudice of all sorts have been erased. But the methods
and fervor of the self-appointed language police can lead to a rigid ortho-
doxy—and unintentional self-parody—opening the movement to the scorn of

conservative opponents and the mockery of cartoonists and late-night television hosts.

It's hard to imagine women earning points for political correctness by saying "ovarimony" instead of "testimony"—as one participant at the recent Modern Language Association convention was overhead to suggest. It's equally hard to imagine people wanting to flaunt their lack of prejudice by giving up such words and phrases as "bull market," "kaiser roll," "Lazy Susan," and "charley horse."

Several books on bias-free language have already appeared, and the 1991 edition of the Random House Webster's College Dictionary boasts an appendix titled "Avoiding Sexist Language." The dictionary also includes such linguistic mutations as "womyn" (women, "used as an alternative spelling to avoid the suggestion of sexism perceived in the sequence m-e-n") and "waitron" (a gender-blind term for waiter or waitress).

8   Many of these dictionaries and guides not only warn the reader against offensive racial and sexual slurs, but also try to establish and enforce a whole new set of usage rules. Take, for instance, "The Bias-Free Word Finder, a Dictionary of Nondiscriminatory Language" by Rosalie Maggio (Beacon Press)—a volume often indistinguishable, in its meticulous solemnity, from the tongue-in-cheek "Official Politically Correct Dictionary and Handbook" put out last year by Henry Beard and Christopher Cerf (Villard Books). Ms. Maggio's book supplies the reader intent on using kinder, gentler language with writing guidelines as well as a detailed listing of more than 5,000 "biased words and phrases."

Whom are these guidelines for? Somehow one has a tough time picturing them replacing "Fowler's Modern English Usage" in the classroom, or being adopted by the average man (sorry, individual) in the street.

The "pseudogeneric 'he,' " we learn from Ms. Maggio, is to be avoided like the plague, as is the use of the word "man" to refer to humanity. "Fellow," "king," "lord" and "master" are bad because they're "male-oriented words," and "king," "lord" and "master" are especially bad because they're also "hierarchical, dominator society terms." The politically correct lion becomes the "monarch of the jungle," new-age children play "someone on the top of the heap," and the "Mona Lisa" goes down in history as Leonardo's "acme of perfection."

As for the word "black," Ms. Maggio says it should be excised from terms with a negative spin: she recommends substituting words like "mouse" for "black eye," "ostracize" for "blackball," "payola" for "blackmail" and "outcast" for "black sheep." Clearly, some of these substitutions work better than others: somehow the "sinister humor" of Kurt Vonnegut or "Saturday Night Live" doesn't quite make it; nor does the "denouncing" of the Hollywood 10.

12   For the dedicated user of politically correct language, all these rules can make for some messy moral dilemmas. Whereas "battered wife" is a gender-biased term, the gender-free term "battered spouse," Ms. Maggio notes, incorrectly implies "that men and women are equally battered."

On one hand, say Francine Wattman Frank and Paula A. Treichler in their book "Language, Gender, and Professional Writing" (Modern Language

Association), "he or she" is an appropriate construction for talking about an individual (like a jockey, say) who belongs to a profession that's predominantly male—it's a way of emphasizing "that such occupations are not barred to women or that women's concerns need to be kept in mind." On the other hand, they add, using masculine pronouns rhetorically can underscore ongoing male dominance in those fields, implying the need for change.

And what about the speech codes adopted by some universities in recent years? Although they were designed to prohibit students from uttering sexist and racist slurs, they would extend, by logic, to blacks who want to use the word "nigger" to strip the term of its racist connotations, or homosexuals who want to use the word "queer" to reclaim it from bigots.

In her book, Ms. Maggio recommends applying bias-free usage retroactively: she suggests paraphrasing politically incorrect quotations, or replacing "the sexist words or phrases with ellipsis dots and/or bracketed substitutes," or using "sic" "to show that the sexist words come from the original quotation and to call attention to the fact that they are incorrect."

16   Which leads the skeptical reader of "The Bias-Free Word Finder" to wonder whether "All the King's Men" should be retitled "All the Ruler's People"; "Pet Sematary," "Animal Companion Graves"; "Birdman of Alcatraz," "Birdperson of Alcatraz"; and "The Iceman Cometh," "The Ice Route Driver Cometh"?

Will making such changes remove the prejudice in people's minds? Should we really spend time trying to come up with non-male-based alternatives to "Midas touch," "Achilles' heel," and "Montezuma's revenge"? Will tossing out Santa Claus—whom Ms. Maggio accuses of reinforcing "the cultural male-as-norm system"—in favor of Belfana, his Italian female alter ego, truly help banish sexism? Can the avoidance of "violent expressions and metaphors" like "kill two birds with one stone," "sock it to 'em" or "kick an idea around" actually promote a more harmonious world?

The point isn't that the excesses of the word police are comical. The point is that their intolerance (in the name of tolerance) has disturbing implications. In the first place, getting upset by phrases like "bullish on America" or "the City of Brotherly Love" tends to distract attention from the real problems of prejudice and injustice that exist in society at large, turning them into mere questions of semantics. Indeed, the emphasis currently put on politically correct usage has uncanny parallels with the academic movement of deconstruction—a method of textual analysis that focuses on language and linguistic pyrotechnics—which has become firmly established on university campuses.

In both cases, attention is focused on surfaces, on words and metaphors; in both cases, signs and symbols are accorded more importance than content. Hence, the attempt by some radical advocates to remove "The Adventures of Huckleberry Finn" from curriculums on the grounds that Twain's use of the word "nigger" makes the book a racist text—never mind the fact that this American classic (written in 1884) depicts the spiritual kinship achieved between a white boy and a runaway slave, never mind the fact that the "nigger" Jim emerges as the novel's most honorable, decent character.

20   Ironically enough, the P.C. movement's obsession with language is accompanied by a strange Orwellian willingness to warp the meaning of words by placing them under a high-powered ideological lens. For instance, the "Dictionary of Cautionary Words and Phrases"—a pamphlet issued by the University of Missouri's Multicultural Management Program to help turn "today's journalists into tomorrow's multicultural newsroom managers"—warns that using the word "articulate" to describe members of a minority group can suggest the opposite, "that 'those people' are not considered well educated, articulate and the like."

The pamphlet patronizes minority groups, by cautioning the reader against using the words "lazy" and "burly" to describe any member of such groups; and it issues a similar warning against using words like "gorgeous" and "petite" to describe women.

As euphemism proliferates with the rise of political correctness, there is a spread of the sort of sloppy, abstract language that Orwell said is "designed to make lies sound truthful and murder respectable, and to give an appearance of solidity to pure wind." "Fat" becomes "big boned" or "differently sized"; "stupid" becomes "exceptional"; "stoned" becomes "chemically inconvenienced."

Wait a minute here! Aren't such phrases eerily reminiscent of the euphemisms coined by the Government during Vietnam and Watergate? Remember how the military used to speak of "pacification," or how President Richard M. Nixon's press secretary, Ronald L. Ziegler, tried to get away with calling a lie an "inoperative statement"?

24   Calling the homeless "the underhoused" doesn't give them a place to live; calling the poor "the economically marginalized" doesn't help them pay the bills. Rather, by playing down their plight, such language might even make it easier to shrug off the seriousness of their situation.

Instead of allowing free discussion and debate to occur, many gung-ho advocates of politically correct language seem to think that simple suppression of a word or concept will magically make the problem disappear. In the "Bias-Free Word Finder," Ms. Maggio entreats the reader not to perpetuate the negative stereotype of Eve. "Be extremely cautious in referring to the biblical Eve," she writes; "this story has profoundly contributed to negative attitudes toward women throughout history, largely because of misogynistic and patriarchal interpretations that labeled her evil, inferior, and seductive."

The story of Bluebeard, the rake (whoops!—the libertine) who killed his seven wives, she says, is also to be avoided, as is the biblical story of Jezebel. Of Jesus Christ, Ms. Maggio writes: "There have been few individuals in history as completely androgynous as Christ, and it does his message a disservice to overinsist on his maleness." She doesn't give the reader any hints on how this might be accomplished; presumably, one is supposed to avoid describing him as the Son of God.

Of course the P.C. police aren't the only ones who want to proscribe what people should say or give them guidelines for how they may use an idea; Jesse Helms and his supporters are up to exactly the same thing when they propose to patrol the boundaries of the permissible in art. In each case, the would-be censor aspires to suppress what he or she finds distasteful—all, of course, in the name of the public good.

28   In the case of the politically correct, the prohibition of certain words, phrases and ideas is advanced in the cause of building a brave new world free of racism and hate, but this vision of harmony clashes with the very ideals of diversity and inclusion that the multicultural movement holds dear, and it's purchased at the cost of freedom of expression and freedom of speech.

In fact, the utopian world envisioned by the language police would be bought at the expense of the ideals of individualism and democracy articulated in the "The [sic] Gettysburg Address": "Four score and seven years ago our fathers brought forth on this continent, a new nation, conceived in Liberty and dedicated to the proposition that all men are created equal."

Of course, the P.C. police have already found Lincoln's words hopelessly "phallocentric." No doubt they would rewrite the passage: "Fourscore and seven years ago our foremothers and forefathers brought forth on this continent a new nation, formulated with liberty, and dedicated to the proposition that all humankind is created equal."

READER RESPONSE

With whom are you more sympathetic: those who advocate politically correct language or those who believe the P.C. movement carries its reform efforts too far?

QUESTIONS FOR DISCUSSION

1. Comment on Kakutani's statement that P.C. "both underscores Americans' puritanical zeal for reform and their unwavering faith in the talismanic power of words" (paragraph 4).

2. Do you agree with Kakutani's objections to the P.C. movement? What effect do you think she intends to achieve by calling proponents of political correctness "the word police"?

3. Select specific words that Kakutani uses as examples of unreasonable substitutions for offensive language suggested by Rosalie Maggio in her book *The Bias-Free Word Finder*. What is Kakutani's objection to the proposed alternatives? What does Maggio find unacceptable in the language for which she proposes substitutions? With whom are you more in agreement, Kakutani or Maggio?

4. Kakutani suggests that one problem with the P.C. movement is that it lends itself so easily to parody and even mockery. Bring to class both a book advocating changes, such as Maggio's *The Bias-Free Word Finder,* and a book that parodies political correctness, such as the *Official Politically Correct Dictionary and Handbook.* Read aloud selected passages from each. Do you and your classmates find the suggestions in the politically correct book to be reasonable? Do you find the parody to be funny?

Symbolic Arguments

William Raspberry

William Raspberry has been writing for The Washington Post
*since 1962. His commentaries on issues such as education,
crime, justice, and drug abuse appear in more than 200 newspapers. In 1994 he won the Pulitzer Prize for Distinguished
Commentary, and in the same year, the National Association of
Black Journalists gave him its Lifetime Achievement Award. Raspberry teaches at Duke University, serving in the Knight Chair in
Communications and Journalism. "Symbolic Arguments" appeared in the August 2, 1999, issue of* The Washington Post.

Confederate flags flying over state buildings, a city slating a picture of Robert
E. Lee for a place of honor and the chief justice of the United States leading
lawyers and judges in singing "Dixie." What the devil is going on?

A resurgence of racism, according to some civil rights activists. An innocent effort at honoring Southern tradition, says a second group. Ho-hum, says a
third.

For many black Americans, the Confederate flag, under which the seces-
sionist South marched into the war to preserve slavery, has become the symbolic equivalent of the "N word;" its meaning is uniform—and negative—no
matter how those who use it describe their intent. It evokes a refusal to accept the outcome of the Civil War (as surely as "Dixie" evokes white Southern
nostalgia for the good old days when black folk were happy slaves).

4   It is not a silly view. The Council of Conservative Citizens, which is
aligned with the pro-Confederate flag movement across the South, might be
thought of as the segregationist White Citizens Councils in a business suit.
Their pro-white positions are hardly distinguishable (save for the more gentle-
manly tone) from the posturing of the Ku Klux Klan.

And although some folk argue that the point of displaying the Stars and
Bars is culture and heritage—honor for forebears who fought bravely to defend principle, not just slavery—it is often a great deal more than that. Ask
black Alabama legislator Alvin Holmes who won a years-long fight to have the
Confederate battle flag removed from atop the state capitol—a site states traditionally reserve only for the U.S. flag and their own state flag.

In Georgia and Mississippi, the state flag incorporates the Confederate
flag, prompting a different sort of battle. But is it reasonable to suppose that
everyone who honors the flags of those two states also despises black folk
and longs for a return to slavery? Does anybody really imagine that Chief Justice William H. Rehnquist, who led a recent 4th Circuit Judicial Conference in
the singing of "Dixie," was signaling his support for the Confederacy and its
discredited ideals? Then what was signaled by the singing of "The Battle Hymn
of the Republic," which he also led?

Sometimes the symbols don't symbolize much of anything. But sometimes they do, and that's the source of the confusion. There was confusion to spare when Richmond, having created Canal Walk along the James River as a tourist attraction, decided to adorn the walk with a mural of Lee, the Confederate general and revered son of Virginia. Black Richmonders exploded, one of them offering this elegant summary: "If Lee had won, I'd still be a slave."

8   The portrait came down. But one wonders how much good that did—which is one of the reasons I hate these battles over symbolism. They can occupy your energies and your resources and still leave you with nothing worthwhile, even when you win. (A friend just reminded me of the jubilation of African Americans a while back when the Pennsylvania legislature passed a Martin Luther King Day amendment to a banking bill. "The main bill affected more black lives, and far more profoundly, than the King Day legislation," he said. "And there weren't two black members of the legislature who could tell you a damn thing about what was in the main bill.")

The dilemma, of course, is that you dare not ho-hum each of these battles as they crop up—even paranoiacs can have real enemies—yet you don't want to be a sucker for every slight, intended or not, that catches your eye. As people who have relied heavily on symbols, from King's Birthday to kente cloth, to assert our pride of heritage, we want to be chary of denying other people the right to their symbols—particularly when they may represent an attempt to retrieve some honor from defeat. What, in such cases, should our attitude be?

Maybe we should borrow the idea of the former U.S. Marine Commandant David M Shoup, who hated those leather-sheathed swagger sticks Marine officers used to carry as much as some of us despise the Stars and Bars. Instead of banning their use, however, Shoup simply announced that the officers could dispense with the swagger sticks—unless they felt a need for them.

READER RESPONSE

What is your opinion on the issue Raspberry addresses?

QUESTIONS FOR DISCUSSION

1. According to Raspberry, what are the implications of flying the Confederate flag, honoring Robert E. Lee, and singing "Dixie" (paragraph 1)? Where do you position yourself on the three possible responses Raspberry suggests in paragraph 2?

2. Summarize, in your own words, the dilemma Raspberry refers to in paragraph 9. How would you answer his question, "What, in such cases, should our attitude be?"

3. Discuss Raspberry's suggestion for how to handle this dilemma by first explaining what he means in the last paragraph and then commenting on its effectiveness as a solution.

The Lesson

Toni Cade Bambara

*Toni Cade Bambara (1939–1995) was born in New York City
and educated at Queens College and City College, New York, with
additional study of theater, mime, dance, film, and linguistics at
eight other institutions in Europe and America. She served as a
social investigator for New York City's Department of Welfare, a
recreation director in New York Metropolitan, a psychiatric hospital; and a program director at Colony House Community Center. In addition, she was an editor of anthologies of black
literature and a well-respected civil rights advocate. Her short
stories have been collected in* Gorilla My Love *(1970) and The
Sea Birds Are Still Alive (1977), and she has published two novels,*
The Salt Eaters *(1980) and If Blessing Comes (1987). "The Lesson"
is from* Gorilla, My Love.

Back in the days when everyone was old and stupid or young and foolish
and me and Sugar were the only ones just right, this lady moved on our block
with nappy hair and proper speech and no makeup. And quite naturally we
laughed at her, laughed the way we did at the junk man who went about his
business like he was some big-time president and his sorry-ass horse his secretary. And we kinda hated her too, hated the way we did the winos who clut-
tered up our parks and pissed on our handball walls and stank up our
hallways and stairs so you couldn't halfway play hide-and-seek without a goddamn gas mask. Miss Moore was her name. The only woman on the block with
no first name. And she was black as hell, cept for her feet, which were fish-
white and spooky. And she was always planning these boring-ass things for us
to do, us being my cousin, mostly, who lived on the block cause we all moved
North the same time and to the same apartment then spread out gradual to
breathe. And our parents would yank our heads into some kinda shape and
crisp up our clothes so we'd be presentable for travel with Miss Moore, who
always looked like she was going to church though she never did. Which is
just one of the things the grownups talked about when they talked behind
her back like a dog. But when she came calling with some sachet she'd sewed
up or some gingerbread she'd made or some book, why then they'd all be too
embarrassed to turn her down and we'd get handed over all spruced up. She'd
been to college and said it was only right that she should take responsibility
for the young ones' education, and she not even related by marriage or blood.
So they'd go for it. Specially Aunt Gretchen. She was the main gofer in the family. You got some ole dumb shit foolishness you want somebody to go for, you
send for Aunt Gretchen. She been screwed into the go-along for so long, it's a
blood-deep natural thing with her. Which is how she got saddled with me and

Sugar and Junior in the first place while our mothers were in a la-de-da apartment up the block having a good ole time.

So this one day Miss Moore rounds us all up at the mailbox and it's puredee hot and she's knockin herself out about arithmetic. And school suppose to let up in summer I heard, but she don't never let up. And the starch in my pinafore scratching the shit outta me and I'm really hating this nappy-head bitch and her goddamn college degree. I'd much rather go to the pool or to the show where it's cool. So me and Sugar leaning on the mailbox being surly, which is a Miss Moore word. And Flyboy checking out what everybody brought for lunch. And Fat Butt already wasting his peanut-butter-and-jelly sandwich like the pig he is. And Junebug punchin on Q.T.'s arm for potato chips. And Rosie Giraffe shifting from one hip to the other waiting for somebody to step on her foot or ask her if she from Georgia so she can kick ass, preferably Mercedes'. And Miss Moore asking us do we know what money is like we a bunch of retards. I mean real money, she say, like it's only poker chips or monopoly papers we lay on the grocer. So right away I'm tired of this and say so. And would much rather snatch Sugar and go to the Sunset and terrorize the West Indian kids and take their hair ribbons and their money too. And Miss Moore files that remark away for next week's lesson on brotherhood, I can tell. And finally I say we oughta get to the subway cause it's cooler an' besides we might meet some cute boys. Sugar done swiped her mama's lipstick, so we ready.

So we heading down the street and she's boring us silly about what things cost and what our parents make and how much goes for rent and how money ain't divided up right in this country. And then she gets to the part about we all poor and live in the slums which I don't feature. And I'm ready to speak on that, but she steps out in the street and hails two cabs just like that. Then she hustles half the crew in with her and hands me a five-dollar bill and tells me to calculate 10 percent tip for the driver. And we're off. Me and Sugar and Junebug and Flyboy hangin out the window and hollering to everybody, putting lipstick on each other cause Flyboy a faggot anyway, and making farts with our sweaty armpits. But I'm mostly trying to figure how to spend this money. But they are fascinated with the meter ticking and Junebug starts laying bets as to how much it'll read when Flyboy can't hold his breath no more. Then Sugar lays bets as to how much it'll be when we get there. So I'm stuck. Don't nobody want to go for my plan, which is to jump out at the next light and run off to the first bar-b-que we can find. Then the driver tells us to get the hell out cause we there already. And the meter reads eighty-five cents. And I'm stalling to figure out the tip and Sugar say give him a dime. And I decide he don't need it bad as I do, so later for him. But then he tries to take off with Junebug foot still in the door so we talk about his mama something ferocious. Then we check out that we on Fifth Avenue and everybody dressed up in stockings. One lady in a fur coat, hot as it is. White folks crazy.

4   "This is the place, " Miss Moore say, presenting it to us in the voice she uses at the museum. "Let's look in the windows before we go in."

"Can we steal?" Sugar asks very serious like she's getting the ground rules squared away before she plays. "I beg your pardon," say Miss Moore, and we fall out. So she leads us around the windows of the toy store and me and Sugar screamin, "This is mine, that's mine, I gotta have that, that was made for me, I was born for that," till Big Butt drowns us out.

"Hey, I'm goin to buy that there."

"That there? You don't even know what it is, stupid."

8   "I do so," he say punchin on Rosie Giraffe. "It's a microscope."

"Whatcha gonna do with a microscope, fool?"

"Look at things."

"Like what, Ronald?" ask Miss Moore. And Big Butt ain't got the first notion. So here go Miss Moore gabbing about the thousands of bacteria in a drop of water and the somethinorother in a speck of blood and the million and one living things in the air around us is invisible to the naked eye. And what she say that for? Junebug go to town on that "naked" and we rolling. Then Miss Moore ask what it cost. So we all jam into the window smudgin it up and the price tag say $300. So then she ask how long'd take for Big Butt and Junebug to save up their allowances. "Too long," I say. "Yeh," adds Sugar, "outgrown it by that time." And Miss Moore say no, you never outgrow learning instruments. "Why, even medical students and interns and," blah, blah, blah. And we ready to choke Big Butt for bringing it up in the first damn place.

12   "This here costs four hundred eighty dollars," say Rosie Giraffe. So we pile up all over her to see what she pointin out. My eyes tell me it's a chunk of glass cracked with something heavy, and different-color inks dripped into the splits, then the whole thing put into a oven or something. But for $480 it don't make sense.

"That's a paperweight made of semi-precious stones fused together under tremendous pressure," she explains slowly, with her hands doing the mining and all the factory work.

"So what's a paperweight?" asks Rosie Giraffe.

"To weigh paper with, dumbbell," say Flyboy, the wise man from the East.

16   "Not exactly," say Miss Moore, which is what she say when you warm or way off too. "It's to weigh paper down so it won't scatter and make your desk untidy. " So right away me and Sugar curtsy to each other and then to Mercedes who is more the tidy type.

"We don't keep paper on top of the desk in my class," say Junebug, figuring Miss Moore crazy or lyin one.

"At home, then," she say. "Don't you have a calendar and a pencil case and a blotter and a letter-opener on your desk at home where you do your homework?" And she know damn well what our homes look like cause she nosys around in them every chance she gets.

"I don't even have a desk," say Junebug. "Do we?"

20   "No. And I don't get no homework neither," says Big Butt.

"And I don't even have a home," say Flyboy like he do at school to keep the white folks off his back and sorry for him. Send this poor kid to camp posters, is his specialty.

"I do," says Mercedes. "I have a box of stationery on my desk and a picture of my cat. My godmother bought the stationery and the desk. There's a big rose on each sheet and the envelopes smell like roses."

"Who wants to know about your smelly-ass stationery," say Rosie Giraffe fore I can get my two cents in.

24   "It's important to have a work area all your own so that . . ."

"Will you look at this sailboat, please," say Flyboy, cuttin her off and pointin to the thing like it was his. So once again we tumble all over each other to gaze at this magnificent thing in the toy store which is just big enough to maybe sail two kittens across the pond if you strap them to the posts tight. We all start reciting the price tag like we in assembly. "Hand-crafted sailboat of fiberglass at one thousand one hundred ninety-five dollars."

"Unbelievable," I hear myself say and am really stunned. I read it again for myself just in case the group recitation put me in a trance. Same thing. For some reason this pisses me off. We look at Miss Moore and she lookin at us, waiting for I dunno what.

"Who'd pay all that when you can buy a sailboat set for a quarter at Pop's, a tube of glue for a dime, and a ball of string for eight cents? It must have a motor and a whole lot else besides," I say. "My sailboat cost me about fifty cents."

28   "But will it take water?" say Mercedes with her smart ass.

"Took mine to Alley Pond Park once," say Flyboy. "String broke. Lost it. Pity."

"Sailed mine in Central Park and it keeled over and sank. Had to ask my father for another dollar."

"And you got the strap," laugh Big Butt. "The jerk didn't even have a string on it. My old man wailed on his behind."

32   Little Q.T. was staring hard at the sailboat and you could see he wanted it bad. But he too little and somebody'd just take it from him. So what the hell. "This boat for kids, Miss Moore?"

"Parents silly to buy something like that just to get all broke up," say Rosie Giraffe.

"That much money it should last forever," I figure.

"My father'd buy it for me if I wanted it."

36   "Your father, my ass," say Rosie Giraffe getting a chance to finally push Mercedes.

"Must be rich people shop here," say Q.T.

"You are a very bright boy," say Flyboy. "What was your first clue?" And he rap him on the head with the back of his knuckles, since Q.T. the only one he could get away with. Though Q.T. liable to come up behind you years later and get his licks in when you half expect it.

"What I want to know is," I says to Miss Moore though I never talk to her, I wouldn't give the bitch that satisfaction, "is how much a real boat costs? I figure a thousand'd get you a yacht any day."

40   "Why don't you check that out," she says, "and report back to the group?" Which really pains my ass. If you gonna mess up a perfectly good swim day least you could do is have some answers. "Let's go in," she say like

she got something up her sleeve. Only she don't lead the way. So me and Sugar turn the corner to where the entrance is, but when we get there I kinda hang back. Not that I'm scared, what's there to be afraid of, just a toy store. But I feel funny, shame. But what I got to be shamed about? Got as much right to go in as anybody. But somehow I can't seem to get hold of the door, so I step away from Sugar to lead. But she hangs back too. And I look at her and she looks at me and this is ridiculous. I mean, damn, I have never ever been shy about doing nothing or going nowhere. But then Mercedes steps up and then Rosie Giraffe and Big Butt crowd in behind and shove, and next thing we all stuffed into the doorway with only Mercedes squeezing past us, smoothing out her jumper and walking right down the aisle. Then the rest of us tumble in like a glued-together jigsaw done all wrong. And people lookin at us. And it's like the time me and Sugar crashed into the Catholic church on a dare. But once we got in there and everything so hushed and holy and the candles and the bowin and the handkerchiefs on all the drooping heads, I just couldn't go through with the plan. Which was for me to run up to the altar and do a tap dance while Sugar played the nose flute and messed around in the holy water. And Sugar kept givin me the elbow. Then later teased me so bad I tied her up in the shower and turned it on and locked her in. And she'd be there till this day if Aunt Gretchen hadn't finally figured I was lyin about the boarder takin a shower.

Same thing in the store. We all walkin on tiptoe and hardly touchin the games and puzzles and things. And I watched Miss Moore who is steady watchin us like she waitin for a sign. Like Mama Drewery watches the sky and sniffs the air and takes note of just how much slant is in the bird formation. Then me and Sugar bump smack into each other, so busy gazing at the toys, 'specially the sailboat. But we don't laugh and go into our fat-lady bump-stomach routine. We just stare at that price tag. Then Sugar run a finger over the whole boat. And I'm jealous and want to hit her. Maybe not her, but I sure want to punch somebody in the mouth.

"Watcha bring us here for, Miss Moore?"

"You sound angry, Sylvia. Are you mad about something?" Givin me one of them grins like she tellin a grown-up joke that never turns out to be funny. And she's lookin very closely at me like maybe she plannin to do my portrait from memory. I'm mad, but I won't give her that satisfaction. So I slouch around the store bein very bored and say, "Let's go."

44   Me and Sugar at the back of the train watchin the tracks whizzin by large then small then gettin gobbled up in the dark. I'm thinkin about this tricky toy I saw in the store. A clown that somersaults on a bar then does chin-ups just cause you yank lightly at his leg. Cost $35. I could see me askin my mother for a $35 birthday clown. "You wanna who that costs what?" she'd say, cocking her head to the side to get a better view of the hole in my head. Thirty-five dollars could buy new bunk beds for Junior and Gretchen's boy. Thirty-five dollars and the whole household could go visit Grand-daddy Nelson in the country. Thirty-five dollars would pay for the rent and the piano bill

too. Who are these people that spend that much for performing clowns and $1000 for toy sailboats? What kinda work they do and how they live and how come we ain't in on it? Where we are is who we are, Miss Moore always pointin out. But it don't necessarily have to be that way, she always adds then waits for somebody to say that poor people have to wake up and demand their share of the pie and don't none of us know what kind of pie she talking about in the first damn place. But she ain't so smart cause I still got her four dollars from the taxi and she sure ain't gettin it. Messin up my day with this shit. Sugar nudges me in my pocket and winks.

Miss Moore lines us up in front of the mailbox where we started from, seem like years ago, and I got a headache for thinkin so hard. And we lean all over each other so we can hold up under the draggy ass lecture she always finishes us off with at the end before we thank her for borin us to tears. But she just looks at us like she readin tea leaves. Finally she say, "Well, what did you think of F.A.O. Schwarz?"

Rosie Giraffe mumbles, "White folks crazy."

"I'd like to go there again when I get my birthday money," says Mercedes, and we shove her out the pack so she has to lean on the mailbox by herself.

48 "I'd like a shower. Tiring day," say Flyboy.

Then Sugar surprises me by sayin, "You know, Miss Moore, I don't think all of us here put together eat in a year what that sailboat costs." And Miss Moore lights up like somebody goosed her. "And?" she say, urging Sugar on. Only I'm standin on her foot so she don't continue.

"Imagine for a minute what kind of society it is in which some people can spend on a toy what it would cost to feed a family of six or seven. What do you think?"

"I think," say Sugar pushing me off her feet like she never done before cause I whip her ass in a minute, "that this is not much of a democracy if you ask me. Equal chance to pursue happiness means an equal crack at the dough, don't it?" Miss Moore is besides herself and I am disgusted with Sugar's treachery. So I stand on her foot one more time to see if she'll shove me. She shuts up, and Miss Moore looks at me, sorrowfully I'm thinkin. And somethin weird is goin on, I can feel it in my chest.

52 "Anybody else learn anything today?" lookin dead at me. I walk away and Sugar has to run to catch up and don't even seem to notice when I shrug her arm off my shoulder.

"Well, we got four dollars anyway," she says.

"Uh hun."

"We could go to Hascombs and get half a chocolate layer and then go to the Sunset and still have plenty money for potato chips and ice cream sodas."

56 "Uh hun."

"Race you to Hascombs," she say.

We start down the block and she gets ahead which is O.K. by me cause I'm going to the West End and then over to the Drive to think this day through. She can run if she want to and even run faster. But ain't nobody gonna beat me at nuthin.

PERSONAL RESPONSE

What is your response to Sylvia's language? Does her language influence the way you view her?

QUESTIONS FOR DISCUSSION

1. What does her very first sentence reveal about Sylvia's character? What does her running commentary on Miss Moore, their field trip, and the other children indicate about her? What do you think of the behavior of the rest of the children?
2. What is the lesson that Miss Moore wants to teach the children? Do the children learn what she wants them to? Could she have taught them the same lesson without taking them to the toy store? Discuss the character of Miss Moore. What difference does it make that she is not from the neighborhood? How do you think she views the children, their parents, and the neighborhood?
3. Sylvia's gets increasingly angry from the moment the children enter the toy store. What is she angry about?
4. What, if anything, does Sylvia learn? What does she mean by her concluding statement, "Ain't nobody gonna beat me at nuthin"?
5. What comments does the story make about economic inequities? To what extent is race a factor in such inequities?

ADDITIONAL SUGGESTIONS FOR WRITING ABOUT PREJUDICE AND DISCRIMINATION

1. Apply Michel Wieviorka's analysis in "The Ruses of Racism" of the identity-related causes of racial violence to a specific area of the world now in conflict over racial or ethnic issues.
2. Referring to Michel Wieviorka's "The Ruses of Racism" when relevant, explain your own theory about the conditions that encourage the growth of racial violence in America.
3. Narrate your first experience with prejudice, discrimination, or bigotry, either as witness to or victim of it. Describe in detail the incident and how it made you feel.
4. If you have been the victim of prejudice for any reason—your sex, your

class, your race, your status as a student, your difference form others around you—describe that experience.

5. Drawing on Stephen Steinberg's "The Affirmative Action Debate," argue your position on the subject of affirmative action in education or employment.

6. Argue your position on the proposition that funding and facilities for men's and women's college sports should be equal.

7. Argue your position on the subject of same-sex or same-race schools.

8. Show the effects of one kind of prejudice—racial, religious, sexual, or the like—on a person or a group of people you are familiar with.

9. With Stephen Steinberg's "The Affirmative Action Debate" in mind, analyze a specific aspect of the system of apartheid: what the system is, how it benefits those in power, what its effect is on those oppressed by it, how those in power maintain it, or what is being done now to end it.

10. Patricia J. Williams, in "Racial Privacy," refers to "civil rights enforcement mechanisms" and "remediation for discrimination" (paragraph 7). Write an essay in which you suggest ways that civil rights can best be enforced or offer ways that remediation for discrimination can best be achieved.

11. Patricia J. Williams, in "Racial Privacy," says that "publicly collected statistics . . . show undisputed racial and ethnic disparities in every realm of American life" (paragraph 8). Write an essay in which you provide examples that either support or refute that statement.

12. Find out more about the Racial Privacy Initiative that Patricia J. Williams writes about in "Racial Privacy," or learn about similar initiatives in other states. Then write a paper arguing your position on the merits of the initiative.

13. Argue for or against the statement that racial profiling is sometimes necessary.

14. Drawing on the selections in this chapter, explore whether racial or sexual discrimination is a thing of the past. Consider interviewing people who lived through the 1950s, 1960s, and 1970s about what they remember of segregation, the civil rights movement, or the women's liberation movement.

15. Michiko Kakutani, in "The Word Police," writes that "the utopian world envisioned by the language police would be bought at the expense of the ideals of individualism and democracy articulated in the 'The [sic] Gettysburg Address.'" Explain in detail what Kakutani means by that statement and your reasons for agreeing or disagreeing with her.

16. What impact has the political correctness movement had on American culture? Is the movement still active, or has it passed its prime?

17. Argue your position on the issue William Raspberry comments on in "Symbolic Arguments." You might want to consider it a First Amendment issue, for instance. Should there be limits on what people can publicly display as symbols of their cultural heritage if such displays can be construed as insulting or demeaning to other people? Where would you

draw the line, if at all, between what is allowable under the First Amendment and what is socially intolerable?

18. Write an essay explaining what aspects of American culture reinforce or even perpetuate stereotypes.

19. Argue in support of or against the proposition that civil protest or rebellion against authority is sometimes warranted.

10

TERRORISM, WAR, AND VIOLENCE

Since the terrorist attacks on New York and Washington, D.C., and the tragically thwarted attempt near Pittsburgh on September 11, 2001, the United States has been engaged in a war on terrorism. While the United States had been the target of other terrorist attacks both at home and abroad, this one was by far the largest in terms of the people killed and injured, the property damaged, and the lives affected. Retaliation for these particular attacks became imperative, but beyond that, many organizations have been actively working to eliminate terrorism worldwide. The selections in this chapter focus on selected aspects of terrorism, war, and violence.

First is Benjamin Netanyahu's "Three Key Principles in the War Against Terrorism," which identifies what he sees as three effective strategies adopted by the United States for defeating terrorism. As an expert on terrorism, Netanyahu speaks from long experience. He offers a reasoned and thoughtful analysis of how the United States can win the War on Terrorism.

Next, Dorothy E. Denning's "Is Cyber Terror Next?" explores the possibility of cyber terrorism as a potential tactic of terrorist groups. She wonders if "terrorists specifically trained in cyber methods [will] conduct future operations using nothing more than a keyboard and mouse? And if they do, will their cyber bombs target critical infrastructures or cause death and destruction comparable to that from physical weapons? Or, will they use cyber terrorism as an ancillary tool to amplify the impact of a physical attack, for example, by jamming 911 services or shutting down electricity or telecommunications after blowing up a building or releasing toxic gases?"

Shifting focus, Ellen Goodman, in her opinion piece "War Culture," insists that, when trying to explain violence such as the Columbine High School shooting in 1999, we must take into consideration this country's attitude toward war. "To have a discussion about violence without talking about war is like talking about war without talking about death," Goodman argues. The terrorist attacks on September 11, 2001, affected the lives of countless numbers of people, not the least of which are children who suddenly had to learn a new vocabulary and to cope with previously unimagined realities. Joan Vennochi takes as her subject in "Parenting Post-9/11" the tough issue of just how frank to be with children when trying to explain evil and the changes brought about by heinous crimes against humanity.

Also presented is an excerpt from Martin Luther King, Jr.'s 1958 book *Stride Toward Freedom*. In "Pilgrimage to Nonviolence," King defines his concept of nonviolent resistance, a strategy he advocated for resisting oppression and gaining true equality. As you read, consider how effective you believe this strategy to be and whether you think King's philosophy is appropriate as a response to today's social problems.

The chapter concludes with Charles Johnson's short story "Menagerie, A Child's Fable," an allegory about mankind's ignorance and intolerance. When a pet-shop owner leaves his animals alone for days, Berkeley, the guard dog, is forced to take control. For a while all goes well, but when the monkey convinces Berkeley to open a few of the cages, chaos ensues. As you read the story, think about the behavior of the different animals in terms of human interaction, especially in the way that individuals, groups, and nations deal with conflict. Is it inevitable that humans will always resort to violence and war to settle their differences?

1. Describe your feelings when you learned of the September 11, 2001, terror-ist attacks.
2. Explain how you think these terrorist attacks have changed America.
3. How, if at all, have the terrorist attacks changed you personally?
4. Explain your observations of the effects of the terrorist attacks on a child or children you know.

Three Key Principles in the War Against Terrorism

Benjamin Netanyahu

Benjamin Netanyahu grew up in Jerusalem but went to high school and college in the United States. He served as Israel's Ambassador to the United Nations from 1986 through 1988, and in 1996 he was elected Prime Minister of Israel. He is author of Terrorism: How the West Can Win *(1986),* A Place Among the Nations *(1992), and* Fighting Terrorism: How Democracies Can Defeat Domestic and International Terrorism *(1995). The following abridgment of a speech he delivered at a Hillsdale College seminar in March 2002 was published in the June 2002 issue of* Imprimis.

The United States is well on its way to winning the war against terrorism because the United States, under President Bush, has espoused three clear principles.

The first principle is moral clarity. President Bush said in his remarkable speech right after September 11 that there are no good terrorists, only bad terrorists—that terrorism is always evil. In saying this, he was saying that nothing justifies terrorism. It is important to state this point clearly and to elaborate on it, because the main weapon that terrorists use against the West is not bombs or guns, but moral obfuscation:"You're terrorists, because you kill civilians, too. America, Britain, Israel—all are terrorist states." We must harden ourselves against this amoral and debilitating charge.

Terrorism is not defined by the identify of its perpetrator. Nor is it defined by the cause, real or imagined, that its perpetrators espouse. Terrorism is defined by one thing and one thing alone. It is defined by the nature of the act. Terrorists systematically and deliberately attack the innocent. That is a very different thing from the unintentional civilian casualties that often accompany legitimate acts of war.

4   For example, in 1944 the British Air Force set out to bomb the Gestapo headquarters in Copenhagen. The British pilots missed, and instead of hitting the Gestapo they hit a hospital and killed 83 children and four nuns. That was not terrorism. That did not make Britain a terrorist state. That was a terrible but unintentional accident of the kind that accompanies every war. But terrorists don't *accidentally* kill civilians. The deaths of innocents are not an unintentional byproduct of their strategy. Terrorists deliberately target the innocent. They intentionally cross the lines that define the conventions of war that have been developed, in accordance with basic morality, to try to limit and regulate conflict. They willfully try to kill as many innocent civilians as they can. And this is never justified, regardless of the cause.

Going back to World War II, consider this hypothetical: You're an American officer. You're fighting for the most just cause in history. But you come

into a German village—maybe even a village next to a concentration camp—
and you line up the women and children in that village and kill them with a
machine gun. You have committed an act of terrorism. You have committed a
war crime and you will be judged guilty and executed, and properly so. Not
even the most just cause can justify terrorism. It is always illegitimate, always
criminal.

Allow me to add one other observation—I think an important one—on
this point. It is not merely that the goals of terrorists do not justify their
means. In addition, the means that terrorists use tell us something about their
real goals. We can see this very simply by looking at what happens when terrorists come to power. They don't establish free societies. They don't establish
governments that respect human rights. They establish dictatorships that tram-
ple human rights. It's the same whether we look at Cuba or at Iran or at Libya
or at Afghanistan under the Taliban. Terrorist movements may talk about fighting for democracy and freedom, but if they're in the business of terror, you
can bet they plan, when they come to power, to grind human rights into the
dust.

So again, terrorism is always criminal, whether practiced by Israel, America, or the Palestinian Authority. The deliberate and systematic assault on innocents is evil. Nor do ratios count. In Afghanistan, when the final tally is over,
America will probably have killed a lot more Afghans than the number of
Americans slaughtered in New York and Washington. But that doesn't make
the Taliban cause just, or America's cause unjust.

8   I think the United States is not and will not be cowed by arguments that
try to delegitimize its war against terrorism—arguments that equate terrorism
with the unintentional killing of civilians. That's what I mean when I say that
President Bush and the American people have moral clarity.

STRATEGIC CLARITY

This brings us to the second principle—strategic clarity. I think the United
States understands that fighting terrorism doesn't really mean fighting the terrorists. Of course it is necessary and right to go after them. But they are not
really the most important target. If you want to fight terrorism—and I've been
saying this for over two decades—you don't go out looking for the needle in
the haystack. You go after the haystack.

To use a different analogy, if you have kamikaze pilots coming at you,
you can shoot down a kamikaze pilot here and there. You can even go after
their squadron leader. But you will still have kamikazes coming in. The only
way that you can stop the attacks from continuing is to go after the aircraft
carrier that is their base. Likewise, if you want to stop terrorism, you have got
to go after the regimes that stand behind the terrorists. You have to understand that the terrorists are not floating up in space. They have to take off
from a certain place and go back to it. They have to have a location to hatch
their grisly plots, and to equip and train themselves. That haven is always the
territory of a sovereign state. If you take away the support of that sovereign

state, the whole scaffolding of international terrorism will collapse into the dust.

That's exactly what the United States is doing now. It went after the Taliban and Al Qaeda began to crumble. There are remnants in Afghanistan. There is perhaps even a residual terrorist capacity. But when the roots are cut off, the grapes left on the vine wither and die. And this is fairly easy to do, because the whole terror network consists of a half-dozen states with about two dozen terrorist organizations affiliated with them—sometimes working directly for them. If you take care of those states, the rest is easy. And there are only two things you can do with terror-sponsoring states: deter them or dismantle them. That means giving them a choice. This choice was well articulated by the British Prime Minister, speaking to the Taliban: "Surrender terrorism, or surrender power." They didn't surrender terrorism, and out they went. There is no third choice.

12   I think the United States is well on its way to handling two other terrorist regimes. One is practicing terrorism this very moment, inciting radicalism and terror and militancy from the Philippines to Los Angeles. I'm talking about Iran. But the first target will be Saddam Hussein in Iraq. Both of these regimes, if unattended, will succeed—fairly rapidly—in the programs they have launched to develop atomic weapons. And once they possess atomic weapons, these two foundations of the terror network could threaten the world and our civilization with a terror that we cannot even imagine today.

President Bush is absolutely right in boldly naming these two countries and going after them—or in the case of Iran, perhaps, waiting for the implosion of its regime after the collapse of Saddam Hussein. So in addition to the moral clarity to identify all terrorism as illegitimate, the United States is demonstrating strategic clarity in moving to root out the terror-supporting regimes.

IMPERATIVE FOR VICTORY

Which brings me to the third principle: the imperative for victory. And when I say this, I don't just mean that the United States wants to win. That's obvious. I mean that the United States understands that the only way to defeat terrorism is actually to defeat it. That sounds redundant, but it isn't. There is a very powerful view today, after all—held even by some former Presidents—that says the root cause of terrorism is the deprivation of national rights or civil rights. This deprivation, according to this view, is what's driving terrorism—which is, of course, what the terrorists themselves say. Anyone who knows modern history, however, can enumerate several hundred battles, struggles, conflicts, and wars that were aimed at the achievement of national liberation, independence, or equal and civil rights, and that did not employ terror. Indeed, one has to look very hard to find the use of terrorism in these conflicts.

For example, if we ask what is the worse occupation in history—the very worst—I think most of us would agree that it was the Nazi occupation of

Europe. Yet when we look, we're hard pressed to find one example of, say, the French Resistance using terrorism. They had plenty of opportunities, but they never once targeted the wives and children of French collaborators, or even the wives or children of German officers stationed in France. Why didn't they? Because they weren't terrorists. They were democrats. Or take an example closer to home: the struggle of blacks for civil equality in the United States during the 1950s and early 1960s. That struggle never employed terror either, because it also proceeded from a democratic mind-set.

16   The only way to persuade people to obliterate buses full of children, or buildings, or cities—the only way to persuade people to abandon the moral constraints that govern human action, even in war—is to inculcate in their minds the idea that there is a cause higher or more important than morality. That cause could be racial. It could be religious. It could be ethnic. It could be social. But whatever it is, it must be *total* if it is going to allow people to circumvent morality even to the point of intentionally blowing up children. That kind of thinking proceeds not from a democratic, but from a totalitarian mind-set. That's why, from its inception, terrorism has been wedded to totalitarianism. From Lenin to Stalin to Hitler, down to the Ayatollahs, terrorism is bred by totalitarianism. It requires a machine that inculcates hatred from childhood, grinding it into peoples' minds and hearts until they are willing even to blow themselves up for the purpose of murdering innocents.

So the root cause of the kind of systemic terrorism we confront today is totalitarianism, and in order to defeat totalitarianism we have to defeat the totalitarian regimes. That was accomplished through war in the case of Nazi Germany. In the case of the Soviet Union, Ronald Reagan won bloodlessly in the end. But he won. Victory over Nazism and communism were imperative for freedom. And in the case of militant Islamic terrorism, the same spirit is required.

Of course, the United States and its allies are often told that if they fight this war, they'll get hundreds of millions of people angry at them. For instance, many said that if America bombed Afghanistan during Ramadan, tens of thousands of Islamic activists would stream into Afghanistan to help the Taliban. Wrong. The United States bombed Afghanistan during Ramadan, but people who oppose America are streaming *out* of Afghanistan, not in. And what about all the governments in the area? Are they attacking the United States or are they trying to line up with it? They are trying to line up, because victory breeds victory and defeat breeds defeat. Insofar as the war against terrorism is victorious, it will compress the forces of Islamic militancy and terrorism and make it harder for them to draw recruits.

ANTIDOTE: FREEDOM

With these three principles—moral clarity, strategic clarity and the imperative for victory—the defeat of terrorism is not as distant as many people think. Beyond that, if I had to point to the one thing that is needed in the Arab and

Muslim world to ensure that the next century will be better than the last—for them and for us—it would be to promote democracy, a free press, debate and dissent. In the end, the only antidote to terrorism is the antidote to totalitarianism. It is freedom. It is what the American flag represents to me and to billions in the world. It is the key to securing not merely peace of mind, but peace between peoples.

20   This peace is within our power. Now we must show that it is within our will.

PERSONAL RESPONSE

Netanyahu says that "the defeat of terrorism is not as distant as many people think" (paragraph 19). What is your view on this point? Do you feel confident that terrorism will be defeated soon? Why, or why not?

QUESTIONS FOR DISCUSSION

1. To what extent do you agree with Netanyahu's definition of terrorism in his opening paragraphs? Would you add anything to that definition?
2. Netanyahu says that "nothing justifies terrorism" (paragraph 2). Do you agree with him? Explain your answer.
3. Where do you position yourself on Netanyahu's second point, that it is necessary "to root out the terror-supporting regimes" (paragraph 13)? Do you agree with him completely? Why, or why not?
4. In his discussion of the third principle, Netanyahu notes "[t]here is a very powerful view today . . . that says the root cause of terrorism is the deprivation of national rights or civil rights" (paragraph 14). To what extent do you agree with that position? What do you think of the reason Netanyahu offers as the root cause?

Is Cyber Terror Next?
Dorothy E. Denning

Dorothy E. Denning is the Patricia and Patrick Callahan Family Professor of Computer Science at Georgetown University and Director of the Georgetown Institute for Information Assurance. Her current work encompasses the areas of cyber crime and cyber terrorism, information warfare and security, and cryptography. She has published 120 articles and four books, her most recent being Information Warfare and Security *(1998). She has*

testified before the U.S. Congress on encryption policy and cyber
terrorism and has served in leadership and advisory positions
with government agencies and private-sector organizations. In
November 2001, she was named a Time *magazine innovator.*
This essay appeared in November 2001 on the Social Science Re-
search Center website's special initiatives archives, "After Sept.
11," and in slightly revised form in the book Understanding September 11 *(2002).*

Shortly after the September 11 terrorist attack against the United States,
hackers took to the Internet to voice their rage. A group called the Dispatch-
ers announced they would destroy Web servers and Internet access in
Afghanistan and target nations that support terrorists. Led by a 21-year-old security worker "Hackah Jak" from Ohio, the group of 60 people worldwide defaced hundreds of Web sites and launched denial of service attacks against
such targets as the Iranian Ministry of Interior, the Presidential Palace of
Afghanistan, and Palestinian ISPs. Another group, called Young Intelligent Hackers Against Terror (YIHAT), claimed they penetrated the systems of two Arabic
banks with ties to Osama bin Laden, although officials from the banks denied
any security breaches occurred. The group, whose stated mission is to stop
the money sources of terrorism, issued a plea on their Web site for corporations to make their networks available to group members for the purpose of
providing the "electronic equivalent to terrorist training camps." Later, they
took down their public Web site, apparently in response to attacks from other
hackers.

One group of Muslim hackers attacking the YIHAT site said they stood
by bin Laden, even as they condemned the attacks of September 11. "Osama
bin Laden is a holy fighter, and whatever he says makes sense," GForce Pakistan wrote on a Web site it defaced. The modified Web page warned that the
group planned to hit major US military and British Web sites and proclaimed
an "Al-Qaeda Alliance Online." Another GForce defacement contained similar
messages along with images of badly mutilated children who had been killed
by Israeli soldiers.

The cyber attacks arising from the events of September 11 reflect a
growing use of the Internet as a digital battleground. It is not at all unusual for
a regional conflict to have a cyber dimension, where the battles are fought by
self-appointed hackers operating under their own rules of engagement. A rash
of cyber attacks have accompanied the conflict between Israel and the Pales-
tinians, the conflict over Kashmir, and the Kosovo conflict, among others. According to iDefense, over 40 hackers from 23 countries participated in the
Israeli-Palestenian cyber conflict during the period October 2000, when the
cyber battles erupted, to January 2001. They also reported that two of the pro-
Palestinian attackers had connections to terrorist organizations. One of these
was UNITY, a Muslim extremist group with ties to Hezbollah. The hackers

launched a coordinated, multi-phased denial of service attack, first against official Israeli government sites, second against Israeli financial sites, third against Israeli ISPs, and fourth, against "Zionist E-Commerce" sites. The other group, al-Muhajiroun, was said to have ties with a number of Muslim terrorist organizations as well as bin Laden. The London-based group directed their members to a Web page, where at the click of a mouse members could join an automated flooding attack against Israeli sites.

4   Cyber protests have emerged in a climate where computer network attacks have become a serious and growing threat. The Computer Emergency Response Team Coordination Center (CERT/CC), for example, reported 2,134 incidents in 1997. This number rose to 21,756 in 2000 and to almost 35,000 during the first three quarters of 2001 alone. Considering that many, perhaps most, incidents are never reported to CERT/CC or indeed to any third party, the numbers become even more significant. Further, each incident that is reported corresponds to an attack that can involve thousands of victims. The Code Red worm, which infected about a million servers in July and August and caused $2.6 billion in damages, was a single incident.

The rise in computer-based attacks can be attributed to several factors, including general growth of the Internet, with corresponding increase in the number of potential attackers and targets; a never-ending supply of vulnerabilities that, once discovered, are quickly exploited; and increasingly sophisticated hacking tools that allow even those with modest skills to launch devastating attacks. The tools used to launch massive denial of service assaults, for example, have advanced command and control capabilities. The attacker runs client software to direct and coordinate the actions of server software running on potentially thousands of previously compromised "zombie" computers. Computer worms like Code Red can be used to find potential zombies and automatically install the attack software.

Although cyber attacks have caused billions of dollars in damage and affected the lives of millions, few if any can be characterized as acts of terrorism: fraud, theft, sabotage, vandalism, and extortion—yes, but terrorism—no. Their effect, while serious and not to be taken lightly, pales in comparison to the horror we witnessed on September 11.

But is cyber terrorism coming? Given that at least some hackers sympathetic to bin Laden are engaging in cyber protests, will they or terrorists specifically trained in cyber methods conduct future operations using nothing more than a keyboard and mouse? And if they do, will their cyber bombs target critical infrastructures or cause death and destruction comparable to that from physical weapons? Or, will they use cyber terrorism as an ancillary tool to amplify the impact of a physical attack, for example, by jamming 911 services or shutting down electricity or telecommunications after blowing up a building or releasing toxic gases?

8   Before addressing these questions, it is important to understand what is meant by cyber terrorism. The term is generally understood to mean a

computer-based attack or threat of attack intended to intimidate or coerce governments or societies in pursuit of goals that are political, religious, or ideological. The attack should be sufficiently destructive or disruptive to generate fear comparable to that from physical acts of terrorism. Attacks that lead to death or bodily injury, extended power outages, plane crashes, water contamination, or major economic losses would be examples. Depending on their impact, attacks against critical infrastructures such as electric power or emergency services could be acts of cyber terrorism. Attacks that disrupt nonessential services or that are mainly a costly nuisance would not.

To assess the potential threat of cyber terrorism, two factors must be considered: first, whether there are targets that are vulnerable to attack that could lead to severe harm, and second, whether there are actors with the capability and motivation to carry them out.

Looking first at vulnerabilities, several studies have shown that critical infrastructures are potentially vulnerable to a cyber terrorist attack. This is not surprising, because systems are complex, making it effectively impossible to eliminate all weaknesses. New vulnerabilities are continually uncovered, and systems are configured or used in ways that make them open to attack. Even if the technology is adequately hardened, insiders, acting alone or in concert with other terrorists, may be able to exploit their access capabilities to wreak considerable harm.

Consultants and contractors are frequently in a position where they could cause grave harm. In March 2000, Japan's Metropolitan Police Department reported that a software system they had procured to track 150 police vehicles, including unmarked cars, had been developed by the Aum Shinryko cult, the same group that gassed the Tokyo subway in 1995, killing 12 people and injuring 6,000 more. At the time of the discovery, the cult had received classified tracking data on 115 vehicles. Further, the cult had developed software for at least 80 Japanese firms and 10 government agencies. They had worked as subcontractors to other firms, making it almost impossible for the organizations to know who was developing the software. As subcontractors, the cult could have installed Trojan horses to launch or facilitate cyber terrorist attacks at a later date.

12   If we take as given that critical infrastructures are vulnerable to a cyber terrorist attack, then the question becomes whether there are actors with the capability and motivation to carry out such an operation. While many hackers have the knowledge, skills, and tools to attack computer systems, they generally lack the motivation to cause violence or severe economic or social harm. Conversely, terrorists who are motivated to cause violence seem to lack the capability to cause that degree of damage in cyberspace. The methods of cyber terrorism are not, to the best of my knowledge, taught in the terrorist training camps of Afghanistan.

In August 1999, the Center for the Study of Terrorism and Irregular Warfare at the Naval Postgraduate School (NPS) in Monterey, California, issued a report entitled "Cyberterror: Prospects and Implications." Their objective was to assess the prospects of terrorist organizations pursuing cyber terrorism. They concluded that the barrier to entry for anything beyond annoying hacks is quite high and that terrorists generally lack the wherewithal and human capital needed to mount a meaningful operation. Cyber terrorism, they argued, was a thing of the future, although it might be pursued as an ancillary tool.

The NPS study examined five types of terrorist groups: religious, New Age, ethno-nationalist separatist, revolutionary, and far-right extremist. Of these, only the religious groups were thought likely to seek the most damaging capability level, as it would be consistent with their indiscriminate application of violence.

In October 2000, the NPS group issued a second report following a conference aimed at examining the decision making process that leads sub-state groups engaged in armed resistance to develop new operational methods. They were particularly interested in learning whether such groups would engage in cyber terrorism. In addition to academics and a member of the United Nations, the participants included a hacker and five practitioners with experience in violent sub-state groups. The latter included the PLO, the Liberation Tigers of Tamil Eelan (LTTE), the Basque Fatherland and Liberty-Political/Military (ETA-PM), and the Revolutionary Armed Forces of Colombia (FARC). The participants engaged in a simulation exercise based on the situation in Chechnya.

16   Only one cyber attack was authorized during the simulation, and that was against the Russian Stock Exchange. The attack was justified on the grounds that the exchange was an elite activity and thus disrupting it would not affect most Russians. Indeed, it might appeal to the average Russian. The group ruled out mass disruptions impacting e-commerce as being too indiscriminate and risking a backlash.

The findings from the meeting were generally consistent with the earlier study. Recognizing that their conclusions were based on a small sample, they concluded that terrorists have not yet integrated information technology into their strategy and tactics; that sub-state groups may find cyber terror attractive as a non-lethal weapon; that significant barriers between hackers and terrorists may prevent their integration into one group; and that politically motivated terrorists had reasons to target selectively and limit the effects of their operations, although they might find themselves in a situation where a mass casualty attack was a rational choice.

The NPS group also concluded that the information and communication revolution may lessen the need for violence by making it easier for sub-state groups to get their message out. Unfortunately, this conclusion does not seem to be supported by recent events. Many of the people in bin Laden's network, including the suicide hijackers, have used the Internet but nevertheless engage in horrendous acts of violence. Groups that foster hate and aggression thrive on the Internet alongside those that promote tolerance and peace.

Although cyber terrorism is certainly a real possibility, for a terrorist, digital attacks have several drawbacks. Systems are complex, so controlling an attack and achieving a desired level of damage may be harder than using physical weapons. Unless people are killed or badly injured, there is also less drama and emotional appeal.

20   In assessing the threat of cyber terrorism, it is also important to look beyond the traditional terrorist groups and to the computer geeks who already possess considerable hacking skills. As noted at the beginning of this essay, some of these folks are aligning themselves with terrorists like bin Laden. While the vast majority of hackers may be disinclined towards violence, it would only take a few to turn cyber terrorism into reality.

Further, the next generation of terrorists will grow up in a digital world, with ever more powerful and easy-to-use hacking tools at their disposal. They might see greater potential for cyber terrorism than do the terrorists of today, and their level of knowledge and skill relating to hacking will be greater. Cyber terrorism could also become more attractive as the real and virtual worlds become more closely coupled, with automobiles, appliances, and other devices attached to the Internet. Unless these systems are carefully secured, conducting an operation that physically harms someone may be as easy as penetrating a Web site is today.

At least for now, hijacked vehicles, truck bombs, and biological weapons seem to pose a greater threat than cyber terrorism. However, just as the events of September 11 caught us by surprise, so could a major cyber assault. We cannot afford to shrug off the threat.

PERSONAL RESPONSE

In what ways, if any, has this article increased your understanding of cyber terrorism—what it is, and what it is capable of?

QUESTIONS FOR DISCUSSION

1. Are you persuaded that a major cyber terrorism attack is a real possibility?
2. Are you convinced that cyber terrorism has the potential to cause the kind of devastating physical damage that more "traditional" forms of terrorism have done?
3. Besides the examples Denning names of the uses cyber terrorists might make of the new technologies, can you think of others? What or who do you think are most vulnerable to possible cyber terrorist attacks?
4. What do you think can be done to defend against the threats posed by the new technologies?

War Culture

Ellen Goodman

Ellen Goodman was born in Boston and began her career as a reporter for Newsweek *after graduating with a bachelor's degree from Radcliffe College. She worked for the Detroit Free Press before becoming a columnist for the* Boston Globe *in 1967. Her column, "At Large," has been syndicated by the Washington Post Writers Group since 1976. In 1980 she won a Pulitzer Prize for distinguished commentary. She has published a study of human change,* Turning Points *(1979), and many of her columns have been collected in* Close to Home *(1979),* At Large *(1981),* Keeping in Touch *(1985), and* Making Sense *(1989). This article was published in the May 20, 1999, issue of the* Boston Globe.

Forgive me for interrupting. It's impolite when everybody around the table seems to have settled into such a familiar, comfortable discussion about violence. Side by side we have folks complaining that Republicans are too meek on gun control and Democrats are too weak in countering Hollywood. Now the president has concluded that "there are far too many vulnerable children who are steeped in this culture of violence . . ."

Something is missing from this discussion. Maybe it is not dinner table conversation, but no one has mentioned the W-word: war. Is it possible that we can understand a culture of violence without talking about war? I don't mean war movies or war video games. I mean the real thing.

Over the last weeks, the news has been full of the massacre at Littleton and the bombing of Kosovo—reports that are simultaneous but stunningly disconnected. This is what sticks in my mind in the aftermath of Columbine High. Remember Eric Harris's essay in which he portrayed himself as a shotgun shell? A worried teacher went to discuss the violence with Harris's father. But, reported the *New York Times,* "after the teacher learned that Mr. Harris was a retired Air Force officer and that his son hoped to enlist in the military, she concluded that the essay was consistent with his future career aspirations." This teenager's hopes and dreams and fantasies and games were about war. As a boy he and his brother played some variation of "Rambo." On the computer he and his friends played war games, "Doom" and "Duke Nukem." But it was OK because his "future career aspirations" were to be a warrior. When Eric heard in his philosophy class that we were on the verge of bombing Yugoslavia he told a classmate, "I hope we do go to war. I'll be the first one there." It was only after his rejection by the Marines that Harris turned his high school into a war zone.

4   Are we so immune that we think of war only as a metaphor for violence? Have we forgotten the background of the socially acceptable, social heroic culture of violence: war?

We have been reluctant to talk about violence as a boy culture. Mothers will tell you that even sons forbidden toy guns will go around the back yard "shooting" with twigs. How many parents train their sons to fight their own battles in the face of bullies? How many of us accept as "normal" boy stuff the video games that we are now told are virtual training sessions for military desensitization?

Do we abandon our sons to the culture of violence out of a subconscious agreement that boys may have to be our warriors? Even in the age of volunteer army and coed battalions, how many raise boys wondering if they will go to war?

At times it seems that everything is turned upside down. In Kosovo we have forgotten that war is hell. We expect surgical strikes—mixing our metaphors of medicine and mayhem. We call our military on the carpet if they hit a Chinese embassy or a field of refugees. And we are shocked—shocked!—when an American plane goes down and a soldier is killed. War isn't supposed to be dangerous.

8   Indeed in August we will celebrate the 50th anniversary of the Geneva Conventions that wrote civilized "rules" for the horror that is war. And in Washington, without any sense of irony, our leaders ask simultaneously for more money for bombs and strong policies for gun control or Hollywood control. They worry more about the effects of war movies than war.

The Marines were proud that they kept Eric Harris out of the corps. The system worked! But isn't war the system, the career aspiration for a young, disturbed war-lover?

I am not speaking as a pacifist. For all its complexity and horror, I don't think we can stay on the sidelines of every dispute between morals and might. There are, as well, times for self-defense. War happens. But let's not deceive ourselves. To have a discussion about violence without talking about war is like talking about war without talking about death. That of course is another impolite interruption.

READER RESPONSE

What are your memories about hearing the news of various school shootings, particularly the one at Columbine High School in Littleton, Colorado, that Goodman features in her article? Were your intellectual and emotional responses different? Explain your answer.

QUESTIONS FOR DISCUSSION

1. What is Goodman's point in her opening and closing paragraphs about "impolite interruption[s]"?
2. Goodman comments that our leaders in Washington "without any sense of irony . . . ask simultaneously for more money for bombs and strong

policies for gun control or Hollywood control." (paragraph 8). What do you think she finds ironic about those requests? Do you agree with her?

3. How would you answer Goodman's question, "Is it possible that we can understand a culture of violence without talking about war" (paragraph 2)?

4. Discuss the extent to which you agree with Ellen Goodman that "to have a discussion about violence without talking about war is like talking about war without talking about death" (paragraph 10).

Parenting Post-9/11

Joan Vennochi

Joan Vennochi is a Boston Globe *columnist who writes regularly on national and local politics and also covers issues relating to business, law and culture. Before joining the op-ed page, she wrote a column on the* Globe's *business page. She began her career at the* Globe *as a researcher on the Spotlight Team, the newspaper's investigative reporting unit, and shared in a Pulitzer Prize awarded to the team for local investigative reporting. This column appeared in the September 10, 2002, issue of the* Boston Globe.

The newly minted fourth-grader was scampering around the house, singing "God Bless America." Suddenly, she started improvising a less appealing version: "God don't bless America, land that I hate."

"That's the way the Taliban would sing it," she explained, her vocabulary reflecting one more truth about the year that has passed since terrorists attacked America in most deadly fashion.

Conversation for young and old, and between young and old, is dramatically different. From anthrax to religious zealot, it includes new words, thoughts, and ethical conundrums.

A routine exchange between a mother and a 9-year-old may now include references to the war in Afghanistan, the collateral deaths of civilians, and the goal of hunting down and killing Osama bin Laden. Until this summer's eruption of scary headlines about abducted children, a child's questions about safety and security were likely to focus on airports and flying rather than on a fear of being snatched from their bed by a stranger.

Since the events of last Sept. 11, parents are challenged to explain complicated geopolitical conflicts they don't fully understand to sons and

daughters who want to know how and why people they don't know could
hate them enough to want them dead.

Many parents believe this is too ugly and too much for them and their *concession*
children to handle. A close friend took a pass recently on buying the Sunday
New York Times after glimpsing a page one reconstruction of wrenching final
moments in the upper floors of the twin towers, with graphic descriptions of
humans hurtling from one certain death to another. He did not want the
newspaper in his house, where his children might see it.

Of course, a parent's first instinct is to protect children and keep them
safe. No one wants to see a child traumatized by images of violence and
death. But knowledge and understanding are antidotes to danger, whether the *# their's*
danger comes from drug dealers or terrorists. In the aftermath of the Sept. 11
attack on America, you could argue that there is a new parental duty to help
our children see a bigger world than many adults did up until a year ago.

8   The history-making events of Sept. 11 are not fantasy, they are reality, just
like the recent wave of suicide bombings that have taken so many lives in Is-
rael. Trying to explain such raw hate to a child is difficult. But, sad to say, hate   *forceful or*
is a universal dynamic that fuels conflict between individuals and countries.   *energetic; a*
Isn't it better to know it exists and grow up trying to understand it than go   *pattern or*
forward in blissful ignorance?   *process of*
      change/
Besides, we cannot stop our children from remembering what they saw   *growth*
one year ago. Images of a plane smashing into a skyscraper, of towers collapsing, cannot be erased by the silliness of SpongeBob SquarePants on Nick-
elodeon. Dwelling on those images is not necessary. Neither is pretending
they will go away.

The 10-year-olds who lived through the assassination of John F. Kennedy
remember the event as if it were yesterday. It was mesmerizing, traumatizing,
overwhelming, and all-consuming, even in black-and-white without 24-7 cable
television access. It triggered a tragic sense of loss and insecurity at a time
when children lived in a much tighter cocoon than they do today, with adults
worrying less about the potential impact on impressionable children. The
world as we knew it stopped on Nov. 22, 1963. Our parents and teachers
wept. A little boy saluted, standing tall next to his pale-faced mother draped in
black. The country mourned, and its children knew that something terrible,
life-changing, and world-changing had happened. For a time the country
seemed under attack, not just a president. We wrote poems and essays and
pored over *Life Magazine*'s commemorative edition on the death of JFK.
There was an unrelenting sadness relived at each anniversary of the assassination.

I am not wishing unrelenting sadness on anyone's children, including my
own, just a glimmer of understanding that the world is bigger than they are.
Tragedies happen, as do triumphs. Context and proportion are important in
12 both.

Above all, they should not tolerate hatred or accept it as immutable, in
the Taliban or anyone else.   *weak conclusion*

Personal Response

Do you think that children, especially very young children, should be shielded from the realities of terrorism and other violent events?

Questions for Discussion

1. How would you/did you explain to children "how and why people they don't know could hate them enough to want them dead" (paragraph 5)?
2. Discuss how you would answer Vennochi's question in paragraph 8: "Isn't it better to know [hate] exists and grow up trying to understand it than go forward in blissful ignorance?"
3. It what ways is Vennochi's discussion on the effects of President Kennedy's assassination (paragraph 10) appropriate as a way of explaining the effects of the tragic events of September 11, 2001?

Pilgrimage to Nonviolence
Martin Luther King, Jr.

Martin Luther King, Jr., was born in Atlanta, Georgia, in 1929. At age 18, he was ordained a Baptist minister in his father's church, the same year that he earned his undergraduate degree from Morehouse College. He earned his B.D. from Crozer Theological Seminary in 1951 and his Ph.D. from Boston University in 1954. In 1955 King organized a successful boycott of the Montgomery, Alabama, bus system and became the leader of the civil rights movement. By the time he founded the Southern Christian Leadership Conference in 1957, he had become internationally known for his philosophy of nonviolent resistance. King was Time *magazine's Man of the Year in 1963, and in 1964 he was awarded the Nobel Peace Prize. He was assassinated in Memphis, Tennessee, in 1968. This selection is from his book* Stride Toward Freedom *(1958).*

When I went to Montgomery as a pastor, I had not the slightest idea that I would later become involved in a crisis in which nonviolent resistance would be applicable. I neither started the protest nor suggested it. I simply responded to the call of the people for a spokesman. When the protest began, my mind, consciously or unconsciously, was driven back to the Sermon on the

Mount, with its sublime teachings on love, and the Gandhian method of nonviolent resistance. As the days unfolded, I came to see the power of nonviolence more and more. Living through the actual experience of the protest, nonviolence became more than a method to which I gave intellectual assent; it became a commitment to a way of life. Many of the things that I had not cleared up intellectually concerning nonviolence were now solved in the sphere of practical action.

Since the philosophy of nonviolence played such a positive role in the Montgomery Movement, it may be wise to turn to a brief discussion of some basic aspects of this philosophy.

First, it must be emphasized that nonviolent resistance is not a method for cowards; it does resist. If one uses this method because he is afraid or merely because he lacks the instruments of violence, he is not truly nonviolent. This is why Gandhi often said that if cowardice is the only alternative to violence, it is better to fight. He made this statement conscious of the fact that there is always another alternative: no individual or group need submit to any wrong, nor need they use violence to right the wrong; there is the way of nonviolent resistance. This is ultimately the way of the strong man. It is not a method of stagnant passivity. The phrase "passive resistance" often gives the false impression that this is a sort of "do-nothing method" in which the resister quietly and passively accepts evil. But nothing is further from the truth. For while the nonviolent resister is passive in the sense that he is not physically aggressive toward his opponent, his mind and emotions are always active, constantly seeking to persuade his opponent that he is wrong. The method is passive physically, but strongly active spiritually. It is not passive nonresistance to evil, it is active nonviolent resistance to evil.

4   A second basic fact that characterizes nonviolence is that it does not seek to defeat or humiliate the opponent, but to win his friendship and understanding. The nonviolent resister must often express his protest through noncooperation or boycotts, but he realizes that these are not ends themselves; they are merely means to awaken a sense of moral shame in the opponent. The end is redemption and reconciliation. The aftermath of nonviolence is the creation of the beloved community, while the aftermath of violence is tragic bitterness.

A third characteristic of this method is that the attack is directed against forces of evil rather than against persons who happen to be doing the evil. It is evil that the nonviolent resister seeks to defeat, not the persons victimized by evil. If he is opposing racial injustice, the nonviolent resister has the vision to see that the basic tension is not between races. As I like to say to the people in Montgomery: "The tension in this city is not between white people and Negro people. The tension is, at bottom, between justice and injustice, between the forces of light and the forces of darkness. And if there is a victory, it will be a victory not merely for fifty thousand Negroes, but a victory for justice and the forces of light. We are out to defeat injustice and not white persons who may be unjust."

A fourth point that characterizes nonviolent resistance is a willingness to accept suffering without retaliation, to accept blows from the opponent without striking back. "Rivers of blood may have to flow before we gain our freedom, but it must be our blood," Gandhi said to his countrymen. The nonviolent resister is willing to accept violence if necessary, but never to inflict it. He does not seek to dodge jail. If going to jail is necessary, he enters it "as a bridegroom enters the bride's chamber."

One may well ask: "What is the nonviolent resister's justification for this ordeal to which he invites men, for this mass political application of the ancient doctrine of turning the other cheek?" The answer is found in the realization that unearned suffering is redemptive. Suffering, the nonviolent resister realizes, has tremendous educational and transforming possibilities. "Things of fundamental importance to people are not secured by reason alone, but have to be purchased with their suffering," said Gandhi. He continues: "Suffering is infinitely more powerful than the law of the jungle for converting the opponent and opening his ears which are otherwise shut to the voice of reason."

8   A fifth point concerning nonviolent resistance is that it avoids not only external physical violence but also internal violence of spirit. The nonviolent resister not only refuses to shoot his opponent but he also refuses to hate him. At the center of nonviolence stands the principle of love. The nonviolent resister would contend that in the struggle for human dignity, the oppressed people of the world must not succumb to the temptation of becoming bitter or indulging in hate campaigns. To retaliate in kind would do nothing but intensify the existence of hate in the universe. Along the way of life, someone must have sense enough and morality enough to cut off the chain of hate. This can only be done by projecting the ethic of love to the center of our lives.

In speaking of love at this point, we are not referring to some sentimental or affectionate emotion. It would be nonsense to urge men to love their oppressors in an affectionate sense. Love in this connection means understanding, redemptive good will. Here the Greek language comes to our aid. There are three words for love in the Greek New Testament. First, there is *eros.* In Platonic philosophy *eros* meant the yearning of the soul for the realm of the divine. It has come now to mean a sort of aesthetic or romantic love. Second, there is *philia,* which means intimate affection between personal friends. *Philia* denotes a sort of reciprocal love; the person loves because he is loved. When we speak of loving those who oppose us, we refer to neither *eros* nor *philia;* we speak of love which is expressed in the Greek word *agape. Agape* means understanding, redeeming good will for all men. It is an overflowing love which is purely spontaneous, unmotivated, groundless, and creative. It is not set in motion by any quality or function of its object. It is the love of God operating in the human heart.

Agape is disinterested love. It is a love in which the individual seeks not his own good, but the good of his neighbor (I Cor. 10:24). *Agape* does not begin by discriminating between worthy and unworthy people, or any qualities people possess. It begins by loving others *for their sakes.* It is an entirely "neighbor regarding concern for others," which discovers the neighbor in every man it meets. There, *agape* makes no distinction between friend and enemy; it is directed toward both. If one loves an individual merely on account of his friendliness, he loves him for the sake of the benefits to be gained from the friendship, rather than for the friend's own sake. Consequently, the best way to assure oneself that love is disinterested is to have love for the enemy-neighbor from whom you can expect no good in return, but only hostility and persecution.

Another basic point about *agape* is that it springs from the *need* of the other person—his need for belonging to the best in the human family. The Samaritan who helped the Jew on the Jericho road was "good" because he responded to the human need that he was presented with. God's love is eternal and fails not because man needs his love. St. Paul assures us that the loving act of redemption was done "while we were yet sinners"—that is, at the point of our greatest need for love. Since the white man's personality is greatly distorted by segregation, and his soul is greatly scarred, he needs the love of the Negro. The Negro must love the white man, because the white man needs his love to remove his tensions, insecurities, and fears.

12   *Agape* is not a weak, passive love. It is love in action. *Agape* is love seeking to preserve and create community. It is insistence on community even when one seeks to break it. *Agape* is a willingness to sacrifice in the interest of mutuality. *Agape* is a willingness to go to any length to restore community. It doesn't stop at the first mile, but it goes the second mile to restore community. It is a willingness to forgive, not seven times, but seventy times seven to restore community. The cross is the eternal expression of the length to which God will go in order to restore broken community. The resurrection is a symbol of God's triumph over all the forces that seek to block community. The Holy Spirit is the continuing community creating reality that moves through history. He who works against community is working against the whole of creation. Therefore, if I respond to hate with a reciprocal hate I do nothing but intensify the cleavage in broken community. I can only close the gap in broken community by meeting hate with love. If I meet hate with hate, I become depersonalized, because creation is so designed that my personality can only be fulfilled in the context of community. Booker T. Washington was right: "Let no man pull you so low as to make you hate him." When he pulls you to the point of working against community; he drags you to the point of defying creation, and thereby becoming depersonalized.

In the final analysis, *agape* means a recognition of the fact that all life is interrelated. All humanity is involved in a single process, and all men are brothers. To the degree that I harm my brother, no matter what he is doing to me, to that extent I am harming myself. For example, white men often refuse federal aid to education in order to avoid giving the Negro his rights; but because all men are brothers they cannot deny Negro children without harming their own. They end, all efforts to the contrary, by hurting themselves. Why is this? Because men are brothers. If you harm me, you harm yourself.

Love, *agape,* is the only cement that can hold this broken community together. When I am commanded to love, I am commanded to restore community, to resist injustice, and to meet the needs of my brothers.

A sixth basic fact about nonviolent resistance is that it is based on the conviction that the universe is on the side of justice. Consequently, the believer in nonviolence has deep faith in the future. This faith is another reason why the nonviolent resister can accept suffering without retaliation. For he knows that in his struggle for justice he has cosmic companionship. It is true that there are devout believers in nonviolence who find it difficult to believe in a personal God. But even these persons believe in the existence of some creative force that works for universal wholeness. Whether we call it an unconscious process, an impersonal Brahman, or a Personal Being of matchless power and infinite love, there is a creative force in this universe that works to bring the disconnected aspects of reality into a harmonious whole.

READER RESPONSE

Do you believe that you would be able to practice nonviolent resistance in the face of threats of harm or other injustice?

QUESTIONS FOR DISCUSSION

1. Identify the following: Gandhi (paragraph 1), the Sermon on the Mount (paragraph 1), the Good Samaritan (paragraph 11), and Booker T. Washington (paragraph 12). If you do not already know, find out who or what they were, and share your findings with your class.
2. Find passages in which King says what nonviolent resistance and *agape* are not (as opposed to those in which he says what they are). Why do you suppose King uses the strategy of saying what things are not when his purpose is to define what they are? Would such an approach work for all definitions? Do you think King has in mind an audience that was opposed to or in favor of his philosophy? Explain your answer.
3. Explain, in your own words, what you understand King to mean by both nonviolent resistance and *agape*. How appropriate do you think King's philosophy of nonviolent resistance is today? In what circumstances would it work? In what circumstances would it not work?

Menagerie, A Child's Fable
Charles Johnson

Charles Johnson began his career as a cartoonist, at one time hosting his own PBS series Charlie's Pad *in the early 1970s. His novels include* Good Thing *(1974)*, Oxherding Tale *(1982), and*

Middle Passage *(1990), for which he won the National Book Award. In 1988 he published a collection of essays,* Being and Race: Black Writing Since 1970. *His collection of short stories,* Sorcerer's Apprentice *(1986), includes "Menagerie, A Child's Fable," which was first published in the* Indiana Review *in 1984. In 1997 Johnson was one of the editors of the volume* Black Men Speaking, *and in 1998 he received a MacArthur Foundation fellowship, popularly known as a "genius" award.*

Among watchdogs in Seattle, Berkeley was known generally as one of the best. Not the smartest, but steady. A pious German shepherd (Black Forest origins, probably), with big shoulders, black gums, and weighing more than some men, he sat guard inside the glass door of Tilford's Pet Shoppe, watching the pedestrians scurry along First Avenue, wondering at the derelicts who slept ever so often inside the foyer at night, and sometimes he nodded when things were quiet in the cages behind him, lulled by the bubbling of the fishtanks, dreaming of an especially fine meal he'd once had, or the little female poodle, a real flirt, owned by the aerobic dance teacher (who was no saint herself) a few doors down the street; but Berkeley was, for all his woolgathering, never asleep at the switch. He took his work seriously. Moreover, he knew exactly where he was at every moment, what he was doing, and why he was doing it, which was more than can be said for most people, like Mr. Tilford, a real gumboil, whose ways were mysterious to Berkeley. Sometimes he treated the animals cruelly, or taunted them; he saw them not as pets but profit. Nevertheless, no vandals, or thieves, had ever brought trouble through the doors or windows of Tilford's Pet Shoppe, and Berkeley, confident of his power but never flaunting it, faithful to his master though he didn't deserve it, was certain that none ever would.

At closing time, Mr. Tilford, who lived alone, as most cruel men do, always checked the cages, left a beggarly pinch of food for all the animals, and a single biscuit for Berkeley. The watchdog always hoped for a pat on his head, or for Tilford to play with him, some sign of approval to let him know he was appreciated, but such as this never came. Mr. Tilford had thick glasses and a thin voice, was stubborn, hot-tempered, a drunkard and a loner who, sliding toward senility, sometimes put his shoes in the refrigerator, and once—Berkeley winced at the memory—put a Persian he couldn't sell in the Mix Master during one of his binges. Mainly, the owner drank and watched television, which was something else Berkeley couldn't understand. More than once he'd mistaken gunfire on screen for the real thing (a natural error, since no one told him violence was entertainment for some), howled loud enough to bring down the house, and Tilford booted him outside. Soon enough, Berkeley stopped looking for approval; he didn't bother to get up from biting fleas behind the counter when he heard the door slam.

But it seemed one night too early for closing time. His instincts on this had never been wrong before. He trotted back to the darkened storeroom; then his mouth snapped shut. His feeding bowl was as empty as he'd last left it.

4   "Say, Berkeley," said Monkey, whose cage was near the storeroom. "What's goin' on? Tilford didn't put out the food."

Berkeley didn't care a whole lot for Monkey, and usually he ignored him. He was downright wicked, a comedian always grabbing his groin to get a laugh, throwing feces, or fooling with the other animals, a clown who'd do anything to crack up the iguana, Frog, Parrot, and the Siamese, even if it meant aping Mr. Tilford, which he did well, though Berkeley found this parody frightening, like playing with fire, or literally biting the hand that fed you. But he, too, was puzzled by Tilford's abrupt departure.

"I don't know," said Berkeley. "He'll be back, I guess."

Monkey, his head through his cage, held onto the bars like a movie inmate. "Wanna bet?"

8   "What're you talking about?"

"Wake *up*," said Monkey. "Tilford's sick. I seen better faces on dead guppies in the fishtank. You ever see a pulmonary embolus?" Monkey ballooned his cheeks, then started breathing hard enough to hyperventilate, rolled up both red-webbed eyes, then crashed back into his cage, howling.

Not thinking this funny at all, Berkeley padded over to the front door, gave Monkey a grim look, then curled up against the bottom rail, waiting for Tilford's car to appear. Cars of many kinds, and cars of different sizes, came and went, but that Saturday night the owner did not show. Nor the next morning, or the following night, and on the second day it was not only Monkey but every beast, bird, and fowl in the Shoppe that shook its cage or tank and howled at Berkeley for an explanation—an ear-shattering babble of tongues, squawks, trills, howls, mewling, bellows, hoots, blorting, and belly growls because Tilford had collected everything from baby alligators to zebra-striped fish, an entire federation of cultures, with each animal having its own distinct, inviolable nature (so they said), the rows and rows of counters screaming with a plurality of so many backgrounds, needs, and viewpoints that Berkeley, his head splitting, could hardly hear his own voice above the din.

"Be patient!" he said. "Believe me, he's comin' back!"

12   "Come *off* it," said one of three snakes. "Monkey says Tilford's *dead*. Question is, what're we gonna *do* about it?"

Berkeley looked, witheringly, toward the front door. His empty stomach gurgled like a sewer. It took a tremendous effort to untangle his thoughts. "If we can just hold on a —"

"We're *hungry!*" shouted Frog. "We'll starve before old Tilford comes back!"

Throughout this turmoil, the shouting, beating of wings, which blew feathers everywhere like confetti, and an angry slapping of fins that splashed water to the floor, Monkey simply sat quietly, taking it all in, stroking his chin as a scholar might. He waited for a space in the shouting, then pushed his

head through the cage again. His voice was calm, studied, like an old-time bar-
rister before the bar. "Berkeley? Don't get mad now, but I think it's obvious
that there's only one solution."

16   "What?"

"Let us out," said Monkey. "Open the cages."

"No!"

"We've got a crisis situation here." Monkey sighed like one of the elderly,
tired lizards, as if his solution bothered even him. "It calls for courage, radical
decisions. You're in charge until Tilford gets back. That means you gotta feed
us, but you can't do that, can you? Only one here with hands is *me*. See, we all
have different talents, unique gifts. If you let us out, we can pool our resources. I can *open* the feed bags!"

20   "You can?" The watchdog swallowed.

"Uh-huh." He wiggled his fingers dexterously, then the digits on his feet.
"But somebody's gotta throw the switch on this cage. I can't reach it. Dog, I'm
asking you to be democratic! Keeping us locked up is fascist!"

The animals clamored for release; they took up Monkey's cry, "Self-deter-
mination!" But everything within Berkeley resisted this idea, the possibility of
chaos it promised, so many different, quarrelsome creatures uncaged, set loose
in a low-ceilinged Shoppe where even he had trouble finding room to turn
around between the counters, pens, displays of paraphernalia, and heavy, bubbling fishtanks. The chances for mischief were incalculable, no question of
that, but slow starvation was certain if he didn't let them in the storeroom.
Furthermore, he didn't want to be called a fascist. It didn't seem fair, Monkey
saying that, making him look bad in front of the others. It was the one charge
you couldn't defend yourself against. Against his better judgment, the watchdog rose on his hindlegs and, praying this was the right thing, forced open the
cage with his teeth. For a moment Monkey did not move. He drew breath
loudly and stared at the open door. Cautiously, he stepped out, stood up to his
full height, rubbed his bony hands together, then did a little dance and began
throwing open the other cages one by one.

Berkeley cringed. "The tarantula, too?"

24   Monkey gave him a cold glance over one shoulder. "You should get to
know him, Berkeley. Don't be a bigot."

Berkeley shrank back as Tarantula, an item ordered by a Hell's Angel who
never claimed him, shambled out—not so much an insect, it seemed to Berkeley, as Pestilence on legs. ("Be fair!" he scolded himself. "He's okay, I'm okay,
we're all okay.") He watched helplessly as Monkey smashed the ant farm, freed
the birds, and then the entire troupe, united by the spirit of a bright, common
future, slithered, hopped, crawled, bounded, flew, and clawed its way into the
storeroom to feed. All except crankled, old Tortoise, whom Monkey hadn't
freed, who, in fact, didn't want to be released and snapped at Monkey's fingers
when he tried to open his cage. No one questioned it. Tortoise had escaped
the year before, remaining at large for a week, and then he returned mysteri-
ously on his own, his eyes strangely unfocused, as if he'd seen the end of the
world, or a vision of the world to come. He hadn't spoken in a year. Hunched

inside his shell, hardly eating at all, Tortoise lived in the Shoppe, but you could hardly say he was part of it, and even the watchdog was a little leery of him. Berkeley, for his part, had lost his hunger. He dragged himself, wearily, to the front door, barked frantically when a woman walked by, hoping she would stop, but after seeing the window sign, which read—CLOSED—from his side, she stepped briskly on. His tail between his legs, he went slowly back to the storeroom, hoping for the best, but what he found there was no sight for a peace-loving watchdog.

True to his word, Monkey had broken open the feed bags and boxes of food, but the animals, who had always been kept apart by Tilford, discovered as they crowded into the tiny storeroom and fell to eating that sitting down to table with creatures so different in their gastronomic inclinations took the edge off their appetites. The birds found the eating habits of the reptiles, who thought eggs were a delicacy, disgusting and drew away in horror; the reptiles, who were proud of being cold-blooded, and had an elaborate theory of beauty based on the aesthetics of scales, thought the body heat of the mammals cloying and nauseating, and refused to feed beside them, and this was fine for the mammals, who, led by Monkey, distrusted anyone odd enough to be born in an egg, and dismissed them as lowlifes on the evolutionary scale; they were shoveling down everything—bird food, dog biscuits, and even the thin wafers reserved for the fish.

"Don't touch that!" said Berkeley. "The fish have to eat, too! They can't leave the tanks!"

28   Monkey, startled by the watchdog, looked at the wafers in his fist thoughtfully for a second, then crammed them into his mouth. "That's their problem."

Deep inside, Berkeley began a rumbling bark, let it build slowly, and by the time it hit the air it was a full-throated growl so frightening that Monkey jumped four, maybe five feet into the air. He threw the wafers at Berkeley. "Okay—okay, give it to 'em! But remember one thing, dog: You're a mammal, too. It's unnatural to take sides against your own kind."

Scornfully, the watchdog turned away, trembling with fury. He snuffed up the wafers in his mouth, carried them to the huge, man-sized tanks, and dropped them in amongst the sea horses, guppies, and jellyfish throbbing like hearts. Goldfish floated toward him, his voice and fins fluttering. He kept a slightly startled expression. "What the hell is going on? Where's Mr. Tilford?"

Berkeley strained to keep his voice steady. "Gone."

32   "For good?" asked Goldfish. "Berkeley, we heard what the others said. They'll let us starve—"

"No," he said. "I'll protect you."

Goldfish bubbled relief, then looked panicky again. "What if Tilford doesn't come back ever?"

The watchdog let his head hang. The thought seemed too terrible to consider. He said, more to console himself than Goldfish, "It's his Shoppe. He has to come back."

36   "But suppose he *is* dead, like Monkey says." Goldfish's unblinking, lidless eyes grabbed at Berkeley and refused to release his gaze. "Then it's our Shoppe, right?"

"Eat your dinner."

Goldfish called, "Berkeley, wait—"

But the watchdog was deeply worried now. He returned miserably to the front door. He let fly a long, plaintive howl, his head tilted back like a mountaintop wolf silhouetted by the moon in a Warner Brothers cartoon—he did look like that—his insides hurting with the thought that if Tilford was dead, or indifferent to their problems, that if no one came to rescue them, then they were dead, too. True, there was a great deal of Tilford inside Berkeley, what he remembered from his training as a pup, but this faint sense of procedure and fair play hardly seemed enough to keep order in the Shoppe, maintain the peace, and more important provide for them as the old man had. He'd never looked upon himself as a leader, preferring to attribute his distaste for decision to a rare ability to see all sides. He was no hero like Old Yeller, or the legendary Gellert, and testing his ribs with his teeth, he wondered how much weight he'd lost from worry. Ten pounds? Twenty pounds? He covered both eyes with his black paws, whimpered a little, feeling a failure of nerve, a soft white core of fear like a slug in his stomach. Then he drew breath and, with it, new determination. The owner couldn't be dead. Monkey would never convince him of that. He simply had business elsewhere. And when he returned, he would expect to find the Shoppe as he left it. Maybe even running more smoothly, like an old Swiss watch that he had wound and left ticking. When the watchdog tightened his jaws, they creaked at the hinges, but he tightened them all the same. His eyes narrowed. No evil had visited the Shoppe from outside. He'd seen to that. None, he vowed, would destroy it from within.

40   But he could not be everywhere at once. The corrosion grew day by day. Cracks, then fissures began to appear, it seemed to Berkeley, everywhere, and in places where he least expected them. Puddles and pyramidal plops were scattered underfoot like traps. Bacterial flies were everywhere. Then came maggots. Hamster gnawed at electrical cords in the storeroom. Frog fell sick with a genital infection. The fish, thought the gentlest of creatures, caused undertow by demanding day-and-night protection, claiming they were handicapped in the competition for food, confined to their tanks, and besides, they were from the most ancient tree; all life came from the sea, they argued, the others owed *them*.

Old blood feuds between beasts erupted, too, grudges so tired you'd have thought them long buried, but not so. The Siamese began to give Berkeley funny looks, and left the room whenever he entered. Berkeley let him be, thinking he'd come to his senses. Instead, he jumped Rabbit when Berkeley wasn't looking, the product of this assault promising a new creature—a cabbit—with jackrabbit legs and long feline whiskers never seen in the Pet Shoppe before. Rabbit took this badly. In the beginning she sniffed a great deal, and with good reason—rape was a vicious thing—but her grief and pain got out of hand, and soon she was lost in it with no way out, like a child in a dark forest, and began organizing the females of every species to stop cohabiting with the males. Berkeley stood back, afraid to butt in because Rabbit said that it was none of his damned business and he was as bad as all the rest. He pleaded reason, his eyes burnt-out from sleeplessness, with puffy bags beneath them, and when that did no good, he pleaded restraint.

"The storeroom's half-empty," he told Monkey on the fifth day. "If we don't start rationing the food, we'll starve."

"There's always food."

44   Berkeley didn't like the sound of that. "Where?"

Smiling, Monkey swung his eyes to the fishtanks.

"Don't you go near those goldfish!"

Monkey stood at bay, his eyes tacked hatefully on Berkeley, who ground his teeth, possessed by the sudden, wild desire to bite him, but knowing, finally, that he had the upper hand in the Pet Shoppe, the power. In other words, bigger teeth. As much as he hated to admit it, his only advantage, if he hoped to hold the line, his only trump, if he truly wanted to keep them afloat, was the fact that he outweighed them all. They were afraid of him. Oddly enough, the real validity of his values and viewpoint rested, he realized, on his having the biggest paw. The thought fretted him. For all his idealism, truth was decided in the end by those who could be bloodiest in fang and claw. Yet and still, Monkey had an arrogance that made Berkeley weak in the knees.

48   "Dog," he said, scratching under one arm, "you got to sleep *some*time."

And so Berkeley did. After hours of standing guard in the storeroom, or trying to console Rabbit, who was now talking of aborting the cabbit, begging her to reconsider, or reassuring the birds, who crowded together in one corner against, they said, threatening moves by the reptiles, or splashing various medicine on Frog, whose sickness had now spread to the iguana—after all this, Berkeley did drop fitfully to sleep by the front door. He slept greedily, dreaming of better days. He twitched and woofed in his sleep, seeing himself schtupping the little French poodle down the street, and it was good, like making love to lightning, she moved so well with him; and then of his puppy-hood, when his worst problems were remembering where he'd buried food from Tilford's table, or figuring out how to sneak away from his mother, who told him all dogs had cold noses because they were late coming to the Ark and had to ride next to the rail. His dream cycled on, as all dreams do, with greater and greater clarity from one chamber of vision to the next until he saw, just before waking, the final drawer of dream-work spill open on the owner's return. Splendidly dressed, wearing a bowler hat and carrying a walking stick, sober, with a gentle smile for Berkeley (Berkeley was sure), Tilford threw open the Pet Shoppe door in a blast of wind and burst of preternatural brilliance that rayed the whole room, evaporated every shadow, and brought the squabbling, the conflict of interpretations, mutations, and internecine battles to a halt. No one dared move. They stood frozen like fish in ice, or a bird

caught in the crosswinds, the colorless light behind the owner so blinding it
obliterated their outlines, blurred their precious differences, as if each were a
rill of the same ancient light somehow imprisoned in form, with being-formed
itself the most preposterous of conditions, outrageous, when you thought it
through, because it occasioned suffering, meant separation from other forms,
and the illusion of identity, but even this ended like a dream within the watchdog's dream, and only he and the owner remained. Reaching down, he stroked
Berkeley's head. And at last he said, like God whispering to Samuel: *Well done.*
It was all Berkeley had ever wanted. He woofed again, snoring like a sow, and
scratched in his sleep; he heard the owner whisper *begun,* which was a
pretty strange thing for him to say, even for Tilford, even in a dream. His ears
strained forward; *begun,* Tilford said again. And for an instant Berkeley thought
he had the tense wrong, intending to say, "Now we can begin," or something
prophetically appropriate like that, but suddenly he was awake, and Parrot
was flapping his wings and shouting into Berkeley's ear.

"The gun," said Parrot. "Monkey has it."

Berkeley's eyes, still phlegmed by sleep, blearily panned the counter. The
room was swimming, full of smoke from a fire in the storeroom. He was short
of wind. And, worse, he'd forgotten about the gun, a Smith and Wesson, that Tilford had bought after pet shop owners in Seattle were struck by thieves who
specialized in stealing exotic birds. Monkey had it now. Berkeley's water ran
down his legs. He'd propped the pistol between the cash register and a display of plastic dog collars, and his wide, yellow grin was frighteningly like that
of a general Congress has just given the go-ahead to on a scorched-earth
policy.

52   "Get it!" said Parrot. "You promised to protect us, Berkeley!"

For a few fibrous seconds he stood trembling paw-deep in dung, the
odor of decay burning his lungs, but he couldn't come full awake, and still he
felt himself to be on the fringe of a dream, his hair moist because dreaming of
the French poodle had made him sweat. But the pistol . . . There was no
power balance now. He'd been outplayed. No hope unless he took it away. Cir-
cling the counter, head low and growling, or trying to work up a decent
growl, Berkeley crept to the cash register, his chest pounding, bunched his
legs to leap, then sprang, pretending the black explosion of flame and smoke
was like television gunfire, though it ripped skin right off his ribs, sent teeth
flying down his throat, and blew him back like an empty pelt against Tortoise's cage. He lay still. Now he felt nothing in his legs. Purple blood like that
deepest in the body cascaded to the floor from his side, rushing out with each
heartbeat, and he lay twitching a little, only seeing now that he'd slept too
long. Flames licked along the floor. Fish floated belly up in a dark, unplugged
fishtank. The females had torn Siamese to pieces. Spackled lizards were busy
sucking baby canaries from their eggs. And in the holy ruin of the Pet Shoppe
the tarantula roamed free over the corpses of Frog and Iguana. Beneath him,
Berkeley heard the ancient Tortoise stir, clearing a rusty throat clogged from
disuse. Only he would survive the spreading fire, given his armor. His eyes

burning from the smoke, the watchdog tried to explain his dream before the blaze reached them. "We could have endured, we had enough in common—for Christ's sake, we're *all* animals."

"Indeed," said Tortoise grimly, his eyes like headlights in a shell that echoed cavernously. "Indeed."

PERSONAL RESPONSE

With whom are you more sympathetic, Berkeley or Monkey? Why?

QUESTIONS FOR DISCUSSION

1. What general human qualities do the animals represent? If Berkeley, Monkey, and Tortoise were humans, how would you characterize them?
2. What is the basic conflict in the story?
3. Why do you think that Berkeley "hated to admit" that the others are afraid of him because of his strength (paragraph 47)? Why does he fret over the idea that "truth was decided in the end by those who could be bloodiest in fang and claw" (paragraph 47)? How does Monkey's use of the store owner's gun undercut this "truth"?
4. Comment on Berkeley's dying statement: "'We could have endured, we had enough in common—for Christ's sake, we're *all* animals'" (paragraph 53). What do you make of the Tortoise's response: "'Indeed'" (paragraph 54)?
5. What do you think is the moral of the story?

ADDITIONAL SUGGESTIONS FOR WRITING ABOUT VIOLENCE

1. Explain how effective you think the three principles that Benjamin Netanyahu discusses in "Three Key Principles in the War Against Terrorism" will be in defeating terrorism.
2. Write your own editorial explaining what the United States must do to combat and/or defeat terrorism.
3. Explore some of the challenges faced by the United States in building an international coalition against terrorism.
4. Argue for or against the statement that countries supporting or aiding terrorists should be held equally responsible for September 11, 2001, attacks in New York and Washington.
5. Argue for or against the position that military retaliation is the proper response to the terrorist attacks of September 11, 2001. Do you agree or disagree that violence should be responded to with violence?

6. Examine the potential of cyberspace to commit terrorist acts.

7. Explore the question of why people resort to terrorism as a means of achieving their goals.

8. Argue for or against Ellen Goodman's thesis in "War Culture" that we cannot "understand a culture of violence without talking about war."

9. Explain how you see terrorism affecting you or your generation in the years to come.

10. Explore ways in which certain everyday realities of our world push children into adulthood too early. If possible, use children you know as examples to support your observations.

11. Write an essay addressed to Martin Luther King, Jr., in which you support or argue against the practicality of nonviolent resistance.

12. Illustrate the concept of *agape* by showing how it is practiced by community groups, organizations, or individuals you know, particularly in the context of violence in society.

13. Explore the question of what must change in American society before the rate of violent crimes can be significantly reduced. Focus on a particular kind of violence. For instance, what can schools and parents do to prevent school shootings like that at Columbine High School in 1999?

14. Argue for or against stricter gun control laws, or argue for or against the statement that the Second Amendment guarantee of a right to bear arms extends to the right of citizens to own semiautomatic machine guns.

15. Examine one aspect of a social problem that is often accompanied by or leads to violence, such as teenage drug abuse, teenage runaways, or teenage pregnancy.

16. Examine one cultural cause often cited as a factor to explain why people commit violent crimes.

17. Select one aspect of the problem of children who murder, rape, or commit other violent crimes, such as how widespread the problem is, how to account for its increase, possible explanations for it, or possible solutions to it.

18. If you have been the victim of a crime, narrate what happened, and describe the effects of the crime. If you personally have not been a victim but someone you know well has, describe the experience of that person and the effects of the crime.

CREDITS

Arnold, David. "Cavalcade of Whimsey: Defending Springfield Against Itself." Reprinted as a shorter version of "Use a Pen" by David Arnold in *Leaving Springfield: The Simpsons and the Possibilities of Oppositional Culture* by John Alberti, editor, 2003, with permission of the Wayne State University Press.

Bambara, Toni Cade. "The Lesson." Copyright © 1972 by Toni Cade Bambara, from *Gorilla, My Love* by Toni Cade Bambara. Used by permission of Random House, Inc.

Beathard, Ron. "Over 40 and Unmarried" from *Newsweek*, June 3, 1996. Copyright © 1996, Newsweek, Inc. All rights reserved. Reprinted by permission.

Begley, Josanne. "'The Gettysburg Address' and the War Against Terrorism." Reprinted by permission of the author.

Berry, Wendell. "Men and Women in Search of Common Ground" from *Home Economics: Fourteen Essays* by Wendell Berry. Copyright © 1987 by Wendell Berry. Reprinted by permission of North Point Press, a division of Farrar, Straus & Giroux, LLC.

Blum, Deborah. "What's the Difference Between Boys and Girls?" *Life*, July 1999. Copyright © 1999 by Time Inc. Reprinted by permission.

Catton, Bruce. "Grant and Lee: A Study in Contrasts," from *The American Story*, ed. Earl Schenk Miers. Reprinted by permission of the U.S. Capitol Historical Society.

Chan, Sucheng. "You're Short, Besides!" Copyright © 1989 by Sucheng Chan. Reprinted from *Making Waves* by permission of the author.

Cisneros, Sandra. "The House on Mango Street" and "My Name." From *The House on Mango Street*. Copyright © 1984 by Sandra Cisneros. Published by Vintage Books, a division of Random House, Inc., and in hardcover by Alfred A. Knopf in 1994. Reprinted by permission of Susan Bergholz Literary Services, New York. All rights reserved.

Conroy, Frank. "Think About It: Ways We Know, and Don't." Copyright © 1988 by *Harper's Magazine*. All rights reserved. Reprinted from the November 1988 issue by special permission.

Corliss, Richard. "Bang, You're Dead," from *Time* magazine, May 3, 1999. Copyright © 1999 by Time Inc. Reprinted by permission.

Crichton, Jennifer. "'Who Shall I Be?': The Allure of a Fresh Start" from *Ms. Magazine*, 1984. Reprinted by permission of the author.

Crow Dog, Mary. "A Woman from He-Dog," from *Lakota Woman* by Mary Crow Dog with Richard Erdoes. Copyright © 1990 by Mary Crow Dog and Richard Erdoes. Used by permission of Grove/Atlantic, Inc.

Davidson, John. "Menace to Society," from *Rolling Stone*, February 22, 1996. Copyright © 1996 by John Davidson. Reprinted by permission of Straight Arrow Publishers Company, Ltd, 1996.

Davis, Katherine. "I'm Not Sick, I'm Just in Love" from *Newsweek*, July 24, 1995. Copyright © 1995, Newsweek, Inc. All rights reserved. Reprinted by permission.

Denne, Michael. "Learning the Hard Way," from *Newsweek*, November 23, 1998. Copyright © 1998, Newsweek, Inc. All rights reserved. Reprinted by permission.

Denning, Dorothy. "Is Cyber Terror Next?" Copyright © 2002 *Understanding September 11* edited by Craig Calhoun, Paul Price, and Ashley Timmer. Reprinted by permission of The New Press. (800) 233-4830.

Dillard, Annie. "Living Like Weasels" from *Teaching a Stone to Talk*. Copyright © 1982 by Annie Dillard. Reprinted by permission of HarperCollins Publishers, Inc.

Doloff, Steven. "Woodstock's Message Is Still

New York. Copyright © 1984, 1988 by Beth Brant.

Raspberry, William. "Symbolic Arguments." Copyright © 1999, *The Washington Post*. Reprinted with permission.

Rose, Tricia. "Rap Music and the Demonization of Young Black Males." Reprinted from *USA Today Magazine*, May 1994. Copyright © 1994 by the Society for the Advancement of Education.

Rosenblatt, Roger. "The Quality of Mercy Killing," from *Time* magazine, August 26, 1985. Copyright © 1985 by Time Inc. Reprinted by permission.

Rosenblatt, Roger. "The Silent Friendship of Men." From *Time* magazine, December 27, 1998. Copyright © 1988 by Time Inc. Reprinted by permission.

Roten, Robert. "Is Hollywood Responsible for 9-11?" Copyright © 2002 Robert Roten. Reprinted by permission of the author.

Safire, William. "A Spirit Reborn." Copyright © 2002 by The New York Times Co. Originally published in the *New York Times*, September 9, 2002. Reprinted by permission.

Saltzman, Joe. "Beating the Same Old Dead Horse." Reprinted from *USA Today Magazine*, November 1993, Copyright © 1993 by the Society for the Advancement of Education.

Segal, David." Where's the Return Fire in Culture Wars?" Copyright © 2002, *The Washington Post*. Reprinted with permission.

Sharrett, Christopher. "Movies, Morality, and Conservative Complaints." Reprinted from *USA Today Magazine*, September 1993. Copyright © 1993 by the Society for the Advancement of Education.

Showalter, Julie. "Vows," first published in *Other Voices*, a publication of the University of Illinois at Chicago, Spring 1996. Reprinted by permission of the author.

Sommers, Christina Hoff. "Are We Living in a Moral Stone Age?" Reprinted by permission from *IMPRIMIS*, the monthly journal of Hillsdale College. Copyright © 1998.

Staples, Brent. "Just Walk on By: A Black Man Ponders His Power to Alter Public Space." Reprinted by permission of the author.

Steinberg, Stephen. "The Affirmative Action Debate," reprinted from the *UNESCO Courier*, March 1996.

Tannen, Deborah. "Sex, Lies, and Conversation," from *The Washington Post*, June 24, 1990. Copyright © 1990 by Deborah Tannen. Reprinted by permission.

Tavris, Carol. "Love Story," reprinted with the permission of Simon & Schuster from *The Mismeasure of Woman* by Carol Tavris. Copyright © 1992 by Carol Tavris.

Thompson, Bill. "It's Too Bad We Don't Have Another Roy," *Fort Worth Star-Telegram*, July 14, 1998. Reprint courtesy of the *Fort Worth Star-Telegram*.

Vennochi, Joan. "Parenting Post-9/11." Copyright © 2002 Globe Newspaper Company. Reprinted by permission.

Watson, Larry. "Silence." Reprinted by permission of the author.

White, E. B. "Once More to the Lake," from *One Man's Meat*. Copyright © 1941 by E. B. White. Reprinted by permission of Tilbury House, Publishers, Gardiner, Maine.

Williams, Patricia J. "Racial Privacy." Reprinted with permission from the June 17, 2002, issue of *The Nation*.

Wilkins, Roger. "I Became Her Target," reprinted by permission of author.

Wills, Gary. "How to Speak to a Nation's Suffering." Copyright © 2002 by The New York Times Co. Originally published in the *New York Times*, August 18, 2002. Reprinted by permission

Wiesenfeld, Kurt. "Making the Grade" from *Newsweek*, June 17, 1996. Copyright © 1996, Newsweek, Inc. All rights reserved. Reprinted by permission.

Wieviorka, Michel. "The Ruses of Racism." Reprinted from *Unesco Courier*. February 1993.

Zinn, Howard. "Unsung Heroes." from *The Progressive*, 6 June 2000. Reprinted by permission from The Progressive, 409 E Main St, Madison, WI 53703. *www.progressive.org*.

PHOTO CREDITS

INDEX